# STRATEGIC INTELLIGENCE

D1457964

# STRATEGIC INTELLIGENCE

**3**

## COVERT ACTION: BEHIND THE VEILS
## OF SECRET FOREIGN POLICY

Edited by
Loch K. Johnson

Intelligence and the Quest for Security

**PRAEGER SECURITY INTERNATIONAL**
Westport, Connecticut • London

**Library of Congress Cataloging-in-Publication Data**

Strategic intelligence / edited by Loch K. Johnson.
      p. cm.—(Intelligence and the quest for security, ISSN 1932-3492)
  Includes bibliographical references and index.
  ISBN 0-275-98942-9 (set : alk. paper)—ISBN 0-275-98943-7 (vol. 1 : alk. paper)—
ISBN 0-275-98944-5 (vol. 2 : alk. paper)—ISBN 0-275-98945-3 (vol. 3 : alk. paper)—
ISBN 0-275-98946-1 (vol. 4 : alk. paper)—ISBN 0-275-98947-X (vol. 5 : alk. paper)
1. Military intelligence.   2. Intelligence service—Government policy.  I. Johnson,
Loch K., 1942–

UB250.S6385 2007
327.12—dc22      2006031165

British Library Cataloguing in Publication Data is available.

Library of Congress Catalog Card Number: 2006031165
ISBN: 0-275-98942-9 (set)
      0-275-98943-7 (vol. 1)
      0-275-98944-5 (vol. 2)
      0-275-98945-3 (vol. 3)
      0-275-98946-1 (vol. 4)
      0-275-98947-X (vol. 5)
ISSN: 1932-3492

First published in 2007

Praeger Security International, 88 Post Road West, Westport, CT 06881
An imprint of Greenwood Publishing Group, Inc.
www.praeger.com

Printed in the Untied States of America

The paper used in this book complies with the
Permanent Paper Standard issued by the National
Information Standards Organization (Z39.48-1984).

10 9 8 7 6 5 4 3 2 1

# CONTENTS

*Appendixes*

# PREFACE

THIS FIVE-VOLUME SERIES IN INTELLIGENCE IS SOMETHING of a landmark in the study of intelligence. Thirty years ago, one would have been hard-pressed to find enough good articles on the subject to fill two volumes, let alone five. In those three decades since 1975, however, the study of intelligence has grown considerably. Today there are several solid professional journals in the field, including the premier publications *Intelligence and National Security* (published in the United Kingdom), *International Journal of Intelligence and Counterintelligence* (the United States), and *Studies in Intelligence* (from the Central Intelligence Agency, in both classified and unclassified form). In just the past two years, bulging anthologies on the general topic "strategic intelligence," as well as a "handbook" on intelligence and a collection of chapters within the more specialized niche of "intelligence and ethics" have appeared, along with a tidal wave of books and articles on one aspect or another of this subject (see the bibliographic essay in volume 1).

Except in times of scandal (Watergate in 1973, CIA domestic spying in 1974, the Iran-*contra* affair in 1987), one could find in this earlier era little newspaper coverage of intelligence activities, so tightly held were these operations by the government. Now, fueled by the events of the September 11, 2001, terrorist attacks and the erroneous prediction in 2002 that weapons of mass destruction (WMDs) were being developed and stockpiled by Iraq, hardly a week goes by without reports on intelligence in the *New York Times* and other leading news-papers. These days, the *Atlantic Monthly* and the *New Yorker*, America's top literary magazines, visit the subject with some regularity, too. The latter has hired Seymour M. Hersh, the nation's most well-known investigative reporter with an intelligence beat.

Intelligence studies has come of age.

Certainly the chapters in these volumes display a breadth of inquiry that suggests an admirable vibrancy in this relatively new field of study. Presented here are empirical inquiries, historical treatments, theoretical frameworks, memoirs, case studies, interviews, legal analyses, comparative essays, and ethical assessments. The authors come from the ranks of academe (twenty-five); the intelligence agencies (thirteen); think tanks (seven); Congress, the State Department, and the National Security Council (three); and the legal world (three).[1] Over a quarter of the contributors are from other nations, including Canada, England, Germany, Israel, Scotland, Switzerland, and Wales. The American writers come from every region of the United States. As a collective, the authors represent a wide range of scholarly disciplines, including computer science, history, international affairs, law, sociology, political science, public administration, public policy studies, and strategic studies. Many of the contributors are from the ranks of the top intelligence scholars in the world; a few young ones stand at the gateway to their academic careers.

Notable, too, is the number of women who have entered this field of study. Thirty years ago, it would have been rare to find one or two women writing on this subject. Seven have contributed chapters to these pages, and another two wrote documents that appear in the appendixes. This is still fewer than one would like, especially in light of the major contribution women have made as intelligence officers. One thinks of the heroic efforts of British women in code breaking and in the Special Operations Executive during World War II, and the American women who contributed so much to the analytic efforts of the Office of Strategic Studies (OSS) during that same war. At least, though, the number attracted to the scholar study of intelligence appears to be rapidly expanding.

The end result of this mix is a landscape illuminated by a variety of methods and appreciations—a rich research trove that examines all the key aspects of intelligence. In addition, each of the volumes contains backup materials in the appendixes. These documents provide the reader with access to significant primary and secondary sources referred to in the chapters.

The volumes are organized according to the major topics of studies in the field. The first volume, titled *Understanding the Hidden Side of Government*, introduces the reader to methods commonly used in the study of intelligence. It imparts, as well, a sense of the "state of the discipline," beginning with a bibliographic essay (by the editor) and continuing with an examination of specific approaches scholars have adopted in their inquiries into this especially difficult discipline, where doors are often shut against outsiders.

In the bibliographic essay that opens the volume, I argue that the literature on intelligence has mushroomed over the past thirty years. Some of this literature is unreliable, but much of it is of high quality. Amy B. Zegart follows my chapter with an important caveat: the literature may be more voluminous these days, but intelligence studies as an academic field has yet to be accepted as a vital part of national security scholarship. The mainstream journals of history, international affairs, and political science have still regarded the study of intelligence as a marginal pursuit. In this regard, Zegart points out, there is a major disconnect between academic scholarship and those who make decisions in Washington, London, and other capitals around the world.

Following this introduction, Len Scott and Timothy Gibbs look at methods that have been used to study intelligence in the United Kingdom; Stuart Farson and Reg Whitaker in Canada; and Michael Warner in the United States. The volume then turns to a more specific inquiry into the central question of how intelligence is interpreted by professionals—the issue of analysis—explored by John Hollister Hedley. An overview of the sometimes turbulent relationship between intelligence officers and the policy makers they serve is explored by James J. Wirtz; and British scholar Peter Gill recalls the failures associated with the 9/11 attacks and the poor judgments about Iraqi WMDs, in hopes of extracting lessons from these intelligence disasters. In the next chapter, the youngest scholar represented in this collection, Harold M. Greenberg, takes us back in time with a remembrance of the legendary CIA officer and Yale history professor Sherman Kent, often known as the dean of CIA analysts. Kristin Lord rounds out the first volume with a look forward into future prospects for a more transparent world—the ultimate goal of intelligence.

As with each of the books, Volume 1 has a set of appendixes designed to supplement the original chapters with supportive materials from government documents and other sources. Appendix A contains the relevant intelligence excerpts from the National Security Act of 1947—the founding charter for the modern American intelligence establishment. Appendix B provides a history of U.S. intelligence since 1947, prepared for the Aspin-Brown Commission in 1995–96 by staff member Phyllis Provost McNeil. These two documents present a contextual backdrop for the Volume 1 chapters. Appendix C provides "wiring diagrams" of the intelligence community, that is, organizational blueprints for the sixteen agencies and related entities. One chart displays the community as it is today, and another displays how it looked in 1985. As the contrast between the two illustrates, the events of September 11, 2001, have led to a larger and more complex intelligence apparatus in the United States. Appendix D shows a photograph of the CIA Headquarters Building, as an example of what one of the secret agencies actually looks like from an aerial perspective. The white dome in the foreground is an assembly hall seating around 600 people and to its left is the main entrance to the original CIA headquarters, built during the Eisenhower years. Behind this older wing is the new green-glass structure erected during the Reagan administration, often known as the Casey addition because William J. Casey was the Director of Central Intelligence (DCI) at the time of its construction during the 1980s.

Appendix E lists the top leadership in the America's intelligence community: the DCIs from 1947–2005 and today's DNI. Included here as well are the leaders in Congress who have been responsible for intelligence accountability in the past, along with the current members of the two congressional Intelligence

Committees: the Senate Select Committee on Intelligence (SSCI, or "sissy" in the unflattering and sometimes true homophone of Capitol Hill vernacular) and the House Permanent Select Committee on Intelligence (HPSCI or "hipsee"). Appendix F presents a 1955 statement from historian and CIA analyst Sherman Kent about the need for a more robust intelligence literature. He would probably be amazed by how much is being written on this subject now. Appendix G offers an overview on the purpose and challenges of intelligence, drawn from the introductory chapters of the Aspin-Brown Commission Report. Finally, Appendix H provides an opening glimpse into the subject of counterintelligence, a world of counterspies and betrayal taken up more fully in Volume 4.

With the second volume, titled *The Intelligence Cycle: The Flow of Secret Information From Overseas to the Highest Councils of Government*, the focus shifts from a broad overview of intelligence to a more detailed examination of its core mission: the collection, analysis, and dissemination of information from around the world. The National Security Act of 1947, which created America's modern intelligence establishment, made it clear that the collection, analysis, and dissemination of information would be the primary duty of the intelligence agencies. As Allen Dulles—the most famous DCI (America's top intelligence official, until this title changed to director of National Intelligence or DNI in 2005)—put it, the intelligence agencies were expected "to weigh facts, and to draw conclusions from those facts, without having either the facts or the conclusions warped by the inevitable and even proper prejudices of the men whose duty it is to determine policy."[2] The collection and interpretation of information, through espionage and from the public record, would be the primary responsibility of America's secret agencies.

At the heart of this mission lies the so-called intelligence cycle. Professional intelligence officers define the cycle as "the process by which information is acquired, converted into intelligence, and made available to policymakers."[3] The cycle has five phases: planning and direction, collection, processing, production and analysis, and dissemination (see Appendix A in Volume 2 for a depiction). As former CIA officer Arthur S. Hulnick notes, however, in the opening chapter, the idea of a "cycle" fails to capture the complexity of how intelligence is collected, assessed, and distributed by intelligence officers.

The next five chapters in Volume 2 take us into the world of the "ints," that is, the specialized "intelligences" (methods) used by intelligence officers to collect information. Patrick Radden Keefe and Matthew M. Aid probe the method of signals intelligence or SIGINT, a generic term used to describe the interception and analysis of communications intelligence and other electronic emissions, from wiretapping telephones to studying the particles emitted by missiles in test flights. Both authors are sensitive to the possible abuse of these techniques, which can be and have been used to spy on Americans without a proper judicial warrant. Jeffrey T. Richelson explores the IMINT domain, that is, imagery intelligence or, in simple terms, photographs taken by surveillance satellites and reconnaissance airplanes (piloted and unpiloted). Telephone conversations can be revealing, but in the old saying, a picture can be worth a thousand words. (Appendix B provides photographic examples of these spy platforms, and Appendix C offers illustrations of the IMINT data they can collect.)

Important, too, is information that can be acquired by human agents ("assets") guided by case officers inside the CIA or the Defense Department, the topic of human intelligence or HUMINT, examined by Frederick P. Hitz. Not all the information needed by policy makers is acquired through SIGINT, IMINT, or HUMINT; indeed, the overwhelming majority—upward of 95 percent—is already in the public domain. This open-source intelligence (OSINT) must be sorted through, organized, and integrated with the secretly gained information. Robert David Steele's chapter looks at OSINT and its ties to the other ints.

In the next chapter, Daniel S. Gressang IV dissects some of the technological challenges faced by intelligence agencies in sorting through the avalanche of data that pours into their headquarters from various intelligence collectors around the world. Here is the Herculean task of sorting out the wheat from the chaff (or the signal from the noise, in another widely used metaphor) in the search for information that may warn the nation of impending peril. Here is the vital task of providing "indicators and warnings" (I&W) to a nation's leaders.

One of the most difficult relationships in the complex process of collection, analysis, and dissemination of information comes at the intersection between intelligence professionals and policy makers—groups of individuals that often have very different training, aspirations, and cultures. Jack Davis sheds light on this often turbulent relationship in the United States, and Michael Herman tackles the same topic in the United Kingdom. Minh A. Luong offers a case study on economic intelligence that underscores some of the difficulties encountered as information travels from the collectors and analysts (the "producers" of intelligence) to the policy makers (the "consumers"). Finally, Max M. Holland takes a look at how intelligence agencies examine their own mistakes ("postmortems") and attempt to make corrections—and how political consideration enter into the process.

By way of supporting documentation, in addition to the appendixes already mentioned, Appendix D outlines the general types of reports prepared by the producers of intelligence, along with a listing of specific examples. Appendixes E and F provide samples of key intelligence products: National Intelligence Estimates (NIEs)—the most important long-range and in-depth forecasting carried out by the U.S. secret agencies ("research intelligence," in contrast to shorter intelligence reports that tend to focus on near-term events, or "current intelligence"); Special National Intelligence Estimates (SNIEs), which concentrate on a narrow, high-priority information requirement (say, the capabilities of the Chinese military); and the *President's Daily Brief* (PDB), the most exclusive current intelligence report prepared by the intelligence agencies for the consumption of the president and a few other high-ranking officials.

In light of the fact that every study of the 9/11 and Iraqi WMD intelligence failures find fault, in part, with America's capacity for human intelligence—

especially in the Middle East and Southwest Asia—Appendix G presents one of the most searing critiques of this int. The critique, by the House Permanent Select Committee on Intelligence, has become all the more significant because the panel's chairman, Representative Porter Goss (R-FL), soon after the completion of the report rose to the position of the DCI. Last, Appendix H provides an excerpt from a key report on the Iraqi WMD mistakes, prepared by the "Roberts Committee": the Senate Select Committee on Intelligence, led by Pat Roberts (R-KS).

The third volume, titled *Covert Action: Behind the Veils of Secret Foreign Policy*, enters an especially controversial compartment of intelligence: the means by which the United States attempts to not just gather and analyze information about the world—hard enough—but to manipulate global events through secret activities in the advancement of America's best interests. An ambiguous passage of the National Security Act of 1947 charged the National Security Council (NSC), the boss over the sixteen U.S. secret agencies, to "perform such other functions and duties related to intelligence [over and beyond collection-and-analysis] affecting the national security as the National Security Council may from time to time direct."[4] The phrase "other functions and duties" left the door open for launching the CIA (and more recently the Pentagon) on a wide range of covert actions around the world.

Covert action (CA), sometimes referred to as the "quiet option," is based on the supposition that this secret approach to foreign affairs is likely to be less noisy and obtrusive than sending in the Marines. Sometimes professional practitioners also refer to covert action as the "third option," between diplomacy and open warfare. As former Secretary of State and National Security Adviser Henry Kissinger once put it: "We need an intelligence community that, in certain complicated situations, can defend the American national interest in the gray areas where military operations are not suitable and diplomacy cannot operation."[5] Still others prefer the euphemism "special activities" to describe covert action. Whatever the variation in terminology, the goal of covert action remains constant: to influence events overseas secretly and in support of American foreign policy.

Covert action operations are often grouped according to four broad categories: propaganda, political, economic, and paramilitary (PM) activities. An example of a propaganda operation was the CIA's use of Radio Free Europe during the Cold War to transmit anti-communist themes into nations behind the Iron Curtain. A political CA during the Cold War was the CIA's clandestine funneling of funds to the anti-communist Christian Democratic Party in Italy. An economic example: the CIA attempted to destroy electric power stations in Nicaragua during the 1980s, as a means of undermining the Marxist-oriented *Sandinista* regime. PM operations can including everything from assassination plots against foreign heads of state to arming and guiding pro-American insurgent armies in one country or another. Little wonder this has been a controversial subject.

Gregory F. Treverton introduces the reader to covert action in the first chapter of Volume 3. He is followed by Kevin A. O'Brien and Ephraim Kahana, who discuss the use of covert action by other nations. The next four chapters illuminate certain aspects of CA, with James M. Scott and Jerel A. Rosati providing an overview of CA tradecraft (that is, the tools used to implement such operations); Michael A. Turner evaluating the merits of CIA covert propaganda operations; William J. Daugherty looking at political and economic examples of covert action; Jennifer D. Kibbe exploring the entry of the Defense Department into this domain; and former diplomat John D. Stempel contrasting the uses of covert action to diplomatic initiatives. Winding up the volume is Judge James E. Baker's legal analysis of covert action.

Supporting documents include excerpts from the Church Committee Report on the evolution of covert action as carried out by the CIA (Appendix A). The supervision of covert action went from an informal to a highly formal process, as a result of a law known as the Hughes-Ryan Act, passed on December 31, 1974. The language of this statute is presented in Appendix B, and the covert action procedures that resulted from the law are outlined in Appendix C. At the center of the covert action decision process since the Hughes-Ryan Act is the *finding*, a term of art that stems from the passage in the law that requires the president to "find" that a particular covert action proposal is important and has the president's approval. Appendix D contains two findings from the Iran-*contra* era in the mid-1980s. Covert actions must have an organizational apparatus to carry them out, and Appendix E displays what that apparatus looked like during the Cold War (and in basic form remains the organizational chart today, with a few name changes in the boxes).

One of the most controversial forms of covert action has been the assassination of foreign leaders. Appendix F presents a case study from the Church Committee on the CIA assassination plot hatched against the leader of the Republic of Congo, Patrice Lumumba, in 1960. The Committee's exposé of this and other plots led President Gerald R. Ford to sign an executive order prohibiting assassination as an instrument of American foreign policy (see Appendix G). The executive order has been waived in times of authorized warfare against other nations, however, leading to failed attempts to assassinate Saddam Hussein in the first and second Persian Gulf Wars (he was eventually captured alive in 2004, hidden away in a hole near his hometown in Iraq) and Al Qaeda leader Osama bin Laden during the Clinton administration. Considerable ambiguity exists regarding the current status of the executive order and under what conditions it might be waived by administrations. Finally, Appendix H—drawing on a presidential commission study and congressional hearings—examines covert action at its lowest state: the Iran-*contra* affair of the 1980s, when this approach to foreign policy subverted the U.S. Constitution and several laws (including the Hughes-Ryan Act).

A third intelligence mission, after collection-and-analysis and covert action, is counterintelligence (CI) and its associated activity, counterterrorism (CT).

Here is the concentration in Volume 4, titled *Counterintelligence and Counter-terrorism: Defending the Nation Against Hostile Forces*. Like covert action, CI went without specific mention in the National Security Act of 1947. By the early 1950s, however, it had similarly achieved a status of considerable importance as an intelligence mission. CI specialists soon waged nothing less than a secret war against antagonistic intelligence services (especially the Soviet KGB); and, after the Cold War, CT specialists would focus on efforts to block terrorists who targeted the United States and its allies. Explaining why the mission of counterintelligence/counterterrorism evolved, a CI expert has pointed out that "in the absence of an effective U.S. counterintelligence program, [adversaries of democracy] function in what is largely a benign environment."[6]

The practice of counterintelligence consists of two matching halves: security and counterespionage. Security is the passive or defensive side of CI, involving such devices as background investigations, fences, sentries, alarms, badges, watchdogs, and polygraphs (lie detection machines). Counterespionage (CE) is the offensive or aggressive side of CI. The most effective CE operation is the infiltration of an American agent or "mole" into the enemy camp, whether a hostile intelligence service or a terrorist cell—a ploy called a penetration. Thus, the practice of security is, according to one of America's top counterintelligence experts, "All that concerns perimeter defense, badges, knowing everything you have to know about your own people," whereas the CE side "involves knowing all about intelligence services—hostile intelligence services: their people, their installations, their methods, and their operations."[7]

Stan A. Taylor and Nigel West clarify these issues in the first two chapters of this volume, then in the next two chapters Katherine A. S. Sibley and Athan Theoharis examine the challenges of keeping the United States spy-free. Rhodri Jeffreys-Jones looks at the efforts in Europe to create a counterintelligence capability similar to that practiced by America's Federal Bureau of Investigation (FBI). Glenn Hastedt takes the reader into the counterterrorism thicket in Washington, DC, explaining how politics influences CI and CT operations. Richard L. Russell and Jennifer Sims discuss the ups and downs of trying to establish an effective counterterrorism response in the United States, complicated by the fragmentation of authority and widely differing cultures among the sixteen U.S. intelligence agencies. Finally, Katharina von Knop looks at the rising role of women in terrorist organizations.

The back-of-the-book documents in Volume 4 begin with a look at the Church Committee findings regarding counterintelligence in 1975 (Appendix A), followed by the notorious Huston Plan—a master counterintelligence spy plan drafted by White House aide Tom Charles Huston in 1970, in response to a nation at unrest over the war in Vietnam (Appendix B). The Huston Plan is a classic illustration of overreaction in a time of domestic strife. In Appendix C, the Senate Select Committee on Intelligence summarizes its findings about the Aldrich H. Ames counterintelligence disaster. Next the appendixes include a series of U.S. commission conclusions about how to improve intelligence in the struggle against global terrorism, whether locating and penetrating their cells in advance of a terrorist attack or thwarting the ability of terrorists to acquire WMDs. The panel reports include: the Hart-Rudman Commission of 2001 (Appendix D); the 9/11 or Kean Commission of 2004 (Appendix E); and the Silberman-Robb Commission of 2005 (Appendix F). For purposes of comparison, the final appendix (G) examines the conclusions reached by a British commission that also probed the Iraqi WMD failure: the Butler Report of 2004.

The fifth volume in the series, titled *Intelligence and Accountability: Safeguards Against the Abuse of Secret Power*, stems from a concern that secret power might be misused by those in high office. This danger was underscored in 1975 when Congress found the U.S. intelligence agencies guilty of spying against law-abiding American citizens, and again in 1987 during the Iran-*contra* affair when some elements of the intelligence community violated the public trust by ignoring intelligence laws. The United States has been one of the few nations in the world to conduct an ongoing experiment in bringing democratic accountability to secret government activities. Democracy and spying don't mix well. Secrecy runs counter to democratic openness, while at the same time openness possesses a threat to the success of espionage operations. Democracies need intelligence agencies to acquire information that may protect them, but thoughtful citizens worry about having secret agencies in an open society.

Until 1975, the nation's remedy for the tension between intelligence gathering and democracy was to trust the intelligence agencies and hope for the best. Elected officials treated the secret services as exceptional organizations, immune from the checks and balances envisioned by the framers of the Constitution. Lawmakers were satisfied with this arrangement, because if an operation went awry they could duck responsibility. When James R. Schlesinger, DCI in 1973, attempted to inform John Stennis (D-MS), a key member of the Senate Armed Services Committee, about an approaching operation, the Senator stopped him short: "No, no, my boy, don't tell me. Just go ahead and do it, but I don't want to know."[8]

This attitude on Capitol Hill—overlook rather than oversight—underwent a dramatic turnabout in December 1974, however, when the *New York Times* reported on allegations of CIA spying at home and questionable covert actions in Chile. Congress might have waved aside the revelations about Chile as just another Cold War necessity in the struggle against regimes leaning toward Moscow, but spying on American citizens—voters—was another matter altogether. In January 1975, President Ford created the Commission on CIA Activities Within the United States (the Rockefeller Commission, led by his vice president, Nelson Rockefeller). Later that month the Senate established a select committee to investigate intelligence activities. The committee was headed by Frank Church, D-ID, and became known as the Church Committee (the editor served as Church's assistant). A counterpart House committee, led by Representative Otis Pike (D-NY), began investigations the following month.

These various panels, especially the Church Committee, found many more improprieties than they had expected. Not only had the CIA engaged in domestic spying in violation of its charter, so had the FBI and several military intelligence units. Furthermore, the FBI had carried out secret operations, known collectively as COINTELPRO, against thousands of civil rights activists, members of the Ku Klux Klan, and Vietnam War dissenters. The objective was to make their lives miserable by disrupting their marriages and employment. The Bureau even attempted to blackmail Dr. Martin Luther King Jr. into committing suicide. Church Committee investigators also discovered CIA assassination plots against foreign leaders and efforts to topple President Salvador Allende of Chile, even though he had been democratically elected.

These revelations convinced lawmakers that the time had come to bring accountability into the dark recesses of government. Congress established intelligence oversight committees in both chambers—the Senate in 1976 and the House a year later—and, by 1980, required by law timely reports on all secret intelligence operations. The new Committees pored over intelligence budgets, held regular hearings (mostly in closed session to protect spy sources and methods) and seriously examined the performance of America's intelligence agencies. No other nation has ever so thoroughly applied democratic principles to its secret services, although a number are now beginning to follow the leadership of the United States toward greater intelligence supervision.[9]

Since 1975, this effort has evolved in fits and starts. Sometimes lawmakers have insisted on close accountability, as when they enacted the Intelligence Oversight Act of 1980 with its stringent reporting requirements for covert operations, or when a series of laws in the 1980s sought to end covert actions in Nicaragua. At other times, members of Congress have loosened the reins—for example, repealing in 1985 a prohibition against covert action in Angola. On still other occasions, Congress has concentrated on helping the intelligence agencies improve their security and performance, as with a law in 1982 that prohibited exposing the names of undercover officers. The Iran-*contra* scandal of 1987 was a major setback to this new oversight, as the Reagan administration bypassed most of these rules and statutes in its conduct of a covert war in Nicaragua against the will of Congress. The scandal was an alert to lawmakers. The Intelligence Oversight Act of 1991 further tightened intelligence supervision by clarifying reporting requirements. Lawmakers also set up an Office of Inspector General in the CIA, confirmed by and accountable to Congress.

The pulling and tugging has continued, most recently over whether President George W. Bush violated the Foreign Intelligence Surveillance Act (FISA) of 1978 by conducting warrantless wiretaps as part of the war against terrorism in the aftermath of the 9/11 attacks. The FISA required warrants, but the White House claimed (when the secret operation leaked to the media) the law had become to cumbersome and, besides, the president had inherit authority to conduct the war against terrorism as he saw fit. This debate aside for the moment (several authors address the issue in these volumes), one thing is certain: the intelligence agencies in the United States are now very much a part of the nation's system of checks and balances. Americans want and deserve both civil liberties and a secure defense against threats; so the search continues for an appropriate balance between liberty and security, democracy and effectiveness—precisely the topic of Volume 5.

The set of chapters on intelligence accountability are introduced with a chapter by David M. Barrett, the foremost authority on the history of accountability in the early years of modern U.S. intelligence (1947 to 1963). The chief counsel of the Church Committee, Frederick A. O. Schwarz Jr., then reflects back on the effects of that watershed inquiry. Next, the editor offers a previously unpublished interview with DCI William E. Colby, who stood at the helm of the intelligence community as it weathered the storm of the investigations into domestic spying during 1975. Mark Phythian presents a chapter on the British experience with intelligence accountability; and, comparing British and American oversight, Lawrence J. Lamanna contrasts the responses on both sides of the Atlantic to the faulty Iraqi WMD assessments in 2002.

The next chapter, written by Cynthia M. Nolan, looks at contemporary issues of intelligence oversight in the United States. Hans Born and Ian Leigh follow with a comparative dimension by contrasting intelligence accountability practices in a variety other nations. Finally, A. Denis Clift and Harry Howe Ransom, who have witnessed the unfolding of intelligence accountability over the past four decades, offer their appraisals of where the experiment stands today.

The first supporting document in this volume is a succinct legislative history of intelligence accountability from 1947 to 1993, prepared by the Senate Select Committee on Intelligence (Appendix A). Then come a series of important oversight laws, beginning with FISA in 1978. With this law, members of Congress sought to rein in the open-ended authority of the executive branch to wiretap and otherwise spy on individuals considered risks to the national security—a privilege abused by a number of administrations from the 1930s forward. Henceforth, FISA required a warrant from a special court (the FISA Court, whose members are appointed by the Chief Justice of the Supreme Court) before such intrusive measures could be carried out. This law, a hot topic in 2005–6 when critics charged the second Bush administration with violation of the warrant requirement, can be found in Appendix B.

The Intelligence Oversight Act of 1980 is presented in Appendix C. This is a brief but nonetheless far-reaching law, enacted by Congress as an attempt to become an equal partner with the executive branch when it came to intelligence. The 1991 Intelligence Oversight Act (Appendix D) emerged after the Iran-*contra* scandal and provided a tightening and clarification of the language in its 1980 precursor, especially with respect to the approval and reporting rules for covert action. The political tug-of-war over the drafting of this currently prevailing oversight statute was intense, leading to the first and only presidential veto of an intelligence act. President George H. W. Bush found the proposal's insistence on prior reporting of covert action objectionable in times of emergency. Lawmakers entered into a compromise with the chief executive, settling on a two-day reporting delay in emergencies. The bill passed Congress again, this time without a presidential veto.

In 1995, the House Permanent Select Committee on Intelligence launched an inquiry into a wide assortment of intelligence issues, stimulated initially by counterintelligence concerns (Aldrich Ames's treasonous activities at the CIA had recently been discovered) but turning into an opportunity for a broad review of new challenges that faced the secret agencies now that the Cold War had ended. In Appendix E, an excerpt from the Committee's final report examines the state of intelligence accountability in the mid-1990s. The next document, in Appendix F, carries the examination into the twenty-first century, with the appraisal of the 9/11 Commission on the same subject. The commissioners were unimpressed, referring to intelligence accountability as "dysfunctional."

At the center of any efforts to maintain accountability for the secret agencies lies the question of funding—the mighty power of the pursue, held in the hands of lawmakers. Appendix G draws on the findings of the Aspin-Brown Commission to provide official documentation about how the United States spends money for spying. Finally, in Appendix H, DCI Robert M. Gates (1991–93) offers observations about oversight from the perspective of the intelligence community management team, located at that time on the Seventh Floor of the CIA.

Here, then, is what the reader will find in these five volumes. The editor and the contributors hope the chapters and documents will help educate the public about the importance of intelligence agencies, as well as stimulate scholars around the world to further the blossoming of this vital field of study. I am pleased to acknowledge my gratitude to Praeger's Heather Staines, senior project editor, and Anne Rehill, development editor, each a pleasure to work with and most helpful in their guidance; Julie Maynard at the University of Georgia for her administrative assistance; Lawrence J. Lamanna, my graduate research assistant, for his good counsel and logistical help; Leena S. Johnson for her indispensable encouragement and support; and the contributors to these volumes for their outstanding scholarship and their much appreciated cooperation in keeping the publishing train running on time.

These volumes are enthusiastically dedicated to Harry Howe Ransom, who has done so much in the United States to lead the way toward a serious discipline of intelligence studies.

Loch K. Johnson

## NOTES

1. Some of the authors have had multiple careers, so in categorizing them I have counted the place where they have spent most of their professional lives.

2. Quoted by Senator Frank Church (D-ID), in *Congressional Record* (January 27, 1976), p. 1165.

3. *Fact Book on Intelligence* (Washington DC: CIA Office of Public Affairs, April 1983), p. 17.

4. National Security Act of 1947, signed on July 26, 1947 (P.L. 97-222; 50 U.S.C. 403, Sec. 102).

5. Comment, "Evening News," NBC (January 13, 1978).

6. Editor's interview with a FBI counterintelligence specialist, Washington, DC (May 16, 1975).

7. Editor's interview with Raymond Rocca, CIA/CI specialist, Washington, DC (November 23, 1975).

8. Editor's interview with James R. Schlesinger, Washington, DC (June 16, 1994).

9. See Hans Born, Loch K. Johnson, and Ian Leigh, *Who's Watching the Spies? Establishing Intelligence Service Accountability* (Washington, DC: Potomac Books, 2005).

# 1

# COVERT ACTION

## Forward to the Past?

GREGORY F. TREVERTON

MY INTRODUCTION TO COVERT ACTION WAS A fascinating one, moving as a graduate student and then freshly minted Ph.D. to Washington to work for the original Senate Select Committee on Intelligence—often called the Church Committee after its chair, Sen. Frank Church (D-ID).[1] The investigations, hard on the heels of Watergate and allegations of covert U.S. intervention in Chile, were the nation's first ever look behind the green wall of intelligence. I had written about presidential decision making and expected to work on the role of intelligence analysis in those decisions.

In fact, I spent virtually all my time on covert action, and much of that on Chile.[2] That stint in Washington was exhilarating and frustrating, and it produced one of very few "aha!" moments I've had researching in deeply classified documents. Press accounts had attributed to Henry Kissinger, then the National Security Advisor, the line: "I don't see why the United States should stand by and watch Chile go communist merely due to the stupidity of the Chilean people." The quote rang true enough, but I hadn't seen a source and didn't expect to. Then, we received a spate of highly classified documents, including minutes from the 40 Committee, the administration's interagency committee for reviewing covert actions.[3]

Kissinger, previously a scholar, had changed the committee's record keeping from the terse notations of previous administrations—"CIA project 123 is approved," with no mention of operation or country—to those of a recording secretary. So there it was at the end of the notes on one meeting: "The chairman [Kissinger] closed the meeting by observing that he didn't see why . . ."

When I reflected some years later on covert action, what struck me was how much the targets of U.S. covert action had changed from the 1940s to the 1990s.[4]

Many of the CIA's early postwar targets, like Iran's Mossadeq or Guatemala's Arbenz, wanted, almost pleadingly, not to be enemies of the United States. However, for later targets, like Nicaragua's Sandinistas or Iran's Khomeini, the United States was more useful as an enemy than a friend. Cuba's Castro bridged the two periods, with America-as-foe becoming the best thing he had going for him.

By the end of the 1990s, a second theme was also apparent: major American "secret" operations, from Nicaragua and Angola to Cambodia and Afghanistan, were not very secret. They had become "overt" covert action, in that actions became public not just when their results were known but while they were in progress. Support for the Nicaraguan rebels, or contras, the most controversial example, was openly debated and openly funded. Neither opponents nor supporters had reason to keep it secret; for its part the Reagan administration regarded covert action as good policy and good domestic politics, a key element of the Reagan Doctrine, which was intended to challenge Marxist-Leninist states around the world. Indeed, when the Reagan administration decided to sell arms to Iran and keep the operation secret, it turned inward, to the White House staff.[5] In embroidering that operation to divert money for the contras, White House aides apparently kept the president ignorant to protect him—providing him with plausible denial of the sort the CIA had long since abandoned.

Now, the United States has come full circle. Not only are most covert actions not very secret, they are mostly paramilitary actions in support of broader, mostly military counterterrorism operations. The campaign against terror has thrown CIA covert operators and Pentagon special forces together in new ways. The successes of that cooperation, in Afghanistan and Iraq, have been impressive. Because the operations are not very secret and because they are part of the broader campaign against a fearsome foe—transnational terrorism—the questions of how to square them with America's values are less evident. Yet the process is making for less clarity about who does what and why. More important, it is complicating who *authorizes* lethal force and on what basis.

This chapter first reviews the early history that set the pattern for U.S. covert action in the half a century after World War II and inquires into how the success or failure of covert actions should be judged. It then looks at the circumstances, both at home and abroad, that changed covert action to "overt covert," and it argues for a bias toward acting openly, not covertly. If covert action is to be employed, what lessons emerge from the history? It then asks how those lessons apply in current circumstances, and it concludes with a coda on how the oversight of intelligence, especially covert action, by Congress has functioned.

## EARLY SUCCESSES SET THE PATTERN

Spying may be the world's second oldest profession, but for the United States it was only the Cold War, coming on the heels of America's wartime experience with secret operations conducted by the Office of Strategic Services, that led to the creation of an intelligence service in peacetime and to covert operations. Notice that spying—human intelligence or HUMINT, in the jargon of the trade—and covert action are superficially similar but in fact quite different. Both involve secret relationships between U.S. intelligence officers and foreigners. But the point of spying is information; the U.S. officer is relatively passive and the process is designed to protect the foreign spy's link to the United States. For covert action, by contrast, the purpose is doing something; the U.S. officer is active and the process carries inherent risks of being blown—the riskier it is, the more ambitious the action.

Wartime success and postwar threat: these were the backdrop for the creation of the Central Intelligence Agency (CIA). In a few years America plunged from the euphoria of victory in World War I1 to the confrontation with a looming Soviet threat, when Western Europe seemed to teeter in the balance. The first line of American response to the onset of the Cold War was overt: the surge of assistance to Europe through the Truman Doctrine and the Marshall Plan. But the second line was renewed interest in what was then called covert psychological warfare— what we could now call propaganda—as a way to respond to the Soviet Union by means that were less than war but more than nothing.

In this atmosphere, the National Security Council approved NSC 1012, a plan that had originated with George Kennan, then director of the State Department's Policy Planning Staff and the author of the famous X article outlining the policy of containment of the Soviet Union. NSC 1012 was the turning point for covert action, expanding it from propaganda to direct intervention. In the words of the document, covert action comprised: "propaganda, economic warfare; preventive direct action, including sabotage, anti-sabotage, demolition and evacuation measures; subversion against hostile states, including assistance to underground resistance movements, guerrillas and refugee liberation groups, and support of indigenous anticommunist elements."[6] NSC 1012 also codified the notion of plausible denial: operations were to be "so planned and executed that any U.S. Government responsibility for them is not evident to unauthorized persons and that if uncovered the U.S. Government can plausibly disclaim any responsibility for them."

The fledgling CIA's first success came that same year, in 1948, when its covert support to the Italian Christian Democrats helped them beat back an electoral challenge from the Italian Communist Party. By 1950 the United States had succeeded in the covert struggle in Western Europe; in Eastern Europe its covert operations wound down to propaganda and intelligence gathering. The center of the battle against communism moved, as Washington saw the world, away from Europe to small, weak countries. Europe had put the CIA into the business of covert political action, but Asia got the agency into secret paramilitary operations in the Korean War, a pattern repeated a decade later in another Asian war, Vietnam.

The incoming Eisenhower administration called for a more active response to the Soviet threat than the passive containment of the Truman administration.

CIA operators soon registered two successes that set the pattern for the next two decades. On August 21, 1953, after a week of turmoil in the streets of Tehran, the Iranian prime minister, Mohammed Mossadeq, who had nationalized that country's oil industry, surrendered. Three days later the shah, who had fled Iran the previous week with his queen, returned to the capital. At his palace a few days later, he offered a toast to Kermit "Kim" Roosevelt, the chief of the CIA's Near East and Africa Division and the man who had improvised Mossadeq's downfall: "I owe my throne to God, my people, my army—and you!"[7]

The next year, on June 16, 1954, Guatemalan Colonel Carlos Castillo Armas crossed the border into his country from Honduras with a few hundred men trained and armed by the CIA. Pilots under CIA contract flew air cover. The president of Guatemala, Jacobo Arbenz Guzmán, was deserted by his air force and his army, which refused his order to arm workers and peasants. The American ambassador hastily arranged a transfer of power to the chief of the armed forces. (In a moment of tragicomedy, that man immediately pledged that he would continue the struggle against Castillo Armas, America's designated successor to Arbenz. Only after complicated negotiations led by the ambassador did Castillo Armas emerge as president.)[8]

The Iran and Guatemala operations—code-named TPAJAX and PBSUCCESS, respectively—coming within a few years of the CIA's success in Western Europe, made the agency's reputation and set the pattern for covert action in the years ahead. Small, cheap, fast, and tolerably secret, they encouraged Washington to think other covert actions could be likewise. When the next administration decided to confront revolution in Cuba, its covert response was the same as in Guatemala. So were the CIA officers who carried it out.

The blush of short-run success amidst the Cold War obscured several warnings. In the early 1950s, both Iran and Guatemala were eminently vulnerable to manipulation by an outside power, particularly the United States. In both, contending political forces were in close balance. Those balances might have tipped against Mossadeq and Arbenz even if the CIA had not intervened. So it appeared that relatively small operations were enough to tip the balance. Yet in both cases, limited interventions might have failed. In fact, Kermit Roosevelt's first plot did fail; CIA Director Allen Dulles was ready to roll up the operation and bring the troops home. And the CIA officers who ran PBSUCCESS were under no illusions: if their deceptions failed and Arbenz were able to get his military into combat, the invaders would be overwhelmed.

Thus, success was purchased at the price of enlarging the intervention. American purposes did not change, but the operational requirements of achieving them did. Once the United States was committed, in secret and in a small way, the stakes increased, and the CIA took the next step. The effort to intimidate Arbenz became a paramilitary campaign, if a small one. In the process, plausible deniability became more tenuous.

Six years later at the Bay of Pigs, deniability evaporated entirely. "How could I have been so stupid, to let them go ahead?"[9] The words were from John

Kennedy. When the CIA trained invasion force of Cuban exiles hit the beach in the early dawn hours of April 17, 1961, everything went wrong: the lives of brave Cubans were spent; the United States was seen to be intervening; and the intervention failed. Once the plan had changed (without anyone outside the CIA quite noticing it) from a guerrilla operation into a full-fledged amphibious invasion, the chance of keeping it tolerably secret diminished to the vanishing point.

## JUDGING SUCCESS

Evaluating covert action in retrospect is speculative, for it is bedeviled by the imponderable of what might have been; history permits no reruns. Failures, such as the Bay of Pigs invasion, are apparent, but successes are harder to judge. Consider the CIA intervention in the Angolan civil war of 1975. On the surface it was a failure: the Cuban- and Soviet-supported faction, the MPLA (Popular Movement for the Liberation of Angola), was installed while the U.S. role in trying to prevent that outcome was being exposed. If, however, the initial purpose was more limited—for instance, to raise the price of victory for the MPLA and its Soviet and Cuban backers—then Angola might be counted a short-run success. Yet American officials did not convey the impression that their aims actually were so limited, either at the time or later.

When, on the one hand, covert actions have succeeded in their short-run purposes, it may be that the action, though marginal, was just the bit of "support for our friends" that tipped the balance in the internal politics of a foreign country. On the other hand, it may be that the American support was entirely superfluous, and the same successful outcome would have ensued without the U.S. involvement. If this is so, all the covert action accomplished was to implicate the United States and tarnish the success by labeling it "made in America" when the existence of the covert action became known.

A case in point was covert American support to opposition political parties and media in Chile during the presidential tenure of Salvador Allende (1970–73), a self-proclaimed Marxist. There is no question that those parties and media were under pressure from the Allende government.[10] The opposition forces survived to fight another day, but there is no telling whether CIA support for them was decisive or irrelevant.

What is clear is the signal conveyed to history by the revelations of American covert action. In retrospect, most reasonably objective observers conclude that Allende's experiment in Chile would have failed on its own terms.[11] Yet history's lesson is not that Allende fell of his own accord but that the United States overthrew him in 1973. That is the public perception, even though this lesson is untrue in the narrow sense: Washington did not engineer his coup, nor did the CIA or the American military participate in it. The very fact of American covert action meant that at a minimum, "it is fair to say that the United States cannot escape some responsibility for [Allende's] downfall."[12]

By the same token, in 1975 when South Africa intervened to back the U.S.-supported Angolan factions, the FNLA (National Front for the Liberation of Angola) and UNITA (National Union for the Total Independence of Angola), a covert action originally intended to counter the Soviet Union and Cuba, then signaled something else. It indicated an alliance with the apartheid regime in Pretoria. In December 1975, when Congress reacted by cutting off the CIA operation, that only ratified what was seen as the inevitable result—defeat—in the eyes of both Washington policy makers and the rest of the world.

In a longer perspective, neither the Iran nor the Guatemala operations can fairly be given too much credit—or too much blame—for what happened afterward in Iran and Guatemala. On one hand, TPAJAX restored the shah of Iran to his throne, where he remained for nearly a quarter century, a pro-Western bastion in a turbulent region. Twenty-five years of stability is no mean feat in international affairs. On the other hand, American covert action identified the shah's Iran more closely with the United States than was good for either of them.

In any case, however, the aspects of U.S. policy that loomed so large in the shah's downfall in 1979 were overt, not covert. They were his image as an American client, the waste and corruption associated with his massive U.S. arms purchases, and his own dependence on the United States. These factors owed much more to American policy during the 1970s than to the event of 1953.

A similar conclusion also applies to Guatemala in 1953. If, in retrospect, the "success" of PBSUCCESS also looks more ambiguous than it seemed at the time, most of the blame or credit lies with American foreign policy, not with covert action. PBSUCCESS did not make it inevitable that Washington would then forget about Guatemala; it only made it possible. David Phillips, a CIA officer who worked on PBSUCCESS, the Bay of Pigs, and Chile, laments that "Castillo Armas was a bad president, tolerating corruption throughout his government and kowtowing to the United Fruit Company more than his own people." But he argues that the United States "could have prevented this with the vigorous exercise of diplomatic pressure . . . to assure that he pursued social reform for the many rather than venal satisfaction for a few. Instead, Washington breathed a collective sigh of relief and turned to other international problems."[13]

Several covert operations of the 1950s remained secret for a long time: The CIA's assistance to Tibetans resisting the domination of their land by the People's Republic of China, regarded in intelligence lore as a successful holding action, is still a little discussed operation, especially because it is an embarrassment now that Sino-American relations have thawed. The effort to unseat President Sukarno of Indonesia, who had earned Washington's opposition for his espousal of nonalignment, ranged from covert political action to a paramilitary operation; it is not much better known than the Tibetan operation.[14]

Even in the 1960s, several brief and limited interventions—small in terms of numbers of people involved, though not in terms of purpose—remained secret for some time. So-called Track II—a secret effort to touch off a military coup in 1970 to prevent Allende from being seated as Chile's president, an operation run without the knowledge of the State or Defense Departments—was not revealed for five years after it happened. And the sad plots in the early 1960s to assassinate Fidel Castro stayed buried for over ten years.[15]

## CHANGING TARGETS, CHANGING TIMES

Yet times changed. Major covert actions became likely to become public knowledge—sooner rather than later, perhaps even before the operation was over. In 1986, the arms sales to Iran became public even though the leak did not initially come from Washington but from an article published in Beirut in Arabic. Americans became more skeptical of their government, of its information, and its capacity, a skepticism that is a legacy of the long history beginning with the label "Watergate." By 1986, when Ronald Reagan, the most popular president in generations, first denied that his administration had traded arms sales to Iran for the release of American hostages in Lebanon, most Americans did not believe him.

This skepticism has been reinforced by the prominence of investigative journalism; every cub reporter aspires to be Woodward or Bernstein of Watergate fame. The media now contain more people asking hard questions, even of secret operations, and probing for leaks; and there are fewer who are prepared to take the government at its word. If reporters are more likely to seek information on "secret" operations, so are they more likely to find it. Leaking, always present, has become routine in Washington; it has become almost acceptable. Officials sometimes leak information merely for the gratification of being pandered to by journalists more famous than they. More often, they leak to rally opposition to or (more rarely) support for a given policy. Administration after administration, regardless of its political persuasion, declares war on leakers. Those wars always fail. They fail for a simple reason: the ship of state is like no other, for it leaks from the top.

Officials at the top of government are precisely those who know of covert actions and thus are most likely to take their opposition to particular programs into the open. This is true of the executive branch, and all the more so of Congress, where this tendency is reinforced by institutional pride and often by partisan politics. On the whole the intelligence committees of the House and Senate have kept secrets at least as well as the executive branch. Yet their role in overseeing covert action means that those who might oppose a particular project are more likely to know of it. The process creates a set of frustrated opponents who will, on occasion, go public with their frustration.

Not every exposé, however, has created a controversy. Even now, not every covert action is controversial. Of the forty or so covert actions under way in the mid-1980s, at least half had been the subject of some press account.[16] Yet only several were controversial enough that the original leaks developed into continuing stories. Most of the rest were open secrets, more unacknowledged than unknown; most members of Congress thought they made sense, as did most Americans who knew or thought about them—and, no doubt, most of the journalists who reported them.

Before September 11, 2001, the biggest open secret, or overt covert operation, was U.S. aid to those in Afghanistan resisting Soviet occupation of their country. Former CIA Director William Colby characterized the reaction to revelations of American assistance to the resistance in Afghanistan: "Afghanistan was a two-column headline in *The Washington Post* for one day, then almost nothing."[17] Americans in and out of Congress broadly supported the cause of the rebels, or *mujahedeen* (often called freedom fighters at the time, which became a cruel irony on 9/11), and the aid was a way to increase the cost of the Soviet occupation. American assistance reportedly begun in a small way in the last year of the Carter administration escalated sharply to reach as much as a half billion dollars a year by the late 1980s.[18]

The secret was an open one; the American role was not so much covert as unacknowledged, by tacit agreement. The reason for circumspection was the delicate position of the Pakistan government, the conduit for the American supplies to the rebels. Pakistan was prepared to support the rebels but was unwilling to be too visible in doing so lest it antagonize its powerful neighbor, the Soviet Union. In those circumstances, resorting to the CIA, rather than the American military, was more a matter of being discreet than of keeping the whole affair secret.

Certainly there will be cycles in American attitudes toward international threats, as there have been before. In the early 1980s most Americans evidently shared their president's concern with the Soviet threat, and their congressional representatives went along with huge increases in defense spending—and in covert action. Ronald Reagan was able to rebuild considerable authority and discretion in the American presidency, the Iran-*contra* debacle notwithstanding. After September 11, 2001, George W. Bush had at least as much of both support and authority. Most Americans enthusiastically supported the war in Afghanistan, and they were prepared, initially at least, to support the war in Iraq as a front in a longer fight against terrorism.

Still, if the changes in American domestic politics since the mid-1970s have made it more difficult for the United States to achieve its purposes secretly, other changes make it harder now than in the 1950s for the United States to intervene successfully at all, covertly or openly. Despite the controversy and mystique that surrounded covert action (and to some extent still do), history suggests that there is no magic to it. It means providing foreigners secretly with money, weapons, or training as tokens of American support.

With the passage of time, however, a little money here, a few weapons there became less likely to achieve grand foreign policy purposes. Castro was a target of a different order than Arbenz. To think in 1975 that a few million dollars might alter the fate of Angola was a faint hope at best, and an illusion at worst, especially given that the CIA recognized that the Soviet Union and other external actors might counter American support with more assistance of their own. Even the CIA officials who planned the Bay of Pigs covert action knew that to delay the invasion until Cuba had received deliveries of advanced Soviet fighter planes would be to condemn the plan to certain failure.

Also, notice the contrast between two Central American cases three decades apart—Guatemala and Nicaragua. Castillo Armas's liberators numbered no more than several hundred. Their "invasion" was more conjured than real. Yet they had control of the air, in large part because Arbenz, unsure of the loyalty of his air force, was unwilling to risk putting his own pilots in the air. *Sulphates*—Spanish for "laxatives," the name Guatemalans gave to the invaders' bombs—plus rumors exaggerating the size of the invasion were enough to induce Arbenz to capitulate. In the case of Nicaragua, the contras numbered about 10,000 by the mid-1980s, yet not even the most ardent advocates of U.S. assistance to them argued that they were about to induce the Sandinistas to say uncle, much less that they posed a threat sufficient to overthrow the regime by sheer force of arms.

The makers of revolutions learned their own lessons from history, including the history of American covert action. They were determined not to repeat the mistakes of Arbenz and Mossadeq. They sought to assure themselves the loyalty of the army or to build revolutionary cadres of their own. Before the fall of communism, they also learned that if the United States threatened them, there were other sources of support to which they could turn. And, unlike Arbenz or Mossadeq, they turned to those sources sooner rather than later. Moreover, they learned that the United States could be very useful as an enemy. Arbenz, Mossadeq, and even Allende sought Washington's approval, or at least its acquiescence. By contrast, if the United States was of use to Castro, the Sandinistas, and the Ayatollah Ruhollah Khomeini, it was primarily as a foreign demon against which their revolutions could rally—even though the Sandinistas were prepared to accept American aid as long as it was forthcoming, and the revolutionary Iranians were not above seeking American spare parts for their military. In 1979 Iranians took Americans hostage and released them only when they ceased to be useful counters in the bargaining within the revolution. Suffice it to say that no one learned the value of America-as-enemy better than Osama bin Laden.

## VALUES AND INSTRUMENTS

In all likelihood, the record shows, covert operations will become known, and America will be judged for having undertaken them. Thus, the practical lessons lead into moral issues. These issues are muted now by the fearsomeness of the terrorist threat. They are hardly unique to covert intervention, though they are powerfully present there, and they risked—and may still risk—being obscured in policy making by the presumption that covert actions will remain secret. Overt interventions, such as the American invasion of Grenada in 1983 or Panama in 1989, or military attacks, such as the bombing of Libya in 1986 or Sudan and Afghanistan in 1998, raise similar moral and instrumental concerns.

These concerns are not absolute; they must be considered against the gravity of the threat and the adequacy of other available responses.

In December 1976, when I was in Washington working with several old friends who were making arrangements for the transition between the Ford National Security Council (NSC) and the Carter NSC, we had decided to retain the basic structure of the Ford operation, with its network of sub-Cabinet committees for particular purposes. Yet of course, as a new administration, it was necessary to change the names of those committees, and so we joked about naming options. The 40 Committee, the Ford administration's group for discussing covert action, would become the "If They Can Do It, So Can We" Committee.

Yet, "if they can do it, so can we" did not seem, even then, to be an unacceptable rationale on either moral or instrumental grounds. What the Soviet Union or other nations did could not settle the issue, nor can how terrorists act. We consider ourselves different from them and imagine that the difference is not only basic to what we are as a people but also a source of American influence in the world, part of this country's moral armor.

We also believe that the example of democracy is powerful, one toward which peoples all over the world will gravitate if given the chance. Believing that, we must also believe that the example is a powerful part of our external behavior, not just of our internal arrangements. If people will choose democracy when given the chance, then democracy is demeaned, perhaps doomed to fail, if it is imposed from the outside. There is something incongruous about helping overthrow governments—especially ones that come to power through elections that we would define as tolerably fair (as in Chile in 1970)—in the name of democracy.

In this view, some of the successes of covert action seem, on the one hand, ambiguous or transient in retrospect, accomplished at significant cost to what we hold dear as a people and to America's image in the world. On the other hand, the world is a nasty, complicated place. The fight against terror has driven home that lesson. In that regard Americans' historical ambivalence between the high moral view and the feeling that international politics is a dirty business is understandable.

Terrorism aside, nations affect each other's politics in so many ways that any too-tidy definition of *intervention* is suspect. In all the examples cited, covert action formed only part of American policy. The United States decided whether to grant economic aid to Cuba, Chile, or Angola, and whether to release Iranian assets held in the United States. Most of these decisions were based on explicitly political criteria. Even if similar decisions toward other countries are not so clearly political, the decisions in any case have political effects on the country in question; foreign political leaders have no doubt of that fact.

The same is true of actions by private American actors. U.S.-based businesses either invest or do not invest in a country, and that decision too has not just an economic but also a political effect. That is the case even if the decision is not political in any narrow sense of the term. Most of the businesses or banks that chose not to invest in Chile under Allende probably did not make that choice for any specific political reason, despite Washington's pressure. Rather, their decision was a business one, based on the climate in Chile. They saw that judgment as an economic one, though political instability surely was a factor in it.

In this context, if a unilateral self-denying ordinance against all intervention—open or covert—seemed too restrictive when the Soviet threat existed, it surely does now in an era of terrorism. Some threats to American national security require responses. Some American friends deserve support. What is imperative to keep in mind is the long-term costs of intervention for a government that is not notable for attending to long-term considerations.

Given that "covert" action is not likely to remain secret, why not act openly? In the case of aid to the FNLA and UNITA in Angola, covert rather than overt aid spared the first identification with the United States for only a few months; as for aid to the contras in Nicaragua, the "covert" form made not one whit of difference. The operation quickly became known, and the same was true of aid to the *mujahedeen* in Afghanistan. Nor is it obvious that in most of these cases that the recipients of American largesse minded the source of the money being known. There is also the risk that covertness creates a self-fulfilling prophecy: If the United States only aids its friends secretly, then any link to the United States may seem sinister, portending much more than is actually the case.

The scope for doing openly what might earlier have been done covertly has increased dramatically since the 1970s. Sovereignty has become less absolute, and international law has come to recognize people, not just nation-states. In that sense, international law has moved in a very "American" direction, even if Americans do not always like the results, as with the creation of the International Criminal Court. But international practice (if not law) has come to recognize that some behavior by national leaders justifies external intervention, even with force of arms.

American radio stations broadcasting into Eastern Europe and the Soviet Union from Munich, Radio Free Europe, and Radio Liberty, were private organizations in form; advertisements exhorted Americans to contribute to them. In fact, they were created and financed covertly by the CIA as propaganda vehicles. When that support was disclosed in 1967, the radio stations nevertheless continued to operate; they became supervised by a board and supported openly by appropriations from Congress.

In the 1980s, the Reagan administration was moved to create the National Endowment for Democracy (NED), on the model of the (then West) German party foundations, like the Konrad Adenauer Stiftung. They are instruments of the major parties but are supported openly by government money. They have openly assisted kindred parties and labor movements around the world. The NED, whose core budget reached $40 million in 2003, channels money to institutes of the two American political parties plus an AFL-CIO group and a business group, which then make grants in support of democratic institutions in a number of countries around the world.[19]

So far, the record of the endowment is mixed but hopeful. Its grants, and those of its four constituent institutes, began by being cautious and close to government policy. It remains an open question whether, given American politics, public funding is compatible with creative (and thus controversial) acts by private groups. The original NED budget was only an eighth of that of the German party foundations. Over the years, Congress has put a variety of restrictions on the endowment—for instance, in 1985 Congress halved the endowment budget and denied any funding to the Republican and Democratic institutes, although that prohibition was relaxed the next year. It may still be easier for the CIA to get money from Congress secretly than for another institution to get it openly—even if the purposes of the two are broadly similar. Funding for the CIA remains wrapped in the cloak of national security, so members of Congress may be prepared to fund particular activities but prefer not to be seen to vote for them openly.

Still, the endowment organizations have become more venturesome as the international and domestic climate has changed. More important, the endowment now works with scores of kindred organizations, both from other governments and from the private sector. To illustrate the change, in the mid-1980s, the NED provided more than $400,000 over two years to the American Friends of Afghanistan to develop educational and cultural facilities inside those portions of the country controlled by the resistance groups—activity that might in other times have been called the civic action component of a paramilitary operation.

By contrast, before Slobodan Milosevic fell from power in 2000, the endowment and other U.S. government sources openly funded opposition parties and groups to the tune of some $25 million.[20] Indeed, the whole operation was almost a carbon copy, done overtly, of what the United States had done earlier covertly in Chile, for instance. In the instance of Serbia, the main difference other than overtness was that U.S. government agencies had lots of company from other countries and private nongovernmental organizations (NGOs). In other respects, the post mortem could have been written by a CIA operative about Chile. For instance: "Foreign assistance should focus not only on political parties but should continue to support a broad range of nongovernmental organizations, labor unions, think tanks, and media."

Acting openly, however, is not always easy or a complete substitute for covert action. It requires an explicitness about influencing the politics of a foreign country that is uncomfortable for Americans and hence likely to be controversial. Moreover, governments that feel threatened by that open assistance can act to prevent it more easily than if it were covert. Yet even that ability is diminishing; national borders are more porous. Milosevic's Serbia did try to limit the assistance to opposition organizations. It had some success keeping foreign advisors out but much less success stopping money flows, and thus ended, somewhat paradoxically, with the worst of outcomes from its perspective: the antigovernment effort was well funded but harder to tar with the epithet "foreign influence" than it would have been had scores of foreign advisors been present. To quote the post mortem again: "While foreign assistance helped to build and sustain the broad anti-Milosevic coalition, indigenous organizations and action were mainly responsible for driving events."

A bias toward openness has it limitations, but surely it is the right long-term direction for American policy. Openness would reflect the reality that, as the century ends, national boundaries are more and more permeable. Given this reality, moreover, those groups the United States would like to support may not be so chary of accepting help, even—perhaps especially—if it is open. The United States would say to them: "We are prepared to support you but only openly. We think that is better for you. In any case, we know it is better for us."

## CHOOSING THE COVERT OPTION: LESSONS FROM HISTORY

The history of covert action before September 11, 2001, suggests that in deciding whether to choose the covert option, prudent policy makers should ask themselves a careful series of "what if" questions. That injunction applies to all policies, foreign and domestic. But it applies with special force to covert action because of the presumption of secrecy.

The most obvious "what if" is "what happens if—or more likely, *when*—it becomes public? What if it becomes public in midstream?" This is the *New York Times* test. Large covert actions will not remain secret, a reminder that is easy to state but hard to embody in the making of policy when the pressures go in the direction of wishful thinking. Witness the reflections on the Bay of Pigs invasion by Richard Bissell, then head of the CIA's clandestine service: "The argument was [not] made that this is now a very public business, and we'd better treat it as such, and either cancel it if we can't stand the publicity, or else do some of the things that will increase the chances of success if we are going to go forward with it."[21]

If the Iran operation of 1985–86 had remained secret for several years after all the U.S. hostages in Lebanon had been released, that success might have outweighed the costs of being seen to have traded arms for hostages when the operations became public. Perhaps. We cannot know for certain. It did not, however, take a sophisticated analysis to show that a covert policy targeted on some Iranians was vulnerable to being publicized by opposing Iranian factions if and when it suited their political purposes. And it was equally likely that when the cover was blown, trading arms for hostages with a nation the United States had denounced as terrorist would be deemed unacceptable—by America's allies, much of the rest of the world, and most important, the American people.

Of course, whether a particular covert operation can bear the test of disclosure is apparent in retrospect but often far from obvious before the fact. Prudence suggests that presidents pay careful attention to such warning signals as the review process throws up—the views of Cabinet officers, people in the White

House who attend to the president's interests, and congressional overseers who are surrogates for public reaction.

One warning signal, however, is evident in advance: Does the intervention contradict overt American policy? If it does, as with arms sales to Iran, it is especially improbable that the operation will withstand the test of disclosure. The arms sales were exactly the opposite of the administration's public policies, which had twisted the arms of America's allies not to sell arms to Iran, had sought an end to the Iran-Iraq war with neither a victor nor a vanquished, and had pledged not to bargain with terrorists over hostages, much less to sell arms to them.

A second "what if" is "what if the first intervention does not succeed? What then?" If covert action is to remain secret, most of the time it will have to be small. Small operations have often begun with grand purposes, objectives incommensurate with the instrument. When the goals could not be achieved, leaders were tempted to take the next step and the next. This happened in the Bay of Pigs invasion, Angola, and Iran in the mid-1980s. Sometimes a limited objective can be achieved, but its achievement makes it appealing to hope for more— witness Angola and perhaps Nicaragua, where the United States did seem to achieve its initial aim of cutting weapons supplies from Nicaragua to the anti-government rebels in El Salvador. Answering this "what if" suggests, at a minimum, careful attention to the CIA's covert operators themselves, for signs of skepticism about whether operations as initially conceived can achieve their purposes. Such signs were present between the lines of Track II in Chile, Angola, and Nicaragua. Some risks are worth running, but few are worth running in ignorance.

A third set of "what if" questions is "what signal will be received, by whom and with what result?" These judgments are also easier with the benefit of hindsight, for they involve calculations of threat and of American interests. Intelligence assessments by the CIA or the State Department provide one set of indicators. In 1985–86, for example, American intelligence on Iran was weak, but what there was offered precious little ground for believing there were moderates who might be detached from their revolutionary colleagues. Later U.S. intelligence cast doubt on the imminence of a Soviet threat to Iran, one of the original premises of the operation. These were cautions that the intended signals might go awry.

The nature of those who are to receive secret American assistance can provide another warning signal. Because their relationship to the United States is meant to be clandestine, the CIA is often in a weak position to compel them to act to suit American purposes, yet the United States inevitably will become associated with their actions, like it or not, if and when the fact of support becomes known. Aid to the contras was dogged by their origins in Somoza's hated National Guard and by charges of human rights violations. Similarly, support for resistance forces in Afghanistan could have been justified as a way to put strategic pressure on Soviet occupation of that country; but given the character of the resistance forces, it was hardly a way to bring democracy to Afghanistan—far from it.

The regional context, in particular the attitude of American friends in the region, is another source of guidance. In the instance of Afghanistan, American assistance to the resistance was supported, though with varying degrees of publicity, by nations ranging from Pakistan and Egypt to Saudi Arabia and China. In Central America this indicator was more ambiguous, for most of the nations of the region publicly expressed qualms about the aid to the contras while privately hoping the Sandinistas could be made to go away.

The second round of covert action in Angola raised these questions of signals given versus those intended, questions for which the 1975 episode provided guidance. In early 1986, the CIA was authorized to provide $15 million in weaponry to Jonas Savimbi's UNITA. For the Reagan administration, the intended signal was anticommunism. For the administration, there was nothing incompatible about supporting anticommunism in Angola and antiapartheid in South Africa. Alas, the reality of southern Africa frustrated that conception in the heads of Washington policy makers. Whatever his attractions, Savimbi had one flaw, a fatal one: he was almost completely dependent on South Africa, his army almost a unit of South Africa's. To support him was to signal to Africans that the United States was throwing its lot in with South Africa, in 1986 just as in 1975.

These rules of thumb amount to establishing a presumption against covert action. The guidance is mostly negative, a series of cautions. It is unwelcome to officials who are looking for something to do rather than something to avoid—a trait that runs deep in the American character and is reinforced by the circumstances in which covert action becomes an option. Yet given how both America and the world have changed over the postwar period, the circumstances in which major covert action makes sense as policy are sharply limited.

Guidelines akin to these were articulated in the 1970s by Cyrus Vance, later Secretary of State. For Vance, the criterion for covert action in the National Security Act of 1974—"affecting the national security"—was too loose. Instead, he recommended covert intervention only as an exceptional measure, when it was "absolutely essential to the national security" and when no other means would do.[22] Decisions would still be matters of judgment under this more restrictive guide, but no one has improved on the Vance standard.

## COVERT ACTION SINCE SEPTEMBER 11, 2001

How has covert action changed since 9/11? And how do those changes relate to the lessons from earlier operations? Most strikingly, 9/11 underscored all too dramatically another theme from my review of earlier covert actions—the problem of control. The very fact that the interventions are meant to be covert gives rise to special problems of control. The link between U.S. intentions and the actions of those foreigners is tenuous at best. They are acting; the United States is only helping. Their purposes may not be ours. They have every incentive to hear from their CIA liaisons what they want to hear or construe it to their own purposes. In the details of earlier operations, that meant that covertly supported groups sometimes engaged in a little unsanctioned drug dealing or killing along the way or tried to overturn regimes when the United States only thought it was keeping opposition forces alive.

In supporting the anti-Soviet *mujahedeen* in Afghanistan, however, the problem of control was strategic. To minimize the American role, the CIA provided mostly money. Most of the contact in Afghanistan with the *mujahedeen* was done by Pakistan's Inter-Services Intelligence (ISI). For its own and Pakistani reasons, ISI gave preference to the radical Islamists among the *mujahedeen*, and in doing so, sowed the seeds for the takeover of Afghanistan by the Taliban and the formation of Al Qaeda as a unified fighting force. "Their" purposes were manifestly not "ours." The two sets of purposes converged only so long as both wanted to expel the Soviet Union from Afghanistan.

In that sense, the problem of control merges with the more general problem of longer term, unintended side effects, one that afflicts not only foreign policy but all of human action. In this case, however, as in most others, it seems unlikely that any amount of asking "what if" could have changed the decisions in the 1970s and 1980s. The "what if" was simply too iffy. The Soviet Union was there in Afghanistan. Getting it out, somehow, was more than U.S. policy makers at the time could hope for. No story about the trail from ISI support to the Taliban to Al Qaeda to collapsing towers could have been made vivid enough to change the decision. The most that might have been accomplished would have echoed David Phillips's comment about Guatemala a half century earlier: support for the *mujahedeen* didn't have to entail that the United States would forget about Afghanistan after the Soviet Union departed.

One big part of the change in covert action happened before 9/11, as Serbia illustrated. Given the end of the Cold War and the changing currents in international law and attitudes, the CIA seems all but out of the business of Chile-style political actions to sustain opposition forces or overturn regimes. In 2006, the Bush administration proposed major funding in support of Iranian opposition groups, but it did so openly, through the State Department. There may arise cases in which covert funding seems imperative—it is hard to imagine supporting North Korean opposition elements at all, and surely impossible openly—but they should be rare. In promoting democracy, or even regime change, the world has transformed enough to allow the bias toward openness to prevail, along with the bias toward company.

To that extent, covert action has become, post-9/11, primarily paramilitary, with the CIA operating either independently or, more often, with military special operators. Surely, the CIA's performance as the first Americans in Afghanistan was impressive.[23] Its operations were secret only in their tactical details, and thus met the *New York Times* test. The national investigation of 9/11 lauded that CIA role and the Afghanistan precedent of joint CIA-military teams. It recommended, though that the CIA cede responsibility for directing and executing operations to the military, with agency officers and capabilities integrated into military-directed teams, giving both the CIA and the Special Forces the opportunity to do what each does best.[24] The December 2004 intelligence reform bill was silent on this issue, and the CIA and the military decided that both would remain in the paramilitary operations business.

Which agency is responsible for conducting paramilitary operations has been at issue well before 9/11, driven by Vietnam and other episodes. The arguments for giving the military control have been, historically, the ones the 9/11 Commission cited: the requisite capabilities are military, the task has not been a continuous priority for the CIA, and it makes no sense for the nation to build two parallel capacities. Operations by the military would give those carrying them out the status of combatants under international law, at least if they were visibly soldiers. On the other side is the concern that the military was never very agile or discreet, let alone covert. That concern may have diminished, but not disappeared, as the special forces have developed a wide variety of units and types of operations.

Whatever else is occurring, the special forces and the CIA are being thrust together, and the CIA is being pushed into counterterrorism operations, both with the military and independently. Both kinds of operations raise thorny questions of authorization and accountability. In 2002, CIA operatives killed five suspected Al Qaeda operatives in Yemen with a Predator missile fired from an unmanned aerial vehicle (UAV). One of the five was a U.S. citizen.[25] The CIA conducted a similar attack in 2006 along the border between Pakistan and Afghanistan.

CIA covert operations require a presidential finding, one transferred in secret to the relevant committees of Congress.[26] Existing findings apparently provided authorization for the CIA to conduct both Predator attacks. By contrast, a similar operation conducted by military special forces could be set in motion simply by the chain of command from the president as commander-in-chief. Unfortunately, the difference may be less than meets the eye, however, if findings have become so broad in the war on terror as to cover almost any CIA operation. If so, however, the problem lies with the breadth of the findings. If they are so broad as to cover almost anything, then the finding process has become a sham.

## COVERT ACTION AND OPEN DEMOCRACY

The United States will remain in the business of covert action. It will continue to confront the paradox of secret operations in a democracy, even if those operations are mostly paramilitary and counterterrorist in character. Unfortunately, the process of congressional oversight of intelligence, including covert action, so carefully crafted in the 1970s, is now regarded as something of a joke in Washington. Terrorism is frightening enough to the body politic to justify almost any action in response—though the controversy in 2006 over eavesdropping on Americans by the National Security Agency in the wake of the terrorist attacks of 9/11 emphasizes the "almost." The House and Senate oversight committees have not escaped the bitter partisanship that has come to afflict Congress as a whole, and for a variety of reasons, the stature of the committee members has declined, though with several sparkling exceptions.

The 9/11 Commission suggested that if a single national intelligence director is to oversee the entire intelligence community—and preside over funding for all of it—Congress also should concentrate its oversight. Accordingly, the commission called on Congress to renew its commitments from the 1970s, having either a single joint committee to oversee intelligence (on the model of the old Atomic Energy Committee) or single committees in each house. Like the House Homeland Security Committee after them, the intelligence committees were never given the monopoly that was intended at their creation, and through the years even more committees have become involved.

The commission also sought to revamp ideas from the 1970s agreements in several other ways. To represent other committees with interests in the field, the new oversight committee or committees would revert to the practice of having a member who also serves on each of the following committees or subcommittees: Armed Services, Judiciary, Foreign Affairs, and Defense Appropriations. To promote continuity and expertise, oversight committee members should serve indefinitely on the new intelligence committees. The new committees should be smaller—perhaps seven or nine members in each chamber of Congress—so that each member feels a greater sense of responsibility and accountability for the quality of the committee's work.

Here, too, the arguments are of long standing, running back to the congressional investigations of the 1970s. However, changing times reshuffle the arguments. Surely the idea of having real focal points is the right one. The objective was identical in the 1970s, but it was never fully achieved and has eroded since then as more committees have gotten into the act. In those days, the model favored by the 9/11 Commission, a single committee for both houses on the Atomic Energy Committee model, was not in favor, for it was regarded as having become the captive of the agency it oversaw. That fear that permanent committee members might become too cozy with the agencies they oversaw also led Congress in the 1970s to give the intelligence committees rotating memberships.

Now, however, those memories are distant and the need for focal points more intense. To try to achieve those points, the commission also favored the 1970s practice of appointing members from other committees with stakes in intelligence to the oversight committees. So, too, by the lights of 2004, when the commission reported, the need for experience on the oversight committees outweighed concerns over cooption, and so the commission favored open-ended assignments to the committee or committees, not rotating ones. But these are details. The real challenge for Congress is not to lag too far behind the executive branch in its own reshaping for the intelligence challenges of the twenty-first century.

The Iran-*contra* affair two decades earlier showed how difficult it can be to manage the paradox of secret operations in an open society. When the president finally signed the finding in January 1986 for the Iran arms sales operation, that finding was explicit: do not tell Congress. The congressional overseers did not find out about the Iran operation until autumn—hardly the law's requirement of "fully and currently informed" by anyone's definition. Later on the president himself apparently was not told, when the Iran and *contra* operations crossed with proceeds from the arms sales to Iran used to fund the contras without congressional appropriation.

In another sense, however, the system worked. In deciding to sell arms to Iran, the president pursued a line of policy opposed by both his Secretaries of State and Defense, about which he was afraid to inform the congressional intelligence committees and which was liable to be revealed by Iranian factions when it suited them. It is hard to imagine any system providing more warning signals. When most of the government's senior foreign policy officials are opposed, it is likely that the policy is wrong. The president thus proceeded at his own peril.

With regard to the diversion of money for the contras, the lesson is a caution for presidents and those who advise them: do not run covert operations from the White House. Before the 1970s it would have been unthinkable for an administration to do so; then the reason was that presidents wanted to stay at arm's length from such things, even if they could not plausibly deny them in a pinch. Now, though, if covert actions are to be undertaken, they should be done by the agency of government constructed to do them—the CIA. It has both the expertise and the accountability.

Moreover, the history of covert action suggests that if the president's closest advisors become the operators, the president loses them as sources of detached judgment on the operations. The president's own circle become advocates, as Allen Dulles did in the Bay of Pigs invasion, not protectors of the president's stakes (even if he does not quite realize his need for protection). So it was with Reagan's National Security Advisors, Robert McFarlane and John Poindexter; once committed, they had reason to overlook the warning signals thrown up by the process. Excluding the designated congressional overseers also excluded one more "political scrub," one more source of advice about what the American people would find acceptable. And the chances increased that someone like Lt. Col. Oliver North would misguidedly interpret the president's interest after his own fashion.

William Miller, the staff director of the first Senate Intelligence Committee, reflected on the Iran-*contra* affair: "If clear lines hadn't been drawn a decade ago, there would have been no hue and cry now."[27] Now is the time to remember again those lines and draw them again, all the more so as the boundary between covert action and military special operations blurs.

## NOTES

1. For an assessment by a fellow staffer, see Loch K. Johnson, "Congressional Supervision of America's Secret Agencies: The Experience and Legacy of the Church Committee," *Public Administration Review* 64 (January 2004), pp. 3–14.

2. See *Final Report of the Select Committee to Study Governmental Operations with Respect to Intelligence Activities of the United States Senate*, 94th Congress, 2nd sess. (1976). For links to these reports, as well as to a rich range of other documents, both historical and contemporary, see www.icdc.com/~paulwolf/cointelpro/cointel.htm.

3. The "40" merely referred to the directive that had created the committee. At other times, in modest attempts at discretion, the committees had been named for the room in which they met.

4. Gregory F. Treverton, *Covert Action: The Limits of Intervention in the Postwar World* (New York: Basic Books, 1987). This chapter draws on an article produced from the book, Gregory F. Treverton, "Covert Action and Open Society," *Foreign Affairs* 65, no. 5 (Summer 1987).

5. For an authoritative account of the affair, see *Report of the President's Special Review Board* (the Tower Commission) (Washington, DC: Government Printing Office, 1987). The *Final Report of the Independent Counsel for Iran/Contra Matters* (1993), is available at http://www.fas.org/irp/offdocs/walsh.

6. Reprinted in William M. Leary, ed., *The Central Intelligence Agency: History and Documents* (Tuscaloosa: University of Alabama Press, 1984), pp. 131–33.

7. Cited in Kermit Roosevelt, *Countercoup: The Struggle for the Control of Iran* (New York: McGraw-Hill, 1979), p. 199. Because Roosevelt's account is not independently documented, his recollections should be taken as evocative, not gospel truth.

8. The most authoritative account of the Guatemala intervention is Richard H. Immerman, *The CIA in Guatemala: The Foreign Policy of Intervention* (Austin: University of Texas Press, 1982), though additional details have been declassified more recently.

9. Quoted in Theodore C. Sorensen, *Kennedy* (New York: Harper & Row, 1965), p. 309.

10. The best account of covert action during this period is *Covert Action in Chile*, staff report to the Senate Select Committee . . . on Intelligence Activities, 94th Congress, 1st sess. (December 1975).

11. See, for example, Conor Cruise O'Brien, "How Hot Was Chile?" *The New Republic*, August 26, 1985, p. 37.

12. Author's press briefing on behalf of the Church Committee, Washington, DC, December 4, 1975.

13. David Atlee Phillips, *The Night Watch* (New York: Atheneum, 1977), p. 53.

14. For accounts of both, see chapters 8 and 9 of John Prados, *Presidents' Secret Wars: CIA and Pentagon Covert Operations Since World War II* (New York: Morrow, 1986).

15. Both Track II and the anti-Castro plots are detailed in *Alleged Assassination Plots Involving Foreign Leaders*, an interim report of the Senate Select Committee . . . on Intelligence Activities, 94th Congress, 1st see. (November 20, 1975).

16. This number is rough, based on my interviews at the time and on press accounts. In any case, the precise number does not mean very much because operations vary widely in cost, not to mention risk and degree of controversy.

17. Interview with author, Washington, DC (January 9, 1986).

18. See Steve Coll, *Ghost Wars: The Secret History of the CIA, Afghanistan, and Bin Laden, from the Soviet Invasion to September 10, 2001* (New York: Penguin Press, 2004).

19. The NED's website contains a careful history of the idea and organization, one that is self-aware of the constraints on NED's operations. See http://www.ned.org/about/nedhistory.html.

20. For this figure, the following quotes, and a nice summary of the Serbian case, see United States Institute of Peace, *Whither the Bulldozer: Nonviolent Revolution and the Transition to Democracy in Serbia,* Special Report 72, 6 August 2001, available at http://www.usip.org/pubs/specialreports/sr72.html.

21. Interview, Columbia University Oral History Research Office (1967), p. 25.

22. Testimony before the Senate Select Committee . . . on Intelligence Activities (Dec. 5, 1975).

23. As usual in Washington, if success didn't have a thousand fathers, it surely did have a thousand chroniclers. Among many accounts of the CIA's role, see Gary C. Schroen, *First In: How the CIA Spearheaded the War on Terror in Afghanistan* (New York: Random House, 2005).

24. Formally, the National Commission on Terrorist Attacks upon the United States, *The 9/11 Commission Report* (Washington, DC, 2004), available at http://www.9-11 commission.gov (accessed August 2, 2004). The specific recommendations are summarized in the Executive Summary and spelled out in more detail in chapter 13, "How to Do It? A Different Way of Organizing the Government."

25. See Dana Priest, "U.S. Citizen Among Those Killed in Yemen Predator Missile Strike," *Washington Post*, November 8, 2002, available at http://www-tech.mit.edu/V122/N54/long4-54.54w.html; Walter Pincus, "U.S. Strike Kills Six in Al Qaeda: Missile Fired by Predator Drone; Key Figure in Yemen Among Dead," *Washington Post*, November 5, 2002, p. A01, available at http://www.washingtonpost.com/ac2/wp-dyn?pagename=article&node=&contentId=A5126-2002Nov4&notFound=true (accessed April 25, 2005).

26. The term *finding* comes from the Hughes-Ryan Act of 1974, which required the president to "find" a particular operation necessary to U.S. national security. Turned into a noun, that became a finding delivered in secret to relevant committees of Congress.

27. Interview with author, Washington, DC (January 16, 1987).

# 2

# COVERT ACTION

## The "Quiet Option" in International Statecraft

KEVIN A. O'BRIEN

## INTRODUCTION

SINCE THE DAWN OF THE NATION-STATE IN international relations, great powers have attempted to control and, if necessary, destroy other powers in a quest for world dominion and control. The nineteenth and twentieth centuries saw the evolution of these policies into refined, fully developed state actions throughout the world, dominated by a few powers alone. The mechanisms and methods used in this quest evolved over time, in most cases becoming more refined and successful—and generally involved three categories of activities: diplomacy, war, and "statecraft," the latter the activities of states when neither of the first two activities were viable options. Indeed, it would appear that these mechanisms of state power developed to their fullest in the post-1945 era, when the third option—statecraft and its primary instrument, covert action—became the mainstay of the Cold War.

Covert action is often been referred to as "the quiet option," both in terms of the intelligence activity and—more broadly—international relations. Used throughout human history, it became—much like the rest of the intelligence activity—a formalized, bureaucratized element of intelligence during the twentieth century. Reaching its height during the Cold War, during which it was used extensively by both East and West blocs in pursuit of both their geostrategic interests and their own rivalry, as a tool it has witnessed a few changes since the end of the Cold War.

Over the past three decades, particularly within the institutions of U.S. governance, covert action has been both far more broadly defined and constrained under legislative and executive statutes and norms; however, this has not meant an end to the use of covert action as a tool of state policy—far from it. Although today covert action would appear to be less of a concern to those interested in the oversight and accountability of intelligence matters and activities, it has remained an often used tool of states around the world. Much like during the Cold War—and for decades, if not centuries, before it—covert action continues to be a tool used to support states' interests and rivalries around the world.

This chapter discusses the "uses and limits" (as Treverton refers to it) of covert action over history, outlining the different categories of covert action witnessed and the utility to which each was put. I provide examples as case studies of these uses and limits, and will consider the implications and impact of the use of each category of covert action outlined. I outline these uses in the different historical periods considered—war, peace, in the shadow world of the Cold War, finally considering "wither covert action today" as the post–Cold War interregnum came to a close in mid-2001 and the twenty-first century's first global war—the war on terrorism—began. My focus centers heavily on the United States (most particularly) and the Soviet Union during the Cold War—both because covert action was very much *the* tool of the Cold War's bipolar confrontation and because assessing quantifiable data on covert activities more recently is difficult (given their recent occurrence)—with other countries providing examples throughout.[1]

## DELINEATING COVERT ACTION

In many ways, covert action (CA)—referred to by the Soviets as active measures—reached its height during the Cold War in terms of the extent of its uses, the bureaucracy that developed to support it, and the interest that was taken in it by the public. The scope of CA is very broad—Johnson calls it the " 'third option' between diplomacy and open warfare"[2] placed firmly between these options; Godson defines it simply as "the attempt by a government to influence events in another state or territory without revealing its involvement."[3] Its covert nature allows states to use it when the first option—diplomacy—is insufficient to achieve an aim, but the second—warfare—is not an option. In British terms, covert action was always seen as "special political action," emphasizing its direct linkage to policy.[4] According to official American definitions—or, at least, delineations of covert activities—it constitutes both "such other functions and duties related to intelligence affecting the national security" and "activities conducted in support of national foreign policy objectives abroad which are planned and executed so that the role of the [government] is not apparent or acknowledged publicly" (according to the 1947 U.S. National Security Act and Executive Order 12333 signed by President Reagan in 1981).[5] This latter element—the fact that this option is chosen by governments when they do not want their presence or hand acknowledged or notable, granting "plausible deniability"—is central to appreciating all aspects of CA. Such catchall phrases have—in the U.S. case, legally speaking—allowed for the undertaking of significant covert activities by

the government in a manner that attempts to find the balance between the stag-
nancy of diplomacy and the risk of overt military force.

The key categories of CA are *propaganda* (also referred to as psychological
operations), *political CA* (CPA), *economic CA*, and *paramilitary CA*.[6] Each will
be explored in greater depth in this chapter.

Godson also provides a distinction between covert action and counterintelligence, where the latter is "targeted at adversary intelligence operatives and their
political masters" compared to the former which targets "non-intelligence
players"—this distinction is as true in the twenty-first century as it was during the
Cold War.[7] Finally, covert action is linked to but not an element of the intelligence process: it can both contribute and react to intelligence. As Steiner warns
recently, CA is "the most sensitive technique for implementing national security
policy.... [CA] is all about making things happen, while intelligence consists of
making the right decisions about what to make happen."[8]

## COVERT ACTION THROUGHOUT HISTORY

Since the dawn of time, CA has been used as an element of societies both
conducting intelligence activities against each other and wishing to undermine
each other. Examples throughout history are manifold—a key example of covert
action was the bribery of foreign officials and rulers as a means of persuasion. As
Blackstock notes, throughout the eighteenth century, the major European powers
used secret state funds extensively (and unsuccessfully) to bribe various foreign
leaders to their cause—such as in Sweden in the 1740s, when England, France,
Russia, and Denmark spent enormous sums on the bribery of political party
leaders, with little result.[9]

During periods of war in the twentieth century, CA was used extensively. In
World War I, the so-called Campaign in the Desert carried out by Lawrence of
Arabia saw a key, covert sabotage and destruction raiding element deployed—
using British officers and Arab (Bedouin) tribes to both distract the Ottoman
Turks (whom, as allies of Imperial Germany in the War, the British were fighting
in the Middle East) and press the British advantage in capturing and securing
large territories in the Middle East against French and American interests. Such
guerrilla warfare tactics that Lawrence developed became the touchstone for
similar activities in the post-1945 decolonization wars and the example on which
most Western covert paramilitary insurgency/counterinsurgency tactics were
predicated.[10]

As World War I drew to a close and the Russian Revolution and subsequent
civil war gathered momentum, the teeter-totter of the twentieth century's global
conflict between the forces of worldwide communism and capitalism began to
deploy CA as a key element of the struggle between them. Though such activities
came into their prime during the Cold War period, during the interregnum of
1917 to 1939, CA was used widely by newly established Soviet Russia to both

counteract the activities abroad of anti-Bolshevik elements (especially in the United Kingdom and United States) and to begin the spread of world socialism through the Communist International as the first stages of worldwide socialist revolution. One of the best (and most successful) examples of this in history was the Monarchist Association of Central Russia, better known as "The Trust": targeting White Russian émigré groups in a massive deception operation aimed at penetrating these groups and flushing out remaining White Russian supporters and sympathizers back in Soviet Russia.[11]

In Ireland, following the 1916 Easter Rising, the newly formed Irish Republican Army under Michael Collins used covert tactics to harass, assassinate, and sabotage institutions and individuals of British power in Ireland during the Irish War of Independence (1919–21)—and later the opposing side in Irish civil war (1922–23)—so successfully that his activities became the template for covert urban and rural paramilitary operations for the rest of that century.[12]

During World War II, CA was used extensively in many forms—economic, political, paramilitary and (certainly) psychological—to support the overt war operations. Indeed, it could be said that the war began with a covert paramilitary operation that simultaneously had an extreme propaganda intention: the deployment of German soldiers, SS men dressed in Polish uniforms (in their own pseudo-operation), and dead concentration camp inmates at the German-Polish border to give the impression that Germany had been provoked into counterattacking Poland on September 1, 1939.

The May 1942 assassination in Prague of SS intelligence chief Reinhard Heydrich by Czech partisans working with the British Special Operations Executive (SOE) is a prime example of assassination as a form of covert paramilitary action. Indeed, the very establishment of the SOE, its sister organization the Political Warfare Executive, and the U.S. Office of Strategic Services (OSS) were all aimed at establishing the ability to conduct covert operations against Axis interests throughout the territories that they occupied during the war. Significant deception operations—such as the Double-Cross System used in the intelligence war between the British and Germans on the personal level and Operation FORTITUDE, the massive deception operation used to support the D-Day landings, on the grand strategic deception level—were played out as a component of both covert political action and psychological operations. Overall, the quantity and variety of covert actions deployed during World War II was massive.[13]

## COVERT ACTION DURING THE COLD WAR

It was truly during the period since 1945—centered on the Cold War period—when covert action came into its prime as one of the key elements of statecraft. The Cold War could be appreciated as "a war carried on by means short of sustained, overt, military confrontation," implicitly conveying the understanding that the confrontation between the Western world (dominated by the United

States) and the communist bloc (dominated by the Soviet Union) was covert in nature—resorting more often than not to nonmilitary means in an attempt to undermine the authority of the opposing power while maintaining control and influence over their own sphere. This clash was not unforeseen: Lenin stated in 1921 that "the existence of the Soviet Republic side by side with the imperialist States is in the long run unthinkable ... a series of the most terrible clashes between the Soviet Republic and the bourgeois States is unavoidable."[14]

In this sense, therefore, the origins of the use of covert action during the Cold War lay with the governments of both the United States and the Soviet Union and their interactions both between the years 1919 and 1939 and during World War II. The main concern of the United States (as well as significant Allied countries, such as the United Kingdom, Canada, and Australia) was the growth in communist influence within Western societies. This increased until, during the period following the early days of the Cold War, it was perceived as "the global challenge of Communism ... to be confronted wherever and whenever it seemed to threaten our interests."[15] Ultimately, as Maurer has pointed out, whereas the United States— like most democratic countries (as well as leading regional powers such as South Africa or India)—tended to distinguish between overt and covert activities, "the Soviet Union [placed] a premium on influencing other countries' beliefs about both itself and the [United States], and that the Soviets [made] little distinction between overt and covert means [in so doing]"—an important distinction to keep in mind throughout this chapter.[16]

Covert action during the Cold War symbolized an ideological conquest for the soul of the world that was the basis of the rivalry between the Western and Soviet (East bloc communist) intelligence services. Within the period of 1945 to 1991, both powers developed their security and intelligence services as a mechanism by which this confrontation could be carried out; in the United States, the Central Intelligence Agency (CIA) was founded in 1947 for (originally) the purpose of intelligence collection and dissemination. In the Soviet Union, the KGB was reorganized out of the previous intelligence and security services following Stalin's death in 1953. Both services soon rapidly developed covert action arms that far outweighed their intelligence collection missions. In the case of the KGB, such activity had been the mainstay of the previous incarnations of Soviet security (Cheka, GPU, OGPU, NKVD, MGB, MVD), whereas the United States had only developed such an ability with the founding of the OSS during World War II—which was disbanded at the end of the war, two years before the founding of the CIA.

### The Development of U.S. Covert Action

In any discussion of covert action—particularly within the Cold War context—the United States provides some of the best (and worst) examples. Covert action is an instrument of statecraft that the United States had long deployed (as with any other power) over the course of its development and expansion (at the least, following the 1898 Spanish-American War). In the post-1945 period in its confrontation with the Soviet Union—both directly and, more frequently, indirectly—the United States used CA extensively and increasingly. Given the nature of the Cold War, CA became the tool for the United States to deploy to both further its interests and undermine its adversaries, particularly the Soviets, in pursuit of their own interests. Indeed, the establishment of the primary tool—the CIA—by which covert actions were developed and used changed the entire raison d'être of the agency as it was originally envisaged. Covert action developed largely due to the plausible deniability implicit in its definition, and the official delineation of CA ("such other functions and duties related to intelligence affecting the national security," as taken from the 1947 National Security Act) provided foreign policy makers the "allowance" to use the CIA to conduct clandestine operations as its primary mission, rather than the collection and dissemination of intelligence as the original formers of its mandate envisioned. This has been further institutionalized by the Executive Orders of successive presidents.[17]

This is not to say that using such means are peculiar to the post-1947 period in U.S. foreign policy. In reality, the use of such covert actions in U.S. foreign policy took flight at the end of the nineteenth century with the Spanish-American War but began their development much earlier. Although a complex subject unto itself, such capabilities and operations that were later inherent to American covert activities abroad were the direct descendants of the methods of intervention, control, and subversion that the United States deployed—particularly in Central and South America—as part of its Monroe-driven hemispheric hegemony during the second half of the nineteenth and first half of the twentieth centuries. These included the processes of direct and indirect interventions, the use of front or partner organizations (such as the United Fruit Company) in assisting with such control, and the deployment of covert economic and political activities to further those methods of control. By the 1950s, these same approaches had matured into fully developed covert action capabilities.

## The Growth of U.S. Covert Action Capabilities

Despite the growth of its covert (and overt) intervention and control capabilities during the previous 100 years, by 1941 the United States—unlike the Soviet Union, the United Kingdom, and virtually every other major power in the world—still did not have an established intelligence service. The attack on Pearl Harbor caused the United States to seriously reexamine their intelligence abilities, as this came to symbolize the worst failure ever of intelligence facilities in modern times.[18] Realizing that it could never again suffer such a surprise attack and to avert it from happening again, the U.S. government determined that it would be necessary to establish a foreign intelligence service with the aim of information collection, covert action, and counterintelligence.

In July 1942, Roosevelt established the Office of Strategic Services (OSS) to coordinate and develop methods of subterfuge and covert warfare. At the end of World War II, Truman abolished the OSS as unnecessary in its current form, having been designed for war. But it was soon apparent that the need for strategic intelligence, which had been divided up under control of the various branches of the military and state departments, would be of increasing importance as tensions began to build with the Soviet Union. The framework for this was pronounced in Kennan's famous article, "The Sources of Soviet Conduct", in which he stated that "in these circumstances it is clear that the main element of any United States policy toward the Soviet Union must be that of a long-term, patient but firm and vigilant containment of Russian expansive tendencies . . . by the adroit and vigilant application of counter-force at a series of constantly shifting geographical and political points, corresponding to the shifts and maneuvers of Soviet policy."[19] The worldview that this professed was further outlined in Eisenhower's secret 1954 National Security Council (NSC) memorandum, which stated: "If the US is to survive, long-standing American concepts of 'fair play' must be reconsidered. We must develop effective espionage and counterespionage services. We must learn to subvert, sabotage and destroy our enemies by more clear, more sophisticated and more effective methods than those used against us."[20] This centered on the idea that the Soviets would need to be confronted throughout the world on an increasingly involved level; this led Truman to institutionalize, through the Department of Defense and the Central Intelligence Group (later Agency), the military and intelligence/covert bureaus as the key arms of conducting this covert foreign policy.

In 1946, Truman established the Central Intelligence Group (CIG), modeled on the OSS; on July 26, 1947, the National Security Act was passed by Congress, replacing the CIG with the CIA and establishing the NSC as the sole advisory committee reporting directly to the president on matters of national security. This was followed two years later by the Central Intelligence Agency Act, which further defined the CIA's mandate.[21] As one of the five directives granted it by the National Security Act, the CIA was authorized to "perform such other functions and duties related to intelligence affecting the national security as the National Security Council may from time to time direct."[22] The ambiguity found in this directive was included to "provide flexibility to the newly created CIA in order to meet unforeseen challenges."[23] In reality, it was perceived to grant the authority to undertake covert actions around the globe as often as it liked without the necessity of congressional approval, some of which came dangerously close to undeclared war operations against foreign governments.

## U.S. Covert Action During the Cold War

Contemporary politics had a great deal to do with the origins of the policies related to covert action. In the case of the CIA, Europe during the late 1940s and into the 1950s was the United States' prime concern. Reconstruction was being carried out in Western Europe, but communist influence was strong. Politically in Italy and France, the communists threatened to destabilize the postwar political and economic balance that the United States was attempting to establish throughout the Western world. In addition, communist unions and organizations posed serious threats to the economic and social welfare of rebuilding Europe. In support of this covert confrontation within the emerging Cold War, the Covert Action Staff (CAS) was established within the CIA and given the Kennan-esque task of rolling back communism, initially in Europe.[24] The CAS—residing initially in the Office of Special Operations, which gave way to first the Directorate for Plans and later the Directorate of Operations—was to serve as a complementary branch to the Office of Policy Coordination (OPC)—itself founded in May 1948 on Kennan's encouragement and intended to "undercut debilitating strikes by Communist trade unions and election advances by Communist parties."[25] These operational roles were laid out in not only the National Security Act of 1947 but also in directives like NSC 10/2 and NSC 5412/2.[26] NSC 10/2, passed on June 18, 1948, by Truman, stated that "the overt foreign activities of the US Government must be supplemented by covert operations," which initiated the CIA's program of propaganda and paramilitary action against the Soviet Union. These operations could involve activities "up to a level just short of armed conflict by recognized military forces."[27]

This policy can be clearly summarized in three points: create and exploit problems for international communism, discredit international communism and reduce the strength of its parties and organizations, and reduce international communist control over any areas of the world.[28] More directly, as Marchetti and Marks state, "in most countries . . . the United States policy [was] usually to maintain the *status quo*, so most [CIA] subsidies are designed to strengthen the political base of those in power."[29] But the status quo could prove difficult to maintain, as Kolko notes: "The credibility of American military power and the emergence of geopolitical analogies and linkages in the form of the domino theory soon subjected US behavior and policies in many areas to new influences that paralleled and sometimes outweighed the more traditional narrower assessments of the economic and political stakes involved in success of failure, action or inaction, in some nation or region." This in turn led to "A growing number of de facto and formal alliances with Developing World surrogates . . . raising for the first time the United States' increasing dependence on inherently unstable men and regimes."[30]

The original policies of the CIA were to stabilize Western politics in favor of the United States as much as possible during the postwar period, while at the same time destabilizing and removing any elements that could threaten economic reconstruction and the political stability that it was intended to bring. The CAS was used extensively in support of this; however, by 1954 with the consolidation of American power in Europe—and the full development of the paramilitary capacity of the CIA—the agency turned its focus onto the developing world.[31] The shift of focus from Eastern Europe to the underdeveloped countries during the 1960s was due to, first, the establishment of the Iron Curtain and the Berlin Wall, lessening availability/opportunities to use classical forms of intelligence collection, leading to heavier reliance on electronic intelligence; and second, the general development of increased activity with policies in developing areas and the shift from a Soviet/Chinese focus to one on the developing world.[32] Furthermore, following African decolonization, CIA activity in Africa increased 56 percent (1959–63) due to fears of Soviet encroachment on these newly independent states.[33]

This shift in focus to the developing world was not solely due to the emerging Cold War confrontation there; it was also a continuation—indeed, reinvigoration—of previous American (and other powers') neocolonial interests in these countries. The 1953 joint CIA–Secret Intelligence Service (U.K.) operation in Iran in support of the shah (and, in turn, his support for the Anglo-Iranian Oil Company) and the 1954 operation in Guatemala (which attempted to use (once again) the United Fruit Company as a covert conduit for intervention, which ultimately was rejected by the company) both exemplified perfectly the growing interlinkage that the United States and other Western powers feared between socialist/communist movements and the efforts of decolonization (including its associated moves to "nationalize" strategic assets previously owned by Western companies, alongside other politico-economic moves that disturbed Western intelligence services and their political masters. Given the assistance that the Soviet Union rendered to these "national liberation" movements, one can find the central interests of Western intelligence in the 1950s and 1960s at this crossroads between the West's attempts to forestall or otherwise control the decolonization process while conducting similar efforts to confront the spread of Soviet influence and interest in the developing world.

These shifts also resulted in the aforementioned overall change in focus and mission of the CIA from an agency dedicated to intelligence collection and counterintelligence actions against its main adversary (the Soviet KGB and its satellite services) to an agency focused heavily on covert actions throughout the developing world—most of these the general (or even specific) continuation of the twin U.S. policies of noninterference and intervention practiced from the nineteenth century onward. The diachronic growth of covert action has been relative to the rapid growth of other aspects of foreign policy implementation due to the leading role the United States has played on the world stage since 1945. As successive presidents have been presented with the opportunity to use this quiet option rather than the other means of intervention, its very use increased immeasurably the number of times it would have to be used.[34] This self-perpetuation is just one of the problems that exist—the other being how successfully congressional oversight has ensured both adherence to mandates by the agencies involved and the accountability of the executive in authorizing covert actions.

In 1975—known as the Year of Intelligence, in which the U.S. intelligence community (and most particularly the CIA) were labeled as a "rogue elephant on the rampage" by the congressional Church Committee, investigating a growing succession of revelations relating to illegal covert activities conducted overseas by U.S. intelligence and military agencies (many dealing with the assassination of foreign nationals and leaders)—Congress moved to regain control over these activities. Starting with the 1974 Hughes-Ryan Act, which established a law requiring the reporting of secret arms sales and covert actions to the congressional intelligence review committees, Congress passed its own succession of legislation attempting to control such operations—including the 1980 Intelligence Accountability Act and the 1982 Boland Amendment.[35] However, as was evidenced by the Iran-*contra* arms dealers, who found their way around even these types of stipulations, serious flaws may continue to exist in the safeguards established to prevent such things from occurring.[36]

## Soviet Covert Action Development

In the case of the KGB, the Soviet intelligence services were carrying out such actions since the time of the Russian Revolution (such as the noted example of the Trust). Covert activities—clandestine political action in particular—were considered to be "the central thrust of the Kremlin's [foreign policy]...the leaders' prime executor of such policies is...the KGB."[37] From 1945, the United States was referred to as the "main adversary" of the KGB, a designation indicating the main focus of all activities, and as such policies were designed to take this into consideration.[38] KGB goals were not laid out as clearly as those of the CIA, but their aims do not seem to differ that much: generally an effort to influence the world toward a policy of friendliness for their parent state. Where they did differ was in their actions and aims against communist dissidents, defectors, and other threats to the continuation of the global communist revolution.

The KGB became the main arm of the Kremlin in dealing with both world communism and communists around the world. On the former, it justified the control it exerted over all aspects of international communism (client regimes, front organizations, proxy armies, etc.) by stating that "to ignore the activities of international progressive public movements...may isolate and weaken national revolutionary forces...fraught with the danger of defeat."[39] On the latter, it used its international reach to undermine and if necessary silence those from the East Bloc communist countries who had defected or otherwise organized external opposition to the supremacy and longevity of the Soviet state.

Soviet interests were essentially the same as in the West: a desire to establish influence throughout as much of the globe as possible. In the 1940s and early 1950s, these activities were focused on Europe. But like the CIA, the KGB shifted its focus to the developing world during the 1950s and 1960s, attempting to establish influence in this uncultivated area. One of the most significant defectors to the CIA throughout the course of the Cold War, Anatoli Golitsyn, stated that in 1959 the KGB's primary mission had changed from conventional espionage to "covert statecraft": the use of agents and other mechanisms to achieve geopolitical goals.[40] One final aspect of the relationship between the KGB and its proxies was that the KGB was itself the sword of another organization, the Communist Party of the Soviet Union (CPSU). All actions the KGB undertook internationally throughout the period were coordinated with the International Department of the Central Committee of the CPSU; the KGB was the conduit for implementing the internationalist policies of the party. The main branch of the KGB that carried out these activities was Department D (later Service A) of the First Chief Directorate; this department coordinated action directly with the International Department.[41] Much of this emerged out of the prewar policies of the COMINTERN: developing international organizations with the "basic aims of promoting the national Communist parties, propagating the Soviet line, and developing political forces subservient to Moscow."[42]

## EXAMPLES OF COVERT ACTIVITIES

### Propaganda and Psychological (Information) Operations

*Propaganda*—often referred to as psychological warfare/operations or *psy ops*—is a broad category under which a wide range of information operations can be undertaken. As part of what he refers to as "political warfare" (i.e., statecraft and covert action), Janowitz defined propaganda as "the planned dissemination of news, information, special arguments, and appeals designed to influence the beliefs, thoughts, and actions of a specific group."[43] Focused generally on activities undertaken as part of both covert and overt action—with corresponding deployment of white and black propaganda—it is often deployed in conjunction with other covert activities (e.g., covert political action) and with a wider aim than simply to propagandize. It can include activities in peacetime (such as benign government spin or malign persuasion activities) or wartime (such as military communications operations, cyber or "information" operations, or active psychological operations on both the tactical and strategic levels). A good example of such activities would involve leaks to various press outlets, either friendly (Western) or national outlets within the target country, in which a certain story or approach to a story is conveyed—for example, a pro–United States or pro-Soviet story in a country where the government opposes said power. Through this medium, native citizens can be seen to be supporting a particular U.S. position contrary to their own government, with the intended outcome often being the aiding or debasing of foreign political figures.[44] In one way, this is nothing new in the twentieth century: in a June 1853 article in the *New York Tribune* titled "The Russian Humbug," Karl Marx discounted widespread European press reports of Russian troop movements toward the Balkans as "nothing but so many ridiculous attempts on the part of Russian agents to strike a wholesome terror into the Western World."[45]

One key aim of propaganda is "persuasion": a term encompassing issues broader than simple propaganda, persuasion may be a mixture of threats and appeals which include a large element of spiritual or physical coercion and violence. This can include the use of bribery, blackmail, and the threat or application of such physical acts of violence as kidnapping, torture, and the use of "controls" over selected targets or agents. In this sense, "persuasion" is directly linked to what Allen Dulles described as the primary interests of "clandestine intelligence collection"—or espionage.

These activities were practiced equally by both Superpowers during the Cold War: in the 1950s, the US established a Psychological Strategy Board directly responsible to the President.[46] The Soviets subscribed to the same principle: "persuasion first, coercion afterward."[47] The media was used extensively in this pursuit by the CIA, the KGB, and virtually all any other intelligence service who wished to promote a particular view. The policies behind media usage were clear: general propaganda and support of one's own policies were the goal. To achieve this, the CIA used

> networks of several hundred foreign individuals ... who provide intelligence for the CIA and at times attempt to influence foreign opinion through the use of covert propaganda. These individuals provide the CIA with direct access to a large number of foreign newspapers and periodicals ... press services and news agencies, radio and television stations, commercial book publishers, and other foreign media outlets.[48]

For the KGB, a distinction was made between propaganda and disinformation: propaganda was described as "directly attributed to the Soviets, the satellites, the client states, or the obviously predisposed," whereas disinformation was "seldom attributable to these sources and depends on its false attribution to an ally, to 'discovered' classified documents that purport to reveal plans to attack the USSR and to other rumors, forgeries and orchestrated deceptions with enough verifiable content to raise serious doubts among allies."[49] Irvine has pointed out, half-jokingly, that "the extension of Communist control over vast areas and populations since the end of the Second World War has owed more to the propaganda and disinformation offensive of the Communist countries than to the power of their arms."[50]

While Radio Free Europe/Radio Liberty—established in 1949 and 1951 respectively, and run by the CIA until the early 1970s—operated overtly,[51] the hand of the U.S. government was covert, as it was assumed that they would "be more effective if the role of the [USG] was not apparent."[52] Other examples of CIA use of radio propaganda include the Voice of Liberation radio used during the coup in Guatemala in 1954;[53] Radio Nejat (Liberation) out of the "Front for the Liberation of Iran" to which the CIA reportedly paid $100,000 per month in 1982;[54] and Radio Swan, established under the Gibraltar Steamship Corporation in Miami, against Cuba from 1960 (this later became Radio Americas and Vanguard Service Corp., respectively, after the Bay of Pigs invasion) until 1969.[55]

The KGB never used radio to the extent the CIA did but preferred to carry out its active measures in disinformation and propaganda through surrogates in the communist world and by influencing the print press. The aim behind such usage was as noted: propagating the Soviet line, encouraging negative reactions to their opponents, and recruiting and developing agents. This was done through a number of methods, the primary of which was the planting of *dezinformatsia* in neutral papers either knowingly or unknowingly. An example of this was the late 1960s reporting of the use of bacteriological weapons by the United States in Indochina in the Bombay *Free Press Journal*. This story was picked up by the *Times* in 1968, as well as other Western print media.[56] Another example was London's *New Statesman*, which was unwittingly used in November 1982 to discredit U.S. Ambassador to the United Nations Jeane Kirkpatrick by linking her with South Africa's infamous security police and South African military intelligence.[57] A final example is the use of the media to better leaders' images: stories picked up by *Time* and *Newsweek* during Andropov's tenure as chairman of the KGB stated that he was "a closet liberal" who "speaks English well ... collects big band records and relaxes with American novels, [and] sought friendly discussions with dissident protesters."[58] The KGB also used press agencies as fronts extensively—such as the Novosti Press Agency, which acted "as one of the vehicles for Soviet 'active measures'—both for the promotion of stories and to act as 'covers' for KGB officers abroad."[59] Finally, individual journalists—such as Danish journalist Petersen who was directed to attack the British Conservative Party, Thatcher, and other anti-Soviet elements in British politics between 1973 and 1981 through pamphlets and articles either written by himself or by Service A under his name[60]—to push the party line covertly. Indeed, Barron states that out of the approximately 500 Soviet journalists abroad at any given time during the later Cold War, although the majority were intelligence officers, the minority (who weren't free to travel outside of the Soviet Union without KGB authorization) could not refuse a request by the KGB to carry out an assignment.[61]

The CIA used similar methods, but not to the same extent. In 1953, Allen Dulles expressed the desire to use the press for both intelligence collection and propaganda.[62] However, rather than doing so blatantly, the CIA relied on U.S. journalists who would want to "help their country,"[63] maintaining a vast network of reporters, magazines, electronic media, and other media personnel to supplement official information to promote current U.S. policies—including covert propaganda and psy ops—through quiet channels.[64] Though most did so unknowingly, the CIA did use journalists directly—both American and foreign nationals—in "clandestine relationships of one sort or another" with the CIA.[65] Carl Bernstein claimed that more than 400 U.S. journalists secretly carried out CIA activities from 1952 to 1976. The Church Committee stated fifty for the same time period, CIA official sources suggest thirty-six.[66]

Finally, the CIA also funded and covertly supported newspapers, journals, and other print media around the world. Some, like its funding of *Der Monat* (FRG), *Encounter* (U.K.), and the *Daily American* (Rome),[67] was within the context of direct rivalry with the Soviets. Others, like *El Mercurio* (Chile) and *Elimo* and *Salongo* (Angola),[68] were to promote CIA interests in a specific region of the globe in support of other operations—for example, during the Vietnam

War, the CIA allegedly wrote whole articles for *The Economist* on the war.[69] Last, numerous books were published with covert CIA funding and support—including *The Dynamics of Soviet Society* and *The Foreign Aid Programs of the Soviet Bloc and Communist China*.

### Covert Political Action

The second and perhaps most extensively used form of CA is *covert political action* (CPA). Treverton defined CPA as "attempts to change the balance of political forces in a particular country, most often by secretly providing money to particular groups."[70] Blackstock further broke down CPA into three stages: *infiltration-penetration, forced disintegration*, and *subversion-defection*. Infiltration ("the deliberate/planned penetration of political and social groups within a state by agents of an intervening power for manipulative purposes") as well as subversion ("the undermining or detachment of the loyalties of significant political and social groups within the victimized state, and their transference, under ideal conditions, to the symbols and institutions of the aggressor") are the most relevant here.[71]

CPA has often provided the central desired outcome in a covert action where other activities—such as paramilitary or propaganda activities—have also been deployed. In some senses, therefore, CPA can be seen as the strategic covert action (encompassing propaganda/disinformation, direct political influencing, paramilitary support, and use of social organizations where related to the Cold War confrontation) and other activities intended on attaining a political outcome.

CPA has been conducted both directly by the state seeking an intended outcome and by proxy or partner organizations working on behalf of the state. The latter have taken many forms: for example, both the CIA and the KGB attempted to influence political parties throughout the world in an effort to directly or indirectly undermine the influence of the other, as well as to further consolidate U.S. or Soviet interests in a region. Social organizations, such as student groups, international front organizations and legitimate bodies, and proxy armies were founded, penetrated, and funded by both services. Media outlets, individuals, and services were utilized either knowingly or unwittingly by the CIA and the KGB. Various corporate organizations or services were used as fronts for CIA or KGB activities across the globe. Finally, individuals fell prey to or were used by such activities in such gambits as false-flag recruitments, the deployment of agents of influence, and the role of defectors and disinformation agents in both Cold War camps.

#### PERSUASION AND INFLUENCE

Blackstock refers to this as manipulative persuasion or control, in which—in the pursuit of intelligence collection activities—the source is controlled or made dependent on his handler through payment in money, goods, drugs, sex, or other perquisites. The latter activity included the use of first- and second-level agents (targets and people with access to the targets) for manipulation and control, as well as the use of bribery or "quiet assistance," as William Colby referred to it. Such activities were nothing new for the United States (as with other powers). Bribery had been used extensively as a form of persuasion for centuries. In the first U.S. congressional appropriation act in 1789, a contingent fund for the bribery of foreign statesmen in the pursuit of American national interests was approved as part of the public purse.[72] More recently, recipients of funds as part of these activities reportedly included the Christian Democratic Party of Italy, King Hussein of Jordan, and various pro-Western factions in Greece, Germany, Egypt, Sudan, Surinam, Mauritius, the Philippines, Iran, Ecuador, and Chile.[73] The influencing of elections—especially in Western Europe, where the United States pushed the opening of Europe to ensure the development and continuation of economic reconstruction along friendly lines—was a prime CPA activity; indeed, Treverton states that these election projects became central to all nonmilitary CA in the future.[74] CPA was developed even further under Dulles in the 1950s: his personal interests in securing democracy against the Soviets in Eastern and Western Europe led to a dominance of CPA during the 1950s, with direct influence on parties and politicians in Western Europe,[75] which continued over the years.

*Case Study: Italian Elections and CIA Funding*

Italy provides the best example of the use of CPA funding to influence elections. Beginning with the 1948 Italian elections, in which the CIA funded heavily the Christian Democrats, between 1948 and 1975, over $75 million was spent by the CIA on Italian elections, $10 million for the 1972 elections alone. The CIA reportedly funded over $1 million to Amintore Fanfani, the secretary-general of the Christian Democrats, in the 1970 elections; at the same time, over $800,000 was given to Gen. Vito Miceli, leader of the neofascist MSI and former head of Italian military intelligence, to ensure success. Even following the Church Report (1976), President Ford approved an additional $6 million for the next election.[76]

The CIA was most often the instrument used to provide clandestine support to such parties and states not only because of its black budget, which allowed for expenditures without justification (unlike, for example, foreign aid budgets) and meant that often the recipient might not even be aware of from whence the funds derived. Finally, it also provided the U.S. government with the all-important plausible deniability should such activities come to light.[77] Other states/parties that received such extensive support included the new Federal Republic of Germany and its Christian Democrat Party (and, reportedly, the Social Democratic Party), as part of wider CPA efforts in West Germany to establish or revive anticommunist, pro-American institutions, discrediting and destroying leftist opposition movements.[78] The Christian Democrats—favorites of the CIA around the world—were also supported in Portugal following the April 1974 coup.[79]

The KGB was also active in this regard. In general, foreign Communist Parties were used as auxiliaries by the KGB as well as recruiting grounds in foreign countries (there is no evidence found to indicate that the CIA recruited within these Communist Parties, although logically this would have often been the case).[80] For example, a great deal of the activities of the French Communist Party were directed from Moscow and were used as a means of penetrating the French government.[81] Moscow Centre's instructions to its stations in this regard states that the main thrust of active measures were to achieve political influence and penetration, such as in Denmark.[82] Overall, although there is indication of attempts made to influence the socialist parties in Western Europe, in general (with the possible exception of the British Labour Party) there has been little success by the KGB in influencing any noncommunist party in Western Europe.[83]

In the developing world, the use of political parties was significantly different. Whereas in Europe, influence over political parties was carried out purely along ideological lines, in the developing world a different pattern emerged. It appears that the CIA operated under the belief that if a party was not aligned with Washington and was not helped along toward that end, then it would automatically fall into Moscow's camp. As is clearly evident with hindsight, nothing could have been further from the truth; indeed, as the example of Castro in Cuba in 1959–60 provides, there were clear cases where such parties were scorned by the CIA or even pushed into the KGB/Soviet camp through CIA action/inaction. Prados refers to these CIA-supported parties as "third force" political movements— generally noncommunist (preferably anticommunist) but also not fascist and politically moderate (usually Christian Democrats). In Latin America, they were usually associated with established oligarchies and in Africa and Asia with tribes. In instances where no third force existed, one was created: examples include the Committee for the Defense of National Interests (Laos), Committee for a Free Albania, Holden Roberto in Angola, and Mobutu Sese Seko in the Congo. The problem that emerged with these groups was that usually, such minorities did little to satisfy general, popular aspirations and often led to further upheaval and, as in Laos, additional obligations for U.S. support. They were generally perceived as "agents of American power."[84]

*Case Study: The CIA in Chile, 1963–74*

The most obvious case of CIA involvement with developing world political parties is that of Chile. Overall political control and penetration was attempted through the Organization of American States to legitimize U.S. anticommunist actions throughout the hemisphere but was largely unsuccessful. But in Chile, after fears that Allende would become another Castro for the United States to deal with, a psy ops action was authorized that started in 1963 and lasted until

Allende was deposed in 1973. Consequently, the CIA intervened in every election in that time. During the Popular Unity coalition government in Chile, the Christian Democrats and the National Party were funded with over $4 million from the CIA; at the same time, monies were used to attempt to lure away factions from the coalition. In 1964, $2.6 million was given to the candidate Frei (who later won) to prevent Allende and the socialists from gaining power.[85] The United States also spent—through the CIA, supported by various private corporations (such as ITT) with business interests in Chile—$12 million to blacken Allende's name.[86]

On its side, the KGB generally helped communist and socialist movements in the developing world, but almost without exception only when they were linked to paramilitary formations involved in war. One clear example is that of the Popular Movement for the Liberation of Angola (MPLA), supported by the KGB until 1974, when Cuba became their prime supporter at the time of the Portuguese coup. This was against not only Jonas Savimbi's South African– and CIA-backed UNITA but also (as noted) Holden Roberto's CIA-supported National Front for the Liberation of Angola (FNLA), the largest anticommunist party in that country.[87] This provides the perfect (and perhaps best) example of a developing country where at least three sides were supported against each other (and their benefactors) to the detriment of the country and its citizens. In Afghanistan, the head of the dominant faction in the Afghan Communist Party, Babrak Karmal, was a KGB agent. Moscow Centre was also reported to have a number of agents directly in Nasser's entourage, including Nasser's head of intelligence.[88] Finally, Andrew and Gordievsky state that the African National Congress (ANC) was greatly penetrated by the KGB due to the ANC's close links with the South African Communist Party, itself deeply tied to Moscow.[89] Finally, a strong example of CPA activities by a Soviet satellite is the extensive operations conducted by Markus Wolf's Foreign Intelligence Division in the East German Ministry for State Security (or Stasi) against the West German government in Bonn (as well as business circles throughout West Germany) over many decades of the Cold War, resulting in the resignation of West German Chancellor Willy Brandt in 1974 after his private secretary was exposed as one of Wolf's moles.

In general, though, neither the KGB nor the CIA were very successful in their usage of political parties in the developing world. The United States and, to a lesser extent, the Soviet Union failed to understand the nature of developing world socialist movements and their links to international ideologies. As already stated, the end result more often than not was additional problems for the individual service, whether on a massive scale such as Indochina and Afghanistan or on a smaller scale such as Central America or Angola. As Prados states, one of the problems of working through proxies is that of suffering political liabilities as a result of acts by such allies, as well as the obvious one of lack of full or even sufficient control over these allies. Examples of such problems would include the drug smuggling carried out by the Indonesian military regime, Li Mi's Chinese, and Vang Pao's Meo.[90]

FRONT ORGANIZATIONS

The extensive development and use of front organizations by both the CIA and KGB—as well as other intelligence services, such as the Israeli Mossad and the apartheid South African National Intelligence Service and Police Security Branch—provides some of the best examples of covert political activities. Some such fronts include the proxy-ized political parties noted above, but the truest of such organizations were those without apparent linkage to any foreign government.

The use of front organizations by both the CIA and KGB was widespread throughout the whole of the Cold War. These organizations took on different guises depending on the requirements of the period, the intended action, and the hoped-for outcome. In the case of the CIA, however, the vast majority of these fronts were direct appendages of the agency. The CIA's policy was to base its support on a wide range of groups and institutions (besides political parties) in various countries to "shift the balance of that country's politics by countering groups perceived as threatening to American interests and aiding those friendly to the United States."[91] In the case of the Soviets, the KGB often acted as a filter for other Soviet organizations (primarily the International Department of the CPSU); therefore, even in instances where a front was not a direct arm of the KGB, it was linked through the committee to other organizations.

For the Soviets, who had established the use of fronts with the GRU (Soviet military intelligence) in the 1920s to obtain monies and economic considerations without it being apparent that these were going to the Soviet Union,[92] their policy was articulated in the March 1926 statement from the Comintern advocating "creating a whole solar system of organizations and smaller committees around the Communist Party . . . actually working under the influence of the Party, but not under its mechanical control." The overall task of these fronts were to "advance the cause of Soviet Communism, to defend the policies of the Soviet Union . . . and to attack the policies of those it opposes." They were also used to recruit agents, provide covers for illegals, and "mould and manipulate public opinion."[93] Most of the fronts that the Soviets used during the Cold War were legitimate in their founding but were captured by the Soviets during the period from the 1920s until 1950.

The CIA's approach to fronts was generally to use a variety of corporate fronts, usually referred to as either "proprietaries" or "Delaware Corporations,"[94] which took many different guises and forms throughout the Cold War, depending on geography, mission, and time. Indeed, it could be argued that the post–Cold War growth in private security and military companies operating internationally—and the role that they fill not only for their client governments or corporations in the Developing World but also in the contracts that they undertake on behalf of Western governments—are a direct descendant of such organizations However, throughout the Cold War and as far back as the U.S. government's use of Vinnell Corporation in Mexico in the early-1930s and throughout World War II (later described by a CIA official as "our own private army in Vietnam"), such private security and military companies provided the same type of service that was secured through these fronts, under very similar circumstances of plausible deniability and ease of use far from the public's eye.

The most well-known type of proprietary was the air corporations. These were established (generally) during the wars in Indochina and in relation to the conflict between Formosa (Taiwan) and communist China; the best known of these was Civil Air Transport (CAT),[95] used in operations involving Li Mi's Nationalist Chinese forces, as well as in support of the French in Indochina, and Air America, which emerged out of the CAT experience and the desire for an International Volunteer Air Group in Southeast Asia.[96] Double-Chek Corporation, listed as a brokerage firm in Florida government records, was in reality a recruiting front for pilots flying against Cuba after 1959; many of the pilots flying B-26s out of Central America against Cuba were recruited by a company called Caribbean Marine Aero Corp. (Caramar), a CIA proprietary.[97] More recent examples include Summit Aviation, which was linked to the CIA during the 1980s with operations in El Salvador and Honduras;[98] and St. Lucia Airways, which, although they deny it, was conclusively tied to the Iran-*contra* operations (along with several other such fronts) as well as to operations in Angola and the Congo (Zaire).[99]

Other types of fronted activities include the use of United Business Associates (Washington) to fund corporate development in the developing world to "offset the Communists from moving in,"[100] and—as a direct continuation of previous U.S. activities—the CIA was supported by the United Fruit Company in developing plans to carry out the 1953 coup against Arbenz in Guatemala, but it never followed through.[101] Finally, one of the best known front organizations of the CIA was Zenith Technical Enterprises, a Miami-based corporation used to organize, direct, fund, and carry out Operation Mongoose, the CIA's war against Castro.[102]

In contrast, no evidence was found to indicate that the Soviets, having pioneered the corporate front with Arcos (All-Russian Cooperative Society, officially the Soviet trade mission in London but in reality the cover for extensive industrial and commercial espionage) in 1921 (and subsequently smashed by MI5 in 1928),[103] continued with corporate fronts after 1945.

South Africa engaged heavily in all manner of covert activity during its wars against the anti-apartheid movements, both in Southern Africa and further afield. Its best-known police intelligence operative—Craig Williamson—was also one of its most successful in conducting CPA operations against the worldwide anti-apartheid movement, particularly in its strongholds in London and Western Europe. In 1972, Williamson, along with Craig Edwards, successfully infiltrated the ANC's structures via the International University Exchange Fund based in Geneva (of which Williamson eventually became deputy director), redirecting virtually all of its fundraising income into South African government secret accounts. He returned to South Africa only after being exposed in 1980, having run the operation for eight years.[104] Indeed, over the course of the 1960s through the 1980s, a triangle of covert support and activities developed between the CIA, South African intelligence, and Israeli intelligence—with British and French intelligence and Zaire's Mobutu sitting somewhat uncomfortably on the edge of the triangle—to confront Soviet/Chinese/general communist influence in Africa while ensuring access to strategic resources.

The CIA also used social and educational organizations—such as the National Student Association, which the CIA had funded (to 80 percent of their budget) between 1952 and 1967 in an attempt to counter Soviet efforts to mobilize world youth,[105] or the European Market Movement to which the CIA provided £380,000 between 1947 and 1953 in an attempt to directly balance KGB activities in the same manner.[106] Finally, anticommunist trade unions were heavily funded by the CIA in Europe and the developing world.[107]

On the Soviet part, Lenin first introduced the idea of propagating communism through trade unions, youth organizations, and other social groups in 1921;[108] over the proceeding years, hundreds if not thousands of Soviet front social organizations existed. Most emerged initially out of Willi Münzenberg's "Innocents' Clubs" of the 1920s where individuals were recruited to the communist cause;[109] since 1945, these have been more concerned with rallying specific social groups across the globe. In 1965, there were eleven official such fronts—such as the World Federation of Trade Unions and the International Union of Students—linked to the Soviet Union.[110] Regionally, such organizations as the Nigerian Trade Union Congress and the Afro-Asian People's Solidarity Organization were funded and utilized by the KGB.[111] The largest such social front was the World Council of Peace/International Institute for Peace, expelled from Paris in 1951 for "fifth column activities," then from Prague to Vienna, where it was banned in 1957 for "activities directed against the interest of the Austrian state," finally establishing itself in Helsinki in 1968.[112] It is believed to have received over $50 million annually through the KGB and even achieved recognition from the United Nations and UNESCO.[113] Finally, although often claiming responsibility for encouraging peace movements (such as the Campaign for Nuclear Disarmament responsible for the protest at Greenham Common), KGB aid could not have motivated them any further, according to Andrew, as they were already in the 1980s very intensely anti–United States.[114]

### Covert Economic Action

The third form is *covert economic action*. This includes the attempt, through covert means, to disrupt or destabilize adversaries' economies. Methods used have included counterfeiting foreign currencies, depressing the world price of agricultural products vital to adversaries (especially one-crop developing nations), trying to control the rainfall over enemy territory through cloud seeding, preparing and introducing parasites for the destruction of crops, contaminating oil supplies (as was done against North Vietnam), dynamiting power lines, and mining harbors to discourage commercial shipping (as Reagan authorized against Nicaragua).[115]

### Covert Paramilitary Action

Finally, the fourth method encompasses both covert paramilitary action (PM) and counterintelligence[116]—or what are collectively sometimes referred to as "secret wars." These include all manner of assassination, coup, raid, counterguerrilla activity and other (generally) armed covert acts. Charters states that these "involve the active direction, deployment, or support of regular or irregular armed bodies of men employing unconventional military means to achieve their (or their sponsor's) political objectives." In this sense, Charters maintains that these activities are closer to military special operations—fitting, given that military special forces and their missions often form part of covert PM actions.[117]

The first American covert PM involved the only time in which the United States engaged in *direct* covert military activities against the Soviet Union—the CIA's (and U.S. military Counterintelligence Corps in occupied Germany) support for anti-Soviet Ukrainian partisans in 1947–48. After that time, the United States did not take direct PM activities within the Soviet Union (unlike, for example, its support for the Afghan *mujahedeen* during the Soviet-Afghan War).

Throughout Africa during the Cold War, the CIA supported Mobutu in the Congo as both a bag man and staging point for all manner of covert paramilitary (and other) activities in Africa—including extensive covert cooperation with apartheid South Africa within the anticommunist Cold War context. The Soviets parried by providing extensive support (alongside and often in competition with the Chinese) to the liberation and revolutionary guerrilla movements across the continent—including especially in Angola, Mozambique, Rhodesia/Zimbabwe, and South-West Africa/Namibia. This, in turn, generated further South African–Rhodesian covert efforts to undermine these revolutionary guerilla movements using their own panoply of covert activities (including the extensive use of assassinations, pseudo-operations, third-force [proxy] counterguerrilla forces, and the like)—creating a spiral of covert action-reaction across the breadth of central and southern Africa throughout the 1970s and 1980s.

In Latin America, covert paramilitary activities against Castro and in Chile, Guatemala, Nicaragua, and El Salvador—culminating in the Iran-*contra* scandal of the 1980s—witnessed the continuation of U.S. interventionist policies from the last century. In Vietnam, initial covert assistance to the French during their Indochinese campaign evolved slowly into the CIA's biggest "war" by the mid-1960s, culminating in the PHOENIX Project. Outside of the Cold War context, the 1985 French special services attack on the Greenpeace *Rainbow Warrior* in Auckland harbor symbolized other aims of covert activities (in this case, acting against a group actively protesting nuclear testing in the South Pacific).

*Case Study: Nicaragua, 1933–87*

The most well-known example of transition from direct to indirect control is the case of Nicaragua. Before pulling the armed forces out of Nicaragua in 1933, the United States trained and equipped the National Guard, whose leader, Anastasio Somoza, instigated a successful coup in 1936. After maintaining very close ties, in all aspects, with the U.S. government for forty-six years, the Somoza government was overthrown in a revolution led by the Sandinistas in 1979. The funding of the National Guard, now called the *contrarevolucionarios* (contras), continued by the CIA from 1979 until it became public in 1987.[118]

At their height in the United States in the 1980s, the combination of both PM and CI authorizations—Reagan's 1981 Executive Order 12333—was the basis for CIA foreign activities under the Reagan Doctrine. As is noted, however, it was long before that the United States developed and deployed its covert paramilitary capability under the Cold War rubric.

The United States was no stranger to counterintelligence operations, having performed their first ones under the Committee of Secret Correspondence, established by George Washington in 1776, against British agents in New England. The first covert action carried out by the U.S. government (in conjunction with France) was the funding of arms to back a coup in Tripoli to place a ruler friendlier to the United States on the throne.[119] But as a prelude to U.S. actions two centuries later, these were child's play.

PM action primarily involves the support of guerilla and other insurgent groups against governments unfriendly or threatening to the United States. For example, from 1963 to 1973, the CIA supported the Meo tribesmen in Laos against the communist Pathet Lao government. Other countries where this type of CA has reportedly taken place include Ukraine, Poland, Albania, Hungary, Indonesia, China, Oman, Malaysia, Iraq, the Dominican Republic, Venezuela, North Korea, Bolivia, Thailand, Haiti, Guatemala, Cuba, Greece, Turkey, Vietnam, Afghanistan, Angola, and Nicaragua, to mention but a few.[120]

These operations were historically carried out jointly by the Directorates of Operations and Administration (responsible for training and support). As well as insurgent support, the CIA has funded various PM training activities throughout the world, provided military advisors (as in Vietnam before full-scale military deployment, and in the recent Afghani war against the Soviets) and transported arms shipments internationally to supply pro-U.S. factions world wide (such as the delivering of Stinger and Blowpipe missiles to the Afghan *mujahedeen* resistance during the 1980s Soviet-Afghan War).[121] Much more recently, as the first U.S. government activity directly against the Taliban and its Al Qaeda supporters in Afghanistan before and during Operation Enduring Freedom, the CIA deployed the "Jawbreaker" team as a covert PM activity aimed at supporting the Afghan Northern Alliance against these foes to foment direct action against them.

As an issue that—like others—intersected CPA and covert PM action, the instigation of physical terror, kidnapping, and assassination serves a double purpose. While political opponents are temporarily or permanently removed from the scene, violence itself is used to create fear and hatred, often discrediting or undermining one entity against another. This is what Blackstock has referred to as "the essence of forced disintegration or atomization," by which the political and social structure of the state is split apart. This use of "executive action" (more commonly referred to as assassination) is something that the CIA has never admitted to, but it is known that several attempts were made on Castro, either by CIA personnel or by CIA-backed assassins (such as the Mafia).

Less well-known, however, are the attempts (and successes) at lower-level assassinations (not prime political figures)—with paramilitary operations such as the PHOENIX Project in Vietnam (see later discussion), the promotion of selected targeting or extrajudicial killings through the School of the Americas at Fort Benning, and other initiatives aimed at decapitating revolutionary or guerrilla movements at the command-and-control level. The death squads run throughout Central America by the CIA during the early 1980s followed similar lines.[122] Following the 1975 Year of Intelligence revelations in the United States and moratoriums on "assassination" initiated by Presidents Ford and Carter, section 2.11 of Executive Order 12333 now prohibits this.

Assassination was also a favored practice of the Soviet intelligence services and their satellites—usually conducted against dissidents from communist countries (such as Georgi Markov of Bulgaria, infamously assassinated in 1978 on London's Waterloo Bridge by a lethal ricin dose delivered by a sharpened umbrella) in exile or those who helped support them and their activities. The Israeli government has made extensive use of assassination—against not only its opponents in the Arab world (such as Hamas bomb maker Yahya Ayyash, known as "The Engineer," assassinated by mobile phone bomb in 1996) but also those who were suspected of helping their enemies (such as Gerald Bull, the Canadian designer of the Iraqi super-gun, assassinated in Brussels in 1990). The apartheid South African government made extensive use of assassination as a covert tool furthering state policies, not only within South Africa but across the front-line states of southern Africa and even as far abroad as London, Brussels, and Paris, where members of the ANC and other liberation movements in exile as well as other players in the anti-apartheid movement worldwide were assassinated with extreme professionalism and success. Indeed, as an example of the success of covert paramilitary activities, the apartheid government's use of assassination (alongside other covert activities) was probably one of the best, forcing the ANC to first withdraw their presence (military bases, offices, and representatives) further from South Africa's borders in southern Africa, and, second, both acknowledge an inability to overthrow the apartheid government by force or revolution and seek a negotiated settlement to the conflict as a result. Israel's assassination activities to this day against Palestinian militants would appear to have had a similar success, at the least in eliminating a considerable cadre of paramilitary technical expertise from among the ranks of the various Palestinian terrorist and militant groups.

Support for paramilitary formations, proxy armies, and similar covert activities followed directly from this: the CIA supported paramilitary formations in Indochina, Angola, Nicaragua, El Salvador, Ethiopia, Afghanistan, and many other regions. The KGB, almost without exception, supported proxy armies in the same areas opposed to the ones the CIA supported. This involved not only direct activities—such as the PHOENIX Program in Vietnam—but also indirect and support activities, such as training. Although good examples of the latter include the training of the GVN police at Michigan State University under a program using USAID cover[123] and the creation and training of Savak (Iranian security service) by the CIA as a means of gathering information on the Soviet Union in exchange for helping repress dissident activity against the shah's regime[124]—the PHOENIX Program represents the best example of this, and probably the most successful CIA covert paramilitary operation ever. Run by CIA-backed South Vietnamese forces against the Viet Cong Infrastructure (VCI), some 20,000 VCI leaders and sympathizers were killed as a result of this program according to Colby. Despite claims that none of them were killed by assassination methods, members of this program have confirmed at least 10,000 assassinations against the VCI. It is never been confirmed whether or not American agents took part as assassins.

The CIA also used Reinhard Gehlen's intelligence network in postwar Germany (called The Organization, the forerunner of the Bundesnachrichtendienst, or BND ) to train Baltic émigrés and refugees to carry out paramilitary CA against the Soviets. These groups acted in concert with the Ukrainian partisan groups in operations against the Soviets in Poland, the Baltics, and the Soviet Union. Eisenhower's Task Force C programs in the 1950s had included the development of a Volunteer Freedom Corps, employing cadres of European émigré fighters, as an aspect of rollback. They failed miserably during the late 1940s and early 1950s.[125] Finally, Vang Pao's Armée Clandestine (Meo units including Operation White Star Green Beret forces) was used to combat Pathet Lao forces in Laos. These included the use of Police Aerial Resupply Units (PARU), not to be confused with the Provincial Reconnaissance Unit (PRU) used in PHOENIX.[126]

For the Soviets, use of such fronts was different from that of the CIA. As already stated, use of proxy armies in the developing world was very similar to that of the CIA. The KGB influenced (and often controlled) the armies of client states (such as Cuba, Angola, Afghanistan, Ethiopia) through replicated Soviet political administrations that placed informers throughout the armies' ranks.[127] The main difference between the two services lay in the KGB's use of "friendly" intelligence services. The KGB directly controlled the intelligence and security services of all the Soviet bloc countries, as well as using the intelligence services of client states, such as Libya. This was done to "give distance and deniability in potentially embarrassing operations," as well as to carry out false-flag recruitment.[128] Examples of this would be the KGB's direction to Czech intelligence to "cause conflict and exploit tension between individual countries, even countries that recently gained their independence."[129] As well, the East German Staatsicherheitsdienst (SSD) was used between 1959 and 1960 as agents provocateurs to try to destabilize West Germany by infiltrating agents into Jewish areas to desecrate graves, spray swastikas on property, and other similar acts. In 1968, the KGB took direct control of Cuba's DGI in a secret agreement with Castro.[130] In international terrorism, although never directly controlled by the KGB, terrorist organizations, such as the Red Brigades in Italy or the Baader-Meinhof Gang in West Germany, were sponsored by Moscow Centre. This was most often accomplished through surrogate intelligence services, such as East German and Romanian secret services. Links existed as well between these organizations and the Palestine Liberation Organization, as well as the Provisional Irish Republican Army for a number of years.[131] No evidence can be found to indicate a similar relationship between the CIA and its allies regarding either of these two categories.

Ultimately, this is the theory and practice of the propaganda of the deed—practiced by both revolutionaries/terrorists and intelligence officials as part of their covert options.[132] However, these activities were not always successful: Mossad estimated that by 1960, Saudi Arabia had already paid out over $3 million in a vain attempt to arrange for the assassination of President Nasser of Egypt.[133] However, Mossad itself was caught in an embarrassing attempt to assassinate Hamas leader Sheikh Khaled Mashal in Amman, Jordan, in 1997 when their assassins not only failed in their direct action attempt but were caught and publicly humiliated by Jordanian police. Mossad has used assassination extensively throughout its existence, not the least of which in its attempts to hunt down and kill every member of the Black September terrorist group responsible for the Munich Olympics massacre.

### Covert Action in Perspective

In all of these actions, overlaps can often be found in practice. A number of these have already been noted—indeed, in most covert actions, multiple outcomes either are intended or are the result (i.e., economic plus political, psychological plus economic, or paramilitary and political). It must also always be kept in mind that these actions are deployed both directly by the instigator—the CIA, the KGB, or another government's instrument—and by the proxies which it supports. Propaganda, for example, can be used to effect or delay political change (as the United States did in Western Europe in the early days of the Cold War or the South African apartheid government did against its ANC enemies) or inspire terror (as was done frequently by both fascist and communist regimes worldwide). Conversely, the actual use of terror—sometimes under the guise of covert paramilitary actions—has its own propaganda effect. A prime example of this mixture between propaganda and covert paramilitary activities is the use of what the British government in Kenya called pseudo-operations—whereby covert units of "turned" guerrillas would visit villages to either gauge local support for the government or the rebels, or (as the Rhodesian and South African apartheid governments conducted to far greater degrees than the British, French, or Portuguese in their decolonization wars) carry out attacks on those villages to make it look like rebels had been responsible.

## COVERT ACTION TODAY

Since the end of the Cold War and across the interregnum of the 1990s CA has evolved to some degree. Indeed, some would argue that it has had to evolve, given that the global environment within which it functions has evolved around it. No longer solely aimed at furthering the aims of intervention, control, or subversion, it has been used by various powers to support more altruistic aims, particularly within the new intervention agenda of the post–Cold War world. With an international security regime driven heavily by humanitarian-led concerns over the rule of law—both domestically and internationally—and a far greater (at least compared to the Cold War context) willingness to push peacekeeping and peace-support operations at the international level and through the United Nations, covert action as a tool of statecraft has been used for support. Part of the reason for this forced evolution is not the least because, in the information age—with the spread and coverage of nonstop news—very few activities can occur unnoticed around the world. Though the original intention of covert activities has not changed—even in those situations where the action is visible, let alone when it occurs under the radar, and the hand of the initiating government is not seen in its undertaking—this rise in media scrutiny combined with ever-increasing public accountability drives the intelligence services (at least in the developed world) has made such undertakings a greater challenge for the intelligence services.

This is not to suggest that covert actions have been undertaken through a United Nations or other regional organizational mandate—but rather that individual powers, acting sometimes with this greater altruistic attitude, have supported a far broader target/interest base than ever was the case during the Cold War. Examples of this include the British government's use of the private military company Sandline International to provide covert support to the exiled government of Sierra Leone in 1999 against the horrendous rebels of the Revolutionary United Front. Another case is CIA support—bungled and dropped in 1995—for the Iraqi Kurds against Saddam Hussein's military and intelligence onslaught after the 1991 Gulf War. In the war on terrorism—really started initially by President Clinton in the mid-1990s—the United States had covert operations against terrorist networks and supporters underway in at least eighty countries by September 2001.[134]

This is not to say that the more traditional state-interest activities have not continued. The CIA's bungles in Haiti in the mid-1990s clashed directly with the Clinton administration's declared intentions and activities aimed at restoring democracy (in the form of Jean-Bertrand Aristide) to that troubled country. In its war with the Chechen rebels, Russia has deployed significant covert paramilitary actions—including especially assassination, but also propaganda and psy ops—against the Chechen rebels, the Chechen people, and (in terms of propaganda) to the outside world. There are even suspicions that Russia's "special services" have conducted pseudo-operations (both inside and outside Chechnya) in an effort to further blacken the reputation of the Chechen rebels.

Probably the best known post–Cold War covert action gone awry was the use of the UN Special Commission on Iraq (UNSCOM) as a cover for CIA and NSA activities in Iraq during the period of international weapons inspections in that country until its exposure in 1998. Greeted with horror and abhorrence, the CIA was vilified for using the United Nations—with its cloak of impartiality and benevolence—as a cover for intelligence activities. The fallout from this operation not only led to the expulsion of the UN weapons inspectors from Iraq but—it could be argued—directly to the 2003 Iraq War.[135] More recently, it has been suspected that the CIA has been ordered to subvert Hugo Chávez's government in Venezuela, much as it did for the better part of a decade against Castro in Cuba and for much the same reasons.

In the war on terrorism, launched following the September 11, 2001, attacks on the United States by Al Qaeda, the known use of covert action has demonstrated the continuation of similar activities from the Cold War period. The use of propaganda—both overtly through media such as Radio Sawa (much like Radio Free Europe in its latter days) and more covertly through attempts to support the promotion of a more understanding and benevolent image of the United States (and the West more generally) across the Muslim world—has seen extensive examination, both by the media and academia. Covert political action, in the form of attempts to influence or support various governments around the world (such as in Pakistan, Uzbekistan, Indonesia, and other regional governments of interest), has continued unabated. The deployment of CIA Counterterrorism Center/ Special Activities Division Jawbreaker teams—armed with both Special Operations Forces and suitcases full of cash—into Afghanistan in the weeks before the launch of Operation Enduring Freedom in October 2001 was the best recent example of this continued practice of nurturing and supporting proxy forces (in the form of the Northern Alliance in this case) through covert paramilitary action. Existing concerns over rogue states or states of concern (such as Iran, Syria, and North Korea) in the first decade of the twenty-first century will likely see the continuation of such activities, both within the context of this war on terrorism and in terms of the broad interests of individual states.

## CONCLUSIONS: THE USES AND LIMITS OF COVERT ACTION

It is clear that by the 1990s, the mechanisms of covert action used by the United States became more refined but not necessarily more successful. Overall, the United States achieved more successes—in this pursuit of statecraft and national interests—during the 1898–1933 period than they have since the 1939–45. Success is a relative concept. In terms of achieving hegemony and maintaining it in their chosen sphere of influence, the United States achieved this by 1914 and maintained it until 1933. The period from 1945 to the present has witnessed the attempts by the United States to reintroduce this concept of hegemony throughout the world with, to a large degree, less success comparatively. The clear difference between the two periods was the evolution of these methods from direct political control and full use of military force, to proxy activities and covert operations spanning the globe. Many of these methods have been, in contrast, very successful in the achievement of immediate goals. In the long run, they had considerably less effect.

During the Cold War, the activities of the United States—and other Western powers—were balanced by those of the Soviet bloc. Since the end of that conflict, the concerns of the CIA—and the United States and other Western powers and their intelligence services—have been redirected to countering regional and local instability and collapse, dealing with humanitarian crises, countering regional and local wars through (generally UN-mandated) interventions, and dealing with rogue states, dictators, and the proliferation of weapons of mass destruction and international terrorism. Although individual states' self-interests have continued to drive not only these activities but also more selfish traditional ones, the geostrategic global balance has now shifted—perhaps irrevocably—to the point where the great (at least Western) powers now act with generally global benevolence in their pursuit of their goals. With the additional challenges that the information age presents to keeping covert actions covert, the pursuit of covert action has become more difficult at the same time that the global public demand for states to be "seen to be acting" with altruistic, globally benevolent interests has increased dramatically. Therefore, *overt* action has come more to the fore in the pursuit of those activities that previously would have been undertaken covertly.

This is not to say that all (or any) states have dropped the pursuit of their own self-interests through the medium of covert action. In the case of previously Soviet (now democratic) Russia, the collapse of Soviet communism and the end of the Cold War also meant the end of the general Soviet pursuit of both supporting the advance of global communism and dealing with those of its citizens abroad who dissented from such a view (along with their supporters), especially in terms of the Cold War covert confrontation between the KGB and CIA in the developing world and all it entailed. The end to these activities symbolizes perhaps the greatest change in covert action goals and aims from the Cold War to the post–Cold War periods. Russia today still covertly pursues its interests abroad through not only its civilian but also (more particularly, in some regards) its military intelligence services. Other states continue to use covert action as a tool of statecraft, such as Israel's pursuit of its national security against its enemies, various rogue states' pursuit of the matériel and capability to develop weapons of mass destruction capability, and China's pursuit of its growing interests globally.

### Assessing Success

At the general level, one may say that the CIA was successful in carrying out many of its covert operations; this is because, as Prados points out, with almost no exception, the actions carried out by the CIA forced the Soviets or the Chinese (the specific opponents named in NSC-5412) to respond in kind without escalating to open military confrontation.[136] This is in contradiction to the general record of CIA covert actions that indicate those CA undertaken over time were more often than not failures in the long or short run. At a more specific level, limited operations were never allowed to stay limited due to the aforementioned problem of escalating commitments, the quagmire of covert action. Thus, even though CA in Angola in 1975 and in Nicaragua in 1980 were initially limited activities aimed at preventing the consolidation of a government in the former case and at harassing the regime in the latter case to prevent its continued support of guerillas in El Salvador, they eventually escalated to such a level that failure was inevitable unless the next step (military intervention) was taken.[137] At this level, the CIA had a number of debacles (Indochina, Cuba) as well as number of limited successes (Chile, Western Europe). Propaganda operations had certain successes; Guatemala is one of the most obvious. Even though the CIA admitted in the post mortem that communism was never a threat in Guatemala, there was not even evidence of contacts with the Soviets.[138] But it was these successes that later led to failures or "problems that rebounded in the face of the [U.S. government]."[139] As far as media successes, opponents of propaganda (or psychological warfare) argue that if overt means had failed, it was unlikely that the target would be persuaded by covert use of media organs. The problem of "blowback" is also of concern; information planted abroad finds its way back into domestic press sources, deceiving one's own citizens.[140] The question is raised as well as to why the U.S. I.A. (United States Information Agency) does not carry out the same role in propaganda because its mission is overt and aimed at spreading U.S. views anyway.[141]

At the most basic level, that of assessing operations individually, the CIA comes up lacking. Mistakes were often made in the planning stages, predetermining failure. This was the case in Libya, where the CIA bypassed the best potential replacement for Qaddafi, and in Iran, where no attempts were made to penetrate religious groups prior to the revolution.[142] In funding support to Tibet, Afghanistan, and Indochina, large portions of CIA assistance was soaked up while still in transit due to corruption. And in some operations, follow-up support could not be granted for various reasons. The most evident case of this was the link between Radio Free Europe (RFE) and the Hungarian uprising in 1956. RFE made vague hints about Western assistance to students and workers in Budapest prior to the revolt; however, once the uprising began, RFE was forced to sit helplessly and listen to broadcasts from Budapest describing the slaughter. An estimated 30,000 died in the Soviet suppression.[143]

On the Soviet side, in many areas successes were more apparent than with the CIA. The use of paramilitary fronts in Eastern Europe linked to deception operations in the years following the war forced the CIA to establish a Counterintelligence Staff (under James JesusAngleton) in 1954 to counter such KGB operations.[144] At the general level, social fronts were by and large successful in that they forced the CIA to always react, one step *behind* the KGB. The KGB's use of the World Council of Peace (WPC) was very successful in coordinating world opinion, through its leadership of the other social fronts, against the United States during the Vietnam War. But even it ultimately failed in 1989 when it admitted that 90 percent of its funding came from the Soviets.[145] Other perceived successes were in reality distinct from KGB operations. For example, in 1984, the KGB launched an anti-Reagan propaganda campaign using the slogan *Reagan: eto voina!* (Reagan Means War!) during his election campaign. The anti-U.S. reaction to Reagan's victory was claimed by the KGB as a sweeping success; however, the fact that this slogan went unused everywhere indicates another area where the KGB had little to do with world opinion.[146] Where the KGB was successful at this level was in gaining recognition for most of its social fronts by the United Nations, UNESCO, United Council of Churches, and other international bodies. This was largely accomplished through the use of developing world surrogates to influence colleagues and decisions. Furthermore, outside of the known social fronts, many splinter committees, action groups, subsidiary organizations, and the like emerged that carried out much the same work as their parent bodies but without apparent Soviet involvement.[147]

Therefore, it is clear that many similarities and differences existed in the use of covert action during the Cold War—not only as part of the bipolar confrontation but also in unilateral activities by many states. In the case of the United States and the Soviet Union, where the CIA generally dealt with any noncommunist political organizations and individuals that would further their cause, the KGB dealt almost exclusively with communist parties or organizations in an attempt to further world communism. But one could argue that both powers were simply looking out for their own interests and using whatever vehicles necessary to fulfill and secure those interests. Prados has concluded about the CIA that "in all these CIA operations, there is a lesson . . . the United States acts in its own interests, which are those of a Great Power. There is little true identity of interest between the restive local minority and the Great Power."[148] This could easily be said for the KGB and the Soviet Union as well. As far as such fronts are concerned, the Soviets proved themselves much more adept at developing and wielding social fronts internationally than the CIA. The use of the media for propaganda, cover and influence was equally successful on both sides. But where the CIA generally failed in its use of proxy armies, the Soviets can be said to have been successful in their use of surrogate intelligence services and armies to accomplish the spread of the Soviet point of view.

Orwell summed up the raison d'être behind the extensive use of covert action when he opined, "We sleep safe in our beds because rough men stand ready in the night to visit violence on those who would do us harm." However, although the Cold War confrontation saw extensive use made of covert actions to further the aims of an individual service or power, more often than not the interests of that power and the deployment of said covert action acted against the wider global interest. Although the complexities of covert action can be found in Treverton's observation that "secret operations in a democracy are a paradox, all the more so if those operations intervene in the politics of another country,"[149] John Le Carré's observation of intelligence as a barely controlled circus may be closer to the truth of the role of intelligence and the need to stay vigilant over its activities: "Now that we had defeated Communism, we were going to have to set about defeating capitalism, but that wasn't really [the] point: the evil was not in the system, but in the man . . . you want to say: 'I slew the dragon, I left the world a safer place.' You can't really, not these days. Perhaps you never could."[150]

## NOTES

1. Although such a vast topic is impossible to tackle adequately within one chapter, there are numerous important academic contributions to be found to this debate within the literature. For excellent discussions of covert action generally—including its uses, links to policy and intelligence, implications, and outcomes—see Paul W. Blackstock, *The Strategy of Subversion* (Chicago: Quadrangle Books, 1964); Loch K. Johnson, *America's Secret Power: The CIA in a Democratic Society* (New York: Oxford University Press, 1989); Walter Laqueur, *A World of Secrets: The Uses and Limits of Intelligence* (New York: Basic Books, 1985); John Prados, *Presidents' Secret Wars: CIA and Pentagon Covert Operations from World War II to the Persian Gulf* (New York: William Morrow, 1996); Gregory F. Treverton, *Covert Action: The Limits of Intervention in the Postwar World* (New York: Basic Books, 1987); Roy Godson, ed., *Intelligence Requirements for the 1980s: Covert Action* (Washington: National Security Information Center, 1981); and David Charters, "The Role of Intelligence Services in the Direction of Covert Paramilitary Operations," in Alfred C. Maurer et al., eds., *Intelligence: Policy and Process* (London: Westview Press, 1985). For studies on the CIA and American democracy specifically, see Loch K. Johnson, *A Season of Inquiry: The Senate Intelligence Investigation* (Lexington: University of Kentucky Press, 1985); Frank J. Smist Jr., *Congress Oversees the United States Intelligence Community, 1947–1989* (Knoxville: University of Tennessee Press, 1990); Gabriel Kolko, *Confronting the Developing World: United States Foreign Policy 1945–1980* (New York: Pantheon Books, 1988); Rhodri Jeffrey-Jones, *The CIA and American Democracy,* 2nd ed. (New Haven, CT: Yale University Press, 1989); Victor Marchetti and John D. Marks, *The CIA and the Cult of Intelligence* (New York: Dell, 1989); Lyman B. Kirkpatrick Jr., *The U.S. Intelligence Community: Foreign Policy and Domestic Activities* (New York: Hill and Wang, 1973); Admiral Stansfield Turner, *Secrecy and Democracy: The CIA in Transition* (Boston: Houghton Mifflin, 1985); *New York Times, The Tower Commission Report* (Toronto: Bantam Books, 1987); Bob Woodward, *Veil: The Secret Wars of the CIA 1981–1987* (Toronto: Pocket Books, 1987); Rhodri

Jeffrey-Jones, *Cloak and Dollar: A History of American Secret Intelligence* (New Haven, CT: Yale University Press, 2002); and U.S. Senate, *Foreign and Military Intelligence: Final Report of the Select Committee to Study Governmental Operations with respect to Intelligence Activities* (Washington: Government Printing Office, 1976). For the best examinations of similar Soviet activities, see Christopher Andrew and Oleg Gordievsky, *KGB: The Inside Story* (London: Hodder & Stoughton, 1990); Jeffrey T. Richelson, *Sword and Shield: Soviet Intelligence and Security Apparatus* (Cambridge, MA: Ballinger, 1986); John O. Koehler, *Stasi: The Untold Story of the East German Secret Police* (Boulder: Westview Press, 1999); Christopher Andrew and Vasili Mitrokhin, *The Mitrokhin Archive—The KGB in Europe and the West* (vol. 1) (London: Allen Lane, 1999), and *The Mitrokhin Archive—The KGB and the World* (vol. 2) (London: Allen Lane, 2005); Peter Deriabin and T. H. Bagley, *KGB: Masters of the Soviet Union* (New York: Hippocrene Books, 1990); John Barron, *KGB Today: The Hidden Hand* (New York: Reader's Digest Press, 1983); and Iain Phelps-Fetherston, *Soviet International Front Organizations* (New York: Praeger, 1965). For examinations of covert activities and operations otherwise, see Peter Grose, *Operation Rollback: America's Secret War Behind the Iron Curtain* (Boston: Houghton Mifflin, 2001); Jeffrey T. Richelson, *A Century of Spies: Intelligence in the Twentieth Century* (Oxford: Oxford University Press, 1995); Edward J. Epstein, *Deception: The Invisible War Between the KGB and the CIA* (Toronto: Simon & Schuster, 1989); Leslie Cockburn, *Out of Control* (New York: Atlantic Monthly Press, 1987); Gordon A. Craig and Alexander L. George, *Force and Statecraft: Diplomatic Problems of Our Time* (Oxford: Oxford University Press, 1983); Allen Dulles, *The Craft of Intelligence* (Toronto: Signet Books, 1965); Chapman Pincher, *The Secret Offensive—Active Measures: A Saga of Deception, Disinformation, Subversion, Terrorism, Sabotage and Assassination* (London: Sidgwick & Jackson, 1985); and Michael I. Handel, *War, Strategy and Intelligence* (London: Frank Cass, 1989). For studies dealing with other national intelligence and covert action activities, see (on the U.K.) Christopher Andrew, *Secret Service: The Making of the British Intelligence Community* (London: Heinemann, 1985), and Stephen Dorrill, *MI6: Fifty Years of Special Operations* (London: Fourth Estate, 2000); (on Israel) Claire Hoy and Victor Ostrovsky, *By Way of Deception: A Devastating Insider's Portrait of the Mossad* (Toronto: Stoddart, 1990), Dan Raviv and Yossi Melman, *Every Spy a Prince: The Complete History of Israel's Intelligence Community* (London: Houghton Mifflin, 1990), and Gordon Thomas, *Gideon's Spies: Mossad's Secret Warriors* (London: Macmillan, 1999); (on World War II) Michael Howard, *Strategic Deception in the Second World War* (London: Pimlico, 1990); and (on Chinese operations) Nicholas Eftimiades, *Chinese Intelligence Operations* (Annapolis: Naval Institute Press, 1990). For an assessment of covert action and intelligence since the end of the Cold War—and, in some cases, since the 2001 declared war on terrorism—see Loch K. Johnson, *Bombs, Bugs, Drugs and Thugs: Intelligence and America's Quest for Security* (New York: New York University Press, 2000); Loch K. Johnson, *Secret Agencies: U.S. Intelligence in a Hostile World* (New Haven, CT: Yale University Press, 1996); John MacGaffen, "Clandestine Human Intelligence: Spies, Counterspies and Covert Action," and Henry A. Crumpton, "Intelligence and War: Afghanistan, 2001–2002," both in Jennifer E. Sims and Burton Gerber, eds., *Transforming U.S. Intelligence* (Washington: Georgetown University Press, 2005); Len Scott, "Secret Intelligence, Covert Action and Clandestine Diplomacy," in Len V. Scott and Peter Jackson, eds., *Understanding Intelligence in the Twenty-First Century: Journeys in Shadows* (London: Routledge, 2004); Roy Godson, *Dirty Tricks or Trump*

*Cards: US Covert Action and Counterintelligence* (London: Transaction, 2001); and Mark M. Lowenthal, *Intelligence: From Secrets to Policy* (Washington: Congressional Quarterly Press, 2000).

2. Johnson, *America's Secret Power*, p. 17.

3. Godson, *Intelligence Requirements for the 1980s*, p. 1.

4. Lowenthal, *Intelligence*, p. 106.

5. Johnson, *America's Secret Power*, pp. 16–17; Executive Order 12333 (1981) (3.4h, also 1.4d/f, 1.8e/f/i).

6. Johnson, *America's Secret Power*, p. 21. Bissell further breaks these down to (1) political advice, (2) subsidies to an individual, (3) financial support and technical assistance to political parties, (4) support of private organizations, (5) covert propaganda, (6) private training, (7) economic operations, and (8) paramilitary operations. Marchetti and Marks, *The CIA and the Cult of Intelligence*, p. 38.

7. Godson, *Dirty Tricks or Trump Cards*, p. xxxi.

8. James E. Steiner, "Restoring the Red Line Between Intelligence and Policy on Covert Action," *International Journal of Intelligence and Counterintelligence* 19, no.1 (Spring 2006), pp. 157, 158.

9. Blackstock, *The Strategy of Subversion*, pp. 78–94.

10. The term *guerrilla* originates with the period of Napoleon's occupation of Spain during the early nineteenth century when Spanish "guerrillas" (from the Spanish term *guerra*—"war"—with the *-illa* ending diminutive, meaning "little war") carried out a harassment, sabotage, and assassination campaign from their mountain hideouts against imperial French forces across Portugal and Spain. Lawrence's desert campaign evinced the exact same activities against the Turkish forces, using the desert (instead of mountains) as their hideout from which to engage in irregular (i.e., not regular) warfare—the epitome of covert paramilitary action witnessed during the Cold War.

11. Andrew and Gordievsky, *KGB: The Inside Story*, pp. 71–78.

12. The Irish Republican Army, formed of the Irish Republican Brotherhood and Irish Volunteers following the 1916 Easter Rising, formed the basis for the new National Army of the Irish Republic following its independence in 1922; this should not be confused with any of the organizations that have used that name since 1922.

13. For more on this, see Howard, *Strategic Deception*.

14. Andrew and Gordievsky, *KGB: The Inside Story*, p. 111.

15. Johnson, *America's Secret Power*, p. 19.

16. Maurer et al., eds., *Intelligence: Policy and Process*, p. 331.

17. As an example, sect.1.8(e) of Executive Order 12333 states that one of the roles of the CIA is to "conduct special activities approved by the President." *Special activities* is defined as "activities conducted in support of national foreign policy objectives abroad which are planned and executed so that the role of the [USG] is not apparent or acknowledged publicly" (3.4(h)-EO12333). Further authorization is given in sect.1.8(i): "conduct such administrative and *technical support activities* within and outside the United States as are necessary to perform the functions described . . . above, including procurement and essential cover and proprietary arrangements" (emphasis added). In this single phrase, Reagan justified the whole arms-for-hostages deal with Iran.

18. Johnson, *America's Secret Power*, p. 13.

19. X (Anonymous), "Sources of Soviet Conduct," *Foreign Affairs* 25, no. 4 (July 1947), pp. 575–76.

20. Johnson, *America's Secret Power*, p. 10.

21. Ibid., p. 14; Central Intelligence Agency, *Factbook on Intelligence* (Washington: CIA Public Affairs Office, 1990), p. 4.

22. Johnson, *America's Secret Power*, pp. 16–17; CIA, *Factbook*, p. 7.

23. U.S. Senate, *Foreign and Military Intelligence: Final Report of the Select Committee to Study Governmental Operations with Respect to Intelligence Activities* (Washington: Government Printing Office, 1976), p. 475.

24. Kolko, *Confronting the Developing World*, p. 51; Ray S. Cline, *Secrets, Spies and Scholars: Blueprint of the Essential CIA* (Washington: Acropolis Books, 1976): 103; Richard Bissell states that the merging of the OPC with the CAS led to a blurring of the lines between the two functions of the CIA and eventual domination of CA over the collection mission (Marchetti and Marks, *The CIA and the Cult of Intelligence*, p. 329).

25. U.S. Senate, *Final Report of the Select Committee to Study Governmental Operations with Respect to Intelligence Activities*, Book 1: *Foreign and Military Intelligence*, p. 145; Book 4: *Supplementary Detailed Staff Reports on Foreign and Military Intelligence*, p. 29.

26. Prados, *Presidents' Secret Wars*, pp. 29, 112–13.

27. Ibid., pp. 28–29.

28. Philip Agee, "Where Do We Go From Here?" in *Dirty Work: The CIA in Western Europe*, eds. Philip Agee and Louis Wolf (Secaucus: Lyle Stuart, 1978), p. 260.

29. Marchetti and Marks, *The CIA and the Cult of Intelligence*, p. 40.

30. Kolko, *Confronting the Developing World*, p. 5.

31. Prados, *Presidents' Secret Wars*, p. 468.

32. Marchetti and Marks, *The CIA and the Cult of Intelligence*, pp. 330–31.

33. U.S. Senate, *Final Report of the Select Committee*, Book 4, p. 68.

34. Ibid., p. 51.

35. Johnson, *America's Secret Power*, pp. 9, 18.

36. Congress attempted repeatedly to bring the intelligence community under legislative control because they feared it was becoming a unilateral security mechanism of the executive. For an in-depth account of this time, see Johnson, *A Season of Inquiry*, or Smist, *Congress Oversees*, as well as Cockburn, *Out of Control*.

37. Deriabin and Bagley, *KGB*, p. 383.

38. Andrew and Gordievsky, *KGB: The Inside Story*, p. 302.

39. Deriabin and Bagley, *KGB*, p. 387.

40. Epstein, *Deception*, p. 78.

41. Andrew and Gordievky, *KGB: The Inside Story*, pp. 57–58, 420, 384–85.

42. William R. Corson and Robert T. Crowley, *The New KGB: Engine of Soviet Power* (New York: William Morrow, 1985), p. 278.

43. W. E. Daugherty and Morris Janowitz, *A Psychological Warfare Casebook* (Baltimore, MD: Johns Hopkins University Press, 1956), p. 2.

44. Johnson, *America's Secret Power*, p. 22.

45. Quoted in Blackstock, *The Strategy of Subversion*, pp. 78–94.

46. Blackstock (*The Strategy of Subversion*) quoting Robert T. Holt and Robert W. van de Velde, *Strategic Psychological Operations and American Foreign Policy* (Chicago: University of Chicago Press, 1960), especially chaps. 1 and 2, pp. 1–54.

47. Blackstock (*The Strategy of Subversion*) quoting Julian Towster, *Political Power in the USSR, 1917–1947* (New York: Oxford University Press, 1948), p. 20.

48. For a discussion of the CIA's use of the media, see the Church Committee, *Final Report* (Washington, DC: U.S. Government Printing Office, 1976), Book 1, p. 192 specifically and pp. 191–201 generally; Johnson, *America's Secret Power*, p. 186.

49. Corson and Crowley, *The New KGB*, p. 379.

50. Pincher, *The Secret Offensive*, p. 1.

51. Prados, *Presidents' Secret Wars*, p. 123; Johnson, *America's Secret Power*, p. 23.

52. Cline, *Secrets, Spies and Scholars*, p. 128.

53. Treverton, *Covert Action*, p. 15.

54. Prados, *Presidents' Secret Wars*, p. 377.

55. Marchetti and Marks, *The CIA and the Cult of Intelligence*, p. 119.

56. Andrew and Gordievsky, *KGB: The Inside Story*, p. 419.

57. Ibid., p. 491.

58. Ibid., p. 406.

59. Ibid., pp. 418, 527.

60. Ibid., pp. 346, 495; Barron, *KGB Today*, p. 277.

61. Barron, *KGB Today*, p. 261.

62. Johnson, *America's Secret Power*, p. 184.

63. Declassified CIA Document DD1984-000091, Scott Library, York University (Toronto).

64. Johnson, *America's Secret Power*, p. 22.

65. Declassified CIA Document DD1984-000083, 1980-9C, Scott Library, York University (Toronto).

66. Johnson, *America's Secret Power*, p. 185; Church Committee *Report*, Book 1, p. 192.

67. Johnson, *America's Secret Power*, p. 186.

68. Treverton, *Covert Action*, pp. 14–15, 19.

69. Johnson, *America's Secret Power*, p. 197.

70. Treverton, *Covert Action*, p. 13.

71. Blackstock, *The Strategy of Subversion*, pp. 43–44, 56.

72. Quoted in Blackstock (*The Strategy of Subversion*): Harry Howe Ransom, *Can American Democracy Survive Cold War?* (New York: Doubleday, 1963), p. 176n.9.

73. Johnson, *America's Secret Power*, p. 25.

74. Ibid., pp. 25–26; Treverton, *Covert Action*, p. 20.

75. Johnson, *America's Secret Power*, p. 102.

76. Victor Marchetti and Panorama, "The CIA in Italy: An Interview with Victor Marchetti," in *Dirty Work: The CIA in Western Europe,* eds. Philip Agee and Louis Wolf (Secaucus: Lyle Stuart, 1978), p. 170; Agee, "Where Do We Go from Here?" p. 267.

77. Treverton, *Covert Action*, pp. 211–12.

78. Philip Agee and *Information Dienst*, "West Germany: An Interview with Philip Agee," in *Dirty Work: The CIA in Western Europe,* eds. Philip Agee and Louis Wolf (Secaucus: Lyle Stuart, 1978), pp. 185–86.

79. Philip Agee, "The CIA in Portugal," in *Dirty Work: The CIA in Western Europe,* Philip Agee and Louis Wolf (Secaucus: Lyle Stuart, 1978), pp. 67–68.

80. Edward Van der Rhoer, *The Shadow Network* (New York: Charles Scribner's Sons, 1983), pp. 6–8.

81. Andrew and Gordievsky, *KGB: The Inside Story*, p. 334.

82. See, for example, Christopher Andrew and Oleg Gordievsky, eds., *More "Instructions from the Centre": Top Secret Files on KGB Global Operations 1975–1985* (London: Frank Cass, 1992), pp. 29–31.

83. Pincher, *The Secret Offensive*, pp. 2–3, 7–12.

84. Prados, *Presidents' Secret Wars*, pp. 469–70.

85. Treverton, *Covert Action*, p. 20; Kolko, *Confronting the Developing World*, p. 217.

86. Johnson, *America's Secret Power*, pp. 22–23.

87. Kolko, *Confronting the Developing World*, p. 242.

88. Andrew and Gordievsky, *KGB: The Inside Story*, pp. 480, 413.

89. Ibid., pp. 466–68.

90. Prados, *Presidents' Secret Wars*, pp. 469–70.

91. Treverton, *Covert Action*, p. 21.

92. Epstein, *Deception*, p. 26; Corson and Crowley, *The New KGB*, p. 278.

93. Phelps-Fetherston, *Soviet International Front Organizations*, pp. 1, 2.

94. Most CIA corporate fronts were incorporated in Delaware due to its more lenient regulations regarding corporations (Marchetti and Marks, *The CIA and the Cult of Intelligence*, p. 118). For a full discussion of the CIA's use of proprietaries, see Church Committee *Report,* Book 1, pp. 205–56.

95. For a complete discussion of CAT, see Marchetti and Marks, *The CIA and the Cult of Intelligence*, pp. 121–24.

96. Prados, *Presidents' Secret Wars*, pp. 114–15, 116; Kirkpatrick, *The U.S. Intelligence Community*, p. 119n; for a complete discussion of Air America, as well as subsidiaries like Air Asia and Southern Air Transport, see Marchetti and Marks, *The CIA and the Cult of Intelligence*, pp. 124–26.

97. Marchetti and Marks, *The CIA and the Cult of Intelligence*, p. 120.

98. Ibid., pp. 408, 431–32, 375.

99. Prados, *Presidents' Secret Wars*, p. 450.

100. John Marks, "The CIA's Corporate Shell Game," in *Dirty Work: The CIA in Western Europe,* eds. Philip Agee and Louis Wolf (Secaucus: Lyle Stuart, 1978), pp. 127, 130.

101. Treverton, *Covert Action*, pp. 102–5.

102. Marks, "The CIA's Corporate Shell Game," p. 137; Prados, *Presidents' Secret Wars*, pp. 195, 211.

103. Arcos was funded through Amtorg (New York) and Wostwag (Hamburg), two fronts for the Comintern, and supported by the Cheka. It was later expelled from the United Kingdom for subversion, sabotage, political intrigue, and so on (Corson and Crowley, *The New KGB*, p. 283; Andrew and Gordievsky, *KGB: The Inside Story*, pp. 82, 84).

104. For more on the apartheid government's covert activities—both foreign and domestic—see Kevin A. O'Brien, "Counter-Intelligence for Counter-Revolutionary Warfare: The South African Police Security Branch," *Intelligence and National Security* 16, no. 3 (Autumn 2001), pp. 27–59; Kevin A. O'Brien, "Special Forces for Counter-Revolutionary Warfare: The South African Case," *Small Wars and Insurgencies* 12, no. 2 (Summer 2001), pp. 79–109; Kevin A. O'Brien, "The Use of Assassination as a Tool of State Policy: South Africa's Counter-Revolutionary Strategy 1979–1992 (Part II)," *Terrorism and Political Violence* 13, no. 2 (Spring 2001), pp. 107–42; and Kevin A.

O'Brien, "The Use of Assassination as a Tool of State Policy: South Africa's Counter-Revolutionary Strategy 1979–1992 (Part I)," *Terrorism and Political Violence* 10, no. 3 (Summer 1998), pp. 34–51.

105. Kirkpatrick, *The U.S. Intelligence Community*, p. 153; Church Committee *Report,* Book 1, p. 184; Marchetti and Marks, *The CIA and the Cult of Intelligence*, p. 41; Richard Fletcher, "How CIA Money Took the Teeth Out of British Socialism," in *Dirty Work: The CIA in Western Europe,* eds. Philip Agee and Louis Wolf (Secaucus: Lyle Stuart, 1978), p. 198.

106. Weissman et al., "The CIA Backs the Common Market," in *Dirty Work: The CIA in Western Europe,* eds. Philip Agee and Louis Wolf (Secaucus: Lyle Stuart, 1978), pp. 202, 203.

107. Johnson, *America's Secret Power*, p. 26; Treverton, *Covert Action*, p. 19.

108. Phelps-Fetherston, *Soviet International Front Organizations*, p. 1.

109. Andrew and Gordievsky, *KGB: The Inside Story*, pp. 57–58.

110. Phelps-Fetherston, *Soviet International Front Organizations*, pp. 3–4.

111. Richard Deacon, *A History of the Russian Secret Service* (London: Frederick Muller, 1972), p. 513; Barron, *KGB Today*, pp. 264–65.

112. Andrew and Gordievsky,*KGB: The Inside Story*, pp. 359, 419.

113. Ibid., pp. 419–20.

114. Ibid., pp. 492, 490, 506.

115. Johnson, *America's Secret Power*, p. 26.

116. *Counterintelligence* is defined as "information gathered and activities conducted to protect against espionage, other intelligence activities, sabotage, or assassinations conducted for or on behalf of foreign powers, organizations or persons, or international terrorist activities" (Executive Order 12333, 3.4a)

117. Charters, "The Role of Intelligence Services," p. 334.

118. Keylor, 221; Cockburn, *Out of Control.*

119. Johnson, *America's Secret Power*, pp. 12–13.

120. Ibid., p. 26.

121. Ibid., pp. 26–27.

122. Ibid., pp. 28–29.

123. Begun in 1952, USAID sent public safety missions to over thirty-eight nations between 1955 and 1962; by 1973, over 73,000 foreign police personnel had been trained. That year, however, Congress banned USAID from continuing such operations, and the project was taken over covertly by the CIA: Johnson, *America's Secret Power*, p. 157, this was exposed in a 1966 issue of *Ramparts*; Kirkpatrick, *The U.S. Intelligence Community*, p. 151; Kolko, *Confronting the Developing World*, pp. 50–51, 131, 210.

124. Church Committee *Report*, p. 269.

125. Prados, *Presidents' Secret Wars*, pp. 40–41, 55–58, 120–21.

126. Ibid., pp. 269–94, 271, 291.

127. Deriabin and Bagley, *KGB*, p. 388.

128. Epstein, *Deception*, pp. 282, 283–90.

129. Deriabin and Bagley, *KGB*, p. 363.

130. Andrew and Gordievsky, *KGB: The Inside Story*, p. 384; Van der Rhoer, *The Shadow Network* 11–12.

131. Deriabin and Bagley, *KGB*, pp. 358–59.

132. Blackstock *The Strategy of Subversion.*

133. Blackstock (*The Strategy of Subversion*) quoting a "former high-ranking Israeli intelligence officer and confirmed by Allen Dulles during a public visit, as a guest lecturer, to the University of South Carolina, April 2, 1963."

134. Bob Woodward, *Bush at War* (New York: Simon & Shuster, 2002), p. 78.

135. For a good summary of this, see Susan Wright, "The Hijacking of UNSCOM," *Bulletin of the Atomic Scientists* 55, no. 3 (May/June 1999), pp. 23–25.

136. Prados, *Presidents' Secret Wars*, p. 466.

137. Treverton, *Covert Action*, p. 22.

138. Kolko, *Confronting the Developing World*, p. 105.

139. Prados, *Presidents' Secret Wars*, pp. 465–66.

140. Johnson, *America's Secret Power*, p. 69.

141. Ibid., p. 196.

142. Ibid., p. 84; Prados, *Presidents' Secret Wars*, p. 383.

143. Prados, *Presidents' Secret Wars*, pp. 469–70, 125.

144. Epstein, *Deception*, p. 41.

145. Andrew and Gordievsky, *KGB: The Inside Story*, pp. 420, 528.

146. Ibid., p. 494.

147. Deriabin and Bagley, *KGB*, p. 364.

148. Prados, *Presidents' Secret Wars*, p. 467.

149. Treverton, *Covert Action*, p. 3.

150. John Le Carré, *The Secret Pilgrim* (Toronto: Viking, 1990), pp. 334–35.

# 3

# COVERT ACTION

## The Israeli Experience

EPHRAIM KAHANA

COVERT ACTION HAS ALWAYS BEEN A SIGNIFICANT element of international politics. When it has served their interests, governments have secretly disseminated propaganda in other countries, manipulated foreign economies, and abetted coups against their adversaries, on either a direct or indirect basis.

Israel, like other countries, has and uses the tool of covert action, with varying degrees of success. Israeli covert action includes the full range of options, inclusive but not limited to paramilitary incursions and the rescue of Jews from foreign territories. In this chapter, the most significant and sometimes most controversial covert actions are described.

## THE BAD BUSINESS

The Bad Business, known in Hebrew as the *Esek Ha'Bish*, was the most controversial Israeli covert action to date in the public domain. This covert action is commonly known as well as either Operation Susannah, or the Lavon Affair, named after the Israeli Defense minister of the period (1954), Pinhas Lavon. In essence, the Bad Business was a paramilitary action of sabotage against primarily American/British targets in Egypt.[1]

Egypt, historically the largest and most powerful of Israel's neighboring Arab countries, was always of primary interest to the Israeli intelligence services. At Military Intelligence (MI), it was decided to set up a network of sleeper agents in Egypt, who, at the appropriate time, would be assigned to carry out secret missions. In May 1951, an Israeli intelligence officer from Unit 131, Maj. Avraham Dar, was secretly dispatched to Egypt under the assumed name of John Darling, using the cover of a British businessman, with a mission to recruit Egyptian Jews for an espionage network. Dar succeeded in this task fairly easily, because several young Egyptian Jews with Zionistic tendencies simply volunteered. Dar set up two espionage cells, one in the port city of Alexandria and the other in Cairo. With respect to the Cairo cell, Dar recruited Ceasar Cohen, Moshe Marzouk, Eli Ya'acov Naim, and Victorine Marcel Ninio as operatives. For the Alexandria cell, he recruited Shmuel Becor Azzar, Robert Nissim Dassa, Victor Moise Levy, Meir Shmuel Meyuhas, Philip Hermann Nathanson, and Meir Yosef Za'afran. Several of the candidate agents were transported secretly to Israel for military training and tradecraft. Despite the fact that many remained rank amateurs after the training, the operatives were nonetheless sent back to Egypt. They "slept" for three years until the agreed code word was broadcast over the army radio channel, *Galei Zahal.*

Toward the end of 1951, Avraham (Avri) Elad, a former major in the Israeli Defense Force (IDF), contacted Dar and the commander of Unit 131, Lt. Col. Mordechai (Motke) Ben-Tsur, to seek employment. Despite certain reservations, the heads of Unit 131 decided to involve Elad in the operation, and he was assigned cover as a German businessman named Paul Frank. Elad resided initially in West Germany to construct and develop his cover story further. In December 1953, Elad arrived in Egypt (as Paul Frank), a wealthy businessman. He soon blended into the expanding colony of expatriate Germans, many of whom were past Nazis. Elad was to take command of the sleeping Jewish espionage network. He contacted all its members and became closely acquainted with their details.

After the revolution in Egypt in 1952, the United States exerted pressure on Britain to withdraw from the Suez Canal zone to keep Egypt in the pro-Western camp. There was concern in Israel concerning the forthcoming British evacuation because the Israeli government regarded the presence of British forces in the canal zone as a check and balance against possible Egyptian adventurism under Gamal Abdel Nasser. However, by the end of June 1954, the British evacuation of the Suez Canal zone appeared imminent. Israeli Defense Minister Lavon asked Binyamin Gibli, the director of MI, to use all of Unit 131's resources in Egypt to prevent the British pullout. Lavon, however, did not immerse himself in the details of strategy, to his discredit. Accordingly, Gibli came up with the idea of preventing or delaying the British withdrawal by staging a series of sabotage acts directed primarily against Western embassies and other institutions that would, according to Gibli, be interpreted by the British as acts being perpetrated by the Egyptians. Gibli believed that under such circumstances the British might reconsider the planned evacuation program.

On June 30, 1954, Gibli instructed Elad to carry out the covert sabotage in Egypt, resulting in small firebombs being placed in mailboxes in Alexandria two days later. On July 14, small, harmless bombs exploded at the U.S. cultural centers in Cairo and the library of the U.S. Information Center in Alexandria, as well as in the luggage storage depot at the Alexandria Railway Station.

However, when Philip Nathanson entered the Rio Cinema in Alexandria, the charge he was carrying went off prematurely, which resulted in his arrest. Within days the Egyptian security police arrested and interrogated the rest of the network's members. They also arrested Max Binnet, another Israeli spy working under cover at the time in Egypt, but who was not directly connected to the group.

Members of the MI's inner circle were forced to accept responsibility for recruiting and training Egyptian Jews for their espionage network, while Gibli admitted the operatives clandestine duties—however, these admissions were not made public. Prime Minister Moshe Sharett knew nothing of the operation. Gibli asserted that the order to activate the operatives was given to him by Lavon.

After the capture of the espionage network's members in Egypt, Gibli tried to activate a European lobby to ease the Egyptians' treatment of their Israeli-trained Jewish prisoners, who were being interrogated under torture in appalling conditions in an Egyptian jail. A trial began on December 11, 1954, with the sentencing a month later. Cohen and Na'im were acquitted. Meyuhas and Za'afran were each sentenced to seven years, and Ninio and Dassa each received fifteen years in prison. Levy and Nathanson were sentenced to life imprisonment, whereas Azzar and Marzuq were sentenced to death and executed. Dar and Elad, the Israeli handlers of the network, were tried in absentia and sentenced to death. Max Binnet, the Israeli spy apprehended with the network but not directly involved in its operations, committed suicide in an Egyptian jail on December 21, 1954, after undergoing severe torture sessions.

For years, Israel denied any connection to the bombing in Egypt, with the local media being barred by the military censor from mentioning the affair. Since the story was published in the foreign press, Israeli inner circles began to demand the establishment of a commission of inquiry. Subsequently, Israeli weekly publication *Ha'Olam Ha'Zeh* printed the story without the censor's permission with an invented name for the country involved.

Ultimately the scandal was made public, and Lavon was forced to resign. David Ben-Gurion returned from retirement and replaced Lavon as Minister of Defense. In 1960, new evidence emerged from a secret trial of Elad, held in 1958. Apparently it is understood that Elad betrayed the Jewish network in Egypt. The Israeli establishment remained anxious, fearing the opening of a Pandora's box regarding the person who gave the order to activate the Jewish network in Egypt. Subsequently, Lavon asked Ben-Gurion to exonerate him, but Ben-Gurion refused.

Several Israeli commissions investigated the Bad Business, but they failed to reach unambiguous conclusions as to who gave the order or who was responsible for the fiasco. In 1960, a commission revealed the forging of a document used by Moshe Dayan and Shimon Peres, then deputy minister of Defense, to attract the responsibility for the botched 1954 Egyptian operation to Lavon. In a subsequent hearing, the results of which were accepted by the government, it was revealed that Peres, Dayan, and Gibli were all involved.

The specific question of "who gave the order?" has been asked countless times by the Israeli public, yet it appears the answer will not be forthcoming. A more important question revolves around who was responsible for the Bad Business, even if it was not that person who actually gave the order. The answer to this question is definitive; as the supreme commander of the IDF, the Israeli government bears the ultimate responsibility for all military intelligence failures, including this one. This also applies to the minister of Defense, even if he did not give the specific order.

In the aftermath of the Sinai Campaign in October 1956, it seemed reasonable to expect negotiations for the release of the prisoners of the Jewish espionage network. Israel held over 5,500 Egyptian POWs after its conquest of the Sinai Peninsula. Among the most senior of the captives was Gen. Fuad el Digwi, who had been the presiding judge at the trial of the members of the Jewish espionage ring in 1954. When he fell into Israeli custody, he was the military governor of the Gaza Strip. All 5,500 Egyptian prisoners were consequently traded for 10 Israeli POWs, including one pilot. The Israeli government did not request the release of the members of the Jewish network from prison because its policy was still to deny any Israeli connection to the events in Egypt in 1954. Top Israeli echelons believed that requesting the prisoners release might endanger Israel's relations with the United States.

After fourteen years of rotting in Egyptian jails, Dassa, Levy, Nathanson, and Ninio were released, as part of the agreement to return 5,237 Egyptian POWs captured during the 1967 Six-Day War. The four members of the network were released separately from the Israeli POWs and reached Israel via Europe. This time the inclusion of the Jewish spy network prisoners in the POW exchange was settled only at the insistence of the director of the Mossad, Meir Amit, who threatened to resign if he would not be allowed to seek their release during negotiations with the Egyptians. For all that, the presence in Israel of the released network members remained an official secret until Prime Minister Golda Meir announced her intention to attend Marcelle Ninio's wedding in 1971 and to inform the Israeli press.

The key result of the Bad Business was that the Israeli government adopted a tenet of never activating Jews in the diaspora for espionage or any other covert action against their own country's government, with a belief that such activity might ruin relations between the Jewish citizens of such countries and their government. In nondemocracies, like the Arab states, activating Jewish spies would in any case have a limited effect, because their access to important governmental positions or secrets, if any, is negligible. The Pollard Affair by definition is dissimilar in nature. Jonathan Jay Pollard was not operated by an official intelligence organization in Israel but by an amateur outfit known as the Bureau of Scientific Liaison, known by its Hebrew acronym as LAKAM.

On March 30, 2005, the three last surviving members of the espionage network in Egypt, Ninio, Dassa, and Za'afran, were accorded recognition by Israel's President Katsav and the chief of the General Staff Lt. Gen. Moshe

Ya'alon, for their services to the state and their years of incarceration and suffering.[2]

## THE KHALED MASHAL FIASCO

The Khaled Mashal fiasco occurred on September 24, 1997, when members of the Kidon (bayonet) Unit of the Mossad arrived in Jordan, where they checked in as tourists at the Intercontinental Hotel in Amman. Two of them, who used fake Canadian passports in the names of Barry Beads and Sean Kendall, were to execute the team's mission, which was to assassinate Khaled Mashal, the leader of Hamas, whom Israel believed to be behind many terrorist attacks that cost the lives of Israeli civilians. The Israeli Committee X, chaired by Prime Minister Benjamin Netanyahu, had decided on the assassination, determining that the mission should be accomplished on Jordanian soil. Although Mashal resided in Jordan, this was a curious decision at best, considering the extremely delicate Israeli-Jordanian relations after the two countries signed a peace treaty in 1994.[3]

The day after their arrival, "Beads" and "Kendall" attempted to poison Mashal in a crowded Amman street by spraying him with a nerve agent. They barely managed to use only half the aerosol can's content when their actions were observed, and they fled the scene immediately but were later arrested. Mashal was hospitalized, while the support members of the Kidon Unit succeeded in departing Jordan.

This fiasco caused enormous embarrassment to both governments and jeopardized Israel's relations with one of its few Middle Eastern allies. King Hussein threatened Netanyahu that he would put the men on trial if the Mossad did not provide an antidote to save Mashal's life. Israel acceded to Hussein's demand and Mashal was saved.

At the demand of Hussein, Israel also released Hamas leader Sheikh Ahmed Yassin, imprisoned in Israel for his role in terrorist acts. The two Mossad agents were delivered to the Canadian embassy in Amman and driven to Israel, with the Israeli government assuring the Canadians that it would never again use false Canadian documents. The Khaled Mashal fiasco was considered the second Bad Business; however, the period was different and this fiasco almost immediately became public, unlike the Bad Business.[4]

## OPERATION WRATH OF GOD

The Munich massacre of the Israeli athletes during the 1972 Olympic Games shook the Israeli defense establishment to its very foundations, and the street demanded vengeance. Golda Meir's government was indeed bent on revenge, and its first response was a massive air bombardment of terror bases in Lebanon. Three days later, the Israel Air Force launched an air raid involving approximately seventy-five aircraft, the largest such attack since the 1967 Six-Day War. Israeli ground troops were additionally ordered into Lebanon to engage Palestinian terrorists who had been mining Israeli roads. Despite this aggressive military response, a select group of high-ranking Israeli officials felt that more had to be done. They decided that a message should be sent not only to those who had perpetrated the Munich massacre but also to those who might consider terrorist attacks against Israelis in the future, so that others might see and fear.[5]

This led to the decision to establish the so-called Committee X, chaired by Meir and Defense Minister Moshe Dayan. The committee authorized the assassination of all the individuals involved, either directly or indirectly, in the Munich massacre. Committee X listed thirty-five main assassination targets. The mission was assigned to several different Mossad teams, formed by the commander of the Caesarea Division in the Mossad, Michael (Mike) Harari. It was carried out mainly by Kidon (bayonet), an ultra-secret subunit of Caesarea.

The operations conducted to assassinate key Palestinian terrorist leaders were known by their unofficial names: Operation Wrath of God and the Sword of Gideon. A general mobilization was declared within the Israeli Security Agency (ISA) and in Unit 504 of the IDF. For the purpose of the assassinations, the most talented intelligence-gathering officers were called up, including Shmuel Goren, commander of Keshet (an intelligence-gathering unit), Baruch Cohen, Zadok Ofir, Raphael (Rafi) Sutton, Eliezer (Geyzi) Tsafrir, and Nahum Admoni, commander of Tevel, the branch in charge of connections with foreign intelligence agencies.

During the search for the terrorists involved in the Munich massacre, it emerged that of the eight who had taken part in the massacre, five had been killed by the German police officers and three had been detained. After the hijacking of a Lufthansa airliner in October 1972, the detained terrorists were released to Libya and then onto Damascus, whereupon traces of them were lost. As far as is known now, they were still alive. However, about twenty other Palestinians with blood on their hands or who had been involved in preparing acts of terror but were not necessarily connected to the Munich massacre met their deaths in strange and mysterious ways.

In any event, the Munich massacre signified a real turning point in Israel's war on terror. This was the beginning of a war to the death against the terror organizations, a campaign of elimination and vengeance. One of the first targeted for assassination, whose name and nickname are still classified, was a Black September Organization (BSO) member who arrived in Athens with the task of sending a container of raisins covering hidden explosives to the Haifa port, where it would be detonated by remote control.

The Mossad received information about this plan, and its operatives left for Athens, where they searched for the perpetrator. They discovered a female customs broker who, unknown to her, was handling that cargo of raisins bound for Israel. Documents were seized, and through them Mossad agents located the storage depot where they hoped to find the raisin bomb, but nothing was discovered. The documents did reveal, however, the man behind the shipment, who was then followed and shot dead. BSO members concluded that the customs broker had given details about their comrade's activities to the Mossad, and they killed her.[6]

According to George Jonas's book *Vengeance*, one of the teams assigned to assassinate Palestinian terrorists was headed by a former IDF officer, who was referred to in his book by the pseudonym Avner, who controlled a team of five operatives and operated in a semi-autonomous fashion. It is, however, impossible to verify the existence of Avner and his specific team. As it is better known today, Kidon's teams were assigned to assassinate a list of targets, as follows: Kamal Adwan, the chief of sabotage operations for the Al Fatah organization in the 1967 occupied territories; Hussein Abad Al-Chir, the Palestinian Liberation Organization (PLO) contact man with the KGB in Cyprus; Mohammed Boudia, the BSO liaison with the European PLO; Abu Daoud, a BSO member; Dr. Wadi Haddad, a chief terrorist linked with Dr. George Habash; Mahmoud Hamshari, a PLO member and coordinator of the Munich Olympic Games massacre; Dr. Basil Raoud Kubaisi, an official of the Popular Front for the Liberation of Palestine (PFLP) in charge of logistics; Kamal Nasser, the official PLO spokesman and a member of the PLO Executive Committee; Ali Hassan Salameh, a developer and executor of the assault on the Israeli athletes at Munich; Abu Yussuf, a high-ranking PLO official; and Wael Zwaiter, a PLO organizer of terror in Europe and Yasser Arafat's cousin. Kidon's teams succeeded in tracking down and killing several of the targets on the list: Zwaiter on October 6, 1972; Hamshari on October 8, 1972; Abad al-Chir on January 24, 1973; Kubaisi on April 6, 1973; and Boudia on June 28, 1973. After killing Abad al-Chir, Ziad Muchassi replaced him as the PLO contact with the KGB, and he was belatedly added to the target list. He was killed on April 12, 1973.

As for the other targets listed by Committee X, six terrorists remained at large. Wadi Haddad was not traced by Israel, but he died of cancer on March 28, 1977 in an East Berlin hospital. Abu Daoud was arrested in Germany in March 1973 and confessed to his involvement in the Munich massacre. Kamal Adwan, Kamal Nasser, and Abu Yussuf were killed by a covert commando raid on April 9, 1973, carried out as a joint Mossad-IDF mission (see Operation Spring of Youth). Ali Hassan Salameh was killed on January 22, 1979, in a Beirut car bomb explosion by another Mossad team.

A high price for Operation Wrath of God was paid by Mossad personnel who collected intelligence data about those marked for elimination. For example, following an arranged meeting with a Palestinian in a café in Madrid, Baruch Cohen was shot dead by another Palestinian as he was leaving the café. Likewise, Zadok Ofir was gravely wounded in Brussels at his meeting with a dubious informer. Other members of the team that mistakenly killed Ahmad Bouchiki (in Lillehammer, Norway) were arrested in Oslo, and four members of the team, Dan Arbel, Marianne Gladnikoff, Sylvia Raphael, and Michael Dorf, were sentenced to prison terms.

## OPERATION DAMOCLES

Operation Damocles was another paramilitary operation of assassination. After the 1956 Sinai Campaign, Egyptian President Gamal Abdel Nasser requested West Germany to build a surface-to-surface missile capability that could be used in future Egyptian wars against Israel. In 1962, Mossad Chief Isser Harel learned that work on the project had begun and requested Israeli Prime Minister David Ben-Gurion to seek the intervention of West German Chancellor Konrad Adenauer to halt it. Ben-Gurion however, was determined not to clash with the West German government. At his own initiative, Harel set in motion subversive actions with the overall title of Operation Damocles against German scientists and their families working on the project in Egypt. This campaign involved abductions and letter bombs, causing the deaths of at least five people between 1962 and 1963. Several letters were mailed by an Israeli spy in Egypt, Wolfgang Lotz. Aharon Moshel, another Israeli spy in Egypt, also engaged in hunting German scientists in that country.

Measures against Germans involved in the missile project were mainly under the command of Joseph ( Joe) Ra'anan, who had joined the Mossad after serving as an intelligence officer in the Israel Air Force, and Yitzhak Shamir, who later became prime minister of Israel. One success was the disappearance of Dr. Heinz Krug, probably murdered in September 1962. In February 1963, Dr. Hans Kleinwachter, an electronics specialist, who in World War II was engaged in Nazi Germany's V2 rocket project, survived an assassination attempt by Shamir's team.

In the 1950s, Israel decided to clandestinely assassinate the chief the Egyptian commanders of the Palestinian terrorism. Col. Hafez Mustafa, then commander of Egyptian Intelligence in the Gaza Strip, was listed as a target and was assassinated. At that time, Egypt customarily sent cells of marauding Arabs (*Fedayeen*) from the Gaza Strip into Israel for the purpose of terrorizing Israeli society by murdering Israelis. Mustafa was in charge of those operations.

In June 1956, the director of Israel's DMI Maj. Gen. Yehoshafat Harkabi proposed a plan to assassinate Mustafa, which was successfully carried out on June 12, 1956, by an explosive device hidden in a book handed to him by an Egyptian double agent. Another book bomb was sent the following day via an East Jerusalem post office to Col. Salah Mustafa, Egypt's Amman-based military attaché, who had dispatched infiltrators via the West Bank into Israel. He opened the package and was killed by the blast. In the 1960s mail bombs became a central assassination tool of Israeli intelligence, especially against (former Nazi) German scientists who were involved in developing a missiles program for Egypt.

These paramilitary covert actions were not designed to be made public; their goals were to enhance Israeli security. The Bad Business and the Khaled Mashal affair became public knowledge because they failed. Operation Wrath of God was never officially connected to Israel, consequently Israel has never admitted partaking in the killings. However, Israeli fingerprints were well stamped on these operations. Two more covert actions of assassination in which Israel has never admitted playing any part were the assassinations of Abu Jihad and Yahya Ayyash.[7]

The Engineer was the nickname of Ayyash, who was born in 1966 near Nablus and studied electrical engineering at Bir Zeit University near Ramallah, where he joined Hamas. During a 24-month campaign of terror beginning on April 6, 1994, Ayyash killed 130 Israelis and wounded nearly 500. As the carnage in the streets of Israeli cities grew, Ayyash became revered by masses of Palestinians. One of the largest manhunts in Israeli history was mounted for Israel's most wanted man, involving the British Secret Service (MI5), the Royal Jordanian Special Forces, the FBI, and the New York City Police Department. In charge of catching Ayash was the ISA. The ISA, among the elite of Israel's security agencies, succeeded in handing Ayyash a mobile phone via an operative. On January 5, 1996, the cell phone was detonated after Ayyash answered an incoming call, and he was killed. More than 100,000 Palestinians attended his funeral.[8]

## THE SPRING OF YOUTH

Other paramilitary covert actions were carried out secretly but became public immediately after the operation ended. These operations were covert for tactical purposes only, to maintain the effect of surprise. Operation Spring of Youth was one of these, and it remained covert as long as the forces were engaged in the field. The operation was launched on April 9, 1973, and was carried out by approximately forty highly trained commandos of the most elite unit of the IDF, Sayeret Matkal. Its purpose was to avenge the deaths of the Israeli athletes slaughtered at the 1972 Munich Olympics by eliminating those in any way responsible for the massacre.[9]

In February 1973, Lt. Col. Ehud Barak, the commander of Sayeret Matkal, obtained photographs and precise information as to the whereabouts of three Palestinians involved in the massacre, Kamal Adwan, Kamal Nasser, and Mahmoud Yussuf Najjer, better known as Abu Yussuf, who were all then residing in Beirut. The Mossad obtained information that two of them lived on the second and third floors of the same building in Beirut, and the third lived across the street. The information also specified the exact architectural plans of the buildings.

After cross-referencing the intelligence, the strategy selected and executed by Sayeret Matkal was for the commando teams to infiltrate the Lebanese border by sea, disguised as tourists, with their weapons hidden. The distance from the beach landing point to the Beirut target apartments was approximately six miles. Three commando units would attack the individual apartments, and a guard unit would be positioned outside the apartment to contain any Lebanese police, army, or Palestinian reinforcements. The operation was calculated to last twenty minutes from the time of the initial shots until Lebanese or Palestinian reinforcements arrived on the scene. By then the commandos were expected to be back on the beach boarding the craft that would return them to Israel.

Barak, dressed as an Arab woman, commanded the operation and lead the guard unit. Another officer, Amiram Levine, was also disguised as an Arab woman. This unit maintained contact with their forward operational headquarters located aboard Israeli navy boats, offshore from Beirut.

Alighting on the Lebanese coast, the commandos were met by three cars driven by Mossad operatives, planted in Lebanon beforehand, who had intimate knowledge of the city. They drove the commandos to the apartments and returned them to the beach once the operation was accomplished. The drivers were Gilbert Rimbaud (Belgian) and Dieter Altnuder (German). In addition to the three apartments, a unit from the Israel Paratroop Regiment, led by Amnon Lipkin-Shahak, was assigned to strike the six-story headquarters of the world's most notorious hijacker, Dr. George Habash of the PFLP. Another paratrooper unit, as well as the Naval Commando Unit Sayetet 13, were to raid weapons manufacturing facilities and fuel dumps that the PLO maintained in the Tyre-Sidon area.

Among other well-known officers who took part in Operation Spring of Youth were Muki Betser and Yoni Netanyahu; the latter was killed in 1976 in Operation Yehonathan (also commonly known as Operation Entebbe).

Operation Spring of Youth succeeded because of excellent intelligence and ground assistance carried out by the Mossad. All the commandos of the Sayeret Matkal returned alive from the operation, with one wounded. During the (paratrooper) raid led by Lipkin-Shahak, two soldiers were killed.[10]

## OPERATION YEHONATHAN

Operation Yehonathan was another covert operation carried out for tactical purposes of surprise: a rescue mission of Israelis who were hijacked by terrorists to Uganda. This operation, which took place on the night between July 3–4, 1976, came belatedly to be known as Operation Yehonathan, in honor of Lt. Col. Yehonathan "Yoni" Netanyahu, who was killed during the operation. The same operation was additionally known as Operation Entebbe, Operation Thunderball, or Operation Thunderbolt.[11]

On June 27, 1976, Air France flight 139 from Israel to Paris with 246 passengers was hijacked after taking off from its stopover point in Athens, Greece. It was diverted to Benghazi Airport in Libya, then onto Entebbe Airport in Uganda, where it landed. Eight of the hijackers were PLO members, and two belonged to the Baader-Meinhof gang. They were apparently supported by the Ugandan regime of pro-Palestinian President Idi Amin. In their ultimatum, the hijackers demanded that the government of Israel release all convicted Palestinian terrorist murderers; they set a 3-day deadline of June 30.

In principle the government of Israel is against any kind of negotiating or bargaining with hijackers, because to do so might serve as a precedent for further hijacking attempts. The alternative option, in this instance, was a rescue attempt by means of a military operation. The IDF chief of the General Staff, Lt. Gen.

Mordechai Gur, was reluctant to recommend a military rescue operation unless relevant and updated intelligence was gathered. The only information at hand concerned the blueprints of the terminal building at Entebbe Airport, obtained from the Israeli construction firm Solel Boneh, which had constructed the building in the 1960s. But this intelligence was insufficient. Parallel to the planning of a military rescue operation of the passengers, the Israeli government stated its readiness to pursue several political paths for the release of the hostages, which was a ploy to gain time for acquiring more intelligence on the situation and planning the rescue operation. As the negotiations proceeded, the hijackers extended their ultimatum to July 4.

The passengers were held in the old terminal's transit hall. The terrorists subsequently freed a large number of them, keeping only Israelis and Jews, whom they threatened to kill if the Israeli government did not meet their demands. The hijackers said they would free the airplane's crew, and an Air France plane was sent to Entebbe for that purpose. The plane's captain, Michael Bacos, and his crew refused to depart without all the passengers and accordingly remained with the hijacked passengers. One hundred three Israelis—men, women, and children— remained hostage in Entebbe.

Following the release of the non-Israeli/non-Jewish hostages, reserve Lt. Col. Amiram Levine in the Collection Department of the DMI flew to Paris on July 1 with Lt. Col. Amnon Biran to collect all possible information from the freed hostages, only two of whom remembered varying levels of detail.

At a preset time, four Hercules transport aircraft flew to Entebbe Airport and night-landed without any ground aid. They were followed by an Israeli air force jet with medical facilities that flew into Nairobi Airport in Kenya. Over 100 Israeli soldiers, including members of the elite Sayeret Matkal Unit, arrived to conduct the assault with Mossad operatives alledgedly taking part by way of providing ground assistance.

The aircraft landed an hour before midnight on July 3, 1976. A black Mercedes Benz limousine with an accompanying jeep convoy were driven toward the airport buildings to divert attention. It was hoped that this cavalcade would be taken to signify the arrival of a high Ugandan official with his escort, possibly Amin himself. Meanwhile the Israeli troops drove from the aircraft to the terminal building.

The raid took place during the early hours of July 4 and lasted about three minutes. Six or eight terrorists were killed, and all the hostages in the terminal were released alive, except for one who was killed when he frantically leaped at the Israeli forces. Another hostage, 75-year-old Dora Bloch, who was recovering from a choking episode in a Kampala hospital on the night of the raid, was left behind in Uganda and later murdered by two Ugandan army officers. During the incursion, Ugandan forces opened fire on Israeli troops, killing Netanyahu. Forty-five Ugandan soldiers were killed during the raid, and the Ugandan Airforce fighter planes parked on the ramp were taken out of action. Shortly after the fighting ceased, the rescued hostages were flown out via Nairobi to Israel.

One of the factors behind the excellent planning of the raid was superior intelligence. The success of Operation Yehonathan was result of the first-class troops of Sayeret Makal, but also, and no less importantly, to the essential information obtained by Israeli intelligence. The successful rescue from Entebbe Airport, a little less than three years after the failure to provide an early warning on the eve of the 1973 Yom Kippur War, afforded a major boost to morale among Israeli intelligence officers.[12]

## COVERT RESCUE MISSIONS

Other covert actions were carried out for purposes of rescuing Jews from hostile Arab dictatorships. In 1970, intelligence began to trickle into the Israeli government from Syria with respect to privations suffered by the Jewish communities in Aleppo and Damascus. The reports told of young Jews making an effort to flee Syria, despite the difficulties and the dangers. The Israeli government, under Golda Meir, resolved to embark on an operation to bring the Syrian Jews to Israel. Operation Blanket began in 1970 and lasted several years; it was in fact a series of individualized and intricate operations. The operations were carried out by combat troops of Naval Commando Shayetet 13 of the Israeli navy, acting under orders of the Mossad, which was charged with the implementation of the operations. As part of the overall plan, Mossad operatives made dozens of incursions into Syria, as did combatants of Shayetet 13.

The Israeli government invested many resources in Operation Blanket, which in total succeeded in taking to Israel only a few dozen young Jews. The operational participants made the Syrian capital almost their home while taking enormous risks. Moreover, this was a mere few years after the capture and execution of an Israeli spy in Syria: Eli Cohen. Other covert actions for purposes of rescuing Jews that became well known were Operations Moses and Solomon. However the first rescue-type operations were Operations Magic Carpet and Tushia.

Operation Magic Carpet involved the secret airlifting of Yemeni Jews to Israel. Toward the end of April 1949, the imam of Yemen agreed to let most of the Jews, some 45,000 out of around 46,000, depart the country of their birth, Yemen. From remote corners of the country, the Yemeni Jews made their way on foot to an airport where they unobtrusively boarded Israeli transport aircraft, totaling 380 flights, to Israel. British and American airplanes were also engaged in the airlift. Most of these impoverished and isolated Jews had never seen an airplane, and on landing in Israel described their flying mode of transport as a "magic carpet." Thus Operation Magic Carpet became the name of this highly complex and dangerous rescue-immigration campaign. Operation Magic Carpet ran from May 1949 to the end of September 1950. Operatives of the Mossad Le'Aliyah Beth were dispatched to Yemen to organize the operation, which was kept secret and revealed to the media only after completion.[13]

Operation Tushia (meaning "initiative" in Hebrew) was carried out in 1956 after the Sinai Campaign. The operation was executed by Israeli intelligence in the hope that its operatives in Egypt would be in a position to contact Egyptian Jews and persuade most to leave for Israel. On November 9, 1956, Maj. Avraham Dar and Aryeh (Lova) Eliav, together with their radio operator, slipped into the war zone pretending to be French officers in French military uniforms and advanced with the British and the French troops. In Port Said they found only 200 mostly elderly Jews with no interest in moving to Israel. In the Jewish synagogue in the town they encountered only sixty-five Jews willing to leave with them for Israel. Secretly the three took them to the harbor and with the assistance of the French army, boarded them onto two French military landing craft. After sailing about one and a half miles offshore, the French craft met up with two tiny Israeli navy vessels camouflaged as Italian fishing boats, which carried the Egyptian Jews to Israel, with Dar and Eliav following days later.[14]

Operation Moses, known in Hebrew as Mivtza Moshe, came to fruition in 1974 after Ethiopian Emperor Haile Selassie was overthrown by a Marxist regime, resulting in the local Jewish community suffering in the Marxist revolutionary chaos. In 1977 and for several more years, Ethiopian Jews began arriving in Israel. As economic and political conditions in Ethiopia deteriorated, tens of thousands of Jews set out to cross the border into neighboring Sudan. In 1979, Israel (and to a lesser degree private organizations) began to evacuate the Ethiopian Jews from Sudan to Israel by various covert means. As word reached the Jewish villages in Ethiopia that the route to Israel was through Sudan, the flow of refugees across the border increased dramatically. The Mossad, through it Tsafririm Unit, was tasked with handling the rescue of the Ethiopian Jews. During winter 1984, it became clear that the refugee camps in Sudan were filling up so quickly that the mode of rescue had to be revamped.[15]

Israeli officials approached the United States for assistance, but the request created a major dilemma because unlike Israel, which was technically at war with Sudan, the United States enjoyed very close relations with President Gaafar al-Numeiry. Accordingly, the United States provided Sudan with large amounts of aid and subsequently exercised leverage over Numeiry. In 1984, Numeiry was in urgent need of further U.S. aid because of Sudan's failing economy, civil unrest, and the need to take care of the nearly half a million refugees, the majority of whom were non-Jews. The problem was that as a member of the Arab League, Numeiry could not afford to be seen to be helping the "Zionists." U.S. officials were well aware of Sudan's instability and were hesitant to do anything that might further endanger Numeiry's regime.

A Sudanese representative traveled to the United States in June 1984 to ask for additional economic aid. In a meeting with Richard Krieger and Eugene Banks of the State Department, Krieger decided to play on his visitor's anti-Semitic feelings; he suggested that the approval of the omnipotent Jewish lobby would be necessary to obtain congressional support for an increase in aid and suggested that Sudan could help by allowing the United States to take the Ethiopian Jews out of the refugee camps. The Sudanese official found this line of argument appealing, and moves were made to arrange a rescue operation. The Refugee Affairs Coordinator at the U.S. embassy in Khartoum, Jerry Weaver, met with Sudanese vice president and security chief Omar Tayeb and secured his agreement to a plan for evacuating the Ethiopian Jews.

According to the plan, the Mossad and the Sudanese secret police would devise the secret operation, known later as Operation Moses. It lasted from November 21, 1984, to January 5, 1985. Altogether 7,800 Ethiopian Jews were rescued in this manner. However, as news of the airlift leaked out, the Sudanese ordered a halt to the operation. As an Arab country, Sudan would not allow its image in the Arab world to be tarnished by way of assisting in enlarging the Jewish population in Israel.[16]

U.S. officials considered the resumption of Operation Moses. On March 3, 1985, Vice President George H.W. Bush met with Numeiry. The latter was reluctant to resume the operation and instead agreed to a quick, one-time secret U.S. (not Israeli) operation in which the flights would not go directly to Israel. The result was that the United States released to Sudan, within a week, US$15 million out of $200 million promised. The remainder was remitted later. To avoid any possibility of disclosure, President Ronald Reagan wanted the operation to be carried out within three or four days. The CIA Station chief in Khartoum thus took an embassy plane to reconnoiter the runway of a remote airstrip near Gedaref and found that it was fit for landings and take-offs.[17]

On March 28, 1985, Operation Sheba began, with Israeli Ethiopian Jews working for Mossad identifying the Ethiopian Jews in the camps and bringing them by truck to the airstrip, eight miles outside Gedaref. Six U.S. Hercules airplanes loaded with food and medical supplies departed to Sudan from a U.S. airbase near Frankfurt, Germany, and landed at twenty-minute intervals to pick up the remaining Ethiopian Jews. However, instead of flying to intermediate destinations, the airplanes flew directly to an Israeli air force base near Eilat, in southern Israel. The original plan of Operation Sheba was to rescue as many as 2,000 Ethiopian Jews from the camps, but they found only 494.

After Operation Sheba concluded, the Israeli government believed that all of the Ethiopian Jews had been evacuated from the refugee camps in Sudan. In fact, many were left, mainly the old and infirm. Soon after Operation Sheba came to an end, Numeiry was overthrown and found asylum in Cairo. The former Sudanese Vice-President Tayeb and other officials were imprisoned or executed for allowing the Ethiopian Jews to leave Sudan for Israel. In sum, out the approximately 76,000 people of the Ethiopian Jewish community, 16,975 were taken to Israel during the 1980s.

Operation Solomon, known in Hebrew as Mivtza Shlomo, was another attempt at the beginning of 1990 at rescuing Jews from Ethiopia. Despite the rescue operations in the 1980s, many Jews still remained in Ethiopia, with numerous families having been divided. Following the resumption of diplomatic relations between Israel and Ethiopia in early 1990, thousands of Jews flocked to the compound around the Israeli embassy in Addis Ababa awaiting their turn to be evacuated to Israel. In 1990 the Mossad embarked on a complex and politically sensitive mission, code-named Operation Solomon, to airlift thousands of Jews from Ethiopia to Israel. The Israeli government had reached an agreement with Ethiopia's ruler, Col. Mengistu Haile Mariam, to allow their departure for US$30 million. On May 24, 1991, with Ethiopian antigovernment rebels closing in on the Ethiopian capital, Operation Solomon was activated and lasted for thirty-three hours, evacuating some 14,325 Ethiopian Jews. The Mossad, which had a key role in the operation, had been assisted on the ground in Ethiopia mainly by Wonderferer Aweke, an Ethiopian Jew.[18]

## THEFT OPERATIONS

Soon after Meir Amit's appointment as director of the Mossad on March 25, 1963, he met with many commanders in the IDF to clarify the Mossad's objectives. He asked what they thought could be the Mossad's most valuable contribution to Israeli security. Maj. Gen. Ezer Weizman, then commander of the Israel Air Force (IAF), remarked that bringing a Soviet-made MiG-21 to Israel would contribute the most to Israeli security. Israel would then have access to the secrets of the most advanced fighter planes the Arab states possessed and, according to the Russians, the most advanced strike aircraft in the world.[19]

The Soviet Union began introducing the MiG-21 into the Middle East in 1961 under heavy secrecy. By 1963 this aircraft had become the major aircraft of the air forces of Egypt, Syria, and Iraq. Few in the West knew much about the MiG-21, but all feared its capabilities. The Mossad had tried unsuccessfully twice to bring a MiG-21 to Israel, and proverbially the third attempt paid off from an unexpected source with little prompting from Israeli intelligence. An Iraqi Jew called Yusuf contacted Mossad officers with somewhat curious information that he might be able to arrange the theft of a MiG-21.

Yusuf had been born to an impoverished Jewish family in Iraq and became an indentured servant to an Iraqi Maronite Christian family at age ten. Although he never attended school and was illiterate, he, not unlike the biblical Joseph, rose to prominence in this family's household. When he was almost sixty, however, the head of the household told Yusuf during a quarrel that without the family he would have had nothing, a taunt Yusuf would not forget. He decided then and there to explore his "otherness"—his Jewish identity, something he had hardly given a thought to. In 1964 he contacted Israeli officials in Tehran (until 1979 Israel had sound relations with non-Arab Iran) and in Europe.

Through Yusuf, Israel made contact with a Maronite Christian pilot in the Iraqi air force, whose family felt the pressure of their Maronite Christian coreligionists under Muslim authoritarian rule. In a previous conversation with Yusuf, the pilot mentioned he would like to leave the country, and this was reported by Yusuf to the Israelis. An American woman, an agent for the Mossad in Baghdad, was assigned to draw out Munir Redfa, an Iraqi Christian air force pilot and a member of Yusuf's adoptive family. The two bonded well, and several salient points were mentioned by Redfa: his disagreement with the war waged by his government against the Kurdish minority in northern Iraq, the fact that although he was a squadron commander he was stationed far from his home in Baghdad, and that because of to his Christian beliefs he was only allowed to fly with small fuel tanks. Furthermore, he commented on his admiration for the Israelis: the few against so many Muslims.

The female agent developed the relationship and suggested they take a holiday together in Europe in July 1966. After a few days of vacation, she suggested to Redfa that he fly with her to Israel, adding that she had friends there who might assist him. Despite initial disquiet from Redfa, the couple arrived in Israel and Redfa was given VIP treatment. After assessing the matter, Redfa was offered Israeli citizenship and US$1 million, an offer he accepted on condition that the Mossad arrange for the escape of his entire family from Iraq as well: his wife, his children, and his parents, along with the rest of his extended family.

The new commander of the IAF from April 1966, Maj. Gen. Mordechai Hod, met Redfa to plan the dangerous MiG flight together. All that remained for Redfa was to fix the date for his flight, which he set for August 16, 1966.

Soon members of Redfa's family began leaving Iraq for a variety of reasons. On that day in August, Redfa went about his business in Iraq as usual, and requested that the ground crew fill his tanks to capacity, an order the Russian advisors generally had to countersign. But the Iraqis disliked the Russian advisors, who seemed to hold them in contempt. This worked to Redfa's benefit, and he took off on his dangerous mission, knowing his fellow pilots would be ordered to shoot him down once Iraqi ground control realized he had diverted from his flight plan. Iraqi ground crew radar picked up a blip on the screen heading west, and they frantically radioed Redfa to turn around, warning he would be shot down. Hundreds of miles away Israeli radar picked up the blip on their screen, and sent a squad of IAF Mirages to escort him, while Redfa went through his prearranged signals, eventually meeting up with the Israeli fighter pilots who escorted him to a base deep in the Negev Desert, in the south of Israel.

On the same day, Mossad agents in Iraq picked up all the remaining members of the pilot's family, who had left Baghdad ostensibly for a picnic, and smuggled them out of the country. Newspapers all over the world carried the sensational story of an Iraqi pilot who had defected with his MiG-21 to Israel. It was no surprise when, during the Six-Day War in June 1967, the IAF demonstrated its superiority over the MiG-21 aircraft of the Arab air forces.

Operation Noah's Ark was the second "theft" covert operation, which involved the "stealing" of five missile boats Israel had ordered and paid for from the French shipyard at Cherbourg at the end of 1969. In 1962, Israel placed an order for missile boats with West German shipyards, as part of the reparations agreement between the two countries. Chancellor Adenauer agreed that the shipyards would build twelve missile boats for the Israeli navy on condition that the transaction be kept secret so as not to incur the wrath of the Arab world. By the end of 1964, three of the twelve missile boats had been built and delivered. However, certain members of the West German government leaked news of the deal to the *New York Times*, with the result that the missile boats would still be financed by the reparations scheme but would be built outside West Germany. The contract for building the remaining boats was given to the Cherbourg shipyards in Normandy on the northern coast of France. In April 1967, the first of the nine boats was delivered to the Israeli navy, and a month later Israel received the second vessel, accumulatively the fifth boat in the purchasing contract.[20]

During the crisis on the eve of the 1967 Six-Day War, on June 2 French President Charles de Gaulle declared that France would no longer supply offensive weapons to the Middle East, which in real terms meant that Israel was to suffer a disadvantage, as the Arab world was being supplied by the Soviet Union. However, since the building of the missile boats in the Cherbourg shipyards was considered a contract in progress, two more boats were delivered to the Israeli navy in the fall of 1967.

Following a Palestinian terror attack on an Israeli aircraft at Athens airport on December 26, 1967, and the Israeli retaliation against Beirut airport two days later with the blowing up of thirteen Lebanese airplanes on the ground, de Gaulle declared that the French arms embargo would now be absolute, including the Cherbourg boats, despite the fact that they had been paid for.

On January 4, 1969, a week after de Gaulle's announcement, small teams of Israeli naval officers and sailors made their way to France and boarded three more missile boats that were almost complete. They spent three hours completing the vessels for sail, after which they hoisted the Israeli ensign and set off. They moved into the English Channel and never returned.

But Israel still desired the remaining boats and, in November of 1969, the clandestine Operation Noah's Ark was implemented. The Israeli Maritime Fruit Company registered the fictitious Starboat Line. A few days later, the Israeli navy informed Cherbourg shipyard management that the Israeli government had decided to seek compensation from the French government for breaching the agreement to deliver the boats to Israel; Israel would concede the boats. Renowned Norwegian shipping expert Ole Martin Siem was invited to join Starboat's board of directors for the specific purpose of purchasing the missile boats. On November 11, 1969, the France-based Israeli coordinator of the naval purchase, Israeli navy reserve Rear Adm. Mordechai Limon, received an acceptable compensation offer from the Cherbourg officials, whereupon Limon gave the go-ahead to Siem for the fictitious purchase of the missile boats.

Shortly thereafter, Siem met the French government's arms vendor, Gen. Louis Bone, and told him that he had heard that several missile boats were for sale and they might be converted to drill for oil. The French general agreed to the sale. One hundred twenty Israeli seamen entered France in pairs as the next stage of the operation and surreptitiously prepared the vessels. On Christmas Eve 1969, despite the unstable weather conditions, final checks were carried out with the boats, which departed France on Christmas Day for Israel.

On December 26, the French authorities realized what had just happened. Although the Israeli government did not admit responsibility for the affair, Limon, who had lived in France for seven years, was declared persona non grata by the French authorities and ordered to leave. Two French generals were dismissed for their part in approving the sale of the missile boats to the fictitious Starboat Line. Seven days after leaving Cherbourg, the missile boats were anchored in Israel.[21]

## OPERATIONS ISORAD AND PLUMBAT

For the purpose of secretly obtaining uranium for the Israeli nuclear reactor in Dimona in the 1960s, Israel used the services of the American company Nuclear Material and Equipment Corporation (NUMEC), a Pennsylvania-based manufacturer of nuclear fuels and specialty metals. For this purpose a dummy company, Isotopes and Radiation Enterprises (ISORAD), was formed in the United States.

During Operation Isorad, Dr. Zalman Shapiro, president of NUMEC, succeeded in diverting large quantities of weapons-grade uranium to Israel. In those years the unaccounted-for uranium missing from NUMEC's plant sparked the curiosity of the American federal authorities, and NUMEC paid almost US$930,000 in fines.[22]

Operation Plumbat, also known as the Uranium Ship Operation, was another covert operation related to stealing uranium. This was a joint operation of LAKAM and the Mossad, in support of the Israeli nuclear weapons effort. A West German chemical corporation named Asmara had bought uranium through subsidiaries from a Belgian company, Société Générale de Mianro. The uranium was loaded in Antwerp onto the vessel *Scheersberg A*. According to the manifest, the ship and its cargo was bound for Genoa. Entering the Mediterranean, the ship sailed east instead of south according to its declared destination, and somewhere between Cyprus and Turkey it rendezvoused with an Israeli freighter chartered by the Mossad. The cargo of some 200 tons of yellow cake uranium in 560 oil drums labeled "Plumbat" (lead) was smuggled onto the Israeli freighter.[23]

The *Scheersberg A* then simply disappeared for a couple of days, showing up later at Iskenderun (a port in Turkey) where the cargo was discovered to be missing. The West German government may well have been directly involved, but if so, this fact remained under wraps to avoid antagonizing the Soviets or the Arabs.[24]

## THE IRANGATE AFFAIR

Israel, along with the United States, suffered a grave loss with the fall of the shah of Iran at the end of 1979. The Israeli leaders assumed that consistent geopolitical interests would eventually triumph over religious ideology and produce an accommodation between Israel and Iran. The onset of the Iran-Iraq war in 1980 gave Israeli leaders the incentive to keep their door open to the Islamic rulers in Iran. The director general of Israel's Foreign Ministry, David Kimche, recommended selling arms to relatively moderate Iranians in positions of power, such as Ayatollah Ali Akbar Hashemi Rafsanjani. His comments were echoed by Uri Lubrani, Israel's chief representative in Iran under the Iranian leader, Shah Pahlavi. The Israeli Defense Minister, Reserve Gen. Ariel Sharon, also supported the idea and believed that Israel's vital interest was a continuation of the war in the Persian Gulf, with an eventual Iranian victory.[25]

The head of the Jaffee Center for Strategic Studies at that time, Aharon Yariv, a retired major general and former director of MI, stated at a scholarly conference at Tel Aviv University in late 1986 that it would be to Israel's advantage if the Iran-Iraq war ended in a stalemate, but it would be even more advantageous for Israel if the war continued. The salient understanding was that once the war ended, Iraq may open up an "eastern front" against Israel.

The first renewed Israeli arms sales to Iran in 1980 included spare parts for U.S.-made F-4 Phantom jets; a later deal that year included parts for U.S.-made tanks, and Israeli officials only informed Washington after the fact, because they believed that the United States would not grant upfront approval of such transactions. The administration of Jimmy Carter was outraged that its embargo had been blatantly violated by the Israelis, especially in light of the hostage crisis with which the United States was being confronted by the Iranians. This had erupted in November 1979 in the early days of the revolution, when Iranian radicals seized the U.S. embassy in Tehran and took sixty-six American diplomats hostage. Thereafter, and until the diplomats were released in January 1981, U.S. Secretary of State Edmund Muskie demanded that Israel cease its shipments.

Israeli Prime Minister Begin promised to comply with the U.S. demands, but in fact Israel continued to sell arms to Iran without U.S. approval. On July 24, 1981, Ya'acov Nimrodi, an Israeli businessman and longtime associate of Ariel Sharon, signed a deal with Iran's Ministry of National Defense to supply arms worth US$135,842,000, including Lance missiles, Copperhead shells, and Hawk missiles. A sale of such a magnitude must have had Israeli government acqui-escence. President Reagan's administration took office in 1981 and, toward the end of that year, Kimche approached U.S. Secretary of State Alexander Haig and National Security Adviser Robert McFarlane to discuss proposed Israeli ship-ments of U.S.-made spare parts worth $10–15 million to a relatively moderate faction in Iran. Haig disapproved the request. In November 1981, Ariel Sharon visited the United States and requested approval from his counterpart, Caspar Weinberger, to sell arms to Iran. Weinberger deferred the decision to Haig, who rejected the request outright. In May 1982 a clandestine gathering took place between Al Schwimmer (an American Jewish billionaire who had founded the Israeli aircraft industry), Nimrodi, Kimche, and Sharon and his wife, Lily, to-gether with Sudanese President Gaafar Numeiry, at a Kenyan safari resort owned

**Table 3-1. Categorization of Covert Operations: Commonly Used Names of the Various Operations That Have Been Used for Practical Purposes**

| PLANNED TO BE TOTALLY COVERT | COVERT FOR TACTICAL REASONS | COVERT YET BEARING ISRAELI FINGERPRINTS |
|---|---|---|
| The Bad Business* | Entebbe† | Abu Jihad† |
| Khaled Mashal fiasco* | Moses† | The Engineer* |
| Wrath of God* | Solomon† | Damocles* |
| Irangate* | Sheba† | ISORAD* |
| | MiG-21* | Plumbat* |
| | Spring of Youth* | |
| | Blanket* | |
| | Cherbourg Missile Boats† | |
| | Noah's Ark† | |

*Nonmilitary.

†Paramilitary. For the purpose of this chapter, *paramilitary* means *auxiliary* military, that is, something not quite military performing military duties. There are political connotations to the term *paramilitary* that often override the original meaning, hence there are contradicting understandings of the term. Those political connotations, however, are localized and at times may again be contradictory. There are paramilitary units that carry out paramilitary activity that are an officially legislated arm of the government. Paramilitary actions carried out by such groups can serve many different functions.

by Saudi business tycoon Adnan Khashoggi. At the meeting, Israel won Numeiry's agreement to allow Ethiopian Jews safe passage through Sudan to migrate to the Jewish state, and in return Numeiry requested Israel's assistance in evacuating him from his country should his regime be toppled

Under U.S. pressure, Israel halted arms sales for a short period, but private Israeli citizens, including Nimrodi, continued making plans to resume trade ties with Iran. In 1985 Nimrodi succeeded in obtaining approval for his plans from Israel's national unity government headed by Shimon Peres. Nimrodi and his partner Schwimmer, a close friend of Peres, were authorized to provide Iran with Lau antitank missiles and antiaircraft Hawk missiles from Israel's stockpiles. These deals were part of what was later known as Irangate—half of the Iran-*contra* affair revealed in 1986.

In the mid-1980s, Schwimmer played a key role in persuading the U.S. administration itself to sell arms to Iran. Through a secret agreement between the United States and the Israeli Defense Ministry in 1985, the arms went to Iran via Nimrodi, with the United States replenishing the supplies Israel transferred to the Iranians. One aspect of the deal was that Iran was to exert pressure on its protégé, the Hezbollah organization in Lebanon, to release U.S. and Western hostages kidnapped after 1982. The Reagan administration was fully aware of attempts at freeing the hostages by means of unsanctioned arms sales to Iran.

News of Irangate, or as it was more commonly known, the Iran-*contra* affair, first began appearing in the media toward the end of 1986. It revealed how deeply the United States was involved in arms sales to Iran, breaching its own laws. One law prohibited the sale of U.S. weapons for resale to a third country listed as a terrorist nation, and this occurred precisely at a time when the Washington was publicly calling for a worldwide ban on selling arms to Iran. Moreover, the monies paid by Iran for the U.S. arms were redirected by senior officials in the Reagan administration to buy arms for the *contra* rebels in Nicaragua. This went against the Boland Amendment of December 8, 1982, which specifically prohibited military assistance to the *contras*. One of the administration officials involved in the scandal was Lt. Col. Oliver L. North, military aide to the National Security Council, who reported in the White House to Robert McFarlane and later to his successor, Vice Adm. John M. Poindexter. The entire scheme was conducted without Congress's knowledge, again contravening a law requiring sales above US$14 million to be reported to Congress.[26]

## CONCLUSION

Although not all of the Israeli covert actions and clandestine collection operations discussed here were carried out in a clandestine manner, of those in the public domain, the most widely known were operationally executed under varying levels of secrecy. In reviewing several of the literally hundreds of diverse covert missions carried out by the different branches of the Israeli intelligence community, it becomes clear that in defense of the homeland, the style and type of operation selected is only limited by the imagination of those involved.

## NOTES

1. Aviezer Golan, *Operation Susannah* (New York: Harper & Row, 1978).
2. Ephraim. Kahana, *Historical Dictionary of Israeli Intelligence* (Lanham, MD: Scarecrow Press, 2006).
3. "The Bungle in Jordan: Mossad Trips Up during an Attempted Hit on a Hamas Leader," *Time*, October 13, 1997.
4. Kahana, *Historical Dictionary of Israeli Intelligence*.
5. Alexander B. Calahan, "Countering Terrorism: The Israeli Response to the 1972 Munich Olympic Massacre and the Development of Independent Covert Action Teams," master's thesis, Marine Corps Command and Staff College, 1995.
6. George Jonas, *Vengeance: The True Story of an Israeli Counter-Terrorist Team* (London: Simon & Schuster, 1984).
7. Kahana, *Historical Dictionary of Israeli Intelligence*.
8. Ibid.
9. Ian Black and Benny Morris, *Israel's Secret Wars: A History of Israel's Intelligence Services* (New York: Grove Press, 1991).
10. Kahana, *Historical Dictionary of Israeli Intelligence*.

11. Yeshayahu Ben-Porat, Eitan Haber, and Zeev Schiff, *Entebbe Rescue*. Transl. Louis Williams (New York: Delacorte, 1977).

12. Kahana, *Historical Dictionary of Israeli Intelligence.*

13. Ibid.

14. Ibid.

15. Claire Safran, *Secret Exodus: The Story of Operation Moses* (New York: Prentice Hall, 1987).

16. Kahana, *Historical Dictionary of Israeli Intelligence.*

17. Ibid.

18. Melissa Crow, *Operation Solomon: A Case Study on the Role of Power Politics in International Negotiation*. Working Paper Series 92-10. Cambridge, MA: Harvard Law School, Program on Negotiation, 1992.

19. Kahana, *Historical Dictionary of Israeli Intelligence.*

20. Ibid.

21. Abraham Rabinovich, *The Boats of Cherbourg: The Secret Israeli Operation That Revolutionized Naval Warfare* (New York: Seaver Books, 1990).

22. Kahana, *Historical Dictionary of Israeli Intelligence.*

23. Elaine Davenport, *The Plumbat Affair* (Philadelphia: J. B. Lippincott, 1978).

24. Kahana, *Historical Dictionary of Israeli Intelligence.*

25. Fred Halliday, *Beyond Irangate: The Reagan doctrine and the Third World* (Amsterdam: Transnational Institute, 1987).

26. Kahana, *Historical Dictionary of Israeli Intelligence.*

# 4

# "SUCH OTHER FUNCTIONS AND DUTIES"

## Covert Action and American Intelligence Policy

JAMES M. SCOTT AND JEREL A. ROSATI

ALTHOUGH THE U.S. GOVERNMENT HAS EMPLOYED COVERT operations since the time of the American Revolution, World War II marks the point at which such activities became a major element of U.S. security policy. Building on the activities of the Office of Strategic Services (OSS) in World War II, U.S. policy makers first established the Central Intelligence Group in January 1946 (by executive order), and then, about eighteen months later, the Central Intelligence Agency (CIA), through the National Security Act. Among other things, the 1947 National Security Act charged the CIA with a variety of intelligence gathering and analysis functions, as well as "such other functions and duties related to intelligence affecting the national security as the National Security Council may from time to time direct." This ambiguous language was the only indication in this seminal legislation that the CIA would be engaged in covert action. Over time, of course, covert action became a signature activity of the agency and perhaps the most controversial as well. In fact, it was only days after the passage of the 1947 act that the Truman administration authorized a series of propaganda activities in Europe.[1] From this relatively modest start, covert action and the CIA's role in it grew considerably.

This chapter reviews the use of covert action in U.S. foreign policy since World War II, focusing on the methods that have been employed over time. After a discussion of the definition of covert action, it surveys covert actions through several periods from the end of World War II until the present. Following this brief overview, the chapter then discusses the range and methods of covert action and concludes by reflecting on key dilemmas associated with the use of covert action as a foreign policy instrument.

## COVERT ACTION

Covert action has often been characterized as the "middle option," "third way," or "quiet approach" to be used when doing nothing and using force are both unacceptable. Accordingly, as other observers have noted, it has more to do with a method than with any particular actions. Indeed, according to Berkowitz and Goodman, almost every activity that has been typically considered a covert action has also been conducted overtly.[2] Hence, what constitutes covert action is somewhat elusive.

As already noted, the 1947 National Security Act mentioned only "such other functions and duties." In mid-1948, George Kennan authored a policy document—NSC 10/2—that characterized covert action as those activities "so planned and conducted that any U.S. government responsibility for them is not evident to unauthorized persons and that if uncovered the U.S. government can plausibly disclaim any responsibility for them."[3] In 1978, President Jimmy Carter issued an executive order that defined covert action as

> operations conducted abroad in support of national foreign policy objectives which are designed to further official United States programs and policies abroad and which are planned and executed so that the role of the United States Government is not apparent or acknowledged publicly, and functions in support of such activities, but not including diplomatic activity or the collection and production of intelligence or related support functions.[4]

Just a few years later, Ronald Reagan's Executive Order 12333 essentially restated this definition, adding that covert actions "are not intended to influence United States political processes, public opinion, polices, or the media and do not include diplomatic activities or the collection or production of intelligence and related support functions."[5] The essence of these definitions was captured in the 1991 Intelligence Authorization Act, which defined covert action as "activities of the United States Government to influence political, economic, or military conditions abroad, where it is intended that the role of the United States Government will not be apparent or acknowledged publicly."[6]

The National Clandestine Service (NCS), the modern-day name for what has been known as the Office of Policy Coordination, the Directorate of Plans, and then the Directorate of Operations, is primarily responsible for U.S. covert operations. The NCS actually involves three types of activities: espionage, counterintelligence, and covert action. Espionage involves human intelligence, such as running spies and double agents abroad to access information, and counterintelligence emphasizes preventing foreign intelligence agencies from penetrating the CIA. Covert actions, by contrast, are influence operations.[7]

A core element of covert action is obviously that the U.S. government conceals its responsibility. As Berkowitz and Goodman have noted, there are two main justifications for such subterfuge: "one is when open knowledge of U.S.

responsibility would make an operation infeasible . . . the other valid reason . . . is to avoid retaliation or to control the potential for escalation."[8] In either case, covert action is fundamentally a foreign policy option, not an intelligence activity.[9] As Loch K. Johnson has noted, "whatever the variation in terminology, the objective of covert action remains constant: to influence events overseas secretly and in support of U.S. foreign policy."[10] As the following historical overview suggests, the use of covert action as a foreign policy instrument has been closely tied to the overarching foreign policy ethos of the time.

## COVERT ACTION SINCE WORLD WAR II: AN OVERVIEW

From its creation until the collapse of the Soviet Union, the CIA and its covert operations have evolved through four stages: (1) the "good old days," 1947 through the early 1970s; (2) the "fall" and reform, early 1970s to 1979; (3) the resurgence, during the 1980s; and (4) the adjustment, in the post–Cold War and post–September 11, 2001, periods.[11]

### The Good Old Days, 1946–73

In terms of budget, personnel, and missions, the CIA grew quickly in the late 1940s and 1950s. All the agency's bureaucratic directorates and functions expanded, but none more so than the operations directorate. Initially, extensive covert operations were probably not envisioned; many observers, including Clark Clifford, George Kennan, Sidney Souers, and President Harry Truman, commented later that the CIA's covert action mission grew well beyond what was imagined at its inception.[12] The CIA was created to provide the president with an intelligence capability to engage in data collection and analysis as well as coordinate the larger intelligence community existing at the time. However, as suggested, one clause of the CIA charter allowed it to "perform such other functions and duties," which provided the later legal justification for involving the CIA in cloak-and-dagger operations.[13] Over time, the CIA soon became the major governmental organization responsible for covert actions abroad in support of the policy of containment.

The rise of the Cold War was the essential factor prompting the growth of the covert action mission. Estimates are that the vast majority of the CIA's budget and personnel throughout the Cold War were devoted to operations. According to Johnson, for example, by the mid-1960s, more than 60 percent of the CIA's budget was dedicated to covert action.[14] The president used the CIA to perform various covert activities that no other agency performed and that were officially denied in public. In fact, the CIA was allowed considerable independence in running its covert operations under presidential supervision.

Although extensive operations were initiated in Europe in the years after World War II, including information campaigns, the provision of political support to preferred parties and individuals, subversion, and other activities, the heyday of covert operations occurred under Director Allen Dulles from 1952 to 1961, a time when his brother, John Foster Dulles, also served as secretary of State.[15] Even though the president often remained distant from the details of an operation, the director responded to presidential initiative and choice. Also, no real oversight existed outside the executive branch, as Congress generally preferred to remain on the sidelines in deference to presidential leadership and the Cold War consensus.[16]

Prevailing Cold War attitudes help explain the vital role that covert action came to play in U.S. foreign policy. American leaders saw a world divided between the forces of good and evil—the free world represented by the United States against the totalitarian, communist bloc represented by the Soviet Union. The Soviet Union was also seen as aggressive, expanding its territorial control and directly threatening American interests and the status quo. Consequently, American policy makers were preoccupied with rearming and creating alliances to deter Soviet expansionism and, if deterrence failed, to fighting a "hot" war. At the same time, American policy makers increasingly came to rely on covert operations to fight the "Cold" War. Such measures were justified in terms of an anticommunist philosophy and a strategy of power politics, in which the ends justifies the means. A secret report authored by Gen. James Doolittle for the 1954 Hoover Commission captured the perspective nicely:

> It is now clear that we are facing an implacable enemy whose avowed objective is world domination by whatever means at whatever cost. There are no rules in such a game. Hitherto acceptable norms of human conduct do not apply. If the U.S. is to survive...We must learn to subvert, sabotage and destroy our enemies by more clever, more sophisticated and more effective methods than those used against us. It may become necessary that the American people will be made acquainted with, understand and support this fundamentally repugnant philosophy.[17]

Driven by this perspective, the CIA became an important tool of U.S. foreign policy immediately after its creation in 1947. The examples discussed next highlight just a few of the important covert activities abroad, which include: (1) manipulating foreign democratic elections; (2) organizing partisan resistance movements; (3) overthrowing foreign governments; (4) participating in foreign assassinations; (5) supporting friendly, often authoritarian governments; and (6) training foreign military, intelligence, and police personnel.

It has been reported that by 1953 the CIA had major covert operations in progress in forty-eight countries.[18] A U.S. Senate select committee investigating foreign and military intelligence in 1975 found that the CIA had "conducted some 900 major or sensitive covert action projects plus several thousand smaller projects since 1961."[19] In other words, the CIA, in its heyday, was engaged in covert operations all over the world, with as much as one-third of its interventions taking place in "pro-Western" democracies.[20] Table 4-1 highlights some of the major covert operations during the "good old days" that have come to light, although much CIA covert activity remains unknown.

In the years after World War II, one frequently employed type of covert activity of the CIA involved influencing foreign elections. In both Italy and France in 1948, for example, the United States worried that the economic and political instability after the war, which strengthened legal communist parties in those countries, would eventually result in communist electoral victories. Consequently, the CIA engaged in a variety of efforts to undermine the communists and strengthen the centrist parties. In Italy, for example, the agency funded and supported the Christian Democratic Party and distributed propaganda and disinformation through a network of Italian media assets (paid agents) employed throughout the print and electronic media to discredit the Communist Party. The Christian Democrats won the election, although the extent of CIA influence remains unclear.

In the late 1940s and 1950s, the CIA also supported partisan resistance movements in communist countries to promote internal instability and domestic uprisings. For example, the agency trained émigrés and secretly transported them into Albania, Poland, Yugoslavia, the Baltic states, Soviet Georgia, and the Ukraine. These partisan resistance efforts made very little headway; in fact, in most cases they were speedy failures. For example, the fairly extensive effort in Albania persisted for a number of years until it became clear that the communist regime had infiltrated the resistance and virtually all the agents had been apprehended almost immediately.

Under President Eisenhower, the CIA became involved in a series of efforts to overthrow foreign governments. For example, with help from the British MI6 (their CIA equivalent), the CIA staged the Iranian coup of 1953 to overthrow the nationalist leader Mohammed Mossadeq and restore the Pahlavi dynasty, headed by the shah. Mossadeq had proclaimed an independent and neutralist state in the growing Cold War and demanded that Great Britain renegotiate its most favorable contract for Iranian oil, and U.S. policy makers feared he was playing into the hands of the communists and the Soviet Union. Once restored, the shah subsequently awarded Gulf, Standard of New Jersey, Texaco, and Socony-Mobil a 40 percent share of Iranian oil rights.[21]

A year later, the CIA staged the 1954 coup in Guatemala, which became the model for many of the agency's subsequent actions. With a history of dictatorial rule, in 1950 Guatemala experienced its first taste of democracy when Jacobo Arbenz Guzmán was elected president. However, when Arbenz promoted agrarian reform and expropriated 234,000 acres of uncultivated land owned by the United Fruit Company, an American company that owned over 40 percent of Guatemalan territory, U.S. policy makers, including President Eisenhower and Secretary of State Dulles, concluded that the Arbenz regime was "playing the communist card" and posed a threat to American national security. The CIA thus

**Table 4-1. Major CIA Covert Operations During the "Good Old Days"**

| | |
|---|---|
| 1947–48 | Propaganda campaign during the 1948 Italian national elections |
| 1947–48 | Propaganda campaign during the 1948 French national elections |
| 1948–52 | Partisan resistance movements in Eastern Europe and Soviet Union |
| 1949 | Anglo-American effort to overthrow the Albanian government |
| 1950–70s | Propaganda campaigns through Radio Liberty and Radio Free Europe |
| 1952–60 | Kuomintang Chinese partisan resistance movement on Sino-Burmese border |
| 1953 | Anglo-American overthrow of Prime Minister Mohammed Mossadegh of Iran |
| 1953–54 | Campaign to support Ramon Magsaysay's presidential candidacy and counter Huk insurgency in the Philippines |
| 1954 | Overthrow of President Jacobo Arbenz of Guatemala |
| 1950s–70s | Subsidization of domestic and foreign groups and publications |
| 1953–70s | Drug testing and mind-control program |
| 1954–70s | Effort to overthrow leader Ho Chi Minh and the North Vietnamese government |
| 1955 | Effort to destabilize President José Figueres's government of Costa Rica |
| 1958 | Support of Tibetan partisan resistance movement in China |
| 1958–65 | Effort to destabilize President Sukarno of Indonesia |
| 1960 | Alleged effort to assassinate Gen. Abdul Kassem, leader of Iraq |
| 1960 | Alleged effort to assassinate President Abdul Nasser of Egypt |
| 1960 | Alleged effort to assassinate political leader Patrice Lumumba of Congo |
| 1961 | Effort to overthrow Fidel Castro, leader of Cuba |
| 1961 | Effort to assassinate Rafael Trujillo, leader of Dominican Republic |
| 1961 | Effort to destabilize President Kwame Nkrumah of Ghana |
| 1960s | Effort to assassinate Fidel Castro of Cuba |
| 1960s | Fought secret war in Laos |
| 1962–63 | Destabilized the Ecuadorean governments of Ibarra and Arosemena |
| 1963 | Destabilized Prime Minister Cheddi Jagan's government of British Guiana |
| 1963 | Supported overthrow of President Ngo Dinh Diem of South Vietnam |
| 1960s | Conducted pacification and Phoenix programs in Vietnam |
| 1964 | Campaign in support of President Eduardo Frei in 1964 Chilean elections |
| 1964 | Supported military coup against President Joao Goulart of Brazil |
| 1967 | Supported military coup in Greece |
| 1967–70s | Domestic campaign against antiwar movement and political dissent |
| 1970–73 | Destabilized Chilean government of President Salvador Allende |

*Sources*: Rhodri Jeffreys-Jones, *The CIA and American Democracy* (New Haven, CT: Yale University Press, 1989); Jonathan Kwitny, *Endless Enemies* (New York: Penguin, 1984); Thomas Powers, *The Man Who Kept the Secrets* (New York: Pocket Books, 1979); John Prados, *Presidents' Secret Wars* (New York: William Morrow, 1986); John Ranelagh, *The Agency* (New York: Simon & Schuster, 1986); David Wise and Thomas B. Ross, *The Invisible Government* (New York: Vintage, 1974); U.S. Congress, Senate, *Alleged Assassination Plots Involving Foreign Leaders*, Congressional Report, 94th Congress, 1st sess. (November 18, 1975); and U.S. Congress, Senate, *Final Report of the Select Committee to Study Governmental Operations with Respect to Intelligence Activities*, Books 1–6, Congressional Report, 94th Congress, 2nd sess. (April 14, 1976).

trained several hundred Guatemalans on a United Fruit plantation in neighboring Honduras and, when it sent the unit into Guatemala, waged an extensive information and psychological warfare campaign to make the force appear larger. The CIA also piloted several small planes in a bombing run over Guatemala City and other key towns. Arbenz lost his nerve and fled the country, and Castillo Armas became the new military dictator.[22]

In the 1950s and 1960s, the CIA also began to be involved in efforts to assassinate foreign leaders, although it appears that the agency was never actually successful in such attempts. For example, during the 1960 independence crisis in the Congo, it is alleged that the CIA attempted to assassinate the first prime minister and nationalist African leader, Patrice Lumumba, who was perceived as being too independent of American interests and open to communist subversion. The CIA was apparently unsuccessful, but Lumumba was assassinated eventually, clearing away for the U.S.–backed dictator, Mobutu Sese Seko, who ruled a corrupt regime for thirty years and impoverished the country.[23] In the 1960s, the CIA made numerous attempts to arrange the assassination of Cuban leader Fidel Castro, none of which came to fruition (see following for more discussion of the anti-Castro campaign).

The CIA also supported foreign governments allied to the United States in such places as Iran, Nicaragua, Cuba, and elsewhere, often participating in an allied government's violent repression of its own people. As George Kennan, in a report to Secretary of State Dean Acheson, stated as early as 1950: "We cannot be too dogmatic about the methods by which local communists can be dealt with. . . . Where the concepts and the traditions of popular government are too weak to absorb successfully the intensity of communist attack, then we must concede that harsh governmental measures of repression may be the only answer."[24]

For example, in Indonesia, after actively destabilizing President Sukarno, a prominent leader of the Third World nonaligned movement beginning in 1958, the CIA actively supported his successor after Sukarno's ouster. The CIA then assisted the new government of General Suharto in eliminating Indonesian Communist Party members and repressing all internal dissent, which included providing the Indonesian army with lists of people to be arrested and killed. Estimates of the number of Indonesians killed in the ruthless campaign range from 300,000 to as many as 1 million, with hundreds of thousands jailed without trial. In South Africa, the CIA supported the white apartheid regime, even providing the regime with a tip from a deep cover CIA agent which led to the August 5, 1962, arrest of Nelson Mandela, the underground leader of the African National Congress, the major force opposing the Afrikaner government and the system of apartheid.[25] Mandela remained imprisoned by the South African government until February 1990; after the transition to black majority rule, he became the first president of South Africa.

The CIA also frequently offered retainers to foreign leaders, putting them on the CIA payroll, and the agency frequently engaged in training of foreign intelligence personnel, including those engaged in covert operations. The armed forces and the national police of many governments allied with the United States also were trained by U.S. military and government personnel. Thus, the U.S. government was heavily engaged in providing overt and covert support with billions of dollars of foreign assistance to friendly governments to ensure their security as part of America's larger campaign to fight the Cold War.

In the late 1950s and 1960s, the CIA relied on a variety of covert operations to be rid of Castro in Cuba. The initial operation was modeled on the 1954 Guatemalan operation. Hundreds of exiled Cubans were recruited and trained by the CIA in Honduras as an invasion force. In 1961, President John Kennedy supported the Bay of Pigs invasion, and the Cubans invaded with limited air cover provided by the CIA. Unlike the Guatemalan operation, however, the Bay of Pigs invasion was a complete failure. The actual invasion strategy was flawed to begin with, and Castro did not flee but used the Cuban military to destroy and capture the invading force. The Bay of Pigs fiasco was the first major CIA covert operation that became public, embarrassing the U.S. government and President Kennedy.[26]

From that point on, President Kennedy and his brother, Attorney General Robert Kennedy, mounted a vendetta against Castro, authorizing the CIA to use all means available to destabilize and assassinate him. The CIA went so far as to turn to the Mafia for assistance, for the Mafia maintained connections in Cuba forged in the days when they ran gambling casinos, before Castro took power. Yet the covert plans to assassinate Castro failed. Most were harebrained schemes that only James Bond could have pulled off, such as attempts to slip Castro the hallucinogen LSD via a cigar, give him a pen with a poison tip, explode clamshells while he dove in the Caribbean, and sprinkle his shoes with an agent to make his beard fall out and with it, according to the psychological warfare experts, his Latin machismo.[27]

Failures did not deter the CIA's involvement in covert operations, nor the president from relying on such operations as a major instrument of U.S. foreign policy. Thus the Americanization of the war in Vietnam not only led to a major overt military effort to keep South Vietnam independent of North Vietnamese communism but included major covert efforts in Vietnam, as well. The U.S. government, with the use of the CIA, supported President Ngo Dinh Diem beginning in 1954. When Diem became less effective and lost credibility as an independent leader of South Vietnam, the U.S. government backed a military coup against him in 1963. The CIA was very active in Vietnam. It trained members of the Meo and Hmong tribes to conduct military operations in support of the American war effort, including a secret war in Laos. It also conducted the infamous PHOENIX program, which targeted thousands of suspected Viet Cong and communist supporters for "neutralization." Not only were many innocent individuals jailed, but torture, terrorism, and assassination were also used as part of the PHOENIX operation.

The last major covert operation during the good old days occurred in the Chilean coup d'état during the Nixon administration. Although Chile had been a democracy since the early 1960s, the Nixon administration worried that the electoral process would bring to power Salvador Allende, an avowed Marxist who believed in socialist democracy. The CIA attempted to influence the elections, but Allende won anyway. The United States then began a campaign to destabilize the Allende regime, highlighted by a CIA covert program to destabilize the Chilean economy and persuade the Chilean military to stage a coup. The military coup came in 1973 and installed Augusto Pinochet as the dictator of Chile for the next sixteen years.

### Fall and Reform in the 1970s

Beginning with the Bay of Pigs fiasco through the 1960s, the CIA faced increasing scrutiny. Operations were less successful than in the 1950s and were being exposed in the media, creating embarrassment and controversy for the U.S. government and American people at home and abroad. The failure of Vietnam politicized segments of American society and contributed to the collapse of the anticommunist consensus. The domestic political environment became even more critical when the revelations of Watergate uncovered abuses of presidential power. In this new political climate, charges were made that the president had become too powerful and abused his office in the name of national security. The CIA was a special focus of attention and was accused of activities that were immoral, illegal, and counterproductive to the long-term interests of the American people.

A period of intense scrutiny ensued. President Gerald Ford appointed the Rockefeller Commission in 1975 to investigate the intelligence community and recommend reforms. But while the Rockefeller Commission was operating, President Ford and Secretary of State Henry Kissinger were supervising a major CIA covert operation in Angola. This involved funding, training, and equipping two independence forces that were battling a Soviet-backed force for control of Angola following the end of Portuguese colonialism. Ford and Kissinger tried to keep the operation secret, but when word of the Angolan operation leaked, Congress voted to abort it and began its own investigation of intelligence.[28]

The House and Senate each conducted major investigations of the intelligence community and covert operations. The Pike and Church Committee investigations (named after the chairman of each chamber's Foreign Relations Committee) led to the first public knowledge of the scale of covert operations conducted by the CIA. Most Americans were, to put it mildly, shocked to discover the degree to which their government was in the business of overthrowing democracies, conducting coups d'état, and planning political assassinations. In this political climate, the intelligence community, especially the CIA and covert operations, experienced a major decline. Under President Ford and to a greater extent under President Jimmy Carter, the CIA budget, personnel, and activities were cut, especially in the directorate of operations, and greater emphasis was placed on the intelligence side of the agency and its technological capabilities. During this time, over 1,800 covert operatives were fired or forced to take early retirement, and most covert operations were cut, including major political and paramilitary programs.

Congress also asserted itself in oversight. For example, in the 1980 Intelligence Oversight Act it established new, permanent intelligence committees in both chambers and required the submission to Congress of a "presidential finding" explaining the need and nature of any covert actions. Presidential executive orders were issued that limited the kinds of covert operations the CIA could conduct, such as forbidding U.S. governmental personnel from becoming involved in political assassinations. Furthermore, the Freedom of Information Act, first passed in 1967, was strengthened to allow public access to classified information. The net impact was that the use of covert operations as a tool of U.S. foreign policy (and morale among covert operatives) reached its nadir by the end of the 1970s.[29]

### The Resurgence of Covert Action in the 1980s

Beginning in 1980, the CIA and covert operations got a new lease on life. The resurgence of the agency began during the last year of the Carter administration, amid growing concern with the threat of the Soviet Union after its invasion of Afghanistan in December 1979. President Carter approved a major covert operation to send money and arms to the Afghan resistance forces through U.S.-controlled sources and agents in Pakistan and Saudi Arabia. Support to the Afghan resistance escalated under presidents Reagan and George H. W. Bush and continued into the early 1990s.[30]

It was under the Reagan administration, however, that the CIA and the use of covert operations became a major force in U.S. foreign policy reminiscent of the early Cold War days. William J. Casey, a strident anticommunist and former member of the OSS during World War II, was selected as Director of Central Intelligence (DCI). Under Casey, the CIA rejuvenated its operations division and rehired many former covert operatives.[31] Under Casey, the CIA again became active in combating communism abroad. The agency launched over a dozen "major" covert operations (defined by the congressional intelligence committees as an operation costing more than $5 million or designed to overthrow a foreign government) in places such as Central America, Angola, Libya, Ethiopia, Mauritius, Cambodia, Afghanistan, and Iran. Among the most significant of these was the huge CIA Afghanistan operation to support insurgents—known as the *mujahedeen*—against the invading Soviet military. Through Pakistan and Saudi Arabia, the CIA provided billions in support for arms and training and played an important role in helping the insurgents force the Soviets to withdraw (although it also inadvertently helped to create the Al Qaeda network that would plague the United States a decade later).[32]

Another major and more controversial operation at the time occurred in Nicaragua and involved creating the *contra* resistance force in an attempt to destabilize and overthrow the new Nicaraguan Sandinista regime. The *contra* covert war was eventually outlawed by Congress in the early 1980s. Nevertheless, the

Reagan administration circumvented the law by pursuing the *contra* operation through the NSC staff and relying on private operatives and groups.[33] The administration attempted to destabilize the country and overthrow the government. The U.S. "rollback" policy under DCI Casey predominantly consisted of a major covert operation devised by the CIA to develop, train, equip, and support a counterrevolutionary force of Nicaraguans, known as the contras, that grew to a 10,000–15,000-strong military force. These activities also included CIA—rather than *contra*—attacks on Nicaraguan oil installations and mining of Nicaraguan harbors; the secret channeling of military equipment to the contras from the Pentagon or cooperative third countries (such as Honduras and Panama); CIA preparation of a training manual for the contras that may have advocated assassination; and efforts to pressure Costa Rica (which was officially neutral) to support the creation of a southern front for the contras (such as the CIA staging phony Sandinista raids on the Costa Rican border).

The Reagan administration took other steps to expand CIA operations. First, the administration eased many restrictions on the conduct of intelligence operations within the United States.[34] In addition, the administration also tightened the security and secrecy system that had developed throughout the intelligence community and the government. It became much more difficult for the public to gain access to information under the Freedom of Information Act. Moreover, to pursue its covert operations, the Reagan administration resisted and circumvented congressional oversight of the intelligence community. It was such actions that triggered the Iran-contra affair and caused Reagan's final two years to be dominated by investigations of this scandal, along with concerns that the CIA was out of control.

### Adjusting to the Post–Cold War and Post–9/11 Periods

The Cold War's end ushered in a set of challenges for the CIA and its covert action mission, which appeared much less central to U.S. foreign policy without the Cold War's context. According to Theodore Draper, "Of all the organizations that miss having the Soviet Union as an enemy, the CIA has undoubtedly been hit the hardest. The reason is that the CIA was specifically established in 1947 to struggle with the Soviet enemy.... But now the enemy has vanished. Its most dedicated American antagonist has been deprived of its mission.... [Now] the CIA wanders about in a wilderness of self-doubt and recrimination."[35] Recent years have not been much kinder, as the spectacular failures of September 11, 2001, and Iraq left the CIA reeling. One recent analysis concluded the CIA has "lost its place and standing in Washington," while a CIA veteran reacted to the 2004 intelligence reforms by saying, "The agency, as we know it, is gone."[36] Yet in late 2005, the CIA's central role in coordinating covert operations was confirmed with the strengthening of the National Clandestine Service, the new name for its directorate of operations. And after September 11, the agency's covert antiterror programs grew into the largest covert action program since the height of the Cold War.[37]

Prior to this recent expansion, however, as the CIA sought new missions in the post–Cold War context, its budget growth first slowed under George H. W. Bush and then began to decline under Bill Clinton. At the same time, challenges to CIA activities began. Congress attempted to enact tighter controls over covert action, but Bush vetoed the legislation in 1992. Not long after, Senator Daniel Patrick Moynihan (D-NY) sponsored legislation to eliminate the CIA entirely, ending covert action and placing the agency's intelligence analysis function in the State Department. Between 1990 and 2001, a spate of studies—some from Congress, some from special commissions, and some from policy think-tanks—all recommended reforms of the intelligence community.[38]

In the midst of this turmoil, the CIA continued some traditional covert operations, and added some new actions as well. For example, the agency applied its traditional instruments in the 1990s against Iraq and Kosovo. In Iraq, starting with a Bush (Sr.) finding that authorized efforts to destabilize the Iraqi economy in 1990 (after the Iran-Iraq War), the CIA engaged in a series of efforts to undermine Saddam Hussein, none of which was particularly effective. Under Bill Clinton, for example, the CIA supported the Iraqi National Congress, spending about $120 million seeking Hussein's assassination or overthrow. These operations collapsed when the resistance was infiltrated by Hussein's forces, although the United States committed itself to regime change in Iraq again in 1998. The initial campaign was an unmitigated disaster, however—"the greatest covert action debacle since Vietnam" in the words of two observers.[39] In Kosovo in 1999, the CIA launched a campaign against Serbia and Slobodan Milosevic that combined propaganda, destabilization, support of opposition groups, and other methods to undermine the regime.[40]

At the same time, the CIA took up a role in new areas as well, including drug trafficking, economic intelligence, and counterterrorism. On the drug war, the CIA began to cooperate with other agencies, including the FBI and the Drug Enforcement Agency, to break up drug rings. The CIA also increased its activities in the highly controversial arena of economic espionage, not only collecting information on trade practices but even attempting to steal trade secrets. Finally, with rising concerns about terrorism after the 1993 World Trade Center bombing, the CIA accelerated its counterterrorism operations as well. Osama bin Laden and theAl Qaeda network were especially important targets, and the CIA established a new counterterrorism center and a "bin Laden station" to oversee its efforts. Although some success occurred, the attacks in 1998 on U.S. embassies in Kenya and Tanzania, the 2000 bombing of the USS *Cole* in Yemen, and, of course, the September 11, 2001, attacks amply demonstrate the limits to the efforts.[41]

The attacks of 9/11 initiated a new season for the CIA and its covert operations mission. Just a few days after the attack, George W. Bush signed a presidential finding starting what has grown into the largest covert operation since the heydays of the Cold War, dwarfing even the decade-long Afghanistan operations of the 1980s. In addition to activities in advance and support of U.S. operations in Afghanistan and Iraq, the CIA began a host of interrelated programs to break up terror cells, assassinate terrorists, capture and interrogate Al Qaeda suspects, gain access to and disrupt financial networks, eavesdrop, and a variety of other activities.[42] As Bob Woodward reported, "The gloves are off. The president has given the agency the green light to do whatever is necessary. Lethal operations that were unthinkable pre-September 11 are now underway."[43] The CIA budget was again increased, rising from about $27 billion in 1998 to over $44 billion in 2005. For the first time in a decade, the CIA began to expand its operations directorate as well, and the counterterrorism center at the agency more than doubled in size, becoming the center of covert actions against terrorism.[44]

At the same time, however, the CIA came under criticism for its failures to prevent the 9/11 attacks and then, later, for its role in the prewar Iraq intelligence fiasco. A number of investigations issued scathing reports of CIA failures. Additionally, as some of the covert actions become public—especially the CIA programs for assassination, capture and interrogation, rendition, and its secret prison system—heightened scrutiny was instigated. Hence, by 2006, with major intelligence reform weakening the CIA's role, sagging morale from the failures of the previous five years, and new challenges from the Defense Department for roles in covert operations, the future of CIA activities in this arena was far from certain.[45]

## METHODS OF COVERT ACTION

In light of this brief overview, it is perhaps no surprise that when most people think of the CIA, they think of covert operations and "dirty tricks." Covert operations involve a variety of operations, where so-called dirty tricks and coercive force are most commonly practiced. According to an important NSC document from the Eisenhower administration, covert action included

> Propaganda, political action; economic warfare; escape and evasion and evacuation measures; subversion against hostile states or groups including assistance to underground movements, guerrillas and refugee liberation groups; support of indigenous and anticommunist elements in threatened countries of the free world; deception plans and operations; and all activities compatible with this directive necessary to accomplish the foregoing.[46]

Most observers lump such covert actions into four or five broad categories. According to Johnson, for example, covert action includes propaganda, political, economic, and paramilitary operations.[47]

### Propaganda

Propaganda involves the use of information to influence the climate of opinion. Much of this activity is done overtly, through government statements, published information in the media and other outlets, television and radio broadcasts, and a wide variety of other means. When such information is disseminated in a way that keeps the true sponsor secret, it becomes a covert action. By far the most common covert action, propaganda of a variety of kinds has been a staple of American covert policy since World War II.[48] The brief survey above includes a number of examples of propaganda ranging from so-called white propaganda to gray and black propaganda. White propaganda is overt, essentially truthful information disseminated through official government pronouncements, broadcasts, and other means. The activities of the U.S. Information Agency (until its dissolution in 1999), as well as Radio Liberty/Radio Free Europe are good examples. According to Godson, "Gray propaganda hides its sources from the uninitiated public, but not from sophisticated observers."[49] The information itself may range from essentially true to one-sided to false. Black propaganda occurs "when the source is false and well concealed, or when the information itself is false" or both.[50] Examples include forgery, rumor, disinformation and the like. According to Loch K. Johnson, "the CIA provides a flood of supportive but unattributed propaganda, distributed through its vase network of media 'assets' (paid agents): reporters newspaper and magazine editors, television producers—the whole range of personnel in the print and electronic media. . . . the extensive CIA propaganda capability produces a great tide of information flowing secretly from Washington into hundreds of hidden channels around the world."[51]

### Political Activity

Usually in combination with propaganda, political activity involves more direct action to affect the political situation in a given country. Typically, such actions involve secret support provided to nationals, parties, or organizations of another country. For example, when the CIA provided covert assistance to political parties in Italy or France in the 1948 elections, anti-Allende parties in Chile in the 1960s, and anti-Milosevic factions in Yugoslavia in 1999, these were instances of political activity. According to Treverton, political activity might typically involve support for media, labor unions, and political parties; influencing elections; and support for individuals or other groups.[52] Such support may range from simple financial aid to more complex campaigns of support. At times, as one long-time analyst of the CIA has described, "the Covert Action Staff at CIA headquarters has resembled nothing less than a group of political campaign consultants, producing slick materials for favored foreign candidates."[53] Not only do propaganda and political action work together, but many major paramilitary operations of the kind already discussed began as political action.[54]

### Economic Activity

A third category of covert action involves efforts to disrupt the economy of another country. Of the examples presented in the preceding summary, operations in Cuba and Chile provide good representations. In Cuba, the CIA engaged in numerous activities to undermine the economy, including an abortive plan to contaminate Cuban sugar with chemicals, the sabotage of shipments of machinery and spare parts, and raids against railroads, oil and sugar refineries, and other factories.[55] In Chile, a variety of efforts were undertaken to destabilize the economy and create unrest to undermine the Allende regime. More recently, economic activities were central to the range of covert actions designed to bring pressure to bear on Slobodan Milosevic in Yugoslavia and currently play a key role in the extensive covert actions in the war on terrorism.

### Paramilitary Operations

The most intrusive—and, paradoxically, high profile—type of covert action are extensive secret wars directed against hostile states (or other targets). According to John Prados,

> American secret wars have been carried out on almost every continent since . . . 1947. These covert operations have involved thousands of native fighters, significant numbers of American clandestine agents, and even regular United States military forces. United States involvement has run the gamut from advice to arms, from supplying full support for invasions of independent nations to secret bombing in support of clandestine military operations.[56]

The paramilitary campaigns in Guatemala, Cuba, Angola, Afghanistan, Nicaragua, and Iraq discussed earlier provide good examples and illustrate the range of activities involved in such operations, from full-scale wars to "little more than the clandestine transfer of a few weapons or of small amounts of training."[57] Also included in this category are assassinations, prohibited since the 1970s by executive order. However, in the wake of the 2001 terrorist attacks on New York and Washington, George W. Bush signed an intelligence order authorizing assassinations of terrorist leaders through such high-tech means as the use of the unmanned Predator drones equipped with Hellfire missiles.[58]

With respect to these categories, one last point bears mentioning. As the descriptions of Guatemala in the 1950s, Nicaragua in the 1980s, and the covert operations against terrorism in the early twenty-first century indicate, covert action typically involves a *campaign* of activities from these categories. At their most successful, such campaigns are carefully orchestrated and integrated into broader foreign policy plans and purposes.

### The "Ladder of Escalation" for Covert Operations

According to Loch K. Johnson, covert actions such as those summarized in the preceding pages can be arrayed along a ladder of escalation as modest intrusions, high risk, and extreme categories (see Table 4-2). Covert actions all fall above the first "threshold" on the ladder dividing "routine intelligence operations" from

**Table 4-2. Covert Action and the "Ladder of Escalation"**

| | |
|---|---|
| Extreme Options | Use of chemical-biological, other deadly agents |
| | Major secret wars |
| | Assassination plots |
| | Small scale coups d'état |
| | Major economic dislocation |
| | Environmental alterations |
| | Pinpointed retaliations against noncombatants |
| | Torture |
| | Hostage taking |
| | Major hostage rescue attempts |
| | Theft of sophisticated weapons or matériel |
| | Sophisticated arms supplies |
| High-Risk Options | Massive increases of funding in democracies |
| | Disinformation against democratic regimes |
| | Disinformation against autocracies |
| | Small-scale hostage rescue attempts |
| | Training of foreign military forces for war |
| | Limited arms supplies for offensive purposes |
| | Limited arms supplies for balancing purposes |
| | Economic disruption without loss of life |
| | Large increases of funding in democracies |
| | Truthful, contentious information in democracies |
| | Truthful, contentious information in autocracies |
| Modest Intrusions | Low-level funding of friendly groups |
| | Truthful, benign information in democracies |
| | Truthful, benign information in autocracies |

*Source*: Adapted from Loch K. Johnson, "On Drawing a Bright Line for Covert Operations," *American Journal of International Law* 86 (April 1992), p. 286.

more intrusive actions.[59] For the purposes of this chapter, the ladder of escalation provides a convenient means to organize the methods of covert activity. With each step up the ladder, the activities become more risky and more likely to trigger a response. Actions on the highest end of the ladder are also the most controversial in terms of both domestic accountability and international law. As such, they must be carefully considered and tightly integrated into foreign policy tactics, strategies, and objectives. Because the options at the high end of the ladder increase in both risk and controversy, such methods demand greater accountability

## DILEMMAS AND CONSIDERATIONS

We conclude this chapter with a few observations on the dilemmas posed by the methods of covert action, followed by a synthesis of guidelines for increasing their legitimacy and effectiveness. First, and most broadly, use of and attitudes toward covert action are strongly shaped by the foreign policy ethos of the time, which is strongly influenced by the nature of threat. When perceptions of enemy threat are high, the demands of national security tend to prevail, resulting in the rise of intelligence activities, particularly covert operations. When threat perceptions decline, democratic considerations tend to rise, and the legitimacy of intelligence functions, especially covert operations, is often questioned.[60] This helps explain the major patterns in our historical overview: (1) During the Cold War years of high threat perceptions, acceptance of and latitude for covert action was greatest; (2) after the Vietnam War, lower threat perceptions prevailed and covert actions received more scrutiny; (3) the 9/11 attacks and the war on terrorism have so far resulted in a similar pattern, with national security demands—and thus support for covert action—ascendant in the immediate postattack period, whereas concerns for the methods and legitimacy of covert action growing after 2003 when the threat environment appeared less urgent. As Godson explains,

> The acceptance of covert action in the 1940s and 1950s, based on the perception of external threat, gave way, beginning in the 1960s and continuing on into the 1980s, to a quite different ethos. That new ethos, "exceptionalism," has over the course of its development wreaked havoc on American covert action capabilities.... Exceptionalism holds that covert action should not be engaged in unless there are grave and unusual circumstances.[61]

Within this context, both policy and accountability dilemmas exist.

### Policy Dilemmas

With respect to policy dilemmas, as many observers have routinely noted, there are legal, moral, and practical dilemmas posed by the methods of covert action. Legally, covert action poses dilemmas because "many covert operations, if carried out by different persons and under other circumstances, would be plainly and seriously criminal," as Berkowitz and Goodman have characterized it.[62] This is true in terms of national laws, but there are also international legal concerns posed by the methods we have discussed, beginning with their implications for norms of sovereignty.[63] As well, morally, dilemmas arise from the dirty tricks and coercive nature of many of the methods. Practically the dilemmas stem from the costs, trade-offs, and long-term implications of covert actions. For example, resort to propaganda bears with it the potential for blowback, whereby disinformation intended to influence a foreign target is recycled into the American media, thereby impacting the U.S. public.

Similarly, the excesses of CIA covert operations often damaged the reputation of the U.S. government and its foreign policy. In Iran, for example, the U.S. government overthrew a nationalist leader, installed the shah on the throne, and backed his ruthless dictatorship for over twenty-five years. This knowledge should allow Americans to better understand the hatred that so many Iranians felt toward the U.S. government and why the United States was portrayed by many Iranians as the Great Satan since the 1970s, especially under Ayatollah Khomeini. CIA excess has also bred mistrust among U.S. allies, whose secrets have been compromised and whose involvement risks considerable political embarrassment. Finally, it has bred distrust and cynicism among the American public about their own government.[64]

## Accountability Dilemmas

In terms of accountability dilemmas, the crux of the matter concerns the extensive secrecy and deniability demanded by covert action, on one hand, and the demands of democracy on the other. Since the erosion of the Cold War consensus, serious concerns about the potential for excess has driven repeated searches for appropriate and effective oversight measures whereby the activities of the intelligence community can be reconciled with the demands of democracy. In the wake of the controversies of the 1970s, the Iran-*contra* episode, and the more recent failures and excesses concerning the war on terror, adequate and appropriate oversight remains a concern.[65] Congress asserted itself in the 1970s after the first wave of revelations, establishing new intelligence committees and oversight procedures, but problems continued. On one hand, democracy requires that governmental agencies be held accountable to elected leaders and the public. The demands of national security, on the other hand, often require a quick and efficient foreign policy response. A premium is placed on the independence and secrecy of governmental operations to keep the enemy at bay. The use of all available means to protect and further national security is often considered a necessity in a world where morality is seen to have little relevance. Covert action, by its nature, therefore generates a fundamental tension in a democratic society.

## Guidelines for Legitimacy and Effectiveness

Given the methods and controversies of covert action, it is no surprise that many policy makers, practitioners, observers, and analysts have expressed concern for guidelines for employing such options. Table 4-3 presents a select list of such concerns, synthesized from the work of leading analysts.[66] As the table indicates, we organize them into three categories: relevance, coherence, and consequences. For relevance, the guidelines urge consideration of the desirability and applicability of covert methods. In particular, they recommend careful weighing of such issues as the need and possibility for deniability, the nature of the target, the relevance of other options, and perhaps most significant, the unsuitability of covert action as a way to take action in the face of pressure to do something when other options appear impossible. Those guidelines related to coherence build on this last point and emphasize, first, the need to embed covert action into a broader foreign policy strategy with explicit goals and objectives (including assessment

**Table 4-3. Guidelines for Covert Action Legitimacy and Effectiveness**

| | |
|---|---|
| Relevance | Make sure deniability is necessary and possible |
| | Consider the nature of the target |
| | Carefully consider other options, including diplomacy, first |
| | Consider proportional response and opt for actions at the lowest end of the "ladder of escalation" |
| | Do not resort to covert action for crisis resolution |
| | Do not resort to covert action as a last resort in the absence of other viable policy options |
| | Do not resort to covert action to rescue a failed policy |
| Coherence | Embed covert action in a strategy that makes geopolitical sense |
| | Tie covert action to specific goals and carefully defined objectives |
| | Ensure that covert action is in harmony with publicly stated policy objectives |
| | Evaluate covert action options through the full interagency process, including consultation with intelligence analysts, not just covert action specialists |
| | Never violate U.S. laws, including reporting requirements |
| Consequences | Consider blowback possibilities and consequences |
| | Consider consequences of the covert action becomes public, including the possibility of embarrassment and the impact on reputation |
| | Consider consequences if first step in covert action is unsuccessful |
| | Consider what signal the covert action will send, to whom, and with what result |

of the nature of the threat) and, second, to ensure that the covert options are carefully vetted through the interagency process and consistent with U.S. laws (including procedural rules for reporting, oversight, and the like). The guidelines related to consequences urge careful consideration of the short- and long-term consequences of the covert action, including key questions about the implications of exposure, failure, and blowback. As Godson suggests, a key question that must be asked is "what if—or more likely, when—it becomes public."[67]

## CONCLUSION

Since World War II, the U.S. has engaged in a wide variety of covert actions all over the globe. During the Cold War, such activities were widely accepted and justified as a necessary part of the intense ideological and geopolitical struggle with the Soviet Union. After the Vietnam War and the revelation of the extent and consequences of covert actions in highly controversial settings such as Cuba, Vietnam, and Chile, to name a few, covert action came under increased scrutiny as Congress in particular sought to exercise greater oversight. For many, the gung-ho enthusiasm of the Cold War gave way to a reluctant exceptionalism that has generated considerable tension since the 1970s. The emergence of terrorism as a central concern in the twenty-first century injected new life into covert action as a foreign policy tool, especially since the shady world of terrorism would seem to be an especially rich target for covert action. The demands of such a "war" would seem to ensure that policy makers will continue to reach for covert action methods of the kinds reviewed here—and new ones to contend with the new environment—to address threats and achieve objectives.

## NOTES

1. David F. Rudgers, "The Origins of Covert Action," *Journal of Contemporary History* 35, no. 2 (April 2000), p. 252.

2. Bruce D. Berkowitz and Allan E. Goodman, *Best Truth: Intelligence in the Information Age* (New Haven, CT: Yale University Press, 2000).

3. Quoted in John Ranelagh, *The Agency: The Rise and Decline of the CIA* (New York: Touchstone, 1987), p. 134.

4. Loch K. Johnson, "Covert Action and Accountability: Decision-Making for America's Secret Foreign Policy," *International Studies Quarterly* 33 (March 1989), p. 82.

5. Executive Order 12333, *United States Intelligence Activities*, December 4, 1981.

6. Intelligence Authorization Act of 1991, Public Law 102-88, 105 Stat, 429 (1991), Section 503 [c][4][e].

7. William J. Daugherty, *Executive Secrets: Covert Action and the Presidency* (Lexington: University Press of Kentucky, 2004), p. 12.

8. Berkowitz and Goodman, *Best Truth*, pp. 129–30. See also Daugherty, *Executive Secrets*, p. 16.

9. Daugherty, *Executive Secrets*, p. 13.

10. Johnson, "Covert Action and Accountability," p. 84.

11. See Rhodri Jeffrey-Jones, *CIA and American Democracy*, 3rd ed. (New Haven, CT: Yale University Press, 2003); Loch K. Johnson, *America's Secret Power* (New York: Oxford University Press, 1991); Jonathan Kwitny, *Endless Enemies: The Making of an Unfriendly World* (New York: Penguin, 1984); John Prados, *Presidents' Secret Wars: CIA and Pentagon Operations Since World War II* (New York: William Morrow, 1986); Ranelagh, *The Agency*; U.S. Senate, *Alleged Assassination Plots Involving Foreign Leaders*, Congressional Report, 94th Congress, 1st sess. (November 18, 1975); and U.S. Congress, Senate, *Final Report of the Select Committee to Study Governmental Operations with Respect to Intelligence Activities*, Books 1–6, Congressional Report, 94th Congress, 2nd sess. (April 14, 1976). See also Loch K. Johnson, "The Contemporary Presidency: Presidents, Lawmakers, and Spies: Intelligence Accountability in the United States," *Presidential Studies Quarterly* 34 (December 2004), pp. 828–37 for a similar set of stages in the evolution of covert activities.

12. For example, see Rudgers, "The Origins of Covert Action," pp. 259–61.

13. In interpreting the meaning of the act's phrase, the CIA's first general counsel, Lawrence Houston, concluded that "taken out of context and without knowledge of [the act's] history, these Sections could bear almost unlimited interpretation. In our opinion,

however, either [propaganda or commando type] activity would be an unwarranted extension of the functions authorized" by the act. "We do not believe that there was any thought in the minds of Congress that the Central Intelligence Agency under this authority would take positive action for subversion and sabotage." Any such missions would necessitate going to Congress "for authority and funds." Such authority eventually was provided by passage of the Central Intelligence Act of 1949 (Jay Peterzell, "Legal and Constitutional Authority for Covert Operation," *First Principles* 10 [Spring 1985], pp. 1–3). See also Jeffrey-Jones, *CIA and American Democracy*, chapter 3.

14. Johnson, "Covert Action and Accountability," p. 87.

15. See Peter Grose, *Gentleman Spy: The Life of Allen Dulles* (Boston: Houghton Mifflin, 1995); Jacob Heilbrunn, "The Old Boy at War," *New Republic,* March 27, 1995, pp. 32–37.

16. David Barrett, *The CIA and Congress: The Untold Story from Truman to Kennedy* (Lawrence: University of Kansas Press, 2005); see also Harry Howe Ransom, "The Politicization of Intelligence," in Steven J. Cimbala, ed., *Intelligence and Intelligence Policy in a Democratic Society* (Dobbs Ferry, NY: Transnational, 1987), pp. 25–46.

17. Senate, *Final Report*, p. 9.

18. Harry Howe Ransom, "Strategic Intelligence and Intermestic Politics," in *Perspectives on American Foreign Policy: Selected Readings,* eds. Charles W. Kegley Jr. and Eugene R. Wittkopf (New York: St. Martin's, 1983), p. 303.

19. U.S. Congress, Senate, *Final Report of the Select Committee to Study Governmental Operations with Respect to Intelligence Activities, Foreign and Military Intelligence,* Book I, Congressional Report, 94th Congress, 2nd sess. (April 14, 1976), p. 445.

20. Jeffrey-Jones, *CIA and American Democracy*, p. 51.

21. See James A. Bill, *The Eagle and the Lion: The Tragedy of American-Iranian Relations* (New Haven, CT: Yale University Press, 1988), and Jonathan Kwitny, *Endless Enemies: The Making of an Unfriendly World* (New York: Penguin, 1984).

22. See Richard H. Immerman, *The CIA in Guatemala: The Foreign Policy of Intervention* (Austin: University of Texas Press, 1982), and Stephen Schlesinger and Stephen Kinzer, *Bitter Fruit: The Untold Story of the American Coup in Guatemala* (New York: Doubleday, 1982).

23. See Madelaine G. Kalb, *The Congo Cables: The Cold War in Africa from Eisenhower to Kennedy* (New York: Macmillan, 1981).

24. U.S. Department of State, *Foreign Relations of the United States* (1950), vol. 2, p. 607.

25. Joseph Albright and Marcia Kunstel, "CIA Tip Led to '62 Arrest of Mandela: Ex-Official Tells of U.S. 'Coup' to Aid S. Africa," *Atlanta Constitution,* June 10, 1990, p. A14.

26. See Peter Wyden, *Bay of Pigs: The Untold Story* (London: Jonathan Cape, 1979).

27. Jeffrey-Jones, *CIA and American Democracy*, p. 132.

28. See John Stockwell, *In Search of Enemies: A CIA Story* (New York: Norton, 1978).

29. Loch K. Johnson, "Accountability and America's Secret Foreign Policy: Keeping a Legislative Eye on the Central Intelligence Agency," *Foreign Policy Analysis* (March 2005), pp. 99–120; Loch K. Johnson, "Covert Action and Accountability," pp. 81–109.

30. See Steve Coll, *Ghost Wars: The Secret History of the CIA, Afghanistan, and Bin Laden, from the Soviet Invasion to September 10, 2001* (New York: Penguin, 2004).

31. Philip Taubman, "Casey and His CIA on the Rebound," *New York Times Magazine* January 16, 1983, p. 21.

32. On the Afghanistan operation, see Coll, *Ghost Wars*; George Crile, *Charlie Wilson's War* (New York: Atlantic Monthly Press, 2003); and James M. Scott, *Deciding to Intervene: The Reagan Doctrine and American Foreign Policy* (Durham, NC: Duke University Press, 1996).

33. On the Nicaragua operation, see Robert Kagan, *A Twilight Struggle: American Power and Nicaragua, 1977–1990* (New York: Free Press, 1996), and Scott, *Deciding to Intervene*.

34. See, for example, Duncan L. Clarke and Edward L. Neveleff, "Secrecy, Foreign Intelligence, and Civil Liberties: Has the Pendulum Swung Too Far?" *Political Science Quarterly* 99 (Fall 1984), pp. 493–513, and Stansfield Turner and George Thibault, "Intelligence: The Right Rules," *Foreign Policy* 48 (Fall 1982), pp. 122–38.

35. Theodore Draper, "Is the CIA Necessary?" *New York Review of Books*, August 14, 1997, p. 18.

36. James Risen, *State of War: The Secret History of the CIA and the Bush Administration* (New York: Free Press, 2006); Siobhan Gorman, "New Intelligence Director Shakes up Hierarchy," available at www.govexec.com/dailyfed/0505/050905nj1.htm.

37. Siobhan Gorman, "New Clandestine Service to Coordinate U.S. Spying," *Baltimore Sun*, October 14, 2005, p. 2A.

38. See, for example, U.S. House of Representatives, Permanent Select Committee on Intelligence, *Intelligence Community in the 21st Century* (1996); Commission on the Roles and Capabilities of the United States Intelligence Community, *Preparing for the 21st Century: An Appraisal of U.S. Intelligence* (1996); and Council on Foreign Relations, *Making Intelligence Smarter: The Future of U.S. Intelligence*, Report of an Independent Task Force for the Council on Foreign Relations (1996).

39. Bruce D. Berkowitz and Allan E. Goodman, "The Logic of Covert Action," *National Interest* 51 (Spring 1998), p. 44.

40. See, for example, Roy Godson, *Dirty Tricks or Trump Cards: U.S. Covert Action and Counterintelligence* (New Brunswick, NJ: Transaction, 2000); Loch K. Johnson, *Bombs, Bugs, Drugs, and Thugs: Intelligence and America's Quest for Security* (New York: New York University Press, 2000); James Risen, "The Clinton Administration's See-No-Evil CIA," *New York Times,* September 10, 2000, p. 5.

41. On these activities, see Robert Baer, *See No Evil: The True Story of a Ground Soldier in the CIA's War on Terror* (New York: Arrow Books, 2002); Berkowitz and Goodman, *Best Truth*; Richard Clarke, *Against All Enemies* (New York: Free Press, 2004); Godson, *Dirty Tricks or Trump Cards*; Johnson, *Bombs, Bugs, Drugs, and Thugs*; and Timothy Naftali, *Blind Spot: The Secret History of American Counterterrorism* (New York: Basic Books, 2005).

42. See, for example, Clarke, *Against All Enemies*; Risen, *State of War*; Dana Priest, "Covert CIA Program Withstands New Furor," *Washington Post*, December 30, 2005, p. A1; Gary Schroen, *First In: An Insider's Account of How the CIA Spearheaded the War on Terror in Afghanistan* (New York: Presidio Press, 2005).

43. Bob Woodward, "CIA Told to Do 'Whatever Necessary' to Kill Bin Laden," *Washington Post*, October 21, 2001, p. A1.

44. Walter Pincus, "Intelligence Shakeup Would Boost CIA," *Washington Post*, November 8, 2001, p. A1.

45. See the 9/11 Commission Report, U.S. Senate, Select Committee on Intelligence, *Report on the U.S. Intelligence Community's Prewar Intelligence Assessments on Iraq* (2004); Commission on the Intelligence Capabilities of the United States Regarding Weapons of Mass Destruction in Iraq, *Report of the President* (March 3, 2005); and Risen, *State of War*.

46. Jeffrey-Jones, *CIA and American Democracy*, p. 83.

47. Roy Godson discusses propaganda, political action, paramilitary activity, and intelligence assistance in *Dirty Tricks or Trump Card*, and Daugherty discusses propaganda, political action, paramilitary operations, and information warfare in *Executive Secrets*. Lowenthal uses a five-part scheme of propaganda, political activity, economic activity, coups, and paramilitary operations in *Intelligence: From Secrets to Policy* (Washington, DC: Congressional Quarterly Press, 2006). Treverton, by contrast, only discusses propaganda, political action, and paramilitary operation in *Covert Action: The Limits of Intervention in the Postwar World* (New York: Basic Books, 1987).

48. See, for example, Treverton, *Covert Action*; Johnson, "Covert Action and Accountability," p. 84.

49. Godson, *Dirty Tricks or Trump Cards*, p. 152.

50. Ibid., p. 154.

51. Johnson, "Covert Action and Accountability," p. 84.

52. Treverton, *Covert Action*, pp. 17–25.

53. Johnson, "Covert Action and Accountability," p. 85.

54. For example, Johnson, "Covert Action and Accountability," p. 85; Treverton, *Covert Action*, p. 17.

55. Prados, *Presidents' Secret Wars*, p. 212.

56. Ibid., p. 15.

57. Treverton, *Covert Action*, p. 26.

58. Bob Woodward, "CIA told to do 'whatever necessary,'" p. A1.

59. Loch K. Johnson, "On Drawing a Bright Line for Covert Operations," *American Journal of International Law* 86 (April 1992), pp. 284–309.

60. Ransom, "Strategic Intelligence and Intermestic Politics," pp. 299–319.

61. Godson, *Dirty Tricks or Trump Cards*, p. 64.

62. Berkowitz and Goodman, "The Logic of Covert Action," p. 38.

63. A good discussion is Johnson, "Drawing a Bright Line."

64. See Anthony Lake, "Lying Around Washington," *Foreign Policy* 2 (Spring 1971), pp. 91–113.

65. On this matter, see Frank Smist, *Congress Oversees the Intelligence Community, 1947–1994* (Knoxville: University of Tennessee Press, 1994); Loch K. Johnson, "Acountability and America's Secret Foreign Policy"; Johnson, *America's Secret Power*; Jeffrey-Jones, *CIA and American Democracy*, among others.

66. These guidelines are synthesized from Johnson, "Drawing a Bright Line"; Berkowitz and Goodman, "The Logic of Covert Action"; Lowenthal, *Intelligence*; Daugherty, *Executive Secrets*, and Godson, *Dirty Tricks or Trump Cards*.

67. Godson, *Dirty Tricks or Trump Cards*, p. 216.

# 5

# COVERT ACTION

## An Appraisal of the Effects of Secret Propaganda

MICHAEL A. TURNER

SECRET PROPAGANDA IS AN ESSENTIAL PART OF America's covert action capabilities. The 1991 Intelligence Authorization Act, which currently governs the covert action reporting process, defines covert action as an "activity or activities of the U.S. Government to influence political, economic, or military conditions abroad, where it is intended that the [U.S.] role will not be apparent or acknowledged publicly." Implicit in this definition is the fact that covert actions involve interference in the domestic affairs of other states or the internal workings of nonstate groups. This invariably makes such operations highly problematic from operational and ethical viewpoints. The generally accepted standard today, first embodied in Executive Order 12036 of 1978 and reaffirmed in various other orders since then, is that covert actions are to be employed only when essential to the national security of the United States and as a last resort. Secret propaganda, a form of covert action, has historically been excluded from this formulation despite its dubious benefits.

## COVERT ACTION TYPES

The U.S. government engages in three categories of covert actions, each of which contains a bewildering range of activities. Political and economic actions are the most obvious and historically the most notorious, in that they involve instigating changes in governments, leadership, or social conditions. For example, the covert operations to prevent Salvador Allende from winning Chile's presidency in 1970 and then to oust him from office in 1973 fell into this category. This category of actions also includes assistance to political parties and labor unions as well as political assassination attempts—of Cuba's Fidel Castro or the Congo's Patrice Lumumba, for example. It says a good deal about their controversial nature that the Chilean operations and the attempts against Castro served as catalysts for the public investigations of U.S. intelligence in general and the Central Intelligence Agency (CIA) in particular during the mid-1970s.

Political and economic actions also include covert support to paramilitary groups and insurgents. According to press reports, the United States, for example, gave military assistance to moderate Afghan dissident groups during the Carter administration in the late 1970s and, following the Soviet invasion in 1979, to Afghan rebels, some of whom were Islamic extremists who later turned their insurgent capabilities against the United States.[1]

The second category of covert actions is paramilitary activity, which often involves the use of CIA's own paramilitary forces or joint arrangements with the U.S. military for combat operations and activities like sabotage. Most paramilitary (as well as political and economic) actions make liberal use of the third type of covert action—propaganda—as the lead or supplemental covert activity. *Propaganda* is defined as the dissemination of information intended to manipulate perceptions in support of one's cause or to damage an adversary.

From the start, when the 1947 National Security Act set up the CIA and later legislation gave the agency responsibility for managing America's covert actions, there has been a symbiosis among the three types of covert operations. By 1953, the CIA's Office of Secret Operations had merged with the Office of Policy Coordination (OPC), the government's covert action arm, to set up CIA's Directorate of Plans. According to the *Los Angeles Times*, this directorate established a massive propaganda machine, with thousands of employees who were adept at not only placing press and radio stories but also in simultaneously carrying out such covert acts as engaging with labor unions, applying economic pressure, offering direct money payments, and waging political and cultural warfare—all to prevent European countries from falling to the communists. The *Los Angeles Times* also asserts that the congressional investigations in the mid-1970s revealed that by then CIA owned or subsidized at various times more than fifty newspapers, news services, radio stations, periodicals, and other communication facilities, most of them abroad. In some cases, these assets were used for propaganda purposes; in other instances, they served as covers for other operations. In any event, paid CIA agents infiltrated a dozen foreign news organizations, and at least twenty-two American news outlets employed journalists working for the CIA. Nearly a dozen U.S. publishing houses printed more than a thousand books that had been produced or subsidized by the CIA.[2]

Of the three types of covert actions, propaganda is an integral part of the government's influence operations. The most overt of these operations, public diplomacy, seeks to explain government policy and project soft power without attempting to hide government sponsorship. Soon after the terrorist attacks of September 11, 2001, the U.S. government began a public diplomacy effort, characterized by fits and starts, that has focused on three strategic imperatives. First, the United States must offer a positive vision of hope and opportunity to people around the world, rooted in America's commitment to freedom. Second, the United States must isolate and marginalize violent extremists and undermine their efforts at terror. Third, the United States must foster a sense of common interests and common values between Americans and people of different countries, cultures, and faiths.[3]

Strategic influence operations, the second type of influence venture, are generally the domain of the U.S. military and attempt to alter attitudes and behaviors in favor of policy stands the U.S. government favors. Winning the hearts and minds of foreign populations is always a tricky proposition, but the *Quadrennial Defense Review Report* of 2006 says that victory in the war on terror depends on strategic communication.[4] Such operations may include information warfare, which is quickly becoming an important part of America's strategic posture.

Secret propaganda, the last of the three types of influence operations, may incorporate aspects of the previous two, in addition to psychological warfare operations. Though conceptually discrete, the three categories of influence operations overlap to such an extent that the best and most effective operation is one that employs the resources of all three and intermixes the capabilities in strategically significant ways.

## SECRET PROPAGANDA

Because propaganda is often built around incomplete or false news stories in an effort to alter perceptions and elicit conditioned responses, its effectiveness often depends on such factors as the way statements are presented, the timing of the story's release, and the path it takes to get it into the media outlets. Experts agree that secret propaganda has three intended effects—mobilizing the target audience toward an intended objective, achieving concealment or surprise, or protecting legitimacy. Secret propaganda that seeks to mobilize does so either to persuade the target to commit itself in support of a cause or provide the illusion that old and new causes are compatible. An example of secret propaganda intended to mobilize is the British efforts prior to the onset of World War II to rally Americans to support the British cause. Another example is the effort by American senior military officers just prior to the 1968 Tet Offensive in Vietnam possibly to falsify Viet Cong order-of-battle figures and underreport North Vietnamese infiltrations of South Vietnam, all intended to strengthen the president's hand and convince the country and ultimately the North Vietnamese of America's determination to stay the course.

Secret propaganda to achieve surprise or to conceal plans usually occurs in wartime. Examples are the propaganda that accompanied the American interventions in the first Gulf War in 1991 and also just prior to the Iraq war in 2003, Soviet deception over the installations of the missiles in Cuba in 1962, and myriad efforts by various governments to mask weakness through a show of strength.

Secret propaganda to achieve, maintain, or restore legitimacy typically occur prior to, during, or just after military operations and are usually defensive in nature. Soviet interventions in Hungary, Suez, Czechoslovakia, Afghanistan, and Poland were accompanied by deceptions to protect legitimacy. The United States also engaged in secret propaganda to establish and defend the legitimacy of the Bay of Pigs operation in 1961. Propaganda to protect legitimacy also includes attempts to shift the blame for fiascoes, as did the Soviets after they shot down Korean Air flight 007 in 1983.

Today, numerous U.S. agencies, including the Department of Defense, engage in propaganda activities, but under U.S. law, propaganda is part of the covert action repertoire of the CIA. Propaganda activities range from overt (or white) propaganda—broadcasting news about the United States by Voice of America (VOA), for example—to black propaganda, which is spreading disinformation. Gray propaganda falls somewhere in between and includes broadcast activities intended to cast the United States in a positive light.

### White Propaganda

White propaganda is the overt dissemination of factual but often biased information for strategic objectives. The activities of the U.S. Information Agency (USIA) during the Cold War, for example, were in the category of white propaganda, for that agency openly disseminated the U.S. policy line through libraries, cultural exchanges, publications, and media outlets. Although the USIA was disbanded in 1999, the U.S. government today floods the Iraqi and Afghan airwaves and print media with good news of schools opened after the U.S. military refurbishment, water systems repaired, or terrorist leaders captured—all truthful reports that essentially leave out items that may not be complimentary to U.S. interests.

### Gray Propaganda

Gray propaganda, the second category, is the covert and unacknowledged dissemination of the official policy lines. Paying a journalist in a target country to write favorable reports about the United States, for example, would fit in this category. So would the surreptitious placement of favorable news items in foreign media outlets, as was the case for the past several years with the Pentagon's secret operations to provide a positive spin to America's efforts in Iraq. According to press reports, the Defense Department has secretly operated radio stations and newspapers in Iraq, placed editorials in Iraqi newspapers and websites, offered TV stations money to run unattributed segments, and contracted with writers of newspaper opinion pieces.[5] Furthermore, Pentagon contractors may have paid Iraqi Islamic religious leaders to offer propaganda advice and print positive articles about the American mission.[6]

This kind of unattributed propaganda has a long pedigree. At the onset of the Cold War, the U.S. government began employing propaganda as an instrument of its foreign policy, intended to "expose the fallacies of communism," warn of its dangers, strengthen Western-oriented regimes, increase awareness of the Soviet threat, and build greater willingness to cooperate with the West.[7] In June 1949, the CIA established the National Committee for a Free Europe to provide cover for a psychological warfare program that included radio propaganda to Eastern Europe. In July, Radio Free Europe (RFE) began broadcasting prodemocracy, anticommunist messages to Poland, Czechoslovakia, Hungary, Romania, and Bulgaria. It also beamed talks by exiles, personal messages, replies to mail from listeners, names of communist secret agents and informers, news items embarrassing the communist regimes, and American popular music banned in Eastern Europe. The CIA also founded RFE's sister station, Radio Liberty (RL), which broadcast similar messages to the Soviet Union in both Russian and the languages of the non-Russian peoples.[8]

The genius of these propaganda efforts was that far from lauding American popular culture or the Western way of life, they focused on issues closest to their listening publics, such as agricultural collectivization, the persecution of religion, the suppression of culture, party purges, and the like.[9]

Some American critics of the stations in the 1970s tried to shut them down, claiming that they were relics of the Cold War and served no useful purpose other than to goad the Soviet Union and its puppet regimes in Eastern Europe. This attempt failed, but the management of RFE/RL eventually was transferred from the CIA to an independent agency. RFE and RL were officially closed down on November 28, 2003, as a cost-saving measure.

One of the CIA's more daring and effective Cold War secret propaganda actions was the establishment of the Congress for Cultural Freedom in 1950. Initiated as a conference of intellectuals in West Berlin in June 1950, the congress published literary and political journals and hosted dozens of conferences bringing together some of the most eminent Western thinkers. Its purpose was to demonstrate that communism, despite its rhetoric, was an enemy of art and thought. By doing so, it sought to negate communism's appeal among artists and intellectuals and at the same time, undermine the communist claim to moral superiority. The CIA's sponsorship of the Congress for Cultural Freedom became publicly known in 1967, effectively ending the operation.[10]

The CIA undertook a similar propaganda venture against Fidel Castro beginning in 1960 as part of a larger covert operation against Cuba. Radio Swan carried programs taped in CIA radio stations in Miami, consisting of news analysis, entertainment, and anti-Castro speeches by Cuban exiles. The CIA also bought time in Caribbean stations for anti-Castro programming. Such programming continued well into the 1970s, stopping only after the congressional investigations of U.S. intelligence activities. Nonetheless, President Ronald Reagan announced plans on September 23, 1981, to revive a radio station to transmit news reports to Cuba. Despite controversy and occasional attempts to disband the station, Radio Marti continues its broadcasts as part of the VOA.[11]

More recently, the United States engaged in psychological operations against Iraqi dictator Saddam Hussein during the first Gulf War in 1990–91 by inciting the Kurds, Shias, and other Iraqis to rise up against the regime. Press reports say that in addition to dropping leaflets over urban areas, messages were broadcast over two "black" radio stations, the Voice of Free Iraq and Radio Free Iraq, both of which were operated by the CIA. Once the ground war began in 1991, the Voice of Free Iraq stepped up its calls for an uprising by suggesting that Saddam Hussein was preparing to flee the country. Although these insurrections failed to materialize in 1991, America's propaganda promises paved the way for rebellions in 1995 that were brutally crushed by Iraq's dictator.[12]

### Black Propaganda

Black propaganda, the purposeful manipulation of the perceptions of a target audience through the use of disinformation or deception, constitutes the third type of propaganda that the United States employs as part of its covert action arsenal. This general category, although used less frequently than the other two types, requires particular specificity to either direct the target into specific types of behaviors or alter attitudes of target audiences to forestall actions detrimental to U.S. interests. Black propaganda may employ white and gray propaganda to fulfill its goals, but its distinguishing characteristic is the nature of its content—information is either exaggerated or false. Given the nature of information technology today, black propaganda may involve spreading disinformation into government or terrorist computer networks.[13] As such, black propaganda more often than not is part of a broader covert action plan.

Black propaganda has been a potent instrument in CIA's arsenal since its inception. Beginning at the onset of the Cold War, the CIA infiltrated Western literature into the totalitarian regimes of the eastern bloc; sponsored anticommunist books written by Soviet and eastern bloc defectors as well as by American scholars; and developed media proprietaries abroad, including a secret propaganda printing plant in West Germany and various press outlets, such as the West German *Der Monat*, the British *Encounter*, and the Italian *Daily American*.[14]

In the campaign to prevent the Italian communists from coming to power in 1948, the CIA's psychological operatives inspired stories in the Italian press and letters from Italian Americans to their relatives in Italy. Funds were handed to Christian Democrats, in part for pamphlets, posters, and other paraphernalia of election campaigns. Publication of the Zorin Plan in *Tempo*, possibly a CIA disinformation story outlining Soviet plans for repressing Italy after the victory of the Italian communists, undoubtedly helped divert voters to the Italian socialists or the right-of-center Christian Democrats instead.[15]

In Guatemala in 1954, CIA engaged in secret propaganda by broadcasting the Voice of Liberation, a dissident station claiming to be based somewhere in the

Guatemalan countryside. The station broadcast the lie that a revolution was under way and an inflated number of troops were marching toward the capital—all calculated to encourage others to rally around the small cadre of CIA-backed insurgents and intimidate president Jacobo Arbenz Guzmán and his supporters into believing that they faced a superior force. This deception ultimately persuaded President Arbenz to flee the country.[16]

The CIA's attempts against Chile's Marxist politician Salvador Allende also involved propaganda in support of a wider covert operation. Much of this propaganda campaign involved discrediting Allende. The CIA spent $3 million in 1964 and another $3 million in 1972 to blacken his name. Between 1963 and 1973, when Allende was ousted by CIA-backed Chilean military officers, the agency spent $12 million on propaganda, employing extensive use of the press, radio, films, pamphlets, posters, leaflets, direct mailings, paper streamers, and wall painting.

On August 25, 1986, the *Wall Street Journal* ran a story that the United States was contemplating military or covert action against Libya and that internal opposition to Libyan leader Muammar Qaddafi was growing. The report in the American newspaper was actually blowback from a U.S. deception operation abroad, designed to create alarm in Libya and possibly precipitate Qaddafi's overthrow by Libyans.

The Soviets also were adept at black propaganda. In 1983 Moscow began a deception operation, first initiated in the Indian daily *Patriot*, designed to attribute blame for the AIDS epidemic to the United States by spreading the false story that the virus had been brought into existence by genetic engineering experiments conducted at Fort Dietrich, Maryland—allegedly to develop new biological weapons. Moscow then spread the story to Africa, South America, and Europe by advertising the investigations of a Soviet biochemist who supposedly had verified the link. The Soviet government acknowledged the disinformation campaign in 1989 and apologized for it, but to this day some extremist Americans and a substantial portion of Africa's population still hold to the fiction that the United States developed the HIV virus for use in the third world.

## APPRAISING EFFECTS

Much of the U.S. government's information machinery, including the USIA and most covert action programs, were dismantled after the Cold War. The Department of Defense created an office soon after the 9/11 attacks to provide news items, both true and false, to foreign news organizations, but the office was quickly shut down after the plan became public and the effort was criticized as damaging U.S. credibility abroad.

Five years after 9/11, however, both the Pentagon and the CIA have undertaken a secret propaganda war to counter the insurgencies in Iraq and Afghanistan. The Pentagon has taken the lead in this effort and, together with CIA's propaganda efforts, has been outsourcing its information campaigns to such contractors as Science Applications International, SyColeman, and the Lincoln Group.[17] For example, these firms have obtained contracts for "media approach planning" on behalf of the Joint Psychological Operations Support Element within the U.S. Special Operations Command.[18] Moreover, an intelligence expert asserts that half of the CIA's efforts have been outsourced to private contractors, which worries many people because these contractors are not subject to the kinds of controls or oversight that CIA employees experience.[19]

On balance, U.S. propaganda activities have had a mixed record. At the operational level, secret propaganda operations are effective (i.e., they succeed) under three conditions: the extent to which (1) their presentation attracts the intended target's attention and holds interest; (2) the effort does not alert the target to its presence; and (3) the target acts in the manner intended. All these factors aligned perfectly in the 1947 propaganda operation to keep the communists from electoral victory in Italy, which cost only about $10 million and resulted in the victory of pro-Western (and anticommunist) Christian Democrats. Logically then, secret propaganda fails if the target takes no notice of the presentation, notices but judges it to be irrelevant, misconstrues its intended meaning, detects the method of deception, or does not behave in the manner intended.

The effectiveness of secret propaganda operations also depends on the degree to which they remain secret. Once they become known, their effectiveness drops precipitously, and in many cases they become either an embarrassment to the government or result in negative and other unintended consequences. For example, in late September 1986, the deceptive nature of the Libyan operation was revealed in the press, and the Reagan administration was criticized for deceiving Americans as well as other publics. A similar result occurred when the *Washington Post* revealed that the U.S. military was planting positive stories in Iraq after the onset of the war in 2003.

On a broader level, secret propaganda can have positive as well as negative consequences. Whether the former outweighs the latter is unclear, but in either case, the legitimacy of secret propaganda appears to rest on the existence of a broad consensus about the country's foreign policy objectives and the means of achieving them. On the positive side, secret propaganda efforts like RFE and RL, whose existence remained unattributed well into the 1980s, benefited from broad consensus about the necessity of opposing the Soviet Union by employing methods short of nuclear war. These radio operations became well known and respected among their listeners. Some Polish leaders, for example, later asserted that the stations played an important role in bringing down at least three Polish Communist Party leaders and were instrumental in sustaining the Solidarity trade union in Poland when it was forced underground by martial law in 1981. During Romanian strongman Nicolae Ceausescu's time, RFE was Romania's most popular source of news. After the end of the Cold War, RFE/RL journalists visiting their target countries were greeted as heroes. Another successful propaganda effort was the CIA's effective campaign in the late 1970s to counter the Soviet propaganda campaign against the U.S. deployment of the neutron bomb in Europe by comparing the bomb to the similarly dangerous Soviet SS-20 missile.

The propaganda effort to foment discontent within the Iraqi population in 1990–91 fell far short of sparking a popular uprising, primarily because of the pervasive internal security Saddam Hussein maintained, but these measures encouraged and gave false hope to the Kurds and the Shias subsequently to launch rebellions. In March 1995, Kurdish guerrillas trained by CIA launched raids against the Saddam Hussein regime, hoping to spark local insurrections, generate defections from government forces, and persuade Saddam that his army would not fight for him. The operation failed because of internal Kurdish defections and when it became clear that the United States would not follow through on its propaganda promises.[20]

Overall, the benefits of successful secret propaganda revolve around the "facts on the ground," that is, secret propaganda may generate greater local credibility than an official (or white) propaganda outlet. In addition, secret propaganda may be the only way for the United States to counter propaganda against it. This may be especially true when the adversary has had success in its propaganda against the United States. This was the case during the Cold War and may be the case now in the counterterrorism fight. It is certainly true that truthful information is essential to counter false information, but the truth may often need the assistance of secret propaganda to overcome preconception, misconception, and prejudice.

An additional benefit of secret propaganda is its possible effects on the actions of leaders. Successful secret propaganda may manipulate the attitudes and perceptions of elites in ways that are desired by the U.S. government. Allied propaganda during the Kosovo war, for example, was directly responsible for Serbian strongman Milosevic's decision in June 1999 to accept NATO's terms for settling the conflict, motivated by his belief that NATO was poised to launch an even more massive bombing campaign if its terms were rejected.

On the negative side, secret propaganda may result in unforeseen consequences that could be detrimental to U.S. interests. One unintended and dire effect of secret propaganda is blowback, the domestic consequences of intended propaganda (and other covert action) program abroad. The issue is particularly relevant today because information flows around the globe at an unprecedented rate with the growing use of computer technology and the Internet. A disinformation campaign abroad, for example, may be reported at home by the American press or American scholars as true, as was the case with the *Wall Street Journal* in 1986 in the Libya operation. This kind of domestic consequence almost certainly skews the domestic political debate and possibly affects its outcome. Activities that may result in blowback also contravene the terms of the 1991 Intelligence Authorization Act, which stipulates that the government will refrain from engaging in actions that may directly or indirectly influence American domestic politics, public opinion, or the media.[21]

Furthermore, there are ethical and moral arguments against secret propaganda programs, especially those that use the press as their conduits. One moral argument holds that secret propaganda undermines the free press, in that journalists in free countries should not be bought and their media corrupted for questionable gains by the U.S. government. Another ethical argument says that recruiting foreign journalists may backfire on the United States. It is possible, for example, for foreign journalists, under covert circumstances, to turn on the United States and reveal their covert recruitment, thus providing pretexts for propaganda against the United States and embarrassment to the government.

## THE BALANCE SHEET

Although propaganda—the dissemination of information for strategic objectives—is part of any government's repertoire, secret propaganda stands on its own to mean the use of information to manipulate, control, or direct a target's preferences in specific ways. The secrecy associated with it gives such propaganda its notoriety and sinister veneer. Though there are legitimate policy reasons for employing secret propaganda to implement aspects of American foreign policy, its success depends to a large extent on highly specific and narrowly construed factors.

On balance, secret propaganda works well when driven by a foreign policy consensus on its utility and when designed in ways commensurate with its intended objectives, as was the case in many of the secret propaganda efforts during the Cold War. Secret propaganda that does not elicit broad-based elite support or that is designed poorly, such as the recent efforts in Iraq and Afghanistan, will almost certainly backfire on the government and result in policy failure.

## NOTES

1. See Jeff Gerth, "Military's Information War Is Vast and Often Secretive," *New York Times*, December 11, 2005.

2. Walter Jajko, "It's Propaganda Time," *Los Angeles Times*, December 2, 2005, p. 13.

3. Testimony of Karen Hughes, Under Secretary of State for Public Diplomacy, Before the House International Relations Committee, November 10, 2005.

4. Office of the Secretary of Defense, *Quadrennial Defense Review Report* (Washington, DC: U.S. Department of Defense, February 6, 2006), pp. 91–92.

5. Gerth, "Military's Information War Is Vast." Also see Jajko, "It's Propaganda Time."; Jeff Gerth and Scott Shane, "U.S. Said to Pay to Plant Articles in Iraq Papers," *New York Times*, November 30, 2005, pp. A1, A18; and "Propaganda Bombards Iraqis on Both Sides," *Associated Press*, September 17, 2005.

6. David S. Cloud and Jeff Gerth, "Islamic Leaders Were Paid to Aid U.S. Propaganda," *New York Times*, January 2, 2006, pp. A1 and A6.

7. Department of State Report on the Conference of Chiefs of Mission, February 21, 1951; U.S. Embassy in Tehran dispatch 1023 on using anti-Soviet materials within Iran,

May 29, 1953; and National Security Council, *Memorandum on U.S. Objectives and Policies with Respect to the Near East*, July 6, 1954.

8. Michael A. Turner, *Historical Dictionary of United States Intelligence* (Lanham, MD: Scarecrow Press, 2006), pp. 167–68.

9. Ibid.

10. Ibid., pp. 38–39.

11. Ibid., p. 168.

12. Gerth, "Military's Information War Is Vast"; Jajko, "It's Propaganda Time"; Gerth and Shane, "U.S. Said to Pay to Plant Articles"; and "Propaganda Bombards Iraqis on Both Sides."

13. See Deborah G. Berger, *Toward a Revolution in Intelligence Affairs* (Santa Monica, CA: RAND Corporation Technical Report, 2005), pp. 116–24.

14. Trevor Barnes, "Democratic Deception: American Covert Operations in Post-War Europe," in David A. Charters and Maurice A. J. Tugwell, eds., *Deception Operations: Studies in the East-West Context* (London: Brassey's, 1990), pp. 297–305.

15. Ibid.

16. David A. Charters, "Breaking Cover: The Bay of Pigs Intervention," in *Deception Operations: Studies in the East-West Context* eds. David A. Charters and Maurice A. J. Tugwell (London: Brassey's, 1990), pp. 353–55.

17. Jeff Gerth, "Military's Information War Is Vast."

18. "Farming out Psyops," *Intelligence Online*, June 17, 2005; Renae Merle, "Pentagon Funds Diplomacy Effort," *Washington Post*, June 11, 2005; and Dean Calbreath, "SAIC to Join Pentagon's Media Blitz," *San Diego Union Tribune*, June 18, 2005.

19. James Bamford, interview on National Public Radio, December 2, 2005.

20. Gerth, "Military's Information War Is Vast"; Jajko, "It's Propaganda Time"; Gerth and Shane, "U.S. Said to Pay to Plant Articles."

21. Intelligence Authorization Act, *Congressional Record* (28 June 1991), p. S9212.

# 6

# POLITICAL ACTION AS A TOOL
# OF PRESIDENTIAL STATECRAFT

WILLIAM J. DAUGHERTY

THE INTELLIGENCE DISCIPLINE OF COVERT ACTION HAS been a policy staple of every post–World War II American president, Democrat or Republican, and most often employed against countries and organizations that were or are hostile toward the United States or U.S. interests. But covert action didn't start with the Cold War; indeed, a number of earlier presidents, going back to George Washington, also relied on what we would call covert action to achieve foreign policy objectives. Thus, covert action is traditional tool of presidential statecraft, the purpose of which is, simply stated, to influence a foreign audience either to do something, or to refrain from doing something, in a direction that coincides with American foreign policy objectives. Put differently, covert action is applied, by specific presidential direction, to compel the target audience to change its policies or its behavior. The target audience might be a foreign government, a foreign nation's general population or distinct part of a population, or members of a hostile nongovernmental organization, such as a narcotics cartel or terrorist group.

Individual covert action operations are managed very much like intelligence collection or counterintelligence operations in that foreign nationals recruited and directed clandestinely to perform a specific mission, usually the provision of confidential information. The difference is that, whereas all aspects of a collection or counterintelligence operation are to remain secret, a covert action operation must ultimately produce some result that is clearly apparent, or overt, at least to the target audience (if not the wider public) if it is have any influence or effect. Although the result must be visible, the sponsorship, for example, the government or intelligence service, of the persons or group that generated the apparent result must remain hidden so as not to undermine the result's credibility with the target audience. In sum, the identity of the sponsor is actually the secret, not the operation itself. For example, if a respected labor leader in a country whose population was generally unsympathetic to the United States were to organize a general strike to emphasize the incompetence of his government, neither he nor the strike would be credible if it were known that the U.S. government was secretly paying him to perform this act.

Purely clandestine operations that are run either to collect sensitive information or to serve a counterintelligence objective are legally considered as routine missions of the U.S. intelligence community. As such, the individual intelligence agencies within the community possess continuing legal authorities to conduct these operations, a great deal of institutional latitude in how they do it, and a fairly low level of congressional oversight. Conversely, covert action programs are not routine intelligence activities: they must have special authorizations to meet federal law requirements, they are denied a good deal of the policy and operational flexibility that other intelligence operations enjoy, and they receive intense oversight from not only Congress but also the National Security Council. Arguably, because they are implemented explicitly to support a president's foreign policy initiative, covert action programs are not even "intelligence" in nature, even though they are executed by the Central Intelligence Agency (CIA) and rely on clandestine methodologies. These differences ultimately remove covert action programs from the realm of general intelligence activities and transform them into highly sensitive instruments of presidential policy.

In essence, covert action programs are secret adjuncts to a particular foreign policy established by the president and employed to support overt policy implementation measures (e.g., diplomacy, trade favoritism or sanctions, foreign aid, military force, training initiatives, and loan guarantees or grants). It is the president, advised by the National Security Council, who decides whether a policy will have a covert component and, if so, how that component will be used. For each covert action program, under which dozens or even hundreds of individual operations may be run, federal law dictates that the president sign a document declaring that he "finds" that the covert action program is necessary for national security purposes. This finding (as it is known in the parlance) spells out the objectives and implementation limits of each program, sets a program budget, defines the role of the CIA and any supporting agencies in executing the program, and includes a risk versus gain assessment. Furthermore, all findings must be sent to the intelligence oversight committees in Congress within forty-eight hours of the president signing the document. Once begun, covert action programs receive nearly continuous scrutiny from CIA senior management, Congress, and the president and his national security team. This oversight is conducted until the program is abolished, a move that again requires a presidential signature. These extra measures necessary to initiate, execute, and terminate covert action programs truly make them "presidential" in all respects.

Covert action programs fall under one of four general operational categories: propaganda, political action, information warfare, and paramilitary operations. Political action programs, the focus of this chapter, generally seek to achieve influence through covert activities that involve the manipulation, legitimate or otherwise, of a foreign nation's political and/or economic system, with the instigating hand of the U.S. government remaining hidden from view. Political action operations are always provocative to some degree, ranging from operations that slightly irritate (e.g., paying a few individuals to carry protest signs in front of a government office or bribing public officials) to the highly antagonistic and hostile (e.g., flooding a country with counterfeit currency or creating a major strike to cripple the economy and undermine the ruling regime). Regardless, political action operations, whether directed at a nation's political institutions or its economy (and often both), seek to change the behavior or policies of a government. Such meddling is contrary to international law and the United Nations Charter and may, if compromised with the sponsorship of the American government exposed, generate many problems, both political and practical, for the president at home and abroad.

But offsetting this risk—and hence its attractiveness to presidents—is the fact that operations that covertly manipulate a country's political processes or economic system are usually much less costly than other forms of pressure, especially military force. For example, if a covert political action program to oust Panamanian dictator Manuel Noriega in 1989 had been attempted and succeeded, the financial and political costs of such would have been far less than the costs (including humanitarian) of using the U.S. military to invade and occupy the country until Noriega was captured.

American history is replete with examples of presidents authorizing secret activities intended to foster and further American interests at the expense of foreign governments. In point of fact, George Washington used covert action programs in addition to intelligence collection operations during the American Revolution and continued doing so after his election to the presidency in 1791 to secure the fledgling democracy. Arguably, the first use of covert action in the new administration was not against an overseas government but against the sovereign governments of Native American tribes.

Once in office, Washington was abetted by his secretary of state, Thomas Jefferson, in implementing a covert action program—a classic example of a political action operation—intended to create confidence and goodwill with various tribes whose lands lay between the settled East Coast and the interior of the continent, awaiting further exploration. Jefferson's objective was to lay the foundation for the U.S. government eventually to acquire their lands for the development or construction of inland transportation systems, such as roads, bridges, and canals, an infrastructure vital to the movement of commercial goods and people within the country. The need to grow the economy was critical to sustaining the faith of the Americans in the newly created democracy, the permanence of which was by no means assured just because the U.S. Constitution was ratified. Quite simply, if Americans were not better off economically under the new Constitution, there would little reason for them to continue to support it. Gaining access to tribal lands for the movement of goods, as well as to encourage the migration to and settlement of the West was, hence, an important part of Washington's economic policy.

The methods Washington and Jefferson employed are easily recognized as basic political action tactics. First, the secretary of War was given visible responsibility for this program, putatively acting autonomously to insulate the president and secretary of State from any negative consequences that might occur. The War secretary then proceeded, through the help of clandestine agents, to bribe tribal chiefs, selectively dole out financing for trading posts and other businesses, extend (or threaten to foreclose) loans granted to tribal leaders, and manipulate the chiefs' human foibles (here, greed) to run them into heavy debt. Owing monies that they had no way of repaying left the tribal leaders vulnerable to exploitation by government agents, who agreed secretly to swap tribal debts for treaties transferring Indian land titles to the United States.

When Jefferson acceded to the White House, he was bedeviled by the predatory actions of the Barbary pirates, seagoing thugs who plundered American commerce in the western Mediterranean and captured American sailors for ransom. Jefferson's solution was the same that later presidents, including Dwight D. Eisenhower, John F. Kennedy, and Richard M. Nixon, found so attractive—implementing a political action program to undermine covertly the offending government (the Tripolitan Pasha) and affect a change of regime by placing a rival on the throne. Jefferson's scheme also involved bribery, secret funding of opposition groups, and a small paramilitary operation conducted by U.S. Marines. The Pasha, seeing the writing on the wall, decided to deal with Jefferson, resulting in an accord that halted acts of piracy against the U.S. merchant fleet and released the American hostages, while allowing the Pasha to retain his throne.

Covert actions, particularly political/economic action programs, were employed through the mid-1800s as America expanded westward, to gain land for the United States from European colonial powers and neighboring Mexico. Under James Madison's direction, two territorial administrators infiltrated secret agents into the Florida panhandle, at the time under Spanish control, to foment a rebellion that would appear to be the actions of local, pro-U.S. residents. The anticipated Spanish reaction would then provide the pretext for the president to order the occupation of the land by U.S. troops to protect lives and property, followed by a proclamation granting the locals their proclaimed wish for independence from Spain. The operation relied on individuals who, in today's intelligence lexicon, would be labeled "agents provocateur" and who were well supplied with secret funds and used a clandestine communications system to coordinate their schemes. A supposedly spontaneous insurgency against the Spanish did break out, with the rebels declaring independence and asking for assistance from the American government. Madison responded by proclaiming that west Florida was actually already a U.S. possession by dint of its (rather suspect) inclusion with the Louisiana Purchase, and soon the Stars and Stripes flew over Pensacola and Mobile.

Madison followed this land expansion with similar covert tactics (i.e., a spontaneous uprising and call for independence) from pro-U.S. inhabitants in eastern Florida, to acquire that territory before the British could seize it from the steadily weakening Spanish empire. His successors—James Monroe, John Quincy Adams, and Andrew Jackson—all employed elements of covert political action operations in their policies toward Mexico. Monroe maneuvered to reduce British influence with the Mexican regime, and Jackson attempted to induce the Mexicans to sell or cede land north of the Rio Grande to the United States. Bribery, support for underground opposition groups, inflammatory propaganda, the public dissemination of erroneous information (disinformation, in espionage parlance), and secret slush funds were all covert methods set in motion by these presidents. That Jackson was ultimately unsuccessful in gaining any Mexican land does not obviate the fact that he carefully and skillfully employed political action operations to further his overt foreign policy.

In an interesting parallel to a large covert political action program initiated in the 1980s under President Ronald Reagan that used a variety of means to deny sensitive emerging technologies to the Soviet Union, Abraham Lincoln established a clandestine network in Europe to prevent those nations from providing much-needed military supplies to the Confederate States during the Civil War. The complex program began with the collection of raw intelligence, the analysis of which identified individuals and companies secretly trading with the South. Political action operations were then run against the traders to disrupt the production of the war matériel, sabotage the factories, and intercept the matériel en route to the Confederate States. Knowing that the Union navy could not always snare the South's blockade runners, waging a covert interdiction campaign in Europe to prevent war matériel from being loaded on a Confederacy-bound ship in the first place proved an effective and economical way to deny the South vital war-making capabilities.

Prior to the Civil War, American presidents essentially used covert action in general and political action operations in particular to expand the land territory of the nation and protect American lives and commerce from foreign interference. But within two decades of the ending of the American insurrection, and well before the United States became a world military force, presidents began using these covert methodologies to strengthen foreign commercial ties, protect American economic interests, and expand international trade. In the 1880s, the American government became cognizant of the tremendous economic potential of Asia as a source of raw materials and a destination for the export of finished goods. It became the goal of presidents to open these markets to trade and to protect the markets once established. A concomitant objective was to reach agreements with Asian regimes for coaling stations for the U.S. Navy's growing Asiatic fleet. Korea drew the interest of the navy and, hence, of President Chester A. Arthur (not a president one usually associates with an aggressive foreign policy), early in that decade for both a trading partner and a refueling post. But Japan and China had squared off over which was to exercise the dominant political and economic influence over the Korean Peninsula, leaving Korea much like a fish caught between two cats. Arthur relied on covert political activities, particularly the supply of arms and funds to a Korean group interested in upsetting the pro-Chinese regime that held power (with the U.S. involvement remaining under the table), to drive a wedge between Tokyo and Beijing in hopes of creating and then filling a power void. A quick-rising squabble between France and China distracted the latter and provided a fortuitous opening for the American-supported clique, which then moved into power.

Under President Benjamin Harrison, America's annexation of Hawaii, whose natural port at Pearl Harbor was a matter of strategic import for the Asiatic fleet, was the consequence of a political action operation bearing similarities to Madison's grab of west Florida. It likewise involved, in 1893, the clandestine fomenting of a "popular" insurrection that portended bloodshed and justified intervention to protect American diplomatic facilities and citizens. Navy sailors and marines occupied Hawaiian government buildings, and the American ambassador soon thereafter declared the establishment of a provisional—and pro-American—government.

But it was, of course, the Cold War and the creation of the CIA that truly made covert political action a critical component of presidential statecraft. Throughout the Cold War, it was the fundamental objective of the United States to (1) counter Soviet expansionary policies; (2) support pro-West governments that were targets of Soviet subversion; and (3) weaken or undermine foreign governments that had fallen into the Soviet orbit. (Policies of transforming oppressive regimes into democracies had to wait until the presidencies of George H. W. Bush and his son, George W. Bush.) The attraction for American presidents in employing political and economic covert actions against the Russian bear was that it permitted the U.S. government to apply a varying degree of pressure against the Moscow regime, but to do so without generating a clear and direct threat to core Soviet interests that might eventually invite a military response. Because covert action programs used a broad spectrum of capabilities that allowed presidents to calibrate the intensity of the pressure felt or perceived by the Soviet leadership, the interests of the United States were protected and advanced but without backing the Soviets into a corner that might have left them no recourse but war. (Of course, the Soviets were concurrently doing the same things against the United States, using the term "active measures" in place of covert action.)

Although at first rather reluctant to open an intelligence war against the Soviet Union, which had been, after all, America's ally in the recent world war, by 1947 President Harry S. Truman had become convinced that Soviet hostility toward the United States, the Western democracies, and capitalist systems would only increase, ultimately threatening democracies and nations seeking to become democratic. To counter Soviet subversive operations in regions considered vital to U.S. national security, Truman implemented overt policies such as the Truman Doctrine (for Greece and Turkey) in March 1947, and the Marshall

Plan (for the reconstruction of Western Europe) just three months later. But overt programs intended to strengthen democratic political systems and rebuild devastated economies in Europe and the Near East were also judged to be insufficient when considering the scope and depth of Soviet covert machinations to undermine those same countries. Under Truman's personal initiative, his newly established National Security Council (NSC) drew up its first national security directive—an order for the CIA (created concurrently with the NSC by federal statute) to counter Soviet political and economic subversive programs in Italy and France, operations by which the Stalinist regime in Moscow sought to acquire control of those governments through manipulation of legitimate electoral processes.

To be sure, there were precedents from which one could learn. Elections in Eastern European countries following the war found the local communist parties legitimately winning seats in those parliaments, from which party members were then chosen to fill key Cabinet positions in the government. With covert assistance from Moscow, the democratic processes were subverted from within (Czechoslovakia was particularly instructive), resulting in the establishment of oppressive pro-Soviet communist regimes. In France and Italy, Soviet agents were likewise seeking to gain control of those elements of society that are fundamental to democracy—political parties, newspapers, labor unions, publishing houses, student groups, and more—through the provision of nearly unlimited funds and then employ these societal influences as front organizations for Soviet intelligence to use to corrupt the democratic processes.

NSC documents from 1947 and 1948 show that the Truman administration viewed a victory for the French and Italian communist parties as an unacceptable outcome and, should that happen, reached the conclusion that all governments in Western Europe would be menaced. The CIA was given the responsibility of countering the Soviet operations, in part by political action—the provision of secret funding to individual candidates for political office as well as to the multiple political parties. In this, neither the U.S. government nor the CIA had a preferred candidate or party. The funds, millions of dollars, were given liberally to groups, organizations, unions, and politicians across the political spectrum, from the far right to the left of center. It mattered not so much who won, but who had to be defeated. Ultimately, between overt U.S. policies and the covert program, the communists lost at the polls. Still, it terms of the role that political action operations played in the greater scheme of things, it is important to understand that the millions of dollars in covert funding constituted only a small percentage of the monies expended in the overt diplomatic programs meant to strengthen governmental institutions and to rebuild the economies devastated from war. Covert action programs, certainly including political and economic operations, are most effective when supporting well-established overt policies, and the operations in Italy and France are proof of this. The perceived need to secretly fund Italian politicians and parties continued through the administration of Lyndon B. Johnson, ending only in 1967.

Perhaps the most familiar—or notorious—political action operations are those in which the president directs the CIA to oust a foreign government or regime. Again, the idea is to make it appear as though local opposition groups act on their own initiative and through their own resources. Presidents Eisenhower, Kennedy, and Nixon each issued orders to the CIA to do overthrow regimes deemed to be politically too close to the Soviet Union, but with varying degrees of success. Operations to reverse regimes in Iran and Guatemala managed to achieve their objective, but similar efforts in Indonesia, Cuba (after paramilitary operations failed in each), and Chile did not. Kennedy furthered toyed with the idea of ordering political action programs to unseat regimes in Santo Domingo and British Guyana as did Reagan early in his administration with Surinam.

The covert overthrow of a foreign regime by the United States is never as easy as its proponents seem to believe, nor are successes truly positive or unalloyed in the long term. For many intelligence professionals, the overthrow of the Iranian regime of Mohammed Mossadeq in 1953 was a double-edged sword, for the ease with which it seemingly occurred served to mislead future presidents and CIA directors into attempting similar operations with less fortunate results. In the case of Iran, the fact is that the CIA itself did not cause the overthrow of Mossadeq. What the CIA did was to provide, in essence, a push at the margins of an already developed and much larger indigenous political movement unhappy with Mossadeq and his policies. It is unknown whether the anti-Mossadeq forces would have prevailed had the CIA not stepped in at a key moment, but it is beyond doubt that the CIA as an institution did not itself effect the change. Indeed, the operation at first appeared to be an abject failure, and it was only the fortuitous appearance of a popular Iranian general to rally the mobs at a critical moment that brought about the ouster of Mossadeq. It is not an oversimplification to say that the Americans contributed just the right amount of pressure, at just the right moment, with just the right people. Said differently, the operation succeeded mostly (or even only) because of luck.

Yet the lesson the CIA and the Eisenhower (and later Kennedy) administration took away from the Iranian program was that the reversal of hostile regimes was nothing particularly difficult; that American ingenuity and righteousness of purpose were enough to prevail. Interestingly, the one person who realized differently was the man who orchestrated the Iranian program, Kermit Roosevelt. Asked to lead the next such operation, the removal of Guatemalan leader Jacobo Arbenz, barely a year later, Roosevelt declined and left the agency. That the Guatemalan operation, a blend of paramilitary, political action, and propaganda operations went well further solidified the belief in the Washington circle that the United States could replace governments at will and without fear of failure.

After the Guatemalan program, the Eisenhower administration took aim at the Indonesian government of Sukarno, who announced his intentions of allowing Communist Party members to hold positions in his Cabinet. Eisenhower, duly alarmed at the prospect of a pro-Soviet regime in that county, authorized a robust covert action program, including operations aimed at manipulating the political and economic processes, to remove Sukarno from power. This effort failed miserably, with the consequence that Sukarno's hold on power was stronger. An astute, objective student analyzing this program might have reached the conclusion that maybe, just maybe, political action operations to change an entrenched regime might not be as easy nor as useful as thought. But with the apparent successes of Iran and Guatemala in the background, the lessons of Indonesia were lost.

It is instructive to note that the definition of *success* as applied to a political action program, especially one in which the change of a regime through subversive measures is the objective, can be elusive. Eisenhower, Kennedy, and Nixon each believed that success constituted the replacement of a pro-Soviet or potentially pro-Soviet government with a right-wing, pro-American regime. And in the short term, that was perhaps so. But over the longer run, arguably more harm was done. The hapless Mossadeq was replaced by a monarchy that grew more oppressive and dictatorial over the years, itself eventually overthrown by indigenous elements, transforming America's most important ally in the Middle East into radical Islamic fundamentalist state that has now waged a war of terrorism against America for a quarter century. Although communist forces were thwarted in Guatemala in 1954, the resulting oppressive right-wing military dictatorship murdered hundreds of thousand of its own citizens over the next forty years, leaving an impoverished nation in its stead.

Chile was the target of covert electoral manipulations beginning with Kennedy, who sought to forestall socialist or communist regimes by directing the provision of secret funds to several Chilean political parties and, especially to one presidential candidate, Eduardo Frei. The program continued through President Nixon, who at one time toyed with instigating a military coup to prevent the election of socialist Salvador Allende. When this proved unfeasible and Allende was elected, Nixon turned his efforts toward destabilizing the new regime. Included in his bag of tricks were monies given to political parties and candidates, payments to various mass media outlets to produce political advertisements or messages, and funds to social and professional organizations—labor unions, student groups, women's clubs, and business and civic associations. In the end, the military acted unilaterally, instigating a coup that left Allende dead and the government in the hands of an oppressive right-wing military cabal that endured for two decades.

But not all political action programs are failures. The CIA managed a number of covert political action operations against the Soviet Union, some for nearly the length of the Cold War. These programs picked up strength and importance during the administration of Jimmy Carter, including operations that fostered the printing and underground distribution within the Soviet Union of prohibited political tracts, the writings of banned Russian authors like Aleksandr Solzhenitsyn and Boris Pasternak, and religious works (Bibles and Korans). Along with the infiltration of printed materials, these political action operations provided, through secret channels, desktop publishing equipment to Soviet dissidents to print and disseminate their writings, known as *samizdat*, within the Soviet Union. Additionally, operations funded Soviet exiles in Western Europe, enabling them to write and publish books, journals, and monographs that, though intended primarily for distribution within émigré circles, likewise found their way clandestinely with to readers inside the Soviet Union. An adjunct initiative known as the Nationalities Program, funded the printing and distribution of journals and pamphlets directed towards the non-Russian ethnic minorities in the Soviet Union, keeping alive their history, culture, and language at a time when the Soviet government was attempting to suppress them. Other CIA political action programs in Europe funded human rights and prodemocracy organizations as part of a larger effort to counter anti-Western Soviet propaganda. These programs and more were continued and expanded during the administration of Ronald Reagan, effectively and inexpensively applying pressures on the Soviet government that contributed to the ultimate demise of the Soviet Union.

But perhaps the most successful political action program ever was a broad-based effort to undermine the legitimacy of the Polish military government that came to power in 1980 while concurrently supporting the independence movement headed by Polish labor union Solidarity. If a critical attribute of any covert action program is that it would, if exposed, meet with the approval of the American public, this was one such program. Although much of the program remains classified, despite its overwhelming success, elements of it have come into the public eye.[1]

As the end of the Carter administration drew near, it was faced with the Soviet Union pressuring the Polish government to outlaw Solidarity and its supporters, as well as threatening to move its military across the border if the Polish power structure failed to contain the growing influence of the union. In response, Carter directed his National Security Advisor, Zbigniew Brzezinski, to advise the Vatican that the United States had clandestine intelligence resources available to aid Solidarity. Moreover, with European governments reluctant to openly confront the Soviet Union over its aggression, Brzezinski bluntly asked Pope John Paul II if he would consent to joining with the United States to isolate economically, culturally, and politically the Soviets if they openly intervened in Poland. The Pope would and did.

The Reagan administration thus inherited an expanding covert political action program that first deterred a Soviet military intervention in Poland (similar to the Soviet invasions of Hungary in 1956 and Czechoslovakia in 1968) and then enabled Solidarity and other underground organizations to survive and resist the martial law government of Gen. Wojciech Jaruzelski. But the CIA's covert operations did not end with just Poland: Reagan believed that if Poland was able to throw off the communist system and emerge as a free and democratic nation, the other five Eastern European countries would follow. The Polish program thus expanded into a worldwide confrontation of the legitimacy of the communist governments of Eastern Europe and the Soviet Union itself. Poland held its first free elections in 1989, and within two years not only were Eastern European countries free of Soviet domination, but the Soviet Union as a political system disappeared into the dustbin of history. Of course, Eastern Europe did not gain its independence nor did the Soviet Union collapse solely because of the covert action operations initiated by the Reagan administration, but these missions did fulfill their intended goal and then some, supporting a vast array of overt United States political, economic, and military policies that collectively made it impossible for Moscow to continue the Cold War.

This abbreviated introduction to covert political action programs operations is meant neither to convince the skeptical of their efficacy nor to provide support to those who see them as a solution to difficult or seemingly insoluble foreign policy issues.[2] Truman and Eisenhower employed political action operations against the Soviet threat with mixed results. Truman's use of covert action in Italy and France must be judged as highly successful, whereas the long-term consequences of the Iran and Guatemalan operations, as well as the clear failure of the Indonesian venture, place into question the wisdom of Eisenhower's decisions to use covert methods against those regimes. Kennedy's efforts in influencing the Chilean elections was successful only in the short term, with a socialist government eventually coming to power despite his efforts, as well as Johnson's, and Nixon's use of multiple political action operations to forestall it. Similarly, Kennedy's intense efforts to overthrow the Cuban regime of Fidel Castro were not only unmitigated failures but might well have placed his administration in serious jeopardy, had the operations become public knowledge during his tenure in office. Unrecognized by many historians, Carter's reliance on covert programs, political action especially, was more successful than not, especially in that he laid the foundation for many of Reagan's programs against the Soviet Union directly and in countering Soviet interventions in places like Afghanistan and Central America.

Whether or not political action programs are an appropriate tool for the president in implementing foreign policies depends on a number of factors, not the least of which is the ability of the president and the national security team to recognize and accept the limits of any covert action program. Certainly it should be clear that these political action operations are not suitable for crisis resolution; rather, they are most wisely employed in consonance with a thoughtfully developed, comprehensive, foreign policy with well-defined objectives implemented in a methodical manner. Successful foreign policies are never the responsibility of just one agency of government, and certainly not intelligence agencies. But covert actions that influence the political or economic systems of target audiences may, when wisely employed, serve a president and the country well.

## NOTES

The author thanks Matthew Easterwood, presently a student at Stetson Law School, for his research assistance with this chapter.

1. Robert M. Gates, a former director of the CIA, has provided some detail in his memoir, *From the Shadows: The Ultimate Insider's Story of Five Presidents and How*

*They Won the Cold War* (New York: Simon & Schuster,1996), which was cleared for publication by the CIA. Other partial accounts have appeared in Zbigniew Brzezinski, *Power and Principle: Memoirs of a National Security Advisor 1977–1981* (New York: Farrar, Straus & Giroux, 1985); and Carl Bernstein and Marco Politi, *His Holiness, John Paul II and the Hidden History of Our Time* (New York: Doubleday, 1996), on which the CIA will not comment. This is unfortunate in that the story is generally now in the public domain, but also at a time when the CIA and the intelligence community are under serious attack, a story that is clearly a great success would only redound to the benefit of the CIA.

2. Mention of more recent covert programs, including political and economic action operations, which might provide more enlightenment for this chapter, is precluded by continuing classification of programs after the Reagan era and the CIA's requirement that this author clear his writings with them prior to publication.

# 7

# COVERT ACTION AND THE PENTAGON

JENNIFER D. KIBBE

THE TERRORIST ATTACKS ON SEPTEMBER 11, 2001, brought about a number of changes in the U.S. national security outlook, not the least of which was a renewed willingness to consider covert action as a policy option. During this same period, the single most significant change in the military services has been the expansion (in both size and responsibility) of its special operations forces. The concurrence of these two trends has led to a blurring of the distinction of whether military units are conducting covert operations and has raised questions about congressional oversight. The *Quadrennial Defense Review* issued by the Pentagon in February 2006 stated unequivocally that special operations forces would be leading the war on terror, making it that much more important to understand the issues raised by potential military involvement in covert action.

Covert action is defined in U.S. law as activity that is meant "to influence political, economic, or military conditions abroad, where it is intended that the role of the United States Government will not be apparent or acknowledged publicly."[1] Covert actions are thus legally distinct from clandestine missions: "clandestine" refers to the tactical secrecy of the operation itself, and "covert" refers to the secrecy of its sponsor. Although most often associated with the assassination of leaders or the overthrow of a government, the category of covert action can include a wide range of activity, from propaganda and disinformation to political influence operations, training and support for foreign military forces, to paramilitary operations. Historically, the Central Intelligence Agency (CIA) has been the main agent of U.S. covert action, but the growth of special operations forces over the past two decades and their ability to conduct direct action operations has raised new questions in the debate over congressional versus executive control of covert action.

## EVOLUTION OF SOCOM

The military's unconventional warfare operations, whether covert or clandestine, are part of the U.S. Special Operations Command (SOCOM), a relatively new command that has now been designated as the leader in the U.S. war against terrorism. Although their roots can be traced to various World War II forces, including the Office of Strategic Services (OSS), air commandos, Scouts, and Raiders, American special operations forces were first really built up in Vietnam as a result of President Kennedy's interest in using the Green Berets to conduct unconventional warfare. However, these forces were somewhat resented by the regular troops and officers who felt that the armed forces' conventional training and approach to warfare had always been good enough before and that there was no need to introduce any sort of "special" forces. Thus, when the end of the war in Vietnam led to severe budget cuts, every one of the armed services drastically cut its special operations units.

The event that caused the pendulum to swing back the other way was the failed mission to rescue the American hostages in Iran in 1980. Because the United States had no standing counterterrorist task force, the necessary personnel and equipment were drawn from the various services, leaving a significant gap in overall coordination. When two aircraft collided in the desert outside Tehran, eight members of the operation died and the rest were forced to turn back without attempting to rescue the hostages, leaving behind three intact helicopters to boot. Within weeks, a commission had been formed to review the failed operation and determine how to improve the United States' ability to run such operations in the future. The Holloway Commission, named for its chair, Chief of Naval Operations Adm. James Holloway, emphasized the uncoordinated nature of U.S. special operations, as well as the lack of any independent review of the operational plans and the poor intelligence support. The commission's recommendation for the creation of a Counterterrorist Joint Task Force was adopted and implemented over the next several years.

The early 1980s saw increased funding for special operations forces, an expansion in personnel and the creation of the Joint Special Operations Command (JSOC, pronounced "jay sock"), whose goal was to provide increased coordination. The first real operational test of the improvements was Operation Urgent Fury, the 1983 invasion of Grenada. Special operations forces, including Navy SEALs, Army Rangers, and members of Delta Force, were directly involved in seven of the operation's eight targets, of which only two were fully successful. Three of the operations were costly failures, with special operations forces incurring heavy casualties as a result of poor planning, coordination, and intelligence.

The failures at Grenada fueled a new round of calls for reform, and not just of special operations forces. This time, however, those interested in reform included some on Capitol Hill. This round of investigations eventually resulted in the Department of Defense Reorganization Act of 1986, also known as the

Goldwater-Nichols Act, which substantially strengthened the power of the chairman of the Joint Chiefs of Staff and the unified combatant commanders (the commanders of the various regional theaters). The element of the Goldwater-Nichols Act that most affected special operations, though, was the subsequent Nunn-Cohen amendment that, most importantly, established SOCOM. Although SOCOM was established as a supporting command, meaning that it could not plan or execute its own independent operations and could only operate in support of other commands' operations, the new legislation still represented a significant step forward in the coordination and enhancement of special operations forces. The Nunn-Cohen amendment also specifically laid out in law, for the first time, the types of operations that would be included under the rubric of special operations: "Direct action, strategic reconnaissance, unconventional warfare, foreign internal defense, civil affairs, psychological operations, counterterrorism, humanitarian assistance, theater search and rescue, [and] such other activities as may be specified by the Secretary of Defense."

In the four major conflicts involving the United States since Grenada (the invasion of Panama, the Gulf War, the Afghanistan war, and the Iraq war), special operations forces have proven to be increasingly effective and useful.

## SPECIAL OPERATIONS FORCES TODAY

SOCOM is comprised of both units that conduct overt or "white" operations, and those that conduct "black" operations, including both covert and clandestine missions. Those involved in white special operations include Army Special Forces (Green Berets), most Ranger units, most of the Navy SEALs, and numerous aviation, civil affairs, and psychological operations units. These white special operators are largely involved in training selected foreign forces in counterterror, counterinsurgency, and counternarcotics tactics; helping with various civil government projects; and disseminating information to foreign audiences through the mass media. The black operators fall under JSOC, which commands the elite units of each service's special operations forces, including Special Forces Operational Detachment—Delta (Delta Force), Naval Special Warfare Development Group (DEVGRU, or SEAL Team 6), the Air Force's 24th Special Tactics Squadron, the Army's 160th Special Operations Aviation Regiment and 75th Ranger Regiment, and a highly classified Intelligence Support Activity team (known as ISA, or more recently as Gray Fox, although its name changes frequently). These units (also known as special mission units) specialize in direct action operations such as hunting terrorists and rescuing hostages. Although it is generally understood that these units exist, the Pentagon does not officially acknowledge them.

From the beginning of his term, one of Secretary of Defense Donald Rumsfeld's chief priorities has been to transform the military from a large conventional force built to face another superpower into a leaner, more flexible, and agile force capable of fighting the less conventional conflicts that have dominated the post–Cold War period. Though his desire to expand special operations was part of that original overall goal, it received a huge boost when at the beginning of the war in Afghanistan, the military's special operations units had to rely on CIA operatives to establish links to the Northern Alliance fighters. By all accounts, Rumsfeld was incensed and was determined to build up his special operations capabilities to eliminate any future dependence on the CIA.

That determination has gradually led to significant increases in funding, personnel, and authority for special operations forces. The FY 2007 defense budget called for special operations funding to grow to $5.1 billion, approximately $1 billion more than the previous year and double the amount allocated to them in 2001. The 2006 *Quadrennial Defense Review*, the Pentagon's main planning document for the next four years, aimed to increase special operations troops, which numbered about 50,000 at the beginning of 2006, by 14,000 through 2011, at a cost of nearly $28 billion. (Note that of the 50,000 current special operations forces, only approximately 10,000–13,000 are "trigger-pullers," i.e., those in the field involved in operations. The remainder are support and administrative staff.)

Beyond the actual numbers, Rumsfeld has also effected several substantive changes in the way SOCOM is run. First, he replaced those leaders of SOCOM who were, in his estimation, too cautious about the command assuming a more aggressive role in the war on terror. He also significantly increased SOCOM's authority by changing it from a supporting to a supported command, meaning that it could now plan and execute its own missions (if authorized by the secretary and, if necessary, the president). This change gave SOCOM a considerable amount of increased flexibility, because it meant the chain of command now went directly from SOCOM to the secretary, without having to go through a regional unified command (Southern Command, for example). This change could also be seen as giving the secretary increased control over special operations. Cutting out the regional commands, however, also presents an increased risk that special operations units may plan missions without taking sufficient account of possible regional repercussions.

In March 2004, after an intensive bureaucratic struggle, Rumsfeld was successful in his campaign to install SOCOM as the leader of the war on terror, ahead of the conventional forces whose leaders he perceived as too tentative. President Bush signed the new Unified Command Plan 2004, which designated SOCOM as the "lead combatant commander for planning, synchronizing, and as directed, executing global operations" in the war on terror (although it did leave the regional commanders in charge of counterterrorism operations in their own theaters).

An amendment to the defense authorization bill in October 2004 represented a further step along SOCOM's road to independence as Congress granted its forces the authority, for the first time, to spend money to pay informants, recruit foreign paramilitary fighters, and purchase equipment or other items from foreigners. Previously, only the CIA had been authorized to disburse such funds, meaning that special operations forces had to rely on the CIA to provide the funds for various operations. One other significant step in the special operations forces' rise to prominence came in January 2006 when JSOC's headquarters was raised from a two-star to a three-star command, thus giving its chief more authority and influence in dealing with other military officers.

There is little doubt that Rumsfeld's vision for SOCOM is a long-term one. Indeed, in presenting the 2006 *Quadrennial Defense Review* to the press in February 2006, Rumsfeld described its emphasis on developing special operations forces as a necessary component of U.S. preparation for what he called the "long war" ahead against extremism. The review calls not only for significant increases in forces but also for increased training of conventional troops in "irregular" operations, such as counterinsurgency and stabilization operations, thus freeing up special forces operators for "more demanding and specialized tasks, especially long-duration, indirect and clandestine operations in politically sensitive environments and denied areas." In addition, the document states that for direct action, special operations forces "will possess an expanded organic ability to locate, tag and track dangerous individuals and other high-value targets globally."[2]

Also in February 2006, Gen. Peter Pace, Chairman of the Joint Chiefs of Staff, reportedly signed a new, classified counterterrorism strategy that orders the Defense Department to undertake a broad campaign to find and attack or neutralize terrorist leaders, their havens, financial networks, methods of communication, and ability to travel. According to the *New York Times*, the strategy document specifies that the effort to defeat terrorism requires "continuous military operations to develop the situation and generate the intelligence that allows us to attack global terrorist organizations."[3]

Another major facet of SOCOM's burgeoning role is its wide geographic scope. In the five years since 9/11, special forces operations have been reported in the Philippines, Malaysia, Georgia, Colombia, Indonesia, Pakistan, Yemen, Algeria, Morocco, Mauritania, Niger, Mali, Chad, Nigeria, and Jordan. Although most of the reported operations are of the white variety, usually involving counterinsurgency and counterterrorism training of indigenous forces, there is little doubt that with the Pentagon's stated goal of hunting down terrorists, black special operators are or will be active in many of those same countries.

SOCOM's growth in size, scope, and influence raises the questions of whether it is conducting any covert operations and of the degree and adequacy of congressional oversight of its activities.

## LEGAL REQUIREMENTS

Congress first tried to assert control over covert action in the mid-1970s in reaction to revelations of U.S. involvement in the coup against Salvador Allende in Chile and assassination attempts against Fidel Castro. The Church Committee, named for Sen. Frank Church (D-ID), chair of the Senate Select Committee to Study Governmental Operations with Respect to Intelligence Activities, conducted an investigation that led to the establishment of permanent intelligence committees in both the House and the Senate. The Iran-*contra* scandal in the Reagan administration, however, highlighted important gaps in the new congressional oversight requirements. In response, Congress adopted more stringent provisions in the 1991 Intelligence Authorization Act, which is still the governing legislation on congressional oversight requirements. The act codified two requirements for any covert action. First, there must be a written presidential finding stating that the action is important to U.S. national security, which cannot be issued retroactively. Second, the administration must notify the intelligence committees of the action as soon as possible after the finding has been issued and before the initiation of the operation, unless "extraordinary circumstances" exist, in which case the president must fully inform the committees "in a timely fashion."[4]

The other significant feature of the 1991 Intelligence Authorization Act is that in response to the Reagan administration's use of the National Security Council to conduct covert action in connection with Iran-*contra*, it expressly applied the requirements to "any department, agency, or entity of the United States Government." In other words, Congress no longer assumed that only the CIA could or would conduct covert operations. The law also included, however, a few designated exceptions to the definition of covert action. Under the most significant one, "traditional ... military activities or routine support to such activities" are deemed not to be covert action and thus do not require a presidential finding or congressional notification. Although the act itself does not define "traditional military activities," the conference committee report presenting the legislative history states that the phrase is meant to include actions preceding and related to hostilities that are anticipated to involve (conventional) U.S. military forces or where such hostilities are ongoing, whether U.S. involvement in the action is made public or not, as well as any military action where the U.S. role is apparent or to be acknowledged publicly.[5]

The interpretation of the "traditional military activities" exception has caused considerable controversy as the Bush administration relies increasingly on special operations forces in the war on terror. Covert operations conducted by special operations forces during wartime clearly do not require a presidential finding and congressional notification. The definition leaves a gray area, however, around the interpretation of the word *anticipated*. It is most commonly thought of in the literal sense of "preparing the battle space" and, in fact, the conference committee report of the 1991 law defines "anticipated" hostilities as those for which operational planning has been approved. Defense Department officials, however, have explained that under the Pentagon's interpretation, the language could refer to events taking place "years in advance" of any involvement of U.S. military forces. Critics contend that the Bush administration has been eager to shift more covert activity from the CIA to the military precisely because they see it as giving them more of a free rein.

But the Pentagon's interpretation of *anticipated* raises an obvious and important question: In prosecuting the war on terrorism, when special operations forces conduct an unacknowledged operation in a country where U.S. troops are not already present, how can they prove that it is in anticipation of involvement of the regular armed forces later on, and thus not a covert action that requires a presidential finding and congressional notification (particularly if it is "years in advance")?

An even more difficult question is, who will ask them to prove it? Legally, the ultimate arbiters of what does and does not constitute covert action would be the House and Senate intelligence committees, which exert a type of veto through their control of the intelligence authorization process. However, there are several problems with that argument. First, if it is a special operations mission, the funding would be controlled by the House and Senate Armed Services Committees, creating a crucial split between the authority to determine whether it is a covert action and budgetary control. Second, the Armed Services Committees have ultimate control over the intelligence authorization process in any case, because they must sign off on intelligence authorization bills before they go to the full House and Senate for a vote. As one Senate Armed Services Committee staffer described the relationship, "We prevail because they're subordinate to us." Finally, the fact of the matter is that congressional committees only know about those operations that the administration tells them about. They cannot ask questions about operations they do not know about.

Beyond the technicalities of arguing the meaning of the word *anticipated*, the Bush administration has made an even broader claim regarding its use of the military to conduct what would be called covert action if it were conducted by the CIA. Having defined the broad post-9/11 strategic situation as a "war on terror," administration officials argue that anything the government does to prosecute the fight against terrorism is part of a "war" and thus, legitimately a "traditional military activity." A variant of this argument stems from Senate Joint Resolution 23, the authorization to use force granted by the Congress in response to the September 11 attacks. That resolution authorizes the president "to use all necessary and appropriate force against those nations, organizations, or persons he determines planned, authorized, committed, or aided the terrorist attacks that occurred on September 11, 2001, or harbored such organizations or persons, in order to prevent any future acts of international terrorism against the United States by such nations, organizations or persons." Thus, according to some legal experts, the resolution grants the president virtually unlimited authority, as long as he "determines" that a particular target has some connection to Al Qaeda.

Finally, some Pentagon lawyers have interpreted the post-9/11 landscape even more broadly. Bush does not even need the resolution's authority, they contend; because of the attacks, anything he does in the fight against terrorism can be seen as a legitimate act of self-defense, and thus a "traditional military activity."

## "SPECIAL ACTIVITIES"

Another aspect of the potentially increasing intersection of covert action and special operations forces, and its implications for congressional oversight, concerns whether the Pentagon is actually conducting covert operations but calling them something else. The Department of Defense has defined a category of so-called special activities with four characteristics. These are activities (1) that are conducted abroad; (2) in which the U.S. role is not apparent or acknowledged; (3) that do not include the collection or production of intelligence; and (4) that are not diplomatic activities. It is difficult to obtain precise information about such special activities, but they are conducted under some presidential authority, such as executive orders, and do entail some degree of congressional notification, although it is impossible to know how many and which members that includes. What is clear is that they are not conducted under the covert action requirements of the law and do not involve notification of whole committees, whether intelligence or armed services. The relevant question is, whatever they are called, are these operations subject to effective oversight?

Another overlapping category that includes unacknowledged operations is that of special access programs, or SAPs. SAPs, established by Executive Order 12958, are sensitive programs that impose "need-to-know and access controls beyond those normally provided for access to confidential, secret, or top secret information." This "beyond top secret" designation is to be established only on an agency head's determination that (1) the vulnerability of or threat to specific information is exceptional, and (2) the normal criteria for determining eligibility for access are not deemed sufficient to protect the information.

The standard reporting requirement for SAPs is that the congressional defense committees be given thirty days' notice before the program is initiated. However, the Bush administration has effectively nullified this requirement since January 2002. In various executive orders and presidential signing statements accompanying defense legislation, Bush has included language claiming that the Supreme Court "has stated that the President's authority to classify and control access to information bearing on national security flows from the Constitution and does not depend upon a legislative grant of authority." As a result, he states that although in most situations the thirty-day advance notice can be provided, "as a matter of comity, situations may arise, especially in wartime, in which the President must promptly establish special access controls on classified national security information under his constitutional grants of the executive power and authority as Commander in Chief of the Armed Forces." The statements then make plain that the executive branch will interpret the reporting requirements "in a manner consistent with the constitutional authority of the President."

There are three categories of special access programs: (1) acknowledged programs, which are unclassified; (2) unacknowledged programs, which are classified but reported to Congress in the same form as acknowledged SAPs; and (3) waived programs, where the classifying agency head waives the standard reporting requirement. Waived SAPs are only orally briefed to the so-called Gang of Eight, that is, the chair and ranking (minority) members of both the Senate and House intelligence (or Armed Services) committees, and the House and Senate Majority and Minority Leaders. The controversial program involving the National Security Agency (NSA)'s program of warrantless domestic surveillance that surfaced in late 2005 was one such waived SAP, apparently authorized by the CIA.

Army documents that came to light in early 2006 as a result of the ongoing Freedom of Information Act lawsuit brought by the American Civil Liberties Union against the Defense Department regarding the abuses at Abu Ghraib prison highlight the risks involved in special operations forces being both involved in the war on terror and covered by SAPs. These documents confirm that a special operations unit known as Task Force 6-26 (also known as Task Force Omaha) has been implicated in numerous detainee abuse incidents in Iraq. Moreover, one army file details how—because the unit was part of a SAP—an investigator was unable to continue an investigation into claims that a detainee captured by Task Force 6-26 in Tikrit, Iraq, was stripped, humiliated, and physically abused until he passed out.

There exists yet another process that provides for the protection of classified information. Known as Alternative or Compensatory Control Measures (ACCMs), these are a way of applying "need-to-know" restrictions on information to, in essence, compartmentalize a program. According to a Navy directive, ACCMs are to be used in situations where need-to-know restrictions are deemed necessary but SAP controls are not warranted. These measures are distinct from SAPs in that although they provide the same internal security standards, they do not need the formal approval of the agency head and they do not have to be reported to Congress. Since September 11, hundreds of ACCMs have been established to compartmentalize information regarding a range of sensitive activities, from special operations in specific countries to intelligence collection and processing programs to various war planning contingencies.

One indication of the potential for abuse of ACCMs came in an internal Navy audit conducted in 2005. The audit reportedly found that secrecy was being used to restrict congressional, Defense Department, and internal access to potentially controversial or even illegal activities. As a result of the audit's findings, the Navy's new directive on ACCMs states, "The use of ACCM measures shall not preclude, nor unnecessarily impede, Congressional, Office of the Secretary of Defense, or other appropriate oversight of programs, command functions, or operations."

There have been indications that some members of Congress are becoming uncomfortable with the Pentagon's increasing independence in the area of unacknowledged operations. In June 2005, the House Permanent Select Committee on Intelligence's report on the 2006 Intelligence Authorization Act stated the committee's belief "that it does not have full visibility over some defense intelligence programs" that fall outside of specific budget categories. Speaking to the press, Representative Peter Hoekstra (R-MI), the chair of the House committee, expressed his concern that the Pentagon was trying to hide activities such as information operations programs, including electronic warfare, psychological operations, and counterpropaganda programs from both the newly created Director of National Intelligence and Congress.

Periodically, information about some previously unknown program will reach the public eye, and a few members of Congress will express their concern about whether the Pentagon is evading oversight restrictions. They often issue calls for hearings, which may or may not be held. Momentum for developing a more robust congressional oversight role of special operations, however, tends to be derailed by a combination of factors. Often, the Pentagon sends representatives to Capitol Hill for either closed-door briefings or closed hearings in which they explain how they are not violating the covert action restrictions because, by their own definition, they do not indulge in covert action (unless an individual operative is on assignment to the CIA). Rather, they explain, they are conducting special activities and they have complied with the relevant notification requirements (as interpreted by the administration).

Another factor working against congressional efforts for a larger role is the underlying antagonism between the intelligence and defense committees, and their respective sense of ownership of their particular issues. The concerns raised by today's special operations invariably involve both committees and will not be addressed adequately until this fundamental issue of turf sharing is resolved. Moreover, although members on both sides of the aisle have voiced concern, it has more frequently been expressed by the Democratic minority, which of course opens it up to partisan debate and power struggles, struggles the minority inevitably loses. Finally, members' motivation to increase their oversight role tends to wither in the face of Congress's traditional reluctance to go up against the Pentagon in a time of war.

## ISSUES BEYOND CONGRESS

Another controversy regarding the expansion of special operations forces into the realm traditionally occupied by the CIA's covert operators involves the question of who is better suited to conduct such operations, whatever they are called. Pentagon officials contend that the CIA is not responsive enough to the military's needs, that it is too risk-averse, and that it is simply too small to meet the global terrorist challenge. The CIA has approximately 700–800 covert operators, compared to the roughly 10,000–13,000 special operations forces. On the other hand, their relative sizes are not as unbalanced as these numbers seem to indicate. Of that total, no more than 2,000 are JSOC black operators, that is, directly comparable to CIA operatives. Moreover, according to many analysts, the difference in size of the overall organizations is a significant advantage for CIA operators. Having much less bureaucracy to deal with, they can do things faster, cheaper, and with more flexibility than special operations forces—the main reason, the CIA's advocates contend, that the agency was able to have men on the ground at the beginning of the Afghanistan war quicker than the military. Even though this has clearly been one of the Pentagon's priorities in enacting its SOCOM reforms, most analysts still believe that the CIA continues to retain an advantage in speed and flexibility.

The CIA also has the advantage of experience: It has been conducting this type of operation for a long time and thus has case officers stationed at embassies throughout the world who have built up an extensive network of contacts that the military simply does not have. In addition, conducting operations where the role of the United States is unacknowledged means, by definition, operating out of uniform. If captured, therefore, a special operations soldier is in an inherently different position than a conventional one. Whereas the latter is covered by international legal mechanisms such as the Geneva Conventions, which govern the conduct of war and the treatment of prisoners, a special operations soldier will have no such recourse. People who join the CIA's operations division are aware of and accept the risk that if captured, they will essentially be completely on their own and that their country will not acknowledge them. Soldiers, however, join with a different set of expectations. They generally assume that if they fight for and defend their country, Washington will do its best to protect them if they are captured. Although many special operations soldiers knowingly accept that risk, analysts point out that it is a dangerously slippery slope. Once some contingent of U.S. military personnel is left without protection, they argue, that endangers the protection of all military personnel serving abroad and could damage troop morale as well.

Many CIA and JSOC operators oppose the Pentagon's emphasis on moving special operations forces into the unacknowledged realm for precisely these reasons. There was, for instance, considerable opposition among special operations forces themselves to the 9/11 Commission's recommendation of moving all paramilitary responsibilities to SOCOM. Furthermore, these critics argue, JSOC's direct action units do not have the training for covert action operations, and if they do undertake the training required, that will detract from their readiness for their traditional, highly specialized missions, such as hostage rescue, close-quarters combat, and dealing with weapons of mass destruction. However, though there are other personnel capable of conducting covert action (i.e., in the CIA), if special operations forces are distracted from their traditional missions, there is no one else who can take their place, leaving the United States vulnerable in certain situations.

Critics of the Pentagon have also raised the concern that the military is running its own unacknowledged operations without notifying the "country team" (the CIA station chief and the ambassador) in the relevant location. Not only would this run the risk of embarrassing the United States diplomatically, but if the CIA were conducting an operation in the same area and the operators were unknown to each other, they could conceivably perceive each other as the enemy, a situation known as "conflication." In response to stories about such situations in the press in 2005, some members of Congress asked for an explanation from the

Pentagon. Defense Department officials testified that they had never conducted an operation without first notifying the country team, which allayed congressional concern. In addition, the Pentagon and CIA had various discussions regarding how to coordinate their operations better to avoid any risk of confliction.

Another question revolves around the actual difficulties in expanding special operations forces, particularly black operators. The Pentagon has called for a significant increase in special operations soldiers by 2011. However, the whole point of special operations forces is that they are the best of the best and are put through much more rigorous and thorough training than conventional soldiers. Many analysts have questioned SOCOM's ability to produce that many more operators, particularly when its training infrastructure is already under stress as a result of increased training loads ever since September 11. The command has revamped some of its training to make it more efficient and get more done in less time, but the fact remains that the high level of training for special operations requires a considerable amount of time, and many question whether the Pentagon's push for increased numbers will result in compromising the quality of the resulting forces.

One final issue that arises in weighing the differences between unacknowledged operations conducted by the CIA and by special forces stems from the differences in mission planning procedures between the two organizations. Traditionally, CIA covert operations are developed by an operational planning group and then subjected to several levels of approval within the Agency. After receiving the CIA's approval, the proposal is then reviewed by the deputies' committee at the National Security Council, and possibly by the principals themselves, before being passed on to the president. Military operational planning, however, is conducted quite differently. Because its primary mission is combat, the military has full authority to make its own operational decisions with no input from outside agencies. A military black operation, therefore, is planned completely within the Pentagon and approved by the secretary of defense. This insulated decision-making system raises obvious risks in a situation where special operations forces are conducting unacknowledged operations in a wide range of countries with which the U.S. has a variety of relationships.

## COMMISSION RECOMMENDATIONS

In its final report, the 9/11 Commission stepped squarely into the debate over who is actually better suited to be leading the covert battle against terrorism. The commission recommended, "Lead responsibility for directing and executing paramilitary operations, whether clandestine or covert, should shift to the Defense Department. There it should be consolidated with the capabilities for training, direction, and execution of such operations already being developed in the Special Operations Command."[6] In response, President Bush asked the Pentagon and the CIA to study the commission's conclusion and come up with a joint recommendation. Although many assumed that because of the Pentagon's political muscle and Rumsfeld's expressed goals, it was a foregone conclusion that the Pentagon-CIA study would agree with the commission's recommendation; in fact they ended up rejecting it, as did the President.

When the Commission on the Intelligence Capabilities of the United States Regarding Weapons of Mass Destruction (Silberman-Robb Commission, after its chairs, Judge Laurence Silberman and former Senator Charles Robb) issued its recommendations in mid-2005, it reportedly included a classified recommendation that also would have given the Pentagon greater authority to conduct covert action. Once again, though, the White House rejected the recommendation. While this would seem to run counter to the Pentagon's moves to expand special operations in the years since 9/11, in the context of the definitional issues just explained, it appears likely that in fact the Pentagon does not want more control of covert action. It has the greatest freedom of action in the present system, whereby the CIA conducts covert action per se and is thus subject to more formal congressional oversight, whereas the Pentagon can continue conducting its special activities, SAPs and ACCMs, with minimal, sometimes nonexistent, oversight.

## CONCLUSION

The question of the military's involvement in unacknowledged operations is shaped by four main factors. First is the Pentagon's broad vision of SOCOM's future role in the "long war" against terrorism. Second is the geographic expansion of special operations forces, in terms of the number of different countries in which both black and white operators are present. A third facet of the issue is the Pentagon's definition of unacknowledged operations as special activities, with more lenient congressional notification requirements than the covert action conducted by the CIA. In addition, the military has the special categories of SAPs and ACCMs that restrict information even further. Finally, there are the indications that some past SAPs have led to highly controversial policies, including renditions (the practice of seizing suspects in one country and delivering them into custody in another country), covert media influence operations in Iraq and Afghanistan, and the direct evidence of the involvement of Task Force 6-26 in interrogations at Abu Ghraib. The military's role in unacknowledged operations is an increasingly complex issue and it remains to be seen how Congress will serve the twin goals of protecting the United States from terrorism and ensuring that there is sufficient accountability to the public.

## NOTES

1. 50 U.S.C. § 413(b)(e).

2. *Quadrennial Defense Review Report*, United States Department of Defense, 6 February 2006. Available at http://www.defenselink.mil/qdr/report/Report20060203.pdf

#search=%222006%20quadrennial%20defense%20review%22 (last accessed 24 August 2006).

3. Thom Shanker, "Pentagon Hones Its Strategy Against Terrorism," *New York Times* (February 5, 2006), p. 16.

4. 50 U.S.C. § 413(b)(e).

5. H.R. Conf. Rep. No. 166, 102nd Congress, 1st sess.; reprinted in *Congressional Record* 137, no. 115, H5904-06 (July 25, 1991), pp. 5905–6.

6. *The 9/11 Commission Report: Final Report of the National Commission on Terrorist Attacks Upon the United States* (New York: W. W. Norton, 2004), p. 415.


## BIBLIOGRAPHY

Cogan, Charles, "Hunters not Gatherers: Intelligence in the Twenty-First Century," *Intelligence and National Security* 19 (2004), pp. 304–21.
Fisher, Louis, *Presidential War Power* (Lawrence: University Press of Kansas, 1995).
Hammond, Jamie. "Special Operations Forces: Relevant, Ready and Precise," *Canadian Military Journal* (Autumn 2004), pp. 17–28.
Kibbe, Jennifer D., "The Rise of the Shadow Warriors," *Foreign Affairs* 83 (2004), pp. 102–15.
Marquis, Susan L., *Unconventional Warfare: Rebuilding U.S. Special Operations Forces* (Washington, DC: Brookings Institution Press, 1997).
Paddock, Alfred H. Jr., *U.S. Army Special Warfare: Its Origins* (Lawrence: University Press of Kansas, 2002).
Reisman, Michael W. and James E. Baker, *Regulating Covert Action: Practices, Contexts, and Policies of Covert Coercion Abroad in International and American Law* (New Haven, CT: Yale University Press, 1992).
Robinson, Linda, *Masters of Chaos: The Secret History of the Special Forces* (New York: Public Affairs, 2004).
Stone, Kathryn, *"All Necessary Means"—Employing CIA Operatives in a Warfighting Role Alongside Special Operations Forces* (Carlisle Barracks, PA: U.S. Army War College Strategy Research Project, 2003).

# 8

# COVERT ACTION AND DIPLOMACY

JOHN D. STEMPEL

COVERT ACTION AND DIPLOMACY HAVE HAD A long and checkered career together for over two millennia. From the earliest organized governments, when functions were not sufficiently differentiated, clandestine operations were standard practice in international relations. Beginning with the Achaemenid Persians between the sixth and fourth centuries B.C., the organization of intelligence as part of government was developed to a very high degree and copied by Arabs, Turks, Afghans, Mongols, and Hindus over the following centuries. Activities that we now consider covert action—assassination, coopting the king's counselor (or mistress), paramilitary support for insurgencies, and propaganda—were common. There was little or no distinction between "intelligence" and "covert action" until the nineteenth and twentieth centuries. That developed in the West as a result of the evolution of Westphalian diplomacy in the fifteenth and sixteenth centuries.[1]

The emergence of Western diplomacy was driven by the disastrous desolation caused by the Thirty Years' War. Crude but temporary diplomatic missions began in the fifteenth century in Venice and the Italian states and spread to Europe. Intelligence and eventually secret operations were an integral part of these activities, though they were fairly simple by modern standards. In the Elizabethan period, British covert action multiplied the effective power of England, especially when the use of gold and Protestant mercenaries as diplomatic weapons saved the Protestant cause in France and the Low Countries.

By end of the Napoleonic Wars in 1815, the Treaty of Vienna included the regulation of diplomatic ranks and began the formal organization of diplomacy under international laws regulating diplomatic rights and duties. It included the principles that diplomats are not to interfere in the internal affairs of states and an outright condemnation of espionage.[2] Of course, this did not stop spying, but it forced intelligence services to become more professional and began the differentiation between intelligence and diplomacy in terms of norms, objectives, and means and methods.

As other European societies followed Britain through the Industrial Revolution, and as continental European politics became more complex through the eighteenth and nineteenth centuries, intelligence services and capabilities grew. The United States entered the diplomatic arena in the late eighteenth century after winning its independence from Britain, but distance, communications, and time kept it from playing a serious role in European and world politics until nearly a century later. The 1898 Spanish-American War, coupled with World War I brought the United States into the world arena.

Because of this history, America lagged behind the rest of the world in developing an organized intelligence capability. Throughout most of the nineteenth and early twentieth centuries, both U.S. intelligence and diplomacy were ad hoc affairs, which included secret operations on occasion, where needed and possible. Roosevelt's maneuvers involving the acquisition of the Panama Canal are a good example. In fact, the United States had no professional diplomatic community until the Rogers Act of 1924, and until 1940, no formal intelligence organizations existed except the military service intelligence departments.

George Washington created his own informal intelligence network during the American Revolution, but it dissolved after the American victory at Yorktown. The U.S. Army began to develop intelligence units during and after the Civil War experiment with outsourcing intelligence to Allan Pinkerton's organization. Formal organizations were not created until the 1880s in the Army and Navy Departments.[3]

In World War I, the military services ran their own shows, and a civilian Committee on Public Information under George Creel focused largely on propaganda and internal security. During the interwar years (1919–39), American intelligence lapsed back into previous peacetime routines, with the military service units dominating the field. American code-breaking efforts were terminated in 1929.

As the war clouds grew over Europe again in the late 1930s, President Franklin Roosevelt selected William O. Donovan to create the Office of the Co-ordinator of Information in June 1941, which became the Office of Strategic Services (OSS) the next year. This was the first organized American effort to conduct what became know within the next decade as covert activities—propaganda, political operations, economic operations, and paramilitary activities, as well as sabotage, espionage, and counterespionage during World War II.

When the OSS was disbanded in September 1945, President Truman transferred its intelligence functions to the State Department, where they became the Bureau of Intelligence and Research. He also created the Central Intelligence Group (CIG) a year later to keep the rest of the trained professionals, including covet action operators, together until the United States could sort out its postwar needs.[4]

Most of today's scholarly work cites the creation of the Central Intelligence Agency (CIA) in 1947 as part of the National Security Act as the real beginning of professionalized intelligence in American government.[5] The vast increase in technological capabilities—such as better communications and space photography—required a much greater concentration of resources and manpower to succeed. Cooperation with Allied intelligence services in World War II socialized Americans to international intelligence work. The imperatives of postwar politics and the rise of the Cold War made such an effort necessary on a continuing basis.[6]

The CIA has maintained its links with the State Department and the military in Washington. Abroad, U.S. and other countries' embassies often host resident personnel under "official" cover. However, the overall tension between the utility of covert action and the requirements of diplomacy and foreign policy continue to this day, breaking out in open hostility on occasion.

## COVERT ACTION: METHODS AND OPERATIONS

Covert action is formally referred to in presidential executive orders as "special activities." Perhaps the most inclusive general description is Jeff Richelson's: "Covert action, also known as "special activities," includes any operation designed to influence foreign governments, persons, or events in support of the sponsoring government' s foreign policy objectives while keeping the sponsoring government's support of the operation secret. Whereas in clandestine collection, the emphasis is on keeping the activity secret, in covert action the emphasis is on keeping the sponsorship secret."[7] Such activities are aimed at keeping the sponsoring government's role secret, but they also do violate the diplomatic Vienna Convention injunctions against interference in the domestic affairs of the host country.

When a covert action is uncovered, the sponsoring country's relations with the target country are adversely affected. This generally brings diplomats back into the problem, because they are the ones who take the brunt of criticism and later raise the general foreign policy question of whether such actions were or are worth the cost. Before pursuing this discussion, the following section examines the types of actions and individual issues/problems. Although much is known about historical operations, details on present-day activities are scarce. This circumstance hampers a complete and fully informed discussion.

Propaganda, sometimes called psychological warfare, or psy ops, has both overt and covert aspects. The press and cultural sections of embassies pass out overt, or "white" information that is attributed to official sources and represents the government's official view. "Gray," or partially concealed propaganda and "black" propaganda that are attributed to someone else, such as falsified statements from a foreign government, are concealed variants. All these types of propaganda were used to influence the 1948 elections in Greece and Italy against the communists. The Soviets made heavy use of all three types from 1945 to the demise of the Soviet Union.[8] Other countries consistently use white propaganda (e.g., the British Broadcasting Company and the French Press Agency).

Examples of black operations include the American establishment of a clandestine radio station in Guatemala that broadcast news of a revolutionary army so convincingly that the procommunist president resigned. Soviet efforts to convince Africans that the United States was responsible for creating AIDS are similar black efforts. A similar clandestine operation publicized in late 2005 told of U.S. military officials paying to have stories placed in the Iraqi press lauding the role of American soldiers in trying to enhance security in Iraq.

For many years, Radio Free Europe and Radio Free Liberty dispensed gray information while covertly supported by the CIA as privately supported organizations. In 1973, Congress gave them independent status under the Board for International Broadcasting to "whiten" their offerings. Such activities are estimated to constitute about 40 percent of the CIA's covert activities.

Economic operations have been the least used covert activities by the CIA, accounting for only 10 percent of U.S. covert activities. Economic support in terms of goods shipments to support friendly governments or withholding trade with unfriendly countries occurs on both the overt and covert levels. Sanctions are overt; manipulating a national currency clandestinely is covert. Much of the action against the Allende government in Chile in the early 1970s involved economic issues, including inciting labor strikes and depressing the world copper price. Positive efforts include measures to restore Iraq's economy after the American defeat of Saddam Hussein in 2003 and shipments of food to friendly countries under the Public Law (PL) 480 program. Economic measures are often overt as well as covert, and these include foreign aid as well as favorable trade pacts. Efforts to beef up the cattle and food industries in Africa are normally overt, but given sensitivities in some areas to the HIV/AIDS problem, covert measures to give additional vaccines and medicines to people in certain places may be necessary.

Political action is a more diffuse and complex category, involving everything from financial support for key leaders to creating insurgencies. Such action accounts for about 30 percent of U.S. covert activities. Some known examples include payments to Jordan's King Hussein, giving money and campaign advice to the Solidarity movement in Poland in the 1980s, and supplying political organizational personnel and money to Afghan politicians since 2002.

In addition to major U.S. efforts in Western Europe in the 1940s, there were two campaigns in Chile in 1964 and 1970. The first was a solid success; the second failed to prevent Salvadore Allende from becoming president and led to a campaign to overthrow him that was a major trigger for the Church Commission's 1974–75 investigation of the CIA.

Moving toward activities that present an even greater challenge to international norms, there are instances where both the United States and the Soviets Union supported coupes d'etat against foreign leaders. Soviet support for coups in Czechoslovakia in 1948 and in Afghanistan 1n 1978 are clear-cut cases of the exercise of Soviet political and eventually military power. The Soviets supplied political support to a number of other regimes including Cuba, Angola, Iraq, and Mozambique up to and including use of force over the past 60 years.

The U.S. has been identified with four other coups in addition to the Guatemalan and Chilean examples given. In 1953, some money and organizational skills were supplied to forces loyal to the shah, which brought down Prime Minister Mossadeq's government and restored the monarchy. The overthrow of the shah twenty-five years later drew substantially on Iranian anger at the earlier effort and raised the question of whether the 1953 coup was effective in protecting long-term U.S. interests. Successful U.S. efforts in 1961 to oust Trujillo from the Dominican Republic and acquiescence in an army coup that killed South Vietnamese President Ngo Dinh Diem in 1963 are other cases the Church Commission discussed.The United States also gave political support to those seeking to oust Philippines President Ferdinand Marcos in 1986 and political and active military support to oust the regime in Grenada in 1983, Panamanian President Manuel Noriega in 1989, and the Haitian military dictatorship in 1993–94.

Paramilitary activities, including assassinations, often overlap with or are carried out in conjunction with political action operations. They generally involve more risk and controversy than any other type of covert action. The CIA's Special Operations Unit ran a "secret" war against the North Vietnamese puppet regime in Laos from 1963 until the United States withdrew from Vietnam in 1973. CIA support for other wars/guerilla operations has included action in twenty-six publicly identified countries, including the Ukraine, Poland, Albania, Hungary, Indonesia, China, Oman, Malaysia, North Korea, Venezuela, the Dominican Republic, Bolivia, Guatemala, Cuba, Nicaragua, El Salvador, Angola, Greece, Afghanistan, and Iraq. Soviet operations include at least that many countries over the seventy-two years of the regime's existence.

Some clandestine American activities involved support for or protection of other elements of the clandestine intelligence collection process, including the maintenance in Iran of monitoring stations to track Soviet missile launches and monitoring sites in Laos and Cambodia for following North Vietnamese troop movements. In the 1980s, American covert operations involving Pakistani aid to the Afghan rebels against the Soviet puppet regime there were major factors in the eventual Soviet withdrawal in 1989. As in most other large-scale operations, part of the activity was covert, the rest merely secret, much of which eventually became public.

## THE NEW TERRORISM

One of the spillovers from American Afghan operations in the 1980s and the Gulf War of 1990–91 was the rise of Islamic terrorism, which eventually led to the destruction of the World Trade Center towers and damage to the Pentagon on

September 11, 2001, when Al Qaeda–trained terrorists flew aircraft into these buildings. Subsequent military action in Afghanistan that destroyed Taliban rule there and chased Al Qaeda into Pakistan was greatly facilitated by both overt and covert operations that relied heavily on CIA cooperation with U.S. military forces, and paramilitary efforts were key to early success. Coordination between the CIA and Defense Department forces, however, did not remain uniformly good throughout and remains a subject of concern to intelligence reformers.[9] Failure to destroy or capture a significant number of Al Qaeda forces and leaders was one of the issues that led to the 9/11 hearings and intelligence reform in 2004–5. A related issue was the use of intelligence in the decision to attack Iraq in March 2003. The misreading of Iraqi nuclear and chemical/biological capabilities and the limited American understanding of Iraq and its politics brought forth criticism on both counts.

The concentration on intelligence reform led to a reassessment of American intelligence capabilities and a reorganization of the intelligence community under a new Director of National Intelligence (DNI).[10] Although the most intense focus centered on the more strenuous overt and secret activities, covert action has been affected as well. Information now available suggests there is more increased covert activity in support of penetrating terrorist cells and infrastructures. Support activities related to U.S. invasion and occupation of Iraq, and U.S. support of Afghanistan's democratic experiment post-2001, have grown dramatically. In these areas, paramilitary operations and support are crucial, overt or covert. This concentration suggests there are fewer resources for and less reliance on covert activities elsewhere, but this is speculative at this time (2006).[11]

## COVERT ACTION: ASSESSMENT

As covert action became a bureaucratized activity in U.S. foreign policy after World War II, rather than an ad hoc political or military event, it became controversial. For over twenty-five years after 1945, during the Cold war, Americans treated covert activities with a "don't ask, don't tell" mentality. This followed a familiar pattern: most nations do not now and never have openly discussed their covert activities. There have been some academic discussions of past efforts when material became available or when enterprising journalists uncovered unsuspected connections. However, these tended to be one-shot stories with little follow-up. This began to change in the United States in the early 1970s when U.S. involvement in Chile drew the attention of Senator Frank Church and others. In 1975–76 a congressional commission investigated alleged intelligence abuses.[12] The Church Commission and subsequent government and scholarly efforts have focused on three issues: Is covert action effective? Is covert action under control? Is covert action moral?

Literature on effectiveness from both academic and professional sources stresses several negative points:

1. The "blowback" from failed operations—or even successful ones—damages U.S. foreign policy.
2. Americans are deficient in the cultural understanding necessary to successfully manipulate other cultures, hence covert action often ends badly.
3. Covert action is not an effective mechanism for resolving crises and has to be integrated as part of an effective policy to succeed.
4. Often, the objectives of the covert activity are not compatible with American values.
5. Often, unclear boundaries between covert action and military operations result in failures.
6. Short-term successes often lead to long-term disasters.[13]

Others, including some critics, concede that despite difficulties, covert action is something that can be useful if it is used properly: (1) if covert activities are integrated into coherent overall foreign policy; (2) if active coordination is maintained between all government agencies; and (3) if no overt options will accomplish the mission. Most agree that other options should be exhausted—much of the political and propaganda work should be done openly, and it must be done competently with a good chance of success. Like other choices for effective action, there are pitfalls as well as possibilities.[14]

The dispute over effectiveness spills over to the second issue: Is covert action under proper control? For Americans, this means conforming to relevant legislation and final presidential approval of such action. President Reagan's definition of covert action, published in Executive Order 12333 in 1981 and still in effect today, covers "special activities conducted in support of national foreign policy objects abroad which are planned and executed so that the role of the United States Government is not apparent or acknowledged publicly . . . but which are not intended to influence United States political processes, public opinion, policies, or media and *do not include diplomatic activities or the collection or production of intelligence and related support functions*" (emphasis added).[15]

The U.S. Congress found this definition acceptable and incorporated similar language in its 1991 Intelligence Authorization Act. The common theme was that covert action is *not* an intelligence activity, and the requirements for a presidential finding did not apply to diplomatic activities. Also, such special activities were not to be targeted at or designed to influence the American public or American politics.

The development of a working definition of *covert action* stemmed from the work of the Church Commission, which at first called the CIA a "rogue elephant," but then backed away from that view in its final report. No other country deals with covert action this way. In 1994, the Hughes-Ryan legislation, which required the presidential finding for covert action, also ended the doctrine of plausible denialability for the president.

The presidential finding combines a determination that the activity is important enough to U.S. national security that it should be undertaken despite the risks and possible exposure, and that the purpose for which it is undertaken and the methods used would be approved should it become public—the risk should be worth it. In 1986, the Iran-*contra* scandal underscored the reason for such legislation when it broke. National Security Council officials John Poindexter and Oliver North concocted a scheme to sell weapons to Iran in return for the release of American captives in Beirut and then (illegally) use the proceeds to fund U.S. operations against the Nicaraguan Sandinista government by supporting the contras.

This operation was never a true covert action, because approval was never sought. Some CIA, diplomatic, and military officials were involved in these basically criminal activities that were kept from Congress's attention until the story was revealed abroad. A few were tried in court, others were fired, and some left government voluntarily. There was considerable anger among the professionals in the various agencies. President Reagan escaped serious censure when he apologized to the country in a televised speech following the scandal.[16]

Journalists and students of intelligence had a field day with the Church Commission's initial allegations about rogue elephants and with the Iran-*contra* scandal, as they often do when intelligence operations go awry.[17] Ever since the 1960s, periodic book and magazine exposés have vied with serious analysis for public attention when covert action is the subject. This highlights the continuing tension between the secrecy needed for covert action and intelligence activities and the requirements for democratic transparency in government. A few other democracies have begun to gently question intelligence activities, but in most nations this is a nonproblem—these matters are simply not discussed.

The final question is whether covert action is moral. It is always justified as important or even vital for national security. It has been separated from diplomacy and discouraged in international law because it is not considered an acceptable part of international relations. Nevertheless, it persists—as do efforts to codify and extend international law.

Throughout the Cold War, America operated on the basis of the view developed by a panel appointed by President Eisenhower. Headed by retired Gen. Jimmy Doolittle, its report said that in view of communism's win-at-all-costs approach to foreign affairs, the United States would have to reconsider its concepts of fair play and undertake to subvert, sabotage, and destroy our enemies.[18] America did not fully trade morals for realpolitik, but it certainly erred on the side of a more vigorous covert action policy.

Beginning with the Carter administration and reemerging with the Clinton administration, the question of how moral our foreign policy was continued to bubble. The Reagan administration returned to the more forceful arguments for fewer limits on covert action, and so did the first President Bush; after 9/11, so did President George W. Bush. Key players in his administration consistently made the argument that the brutality and viciousness of the terrorists required the utmost response. However, the president's policy of bringing democracy to the Middle East, which justified the 2003 invasion of Iraq, also raised the question of whether covert actions by their very nature undercut strategies to promote democracy in Iraq and elsewhere.[19]

Several writers have made the argument that covert action must be considered in terms of just war theory and that covert action can be justified in some circumstances, but it should not be used as a "lazy country's way of avoiding hard diplomatic work."[20] Some former agents argue that collecting intelligence and covert action often involve working with amoral characters, especially when terrorists such as Al Qaeda are the targets.[21]

They have a point, and no one has said the choices are easy. Most thoughtful writers suggest that some form of the following guidelines would give a government a solid base for defending covert actions if they went bad, and that most people would support covert action taken for the following reasons:

1. The president approves the covert action after organized deliberation within the executive branch and the legally required consultation with Congress.
2. The action's intentions and objectives are clear, reasonable, and just and are also part of a coherent foreign policy.
3. Overt means of advancing the policy will not work.
4. There is significant probability of success, with minimal damage to innocent people.
5. Damage inflicted should be proportional to the threat reduced or averted.

Of course, such assessments have and could turn out to be wrong, or actions could be botched or turn out badly. There is really no way of averting criticism or political damage, but a defense of just covert action will limit damage to the diplomacy of the country that can so defend itself politically if matters go badly.

Using such guidelines may also assist in minimizing organizational struggles and clashes within the intelligence, defense, and diplomatic communities. If all work from the same page, intragovernmental spats will be minimized because positions will have to be harmonized or adjusted before action can get under way. Legal issues would be minimized, and there will also be more markers for judging the effectiveness of covert action. Those who have put themselves above the requirements for control are those who caused real damage to the system. They have also raised the bar of distrust across both international as well as domestic dimensions.

## CONCLUSION: THE FUTURE

Combining considerations of effectiveness, control, and morality has and will help governments assess and carry out special activities in a future that is coming at us with dizzying speed.

When the United States began its romance with covert action in the late 1940s and '50s, leaders of developing new nations had not yet mobilized masses of people in the developing world for political action. Politics was still very much an elite game when Kermit Roosevelt helped restore the shah to power in 1953. The mobilization of Iran's Islamic population by Khomeini and others made covert action almost impossible. The OSS successes in France and Burma during World War II were difficult to repeat in the Eastern Europe of the 1940s and '50s. Similarly, the triumph of mass movements in other African and Middle Eastern states in the 1960s increased the need for effective diplomacy while simultaneously reducing the productive scope of covert activities.

Similarly today, the explosion of cell phones, computers, and the Internet has complicated covert operations. The geometric increase in surveillance capacities and means for harming others has both helped and hindered cover actions, and foreign policy and intelligence become more complex and interlinked than they have ever been.

The result, certainly for the United States, had been a reassessment of intelligence and the creation of a new Director of National Intelligence. Covert action has come under renewed scrutiny. Paramilitary efforts were stepped up in the wake of 9/11. Efforts have been made to increase public diplomacy and bring politics activities into more transparent light.

All postwar presidents have used covert action with congressional approval since 1974 (the exceptions have resulted in disgrace and/or punishment for the culprits). It is not unreasonable to suggest that they will continue to do so in a dangerous world. To achieve success, however, they will have to keep in mind the pitfalls and problems connected with such activities, as well as the guidelines for success listed above.

Ultimately, all connected with such activities need to bear in mind the words of former National Security Agency Director William E. Odom: "Intelligence performance simply can not be separated from foreign policy making and military operations."[22]

## NOTES

1. For history on these points, see Keith Hamilton and Richard Langhorn, *The Practice of Diplomacy* (New York: Routledge, 1995); G. R. Berridge, *Diplomacy: Theory and Practice*, 3rd ed. (New York: Palgrave, 2002); and Adda Bozeman, *Strategic Intelligence and Statecraft* (Washington: Brassey's, 1992).

2. Berridge, *Diplomacy*, pp. 618ff.; for more detail see Garrett Mattingly, *Renaissance Diplomacy* (New York: Houghton Mifflin, 1995).

3. See Scott Breckinridge, *The CIA and the U.S. Intelligence System* (Boulder, CO: Westview Press, 1986), chap. 1: Jeff Richelson, *The U.S. Intelligence Community* (Boulder, CO: Westview Press, 1995), chap. 1.

4. Charles D. Ameringer, *U.S. Foreign Intelligence: The Secret Side of American History* (Lexington: Lexington Books, 1990). This is an excellent and readable, swift

review of U.S. intelligence from the country's inception through the Reagan administration, including covert action.

5. Richelson, *Intelligence Community*; Rhodri Jeffreys-Jones, *The CIA and Ameri-
can Democracy* (New Haven, CT: Yale University Press, 1989), intro and chaps. 1, 2; Abram
N. Shulsky, *Silent Warfare: Understanding the World of Intelligence* (Washington:
Brassey's, 1991), chaps. 2 and 14.

6. Breckinridge, *CIA and U.S. Intelligence*, part 1.

7. Richelson, *Intelligence Community*, p. 3.

8. Christopher Andrews and Vasili Mitrokhin, *The World Was Going Our Way: The
KGB and the Battle for the Third World* (New York: Basic Books, 2005), is an excellent
review of Soviet activities.

9. Sean Naylor, *Not a Good Day to Die* (New York: Berkley Books, 2005); William
E. Odom, *Fixing Intelligence* (New Haven, CT: Yale University Press, 2003), chap. 4 and
conclusion.

10. Steve Strasser, ed., *The 9/11 Investigations: Staff Reports of the 9/11 Commission* (New York: Public Affairs, 2004).

11. Paul Pillar, *Terrorism and Foreign Policy* (Washington: Brookings Institution,
2001); Strasser, *9/11 Investigations*; Odom, *Fixing Intelligence*, pp. 150–92.

12. Breckinridge, *CIA and U.S. Intelligence*, parts 2 and 3; Loch K. Johnson,
*America's Secret Power: The CIA in a Democratic Society* (New York: Oxford Univer-
sity Press, 1989); Loch K. Johnson and James J. Wirtz, eds., *Strategic Intelligence:
Windows into a Secret World* (Los Angeles: Roxbury, 2004), part 8.

13. Excellent examples and discussions of these points may be found in William
J. Daugherty, *Executive Secrets: Covert Action and the Presidency* (Lexington: University
Press of Kentucky, 2004), chaps. 1–3; Chalmers Johnson, *The Sorrows of Empire* (New
York: Metropolitan Books, 2004); Anonymous [Michael Sheuer], *Imperial Hubris: Why the
West Os Losing the War on Terror* (Washington: Brassey's, 2004); Michael Sheuer,
*Through Our Enemies' Eyes* (Washington: Brassey's, 2002); Odom, *Fixing Intelligence*,
chaps. 7 and 9; Johnson, *America's Secret Power*, chaps. 6–9; Kim Roosevelt, *Counter-
coup: The Struggle for Control of Iran* (New York: McGraw-Hill, 1979); Stephen Kinser,
*All the Shah's Men* (Hoboken, NJ: Wiley, 2003); Naylor, *Not a Good Day to Die*. Of these
authors, four are former intelligence professionals, two are academics, and two are journalists.

14. Daugherty, *Executive Secrets*, conclusion; Odom, *Fixing Intelligence*, chaps.
7–9; Johnson and Wirtz, *Strategic Intelligence*, chaps 17, 19, 21, 28.

15. Executive Order 12333, U.S. Intelligence Activities, December 4, 1981, 3 CFR
200 (1981, 46 FR 59955, as amended by Executive Order 12701, 14 February, 1990, 55
FR 59333).

16. Daugherty, *Executive Secrets*, pp. 34–37; Bob Woodward, *Veil: The Secret Wars
of the CIA, 1981–1987* (Buccaneer Press, 1994). 17. David Atlee Phillips, *The Night
Watch* (New York: Ballantine Books, 1982); Victor Marchetti and John Marks, *The CIA
and the Cult of Intelligence* (New York: Knopf, 1974).

18. Johnson and Wirtz, *Strategic Intelligence*, chap. 22.

19. David Rieff, *At the Point of a Gun: Democratic Dreams and Armed Intervention* (New York: Simon and Schuster, 2005), pp. 173–76; Stephen M. Walt, *Tam-
ing American Power: The Global Response to U.S. Primacy* (New York: Norton, 2005),
pp. 243–47.

20. The source of the quote is a former intelligence officer who also served with the Foreign Service. The same themes can be found in Johnson, *America's Secret Power*, pp. 261–62; Daugherty, *Executive Secrets*, pp. 67–70 and conclusion; Johnson and Wirtz, *Strategic Intelligence* 278–79.

21. Robert Baer, *See No Evil* (New York: Crown, 2002); James Risen, *State of War* (New York: Free Press, 2006).

22. Odom, *Fixing Intelligence*, p. 186. Robert W. Pringle Jr. and Jennifer Griffin aided the author in identifying several sources.

# 9

# FROM COLD WAR TO LONG WAR

## Covert Action in U.S. Legal Context

JAMES E. BAKER

## INTRODUCTION

ALTHOUGH COVERT ACTION HAS HISTORICALLY PLAYED A small part in the overall intelligence budget, as an intelligence function it has played a disproportionately large role in defining public perceptions of "intelligence,"[1] shaping congressional oversight, and policy impact. This reflects the reality that covert activities bear particular policy and legal risks as well as benefits. Covert action has historically included activities on a continuum between diplomacy and acts of war undertaken to hide the national footprint.[2] As a result, these activities are undertaken without the ordinary mechanisms of policy preview and external validation. Thus, although the law pertaining to covert action permits and prohibits, most of all it regulates its use by creating substantive thresholds triggering statutory and executive processes for authorizing and then appraising covert activities. These processes are intended to ensure that the means to effect covert actions are lawful, but also that the policy choices are sound and effective and that the gain from action exceeds the pain, in both the short and long run.

This chapter is divided into two sections. The first places covert action in contemporary policy and legal context. In a global low-intensity conflict against nonstate actors intent on conducting acts of terrorism with high-intensity consequences, clandestine activities of the sort historically identified as covert action play a central role. However, because this conflict is fought over values, including legal values, and because success in this conflict requires intelligence alliance, the when, why, where, and how of covert action takes on added importance. Contemporary law provides a procedural framework for addressing these issues within a context of limited access.

The second section raises three legal policy issues: (1) Will the president's wartime authority as commander-in-chief eclipse or marginalize the statutory framework for addressing covert action? (2) Does the statutory definition of *covert action* remain viable in light of the evolving use of "liaison" and "traditional activities" to combat terrorism? (3) Is the measure of executive preview and review adequate to address the policy and legal risks inherent in covert action, as well as those contemporary activities that bear comparable policy and legal risks?

## LEGAL FRAMEWORK: A THUMBNAIL SKETCH

American covert action predates the Republic. Benjamin Franklin, the colonial envoy in France employed tradecraft like secret writing and dead drops to organize an espionage ring in Paris. Notably for this chapter, he also engaged in the covert planting of disinformation in the Paris press and the clandestine shipment of arms to the Colonies.[3] Covert action has been one of America's national security tools ever since. During the Cold War the United States (and the Soviet Union) engaged in a number of "overt-covert actions," such as the landings at the Bay of Pigs, the supply of the *contras*, and provision of support to the Afghan *mujahedeen*. Such "covert" mechanisms allowed proxies to engage in hot war, while the great power conflict remained "cold." (However, most covert activities, then and now, are secret and remain so.) Resort to covert action also reflected the strategic view that the threat posed by communism warranted resort to all the instruments of national policy.[4]

In a conflict against Islamic Jihadists, the United States should be expected to use all the national security tools, including covert action. Indeed, the instrument is well suited to address a nonstate opponent, acting outside the laws of armed conflict and operating without necessity of a particular territory, base, or even chain of command. In theory and in law, covert action is fast and flexible, allowing prompt response or proactive use against a mobile opponent within states either unwilling or unable to effect their capture. And in theory and in law, covert action is nonattributable and secret. This allows assisting states to otherwise deny complicity in necessary but locally unpopular actions. It also removes the "made in America" label, where for example, an audience might otherwise be receptive to the message, but not the messenger. For these reasons the law related to the authorization and review of covert activity is on the front line of counterterrorism. For these same reasons, the law, process, and practice of covert action will surely evolve from Cold War to "Long War" understandings and applications.

### Constitutional Context

The president's inherent intelligence powers are found in enumerated constitutional authorities over foreign affairs and national defense as recognized in long-standing executive practice as well as in those few Supreme Court decisions that address intelligence.[5] The extent to which the president's inherent authority is magnified as commander-in-chief in time of conflict is a matter of debate, in the intelligence as well as military spheres of security. However, there is surely a wartime gloss that attaches to exercise of executive authority during conflict overseas, but wider debate on whether or how such a gloss applies at home.

Congress's authority over the intelligence function is found in the funding power, the "necessary and proper" clause, its general legislative power, as well as the range of enumerated authorities the Congress possesses over national defense. The law provides for congressional notification of covert action and not consultation or approval, a constitutional acknowledgment of the president's particular authority in this area. However, in constitutional practice, strong legislative resistance can shape or even lead to the termination of a covert action program. Congress's leverage increases when a program requires the authorization and appropriation of new money (as opposed to presidential authorization to spend existing funds) or where Congress chooses to use the power of the purse to "fence" funding.

### Statutory Context

Although there are a number of statutes that address intelligence, the National Security Act of 1947, as amended, remains the bedrock of U.S. intelligence laws. This is true in the area of covert activity. The act, in some manner or another, has served as statutory authorization for covert activity since 1947;[6] however, it was not until 1990, in the wake of the Iran-*contra* affair, that the Congress defined covert action in law. "DEFINITION: Covert Action is defined by what it is, an activity or activities of the United States Government to influence political, economic, or military conditions abroad, where it is intended that the role of the United States Government will not be apparent or acknowledged publicly."[7] Through negative definition, "Covert action . . . does not include—(1) activities the primary purpose of which is to acquire intelligence or traditional counterintelligence activities; (2) traditional diplomatic or military activities or routine support to such activities; (3) traditional law enforcement activities; or, (4) activities to provide routine support to overt U.S. activities abroad."[8]

This definition was intended to capture activities that Congress determined should be channeled through a particularized process of executive authorization and congressional notification because of the nature of and risk inherent to the activities involved. The definition was meant to reflect existing practice, the legislative history stating: "It is not intended that the new definition exclude activities which were heretofore understood to be covert actions, nor to include activities not heretofore understood to be covert actions."[9] As a result, historical practice is particularly relevant to legal interpretation, albeit hard to ascertain using ordinary methods of legal research. The legislative history as well is particularly important in fleshing out the meaning of "traditional" activities exempt from the definition's reach.

Notably, this definition is act-based, not actor-based. This means that the law applies not just to the Central Intelligence Agency (CIA) but also to the Department of Defense and the Federal Bureau of Investigation (FBI) and other government entities, *provided* the contemplated activity fits the positive definition of covert action and is not otherwise "traditional." However, identity *is* relevant in determining whether an activity is traditional. For example, certain activities like raids might be traditional if undertaken by military actors in uniform during armed conflict; however, the same result may not follow if the raid were undertaken by nonattributable U.S. surrogates in peacetime. Of course, activities that were "extraordinary" before September 11, 2001, may have become ordinary and traditional since then.

### FINDINGS

The act also recognizes the president's direct responsibility for covert action. The president is required to find that "an action is necessary to support identifiable foreign policy objectives of the United States and is important to the national security of the United States."[10] Findings must be in writing, "unless immediate action by the United States is required," in which case a contemporaneous notation of the president's decision shall be made and a written finding produced within forty-eight hours. Reflecting some of the issues identified in the Iran-*contra* context, findings must also specify the department or agencies authorized to fund or participate "in any significant way" in an action, as well as specify whether the participation of third parties (e.g., third countries or persons) is contemplated.[11]

### REPORTING

The act also requires the president to ensure that findings are reported to the intelligence committees "as soon as possible after . . . approval and before initiation."[12] The ordinary process of notification is in writing to the full committees. In practice, this means not only to the members but also designated staff with an oral briefing accompanying the underlying document. However, "To meet extraordinary circumstances affecting vital interests of the United States,"[13] the president may limit notification to the so-called Gang of Eight (the chairs and vice chairs of the Intelligence Committees and the Majority and Minority Leaders of each house of Congress) "and such other member or members of the congressional leadership as may be included by the President." Exercise of this option requires a statement from the president indicating why the action in question warrants limited notification. It follows that a limited notification is to members only and may be done orally. The president may, of course, authorize notification to additional members of Congress, or staff, something in between the full committee and the Gang of Eight. Although there may be good tactical reasons to do so, as in the case of members serving on the Appropriations Committees, selective notification to preferred members of Congress or staff would seem to erode the premise behind limited notification.

Finally, the act implicitly authorizes the president to withhold notification altogether by stating that "whenever a finding is not reported [in one of the first two manners], the President shall fully inform the intelligence committees in a timely fashion and shall provide a statement of the reasons."[14] There is no public indication of whether this provision has ever been invoked.

In addition to reporting findings, significant changes to or significant undertakings pursuant to a previously approved action must be reported "in the same manner as findings are reported." This language is implemented through presidential Memoranda of Notification (MONs), which supplement, amend, or clarify previously approved findings. It follows that MONs are reported to the Congress using one of the three mechanisms specified for reporting findings. The triggering threshold for significant undertakings or changes has been the subject of internal executive debate as well as debate in Congress. The legislative history gives two examples. First, "this would occur when the President authorizes a change in the scope of a previously approved finding to authorize additional activities to occur. The second type of change specified in this subsection pertains to significant undertakings pursuant to a previously approved finding. This would occur when the President authorizes a significant activity under a previously-approved finding without changing the scope of the finding concerned."[15] These same terms were addressed in National Security Decision Directive 286, signed by President Reagan in the wake of Iran-*contra*, stating: "In the event of any proposal to change substantially the means of implementation of, or the level of resources, assets, or activity under, a Finding; or in the event of any significant change in the operational condition, country or countries significantly engaged, or risks associated with a special activity, a written Memorandum of Notification (MON) shall be submitted to the President for his approval."[16]

Finally, the act requires the president to "ensure that the Intelligence Committees are kept fully and currently informed of the intelligence activities of the United States, including any significant anticipated intelligence activity as required by this Title."[17] Likewise, Section 503 of the title pertaining to covert action requires the Director of National Intelligence and the heads of any other government entities involved in covert action

> To the extent consistent with due regard for the protection from unauthorized disclosure of classified information relating to sensitive intelligence sources and methods or other exceptionally sensitive matters or other exceptionally sensitive matters ... keep the intelligence committees fully and currently informed of all covert actions which are the responsibility of, are engaged in by, or are carried out for or on behalf of, any department, agency, or entity of the United States Government, including significant failures.[18]

These are important provisions. At the higher levels of the political branches, program initiation receives more attention and consideration than program administration. Moreover, policy-level oversight tends to focus on moments of crisis or failure and less on ensuring that programs are on track and in fact accomplishing what they were intended to achieve and in the manner contemplated and represented to the president.

### Executive Process and Review

In addition to determining whether presidential approval is required, as a parallel matter, the definition of covert action also triggers specific processes of executive review. These processes are classified. However, in the wake of the Iran-*contra* scandal, President Reagan issued and released NSD-286, Approval and Review of Special Activities, describing the process the president intended apply to the review and authorization of covert activities. The document describes a process by which covert actions reviewed at working group level and then by the Deputies Committee and Principals Committee before submission to the president.[19] The public record also reflects that in establishing his National Security Council (NSC) system, President Clinton directed that "the Attorney General shall be invited to attend meetings pertaining to his jurisdiction, including covert actions."[20] Where the president has directed that a particular process of review occur, then he must authorize deviation from that process or otherwise delegate the authority to do so. Law or not, certainly the president should be informed when expected or important views are omitted from NSC consideration.

The special relationship between the president and the intelligence instrument is also recognized in executive directives as it is in statute. Executive Order 12333, for example, states: "The NSC shall act as the highest Executive Branch entity that provides review of, guidance for and direction to the conduct of all national foreign intelligence, counterintelligence, and special activities, and attendant policies and programs."[21]

This observation should not be lost on intelligence officials who disagree with policy or commentators who disagree with the acts of commission or omission placed at the CIA's door, rather than in the NSC Situation Room or the Oval Office.

### Legal Permits and Constraints

In addition to authorizing covert activities, the law imposes certain constraints on the conduct of those activities. Of course, much of the relevant law is found in classified presidential and executive directives (e.g., attorney general guidelines and intelligence directives). "A finding may not authorize any action that would violate the Constitution or any statute of the United States."[22] This means that an otherwise lawful intelligence activity must comply with applicable U.S. law unless the law exempts the government or intelligence actors from its reach. This would include international law to the extent such law is incorporated into U.S. law. For example, the law of armed conflict is found in the U.S. criminal code at Title 18, section 2441. Thus, when the United States placed the threat posed by Al Qaeda into a law of armed conflict construct before the embassy attacks in August 1998, this section of law became applicable to the conduct of covert activities against Osama bin Laden. This is evident in the instructions conveyed to certain Afghan "tribals," as reported by the 9/11 Commission. The instructions reference some of the staples of the law of armed conflict that one might expect to find on a military rules of engagement card, involving the treatment of prisoners and discrimination in attack. "The United States preferred that Bin Laden and his lieutenants be captured, but if a successful capture operation was not feasible, the tribals were permitted to kill them. The instructions added that the tribals must avoid killing others unnecessarily and must not kill or abuse Bin Ladin or his lieutenant if they surrendered."[23]

A prohibition on assassination, originally promulgated by President Ford in 1976, is documented in Executive Order 12333: "2.11 Prohibition on Assassination. No person employed by or acting on behalf of the United States Government shall engage in, or conspire to engage in, assassination." This order continues in force, subject, like other executive orders, to classified presidential interpretation, amendment, or suspension. However, what is acknowledged publicly is that the targeting of legitimate military targets consistent with the law of armed conflict is not considered assassination under the executive order. As former National Security Advisor Samuel Berger testified before the 9/11 Commission with respect to the August 1998 (overt) missile strikes in Afghanistan: "We received rulings in the Department of Justice—[that the] executive order [did] not prohibit our ability—prohibit our effort to try to kill Bin Laden because it did not apply to situations in which you are acting in self-defense or you're acting against command and control targets against an enemy, which he certainly was."[24] As evidenced by parallel executive statements, similar conclusions were reached at the time of the 1986 U.S. air strikes on Tripoli, which included a tent used at times by Col. Muammar Qaddafi, and in April 2003 when the United States targeted buildings where Saddam Hussein was thought located.

In addition, "No covert action may be conducted which is intended to influence United States political processes, public opinion, policies, or media."[25] For example, in the vernacular of intelligence law, the prospect of U.S. covert propaganda influencing the American media and public is known as blowback, a real risk in a global world with around-the-clock news cycles. As criminal lawyers will recognize, the critical term in the prohibition is *intended*, defining the restriction as one of specific intent. Of course, lawyers might find that the United States should be deemed to have intended something that is a predictable and logical consequence of action.

Regardless of legal argument, as a matter of legal policy, decision makers must evaluate the consequences of U.S. covert activities blowing back into the United States even where such a result is not intended. To pick a safe example, the

covert recruitment and insertion of a rebel force may lead unwitting policy observers to make unfounded conclusions about the strength of the opposition to a
regime. Likewise, were the United States to covertly place favorable news articles
in the foreign press, a historical mechanism for disseminating propaganda during
the Cold War, the potential for blowback might hinge on whether the material was
disseminated in English and/or in a forum likely to be covered by the U.S. media.

LEGAL PRISM

For the handful of lawyers who practice in this area, each covert activity will
present questions of domestic, international, and foreign law. For example, in the
context of a hypothetical extraordinary rendition, say, the kidnapping in 1960 of
Nazi war criminal Adolf Eichmann by Israeli agents in Argentina, a lawyer might
first determine whether the operation constitutes covert action, and if so whether
it was authorized by an existing authority or required subsequent presidential
approval. Whether considered covert or not, the operation must be approved in a
manner consistent with internal U.S. directives, unclassified in the case of *The
U.S. Attorney's Manual*, but otherwise generally classified. Depending on the
circumstances, congressional notification might also be warranted or required.

U.S. criminal law and procedure might also be implicated depending on
context. For example, if the subject was intended for U.S. prosecution, then
lawyers would need to consider whether and how Fourth and Fifth Amendment
protections might apply. Lawyers would also need to ensure that the means of
abduction and transfer did not otherwise violate U.S. law, including the *Ker-
Frisbie-Toscanino* doctrine—the concept that U.S. courts will generally not look
to the manner by which a defendant came before the court so long as it did not
involve conduct that "shocks the conscience."[26]

U.S., international, and foreign law relating to the Torture Convention might
also be implicated.[27] In the case of foreign assistance or transfers, assurances
involving the treatment of the subject might be required or prudent depending in
part on the degree of U.S. involvement and direction during and after the rendition. Assurances may take different forms, including oral assurances, diplomatic
notes, and liaison channel agreements. The government of the United Kingdom
and the government of Jordan, for example, have concluded a public Memorandum of Understanding on the subject of rendition.[28] Whether assurances are
required as a matter of law and in what form and level of authority will depend on
context,[29] including for example, the track records of the country or persons involved, with respect to both their treatment of prisoners and adherence to prior
assurances. Of course, the more intrusive the U.S. requirements, the less likely a
third country or U.S. agents will agree to assist with a rendition.

International law might also be implicated with such an Eichmann rendition.
Under international law, abduction without the meaningful consent of the host
government would violate the territorial integrity of the host state and in all likelihood violate local law as well. However, as a matter of international law, the

violation of sovereignty would implicate the rights of the host state and not the subject of rendition. Call this the Eichmann Rule. In the Eichmann hypothetical, we will stipulate that the United States is not acting in self-defense or collective self-defense, but rather to vindicate the Nuremberg principles and the victims of the Holocaust. Such a rendition might also implicate bilateral treaties between the countries affected.

Such a rendition could also implicate the local (foreign) law of the jurisdiction where the rendition takes place and along the route of egress. Thus, even when an operation is conducted in a manner consistent with U.S. law, it may yet subject U.S. actors and others to criminal exposure in foreign states for kidnapping or for violating local law implementing international treaties or prescribing domestic rights. Such risks would need to be balanced against the importance of the seizure in question, the risk to bilateral relations (including the prospects for future extradition cooperation), as well as to multilateral efforts to bring war criminals to justice. Recall as well that in *Ker*, the Court did not object to the manner in which the defendant was brought before the court, but the Court suggested that Peru was not without recourse, for the extradition treaty between the United States and Peru "provides for the extradition of persons charged with kidnapping, and, on demand . . . the party who is guilty of it, *could* be surrendered" (emphasis added).[30]

## LEGAL POLICY ISSUES

There are sometimes tensions between the requirements for successful action and the evaluation of the risks associated with covert action. On the one hand, successful covert action requires secrecy. In context, this is self-evident: if the intended policy effect will be lost if the U.S. hand is apparent; if the cost will outweigh the gain if the United States is held to account; or if the opportunity will be lost if the target is alerted. Secrecy is also generally essential to protect those persons engaged in the action. In context, covert action also requires speed. A terrorist target of opportunity may come and go in the wink of a Predator drone's eye. Moreover, covert activities occur within a context where the president has already determined that the action(s) in question "is important to the national security of the United States." These interests all point in the direction of a rapid, secret, and truncated process of authorization.

On the other hand, covert activities have historically carried significant policy risks. As a result, presidents have subjected covert activities to specialized processes of interagency and intra-agency review within the executive branch, and Congress has enacted a specialized process of notification. The Intelligence Committees have also adopted specialized internal procedures for addressing covert action, including a staff-directed quarterly review in the Senate. These parallel and sometime competing considerations result in a number of legal policy tensions.

### What Is the Scope of the President's Authority over Covert Action in Wartime? What Role Must and Should Congress Play?

Heretofore the National Security Act has successfully served as an agreed mechanism between branches for addressing covert action. The act incorporates the ultimate constitutional positions of both branches (prior reporting and no reporting), without either side having conceded ultimate authority. The act leaves the political branches to work through the constitutional principles and tensions in an informal and contextual manner. In this way, the statute plays an overlooked but important constitutional role by defining expectations and suggesting limits— that is, setting the constitutional rules of the road between the president and Congress on the meaning and reporting requirements for covert action.

Thus, where the president and Congress have disagreed on an important point of law, they have also agreed to disagree and worked out accommodations. For example, when President Bush signed the 1990 Intelligence Authorization Act into law, he stated his constitutional view that he was not required to report findings in advance or at all; but in a side letter to the chairmen of the Intelligence Committees, Bush undertook as a matter of practice not to withhold notification to the Congress beyond a few days after signing a finding, understood on the Hill as within forty-eight hours.[31]

The question presented is whether these same constitutional rules of the road still abide, or should abide during wartime, and in particular during a conflict of indefinite duration. The question is all the more apt in light of presidential assertions of inherent authority to engage in certain electronic surveillance in wartime. The president (by which I mean a president, not necessarily the incumbent president) may assert a coterminous authority during "wartime" to engage in covert action outside the framework of the National Security Act or entirely within that provision of the National Security Act contemplating post facto notification. In the covert action context, there are arguments supporting a broad reading of presidential authority. Moreover, such a claim of authority would be impenetrable, provided the action in question in fact remained covert. However, the question is not just whether such a reading is lawful, but also whether it is a good idea.

APPRAISAL

Both the 9/11 Commission and the WMD Commission included recommendations to reform the manner in which Congress conducts intelligence oversight.[32] In particular, the commissions were critical of the episodic and reactive nature of oversight, as well as the disparate sources of congressional input into the design and funding of intelligence. Congressional oversight is selective. Few members of Congress outside the committees possess the background to address intelligence issues. Moreover, by definition, the intelligence committees operate with the inherently inductive knowledge that comes from periodic briefings rather than daily contact with operators and policy makers. Members see only part of the picture, and then only that part of the picture contained in executive talking points that have survived layers of editing and are designed to fend off policy or partisan attack. Moreover, where members do follow intelligence closely, the interest tends to flow toward the "sexy" areas and not to areas like computer interoperability and funding audits, where appraisal may be needed most. Recall that approximately 85 percent of intelligence funding is directed to the Department of Defense.[33]

Nonetheless, congressional appraisal of the covert action instrument remains an essential source of balance on executive action, in part because in this area it may be the only source of balance. This is not a matter of constitutional idealism, although it pertains to the rule of law, but a matter of national security efficacy. In a system of shared powers and separate branches, Congress can provide a source of legitimacy and constitutional safeguard to intelligence activities that are conducted outside the reach of public knowledge and review. At times, the committee members and staff may be the only persons outside the NSC process and relevant intelligence agencies aware of an activity, and certainly the only persons without a direct policy stake in the success or funding of the activity. Therefore, whether their views are desired or not, they may be the only source of outside perspective at the advent of activity.

Sustained conflict will involve difficult policy trade-offs that will require sustained public support—that means support from a majority of the population, not just the president's political base or party. Chances are if the executive cannot sell a policy to a few members of Congress, the executive will not be able to convince the American public or the international community that a program or activity was prudent and/or lawful if it is disclosed.

The president alone has the authority to wield the covert action tool and the bureaucratic wherewithal to do so effectively. However, that is not to say the president should not strive to maximize his authority through the involvement and validation of Congress. Whatever can be said of the president's independent authority to act, when he acts with the express or implied authorization of Congress he acts at the zenith of his authority.[34] Therefore, those who believe in the necessity of executive action to preempt and respond to security threats should favor legal arguments that maximize presidential authority.

The inclusion of an independent check on executive action also reduces the potential for mistake. That is because the executive takes particular care in what it tells the Congress. War Powers Reports may be bland, for example, but they do necessitate an internal process before they are submitted that causes senior officials to check their assumptions and their arguments one more time before they send the report to the president and then Congress. In similar fashion, in notifying Congress of covert action, executive branch actors may well determine whether they have, in fact, covered all the angles and addressed or mitigated divergent views.

Finally, risk taking in the field increases where the government exercises shared authority. Certainly, this statement is hard to empirically demonstrate; the concept is nonetheless real. As reflected in statements made to the 9/11 Commission, there is a cultural perception in the intelligence community that there is danger in acting too aggressively when the authority to do so is unclear or subject to political change. Where authority is embedded in a written finding provided to Congress, intelligence actors are on surer footing. There can be no legitimate debate as to what was or was not authorized, unless the finding is itself ambiguous, and therefore no excuse for not leaning forward in execution.

Nor does the inclusion of the legislative branch *necessarily* undermine the requirements for speed and secrecy. Although it is hard to prove a negative or demonstrate a general truth from a single point, it is noteworthy that one of the most significant intelligence secrets briefed to the Gang of Eight in the terrorism context—the U.S. effort to capture or kill Osama bin Laden in the late 1990s did not leak.

## Is the Definition of Covert Action Still Viable?

Concerns for security, speed, and flexibility may also drive activities that heretofore received internal and external appraisal as covert action into legal pockets or rubrics subject to less preview and review. The same result may occur as a product of the good faith application of law to fact. For example, activities historically considered covert actions may become common in the context of a global conflict with Islamic Jihadists and thus come to constitute "traditional military, law enforcement, and diplomatic activities." These same activities may also properly fall within the construct of "liaison."

### COVERT ACTION AND LIAISON

Liaison involves the formal and informal ties between allied or like-minded intelligence services. As an intelligence function, it lies somewhere between collection and covert action. Liaison incorporates all that the United States brings to the collection table as well as all that foreign liaison services bring. This is particularly important in the area of human intelligence and counterterrorism where foreign services may have greater access based on ethnicity, nationality, proximity, or security focus. Moreover, a global collection effort is too broad for any one service, however competent, to successfully cover all the gaps.

However, liaison also entails action. Most liaison entails the routine passage of information that one might expect between allies. Closer to the edge of the liaison envelope there is a thin line between liaison and covert action. This line is in sight where, for example, U.S. information may not just inform a liaison ally but predictably result in the ally taking action on the basis of the intelligence provided. The provision of satellite photographs, for example, or information pinpointing the location of a weapons lab, might be used to inform defensive planning or as the missing link in a decision to take military action. In other circumstances, where the United States is itself engaging in action, say, an extraordinary rendition with the participation of the host nation, the activity may fall outside the construct of covert action, because the U.S. role is indeed apparent (at least to the assisting government).

Liaison can carry all the policy implications, benefits, and risks of a covert activity. (Our liaison counterparts would not be any good at intelligence if they were not getting something in return for their assistance other than goodwill.) This is noteworthy because U.S. liaison relationships extend beyond a predictable ring of democracies. Moreover, there is additional policy risk with liaison, because generally liaison activities receive less formal executive review than covert action. Most intelligence liaison is considered internal intelligence agency activity.[35] Returning to the hypothetical extraordinary rendition of Eichmann, one might imagine that an intra-agency review of the operation might identify a different set of policy pros, cons, and risks than an interagency review might.

The legal question, in context, is how much involvement is too much, such that the activities should be considered U.S. covert action? The legal policy question is this: Are such activities subject to an adequate measure of preview and review to confirm that (1) we are accomplishing all that we can accomplish, but (2) that we do so cognizant of the policy and legal risks involved and where appropriate that we mitigate, curtail, or eliminate those risks?

### MILITARY ACTIVITIES AND COVERT ACTION

As noted, the definition of *covert action* is action rather than actor based. However, uniformed military operations have historically not been considered or treated as covert activities. Thus, even if the definition is action-based, the exception for traditional military activities may effectively remove clandestine military operations from its reach. This legal paradigm is reinforced by the military's long-standing cultural aversion to covert action. This antipathy may reflect a desire to avoid the additional internal and external oversight that accrues to covert action, as well as a desire to avoid the occasional tarnish that emerges from the retrospective glitter of certain covert activities. It may also emulate the traditional differences in military outlook and focus between Special Forces and regular units.

The military–covert action bifurcation is significant in light of the importance of special operations in a worldwide conflict against Islamic Jihadists. As with liaison, the critical question is not whether an activity is covert action but whether those activities that raise the sorts of policy and legal risks that covert activities do are subject to a process of rigorous policy and legal preview before they are undertaken. This is important not just as a matter of law but as a matter of national security success.

### The Nature and Scope of Review

With respect to activities that are encompassed within the definition of covert action, two legal policy questions linger: How much executive process is appropriate before a finding or MON is signed or authorization for a specific operation given? How much detail should be specified in these documents beyond that necessary to satisfy the statutory requirements?

There are good arguments for and against process. In the view of some, *process* itself is a euphemism for *bureaucracy*, pejorative meaning intended.[36] Bureaucracy can delay (if not lose) operational opportunity. Bureaucracy increases the prospect of security breach. And bureaucracy usually brings layers of lawyers with it.

At the same time, national security is not subject to the same processes of internal, external, or public evaluation that may occur in other public policy areas. Where appraisal is structural, as in the case of agency inspectors general, the focus of analysis is on the identification of retrospective fault, rather than the ingredients of prospective success. To start, national security programs, and certainly compartmented intelligence programs, are secret. Limits on external appraisal also derive from certain functional and structural aspects of national security decision making and the presidency, especially during war. First, where national security is concerned, the policy pressure to succeed is at its greatest. As James Madison observed, "Safety from external danger is [indeed] the most powerful director of national conduct."[37] For presidents, this responsibility is real, immediate, and sincere. As a result, as Justice Jackson observed of executive deliberation, "The tendency is strong to emphasize transient results upon policies . . . and lose sight of enduring consequences upon the balanced power structure of our Republic."[38] Furthermore, for a presidency conditioned to crisis and command, which is to say the modern presidency, appraisal is a difficult decisional function to implement. There is also less opportunity for appraisal because where national security activities are subject to external review, they are subject to doctrines of judicial and political deference.

Process can be good or bad. Good process should be viewed as a source of policy strength in an area of historical risk, rather than an impediment to operational success. Good process alerts decision makers to the pros and cons of contemplated action, including the benefits and risks of accomplishing the task covertly rather than overtly. Process also helps ensure that secret policies are consistent with overt policies, and where they are not, whether there is good reason for any divergence. In an area where U.S. actions are intended to be kept secret, policy makers and those actors who may become aware of the underlying acts (if not their impetus) must also know of their existence to avoid blowback or inadvertent disclosure.

Clearly, streamlined executive decision has advantages in speed and secrecy. Speed comes in part from the absence of objection or dissent. But there are also benefits in the foreknowledge of objection and the improvements in policy or execution that dissent might influence. Because the conflict against Islamic fundamentalism is a conflict fought over values with words and not just territory with weapons, careful review also allows policy makers to balance the relative benefits and costs represented by both the means and ends of action. We may in fact do harm to our physical security by losing cooperation or moral leverage when we employ arguments and methods that address our safety but are perceived as contradicting the values we otherwise espouse and that will help to undermine the jihadist terrorist movement. This tension is surely found in the area of extraordinary rendition, where there are sometime difficult trade-offs between preventing attacks and intelligence gathering, on one hand, and public diplomacy and human rights, on the other hand. When these decisions are taken solely within security agencies, the trade-offs will invariably balance in favor of action, just as company grade infantry officers will generally lean toward force protection when faced with questions of proportional balance between physical security and securing local support. Generally, executive review tends to be more inclusive, and therefore more rigorous, when a decision is subject to interagency review and senior policy review than when it is subject to single agency review.

Additional checks do not necessarily eliminate mistakes; they diminish the potential for error. In the context of intelligence operations using military means, such as the use of a Predator drone to attack the enemy, covert or not, the value of rigorous process is obvious. The military, for example, uses multiple tiered computer modeling to assess the potential for collateral damage. Targets are validated through a tested and recognized staff process. In short, rigorous but timely processes can demonstrate confidence in policy choice, legal arguments, and a willingness to account for effect.

When process proves bureaucratic, the answer is not to remove internal mechanisms of appraisal but to streamline them. For example, a legal question can go straight to the attorney general sitting in the Oval Office. As noted earlier, in the case of immediate need, the act provides for oral authorization where "immediate action by the United States is required," in which case a contemporaneous notation of the president's decision shall be made and a written finding produced within forty-eight hours.[39]

SPECIFICITY

Policy makers and lawyers must also consider the measure of detail to include in a finding or MON. There exists a tension between the generic authorizing instrument that provides the greatest flexibility and the too-specific instrument, which may need amendment with every change in the field. From the standpoint of legal policy, such documents should be crafted with sufficient specificity so that it is clear to the president what he is approving and the policy implications and risks of doing so, including the risks of taking no action. When flexibility may be required—for example, where the geographic foci of activity may shift—there should also be sufficient authority to adjust in the field or a viable process to garner prompt policy consideration, such as approval by the Principals or Deputies Committees or an appropriate subset of them.

Operators will almost always push for more flexibility, as those familiar with headquarters-field relationships will appreciate. A worldwide threat from Jihadists requires worldwide authority to respond and do so on short or immediate time frames. However, presidents should be careful they do not go too far and surrender authority over the actual substance of decision. For one cannot have effective appraisal and accountability if there is no discernible standard against which to measure result. Moreover, presidential decision is an essential source of democratic legitimacy for actions taken in secret with limited or no external input or review. At the same time, field operatives should press for sufficient detail so that the policy intent is clear and operatives are protected from second-guessing in the event of failure, and therefore will take greater risks in accomplishing the intended objectives. Moreover, clear direction also helps mitigate against the conscious and subconscious bias toward risk taking or risk aversion that individual case officers may possess.

## CONCLUSION

Faced with an intractable opponent intent on catastrophic attack, the United States should respond with all the lawful national security tools. This includes covert action, which is fast, flexible, and often daring. It is also suited to a conflict that is as dependent on public diplomacy as it is on military action.

The success or failure of its use will depend on the successful assessment and allocation of risks. First, intelligence decision makers will have to find the optimum balance between counterintelligence risk and operational need. Effective penetration of terrorist targets requires the employment or utilization of persons with necessary ethnic and cultural background. These persons may not be U.S. citizens, and if they are, the ordinary degree of background inquiry may not be available. If we assume too little risk of counterintelligence penetration, we may forgo important opportunities. If we assume too much risk, we may find our agents and officers dead, our avenues of intelligence attack compromised, and our moral leadership undermined.

Second, the mission requires modulation of the risk the United States is prepared to assume in introducing U.S. personnel into high-risk environments, with the encompassing danger that Americans will be captured or killed. Intelligence operations on this battlefield are exceptionally dangerous where the opponent does not play by the "rules of the road" that state intelligence services generally accepted during the Cold War.

Intelligence policy makers will also have to factor in the risk of moral or legal compromise. Although lawful, is an operation a good idea? Do the potential benefits outweigh the policy costs? Have decision makers identified and weighed the enduring consequences of their actions or just their immediate results? If one, for instance, works back from the threat of a WMD being used in a major U.S.

city or that of an ally, then one must hope that the government is continuously appraising and reappraising how we have balanced these risks.

Covert action law addresses these risks in two main ways. First, in statute and executive directive, the law imposes certain minimum requirements of process to address the policy and legal risks and trade-offs of action. Second, the law establishes clarity in accountability. In some cases this is done through imposition of substantive limits on conduct. But more directly, the law does so by making it clear that the president is responsible. Where covert action is concerned, the buck does indeed stop on the president's desk.

However, law does not dictate results; it provides opportunity for success. Changes in the legal landscape will occur because the definition of covert action is, by its own terms, evolving. Moreover, as the United States moves from Cold War understandings to Long War applications of the intelligence and military instruments, a broad range of activities important to national security will be conducted as liaison or clandestine military operations. As a result, the success or failure of covert operations will not only depend on how the executive uses the covert action instrument but on the measure of process applied to those activities that bear comparable benefits and risks.

## NOTES

1. Covert action is one of the five intelligence functions along with collection, analysis and dissemination, liaison, and counterintelligence. R. Gates, "The CIA and Foreign Policy," *Foreign Affairs* 66, no. 2 (Winter 1987/88), p. 216.

2. For a historical overview see, G. Treverton, *Covert Action: The Limits of Intervention in the Postwar World* (New York: Basic Books, 1987); M. Reisman and J. Baker, *Regulating Covert Action* (New Haven, CT: Yale University Press, 1992).

3. See Central Intelligence Agency (undated), *Intelligence in the War of Independence*, available at http://www.cia.gov/cia/publications/warindep/index.html (accessed March 10, 2006); for additional historic perspective, see S. Knott, "Thomas Jefferson's Clandestine Foreign Policy," *International Journal of Intelligence and Counterintelligence* 4, no. 3 (Fall 1990).

4. The words of the Doolittle Committee capture the tenure: "It is now clear that we are facing an implacable enemy whose avowed objective is world domination by whatever means ate whatever cost. There are no rules in such a game. Hitherto acceptable norms of human conduct do not apply." "Report on the Covert Activities of the Central Intelligence Agency," September 30, 1954.

5. See, for example, *Totten Administrator v. United States*, 92 U.S. 105 (1875) and its 2005 antecedent *Tenet et al. v. Doe et ux, 544* U.S. __ (2005); *Curtiss-Wright Export Corp. v. United States*, 299 U.S. 304 (1936); *United States v. Nixon*, 418 U.S. 683 (1974). See also, Reisman and Baker, *Regulating Covert Action*, pp. 117–18.

6. In addition to the president's constitutional authority, covert action was undertaken pursuant to §102(d)(5) of the National Security Act: "It shall be the duty of the Agency, under the direction of the National Security Council . . . (5) to perform such other

functions and duties relating to intelligence affecting the national security as the National Security Council may from time to time direct." Reisman and Baker, *Regulating Covert Action*, p. 118.

7. 50 U.S.C. § 413b(e) (2006).

8. 50 U.S.C. §§ 413b(e)(1), (2), (3), and (4) (2006).

9. Senate Report No. 102-85, "Legislative History, Intelligence Authorization Act of 1990," P.L. 102-88, p. 235.

10. For a discussion of the etymology of the phrase "national security" see M. Shulman, "The Progressive Era Origins of the National Security Act," *Dickinson. Law Review* 104 (Winter 2000), p. 289.

11. 50 U.S.C. § 413b(a) (2006).

12. 50 U.S.C. § 413b(c)(1) (2006).

13. 50 U.S.C. § 413b(c)(2) (2006).

14. 50 U.S.C. § 413b(c)(3) (2006).

15. Senate Report No. 102-85, p. 234.

16. Ronald Reagan, National Security Decision Directive 286, "Approval and Review of Special Activities," October 15, 1987.

17. 50 U.S.C. § 413(a)(1) (2006).

18. 50 U.S.C. § 413(a) (2006), as amended by the Intelligence Reform and Terrorism Prevention Act of 2004, P.L. 108-458 §1071(a)(Y).

19. The NSC is comprised of the president, vice president, secretary of State, and secretary of Defense. The director of National Intelligence and the chairman of the Joint Chiefs of Staff are statutory advisors to the NSC. The president designates members of the NSC Principals Committee and the NSC Deputies Committee. Membership may vary depending on the subject matter. In general, the Principals Committee is chaired by the assistant to the president for National Security Affairs and is comprised of the secretary of State, secretary of Defense, the DNI, the chairman of the Joint Chiefs, the national security advisor to the vice president, and, depending on the subject matter, the attorney general, and the secretary of the Treasury. Depending on the president, the chief of staff to the president, the secretary of the Treasury, the U.S. Ambassador to the United Nations, and others have been designated members of the Principals Committee. The Deputies Committee generally is chaired by the principal deputy assistant to the president for National Security Affairs and is comprised of the deputies or designated representatives of the Principals. Of course, other senior officials and staff may attend designated meetings of the committees.

20. William J. Clinton, Presidential Decision Directive (PDD) 2, "Organization of the National Security Council," January 20, 1993, para. A.

21. Executive Order 12333, "Intelligence Activities," December 4, 1981, para. 1.2(a). Special activities are "activities conducted in support of national foreign policy objectives abroad which are planned and executed so that the role of the United States Government is not apparent or acknowledged publicly...," in other words "covert action."

22. 50 U.S.C. § 513b(a)(5) (2006).

23. The 9/11 Commission, *Final Report of the National Commission on Terrorist Attacks Upon the United States* (New York: Norton, 2004), p. 132. See also R. Posner, "The 9/11 Report: A Dissent," *New York Times Book Review*, August 29, 2004.

24. September 18, 2002 Testimony before Senate and House Select Committees on Intelligence.

25. 50 U.S.C. § 413b(f) (2006).

26. See generally, *Ker v. Illinois*, 119 U.S. 436 (1886); *Frisbie v. Collins*, 342 U.S. 519 (1952); *Toscanino v. United States*, 500 F.2d 267 (2nd Cir. 1974); and *United States v. Alvarez-Machain*, 504 U.S. 655 (1992). The doctrine is discussed in Reisman and Baker, *Regulating Covert Action*, pp. 128–30.

27. Convention Against Torture and Other Cruel, Inhuman or Degrading Treatment or Punishment, and 18 U.S.C. § 2340A.

28. "Memorandum of Understanding Between the Government of the United Kingdom of Great Britain and Northern Ireland and the Government of the Hashemite Kingdom of Jordan Regulating the Provision of Undertakings in Respect of Specified Persons Prior to Deportation," August 10, 2005, available at http://newsvote.bbc.co.uk/mpapps/pagetools/print/news.bbc.co.uk/1/hi/uk/4143214.stm (accessed March 10, 2006).

29. In the context of detainees transferred from Guantánamo Bay to third countries, the assistant U.S. attorney representing the United States in litigation has stated in court: "We have obtained assurances before they are released that it is more likely than not that they will not be tortured in a country that they go to. In fact it has happened where we have not been satisfied with the assurances that a foreign government has given the United States, and we have not transferred those detainees." V. Blum, "Gaining a Foothold in Guantanamo: Defense Lawyers Want Access to Every Detainee—And Say in Prisoner Transfers," *Legal Times*, March 28, 2005.

30. *Ker*, 444.

31. Senate Report 102-85, p. 233, quoting the text of a letter sent to the chairmen of the Senate and House Intelligence Committees. "Dear Mr. Chairman: I am aware of your concerns regarding the provision of notice Congress of covert action. . . . I anticipate that in almost all instances, prior notice will be possible. In those rare instances where prior notice is not provided, I anticipate that notice will be provided within a few days. Any withholding beyond this period will be based upon my assertion of authorities granted to this office by the Constitution." For an example of an instance when a president might withhold notification occurring before these provisions were enacted see S. Turner, "Covert Common Sense: Don't Throw the CIA out with the Ayatollah," *Washington Post,* November 23, 1986.

32. See 9/11 Commission, *Final Report*, pp. 419–23; Commission on the Intelligence Capabilities of the United States Regarding Weapons of Mass Destruction, *Report to the President of the United States* (Washington: Government Printing Office, 2005), pp. 337–41.

33. Congressional Research Service, "Director of National Intelligence: Statutory Authorities," April 11, 2005, p. 2; Commission on the Roles and Capabilities of the Intelligence Community, p. 45, available at http://www.access.gpo.gov/intelligence/int/pdf/report.html (accessed March 14, 2006).

34. *Youngstown Sheet & Tube Co. v. Sawyer*, 343 U.S. 579, 635–36 (1952).

35. Like covert action, liaison authority is expressly authorized in statute and unclassified executive directive. Section 104(e), for example, of the National Security Act includes within the DNI's authorities "Coordination with Foreign Governments." Specifically, "under the direction of the National Security Council . . . the Director shall coordinate the relationships between elements of the intelligence community and the intelligence security services of foreign governments on all matters involving intelligence related to the national security or involving intelligence acquired through clandestine

means." Liaison might also be conducted solely pursuant to the president's constitutional authority as delegated by directive. Executive Order 12333 directs the (then) DCI to "Formulate policies concerning foreign intelligence and counterintelligence arrangements with foreign governments, coordinate foreign intelligence and counterintelligence relationships between agencies of the Intelligence community and the intelligence and or internal security services of foreign governments, and establish procedures governing the conduct of liaison by any department or agency with such services on narcotics matters."

36. J. Lehman. "Getting Spy Reform Wrong; Sept. 11 Commission's Proposals Were Turned into Bureaucratic Bloat," *Washington Post*, November 16, 2005.

37. A. Hamilton, J. Madison, and J. Jay, *The Federalist Papers,* edited by Clinton Rossiter (New York: Signet, 1961), p. 67.

38. *Youngstown*, 343 U.S. at 634.

39. 500 U.S.C. 413b (a) (2006).

# EXCERPT FROM THE CHURCH COMMITTEE REPORT ON THE EVOLUTION OF CIA COVERT ACTION

## CLANDESTINE ACTIVITIES

### A. ORIGINS OF COVERT ACTION

The concept of a central intelligence agency developed out of a concern for the quality of intelligence analysis available to policymakers. The 1945 discussion which surrounded the creation of CIG focused on the problem of intelligence coordination. Two years later debates on the CIA in the Congress and the Executive assumed only the coordination role along with intelligence collection (both overt and clandestine) and analysis for the newly constituted Agency.

Yet, within one year of the passage of the National Security Act, the CIA was charged with the conduct of covert psychological, political, paramilitary, and economic activities.[21] The acquisition of this mission had a profound impact on the direction of the Agency and on its relative stature within the government.

The precedent for covert activities existed in OSS. The clandestine collection capability had been preserved through the Strategic Services Unit, whose responsibilities CIG absorbed in June 1946. The maintenance of that capability and its presence in CIA contributed to the Agency's ultimate assumption of a covert operational role.

---

*Source*: Select Committee to Study Governmental Operations with Respect to Intelligence Activities (the Church Committee), *Supplementary Detailed Staff Reports on Foreign And Military Intelligence, Final Report,* Book IV, 94th Cong., 2d Sess., Sen. Rept. No. 94–755 (April 23, 1976), pp. 25–41 (written by staff member Dr. Anne Karalekas). Footnotes reflect original numbering.

[21] Psychological operations were primarily media-related activities, including unattributed publications, forgeries, and subsidization of publications; political action involved exploitation of dispossessed persons and defectors, and support to political parties; paramilitary activities included support to guerrillas and sabotage; economic activities consisted of monetary operations.

The United States, initiation of covert operations is usually associated with the 1948 Western European elections. It is true that this was the first officially recorded evidence of U.S. covert political intervention abroad. However, American policymakers had formulated plans for covert action—at first covert psychological action—much earlier. Decisions regarding U.S. sponsorship of clandestine activities were gradual but consistent, spurred on by the growing concern over Soviet intentions.

By late 1946, cabinet officials were preoccupied with the Soviet threat, and over the next year their fears intensified. For U.S. policymakers, international events seemed to be a sequence of Soviet incursions. In March 1946, the Soviet Union refused to withdraw its troops from the Iranian province of Azerbaijan; two months later civil war involving Communist rebel forces erupted in Greece. By 1947, Communists had assumed power in Poland, Hungary, and Rumania; and in the Phillipines the government was under attack by the Hukbalahaps, a communist-led guerrilla group.

For U.S. officials, the perception of the Soviet Union as a global threat demanded new modes of conduct in foreign policy to supplement the traditional alternatives of diplomacy and war. Massive economic aid represented one new method of achieving U.S. foreign policy objectives. In 1947, the United States embarked on an unprecedented economic assistance program to Europe with the Truman Doctrine and the Marshall Plan. By insuring economic stability, U.S. officials hoped to limit Soviet encroachments. Covert operations represented another, more activist departure in the conduct of U.S. peacetime foreign policy. Covert action was an option that was something more than diplomacy but still short of war. As such, it held the promise of frustrating Soviet ambitions without provoking open conflict.

The suggestion for the initiation of covert operations did not originate in CIG. Sometime in late 1946, Secretary of War Robert Patterson suggested to Forrestal that military and civilian personnel study this form of war for future use. What prompted Patterson's suggestion is unclear. However, from Patterson's suggestion policymakers proceeded to consider the lines of authority for the conduct of psychological operations. Discussion took place in the State-War-Navy Coordinating Committee (SWNCC), whose members included the Secretaries of the three Departments, Byrnes, Patterson and Forrestal.[22] In December 1946, a SWNCC subcommittee formulated guidelines for the conduct of psychological warfare in peacetime and wartime.[23] The full SWNCC adopted the recommendation later that month.

Discussion continued within the Executive in the spring and summer of 1947. From all indications, only senior-level officials were involved, and the discussions were closely held. From establishing guidelines for the possibility of psychological warfare, policymakers proceeded to contingency planning. On April 30, 1947, a SWNCC subcommittee was organized to consider and actually plan for a U.S. psychological warfare effort. On June 5, 1947, the subcommittee was accorded a degree of permanency and renamed the

---

[22] SWNCC was established late in 1944 as an initial attempt at more centralized decisionmaking.

[23] In peacetime, psychological warfare would be directed by an interdepartmental subcommittee of SWNCC with the approval of the JCS and the National Intelligence Authority. During war, a Director of Psychological Warfare would assume primary responsibility under a central committee responsible to the President. The committee would consist of representatives from the SWNCC and from CIG.

Special Studies and Evaluations Subcommittee. By this time, the fact that the U.S. would engage in covert operations was a given; what remained were decisions about the organizational arrangements and actual implementation. Senior officials had moved from the point of conceptualization to determination of a specific need. Yet it is not clear whether or not they had in mind specific activities geared to specific countries or events.

In the fall of 1947 policymakers engaged in a series of discussions on the assignment of responsibility for the conduct of covert operations. There was no ready consensus and a variety of opinions emerged. DCI Hillenkoetter had his own views on the subject. Sometime in October 1947 he recommended "vitally needed psychological operations"—again in general terms without reference to specific countries or groups—but believed that such activities were military rather than intelligence functions and therefore belonged in an organization responsible to the JCS. Hillenkoetter also believed congressional authorization would be necessary both for the initiation of psychological warfare and for the expenditure of funds for that purpose. Whatever Hillenkoetter's views on the appropriate authorization for a psychological warfare function, his opinions were undoubtedly influenced by the difficulties he had experienced in dealing with the Departments. It is likely that he feared CIA's acquisition of an operational capability would precipitate similar problems of departmental claims on the Agency's operational functions. Hillenkoetter's stated preferences had no apparent impact on the outcome of the psychological warfare debate.

Within a few weeks of Hillenkoetter's statement, Forrestal, the Secretaries of the Army, Navy, and Air Force, along with the JCS, advanced their recommendations regarding the appropriate organization to conduct covert psychological warfare. In a proposal dated November 4, they held that propaganda of all kinds was a function of the State Department and that an Assistant Secretary of State in consultation with the DCI and a military representative should be responsible for the operations.

On November 24, President Truman approved the November 4 recommendation, assigning psychological warfare coordination to the Secretary of State. Within three weeks, the decision was reversed. Despite the weight of numbers favoring State Department control, the objections of Secretary of State George Marshall eliminated the option advanced by the other Secretaries. Marshall opposed State Department responsibility for covert action. He was vehement on the point and believed that such activities, if exposed as State Department actions, would embarrass the Department and discredit American foreign policy both short-term and long-term.

Apart from his position as Secretary of State, the impact of Marshall's argument derived from the more general influence he exerted at the time. Marshall had emerged from the war as one of America's "silent heroes." To the public, he was a quiet, taciturn, almost unimpressive figure, but as the Army Chief of Staff during the war, he had gained the universal respect of his civilian and military colleagues for his commitment, personal integrity, and ability.

In the transition from military officer to diplomat, he had developed a strong sense that the United States would have to adopt an activist role against the Soviet Union. Immediately after his appointment as Secretary in February 1947, he played a key role in the decision to aid Greece and Turkey and quickly after, in June 1947, announced the sweeping European economic recovery program which bore his name. It was out of concern for the success and credibility of the United States' recently articulated economic program that Marshall objected to State Department conduct of covert action. Marshall favored placing covert activities outside the Department, but still subject to guidance from the Secretary of State.

Marshall's objections prevailed, and on December 14 the National Security Council adopted NSC 4/A, a directive which gave the CIA responsibility for covert psychological operations. The DCI was charged with ensuring that psychological operations were consistent with U.S. foreign policy and overt foreign information activities. On December 22 the Special Procedures Group was established within the CIA's Office of Special Operations to carry out psychological operations.

Although Marshall's position prevented State from conducting psychological warfare, it does not explain why the CIA was charged with the responsibility. The debate which ensued in 1947 after the agreement on the need for psychological warfare had focused on control and responsibility. At issue were the questions of who would plan, direct, and oversee the actual operations.

State and the military wanted to maintain control over covert psychological operations, but they did not want to assume operational responsibility. The sensitive nature of the operations made the Departments fear exposure of their association with the activities. The CIA offered advantages as the organization to execute covert operations. Indeed, in 1947 one-third of the CIA's personnel had served with OSS. The presence of former OSS personnel, who had experience in wartime operations, provided the Agency with a group of individuals who could quickly develop and implement programs. This, coupled with its overseas logistical apparatus, gave the Agency a ready capability. In addition, the Agency also possessed a system of unvouchered funds for its clandestine collection mission, which meant that there was no need to approach Congress for separate appropriations. With the Departments unwilling to assume the risks involved in covert activities, the CIA provided a convenient mechanism.

During the next six months psychological operations were initiated in Central and Eastern Europe. The activities were both limited and amateur and consisted of unattributed publications, radio broadcasts, and blackmail. By 1948 the Special Procedures Group had acquired a radio transmitter for broadcasting behind the Iron Curtain, had established a secret propaganda printing plant in Germany, and had begun assembling a fleet of balloons to drop propaganda materials into Eastern European countries.

Both internally and externally the pressure continued for an expansion in the scope of U.S. covert activity. The initial definition of covert action had been limited to covert psychological warfare. In May 1948, George F. Kennan, Director of the State Department's Policy Planning Staff, advocated the development of a covert political action capability. The distinction at that time was an important and real one. Political action meant direct intervention in the electoral processes of foreign governments rather than attempts to influence public opinion through media activities.

International events gave force to Kennan's proposal. In February 1948, Communists staged a successful coup in Czechoslovakia. At the same time, France and Italy were beleaguered by a wave of Communist-inspired strikes. In March 1948, near hysteria gripped the U.S. Government with the so-called "war scare." The crisis was precipitated by a cable from General Lucius Clay, Commander in Chief, European Command, to Lt. General Stephen J. Chamberlin, Director of Intelligence, Army General Staff, in which Clay said, "I have felt a subtle change in Soviet attitude which I cannot define but which now gives me a feeling that it [war] may come with dramatic suddenness."

The war scare launched a series of interdepartmental intelligence estimates on the likelihood of a Soviet attack on Western Europe and the United States. Although the estimates concluded that there was no evidence that the U.S.S.R. would start a war, Clay's cable had articulated the degree of suspicion and outright fear of the Soviet Union that was shared by policymakers at this time. Kennan proposed that State, specifically the Policy Planning Staff, have a "directorate" for overt and covert political warfare. The director of the Special Studies Group, as Kennan named it, would be under State Department control, but not formally associated with the Department. Instead, he would have concealed funds and personnel elsewhere, and his small staff of eight people would be comprised of representatives from State and Defense.

Kennan's concept and statement of function were endorsed by the NSC. In June 1948, one month after his proposal, the NSC adopted NSC 10/2, a directive authorizing a dramatic increase in the range of covert operations directed against the Soviet Union, including political warfare, economic warfare, and paramilitary activities.

While authorizing a sweeping expansion in covert activities, NSC 10/2 established the Office of Special Projects, soon renamed the Office of Policy Coordination (OPC), within the CIA to replace the Special Procedures Group. As a CIA component OPC was an anomaly. OPC's budget and personnel were appropriated within CIA allocations, but the DCI had little authority in determining OPC's activities. Responsibility for the direction of OPC rested with the Office's director, designated by the Secretary of State. Policy guidance—decisions on the need for specific activities—came to the OPC director from State and Defense, bypassing the DCI.

The organizational arrangements established in 1948 for the conduct of covert operations reflected both the concept of covert action as defined by U.S. officials and the perception of the CIA as an institution. Both the activities and the institution were regarded as extensions of State and the military services. The Departments (essentially the NSC) defined U.S. policy objectives; covert action represented one means of attaining those objectives; and the CIA executed the operations.

In a conversation on August 12, 1948, Hillenkoetter, Kennan, and Sidney Souers discussed the implementation of NSC 10/A. The summary of the conversation reveals policymakers firm expectation that covert political action would serve strictly as a support function for U.S. foreign and military policy and that State and the services would define the scope of covert activities in specific terms. The summaries of the participants' statements as cited in a CIA history bear quoting at length:

> Mr. Kennan made the point that as the State Department's designated representative he would want to have specific knowledge of the objectives of every operation and also of the procedures and methods employed in all cases where those procedures and methods involved political decisions.
>
> Mr. Souers indicated his agreement with Mr. Kennan's thesis and stated specifically that it has been the intention of the National Security Council in preparing the document that it should reflect the recognition of the principle that the Departments of State and the National Military Establishment are responsible for the conduct of the activities of the Office of Special Projects, with the Department of State taking preeminence in time of peace and the National Military Establishment succeeding the pre-eminent position in wartime.
>
> Admiral Hillenkoetter agreed with Mr. Kennan's statement that the political warfare activity should be conducted as an instrument of U.S. foreign policy and subject in peacetime to direct guidance by the State Department.
>
> Mr. Kennan agreed that it was necessary that the State Department assume responsibility for stating whether or not individual projects are politically desirable and stated that as the State Department's designated representative he would be accountable for providing such decisions.

Likewise, reflecting on his intentions and those of his colleagues in 1948, Kennan recently stated:

> ... we were alarmed at the inroads of the Russian influence in Western Europe beyond the point where the Russian troops had reached. And we were alarmed particularly over the situation in France and Italy. We felt that the Communists were using the very extensive funds that they then had in hand to gain control of key elements of life in France and Italy, particularly the publishing companies, the press, the labor unions, student organizations, women's organizations, and all sort of organizations of that sort, to gain control of them and use them as front organizations....
>
> That was just one example that I recall of why we thought that we ought to have some facility for covert operations....
>
> ... It ended up with the establishment within CIA of a branch, an office for activities of this nature, and one which employed a great many people. It did not work out at all the way I had conceived it or others of my associates in the Department of State. We had thought that this would be a facility which could be used when and if an occasion arose when it might be needed. There might be years when we wouldn't have to do anything like this. But if the occasion arose we wanted somebody in the Government who would have the funds, the experience, the expertise to do these things and to do them in a proper way.[24]

Clearly, in recommending the development of a covert action capability in 1948, policymakers intended to make available a small contingency force that could mount operations on a limited basis. Senior officials did not plan to develop large-scale continuing covert operations. Instead, they hoped to establish a small capability that could be activated at their discretion.

## B. THE OFFICE OF POLICY COORDINATION, 1948–1952

OPC developed into a far different organization from that envisioned by Forrestal, Marshall, and Kennan in August 1948. By 1952, when it merged with the Agency's clandestine collection component, the Office of Special Operations, OPC had expanded its activities to include worldwide covert operations, and it had achieved an institutional independence that was unimaginable at the time of its inception.

The outbreak of the Korean War in the summer of 1950 had a significant effect on OPC. Following the North Korean invasion of South Korea, the State Department as well as the Joint Chiefs of Staff recommended the initiation of paramilitary activities in Korea and China. OPC's participation in the war effort contributed to its transformation from an organization that was to provide the capability for a limited number of *ad hoc* operations to an organization that conducted continuing, ongoing activities on a massive scale. In concept, manpower, budget, and scope of activities, OPC simply skyrocketed. The comparative figures for 1949 and 1952 are staggering. In 1949 OPC's total personnel strength was 302; in 1952 it was 2,812 plus 3,142 overseas contract personnel. In 1949 OPC's budget figure was $4,700,000; in 1952 it was $82,000,000. In 1949, OPC had personnel assigned to seven overseas stations; in 1952 OPC had personnel at forty-seven stations.

Apart from the impetus provided by the Korean War several other factors converged to alter the nature and scale of OPC's activities. First, policy direction took the form of condoning and fostering activity without providing scrutiny and control. Officials

[24] George F. Kennan testimony, October 28 1975, pp. 8–10.

throughout the government regarded the Soviet Union as an aggressive force, and OPC's activities were initiated and justified on the basis of this shared perception. The series of NSC directives which authorized covert operations laid out broad objectives and stated in bold terms the necessity for meeting the Soviet challenge head on. After the first 1948 directive authorizing covert action, subsequent directives in 1950 and 1951 called for an intensification of these activities without establishing firm guidelines for approval.

On April 14, 1950, the National Security Council issued NSC 68, which called for a non-military counter-offensive against the U.S.S.R., including covert economic, political, and psychological warfare to stir up unrest and revolt in the satellite countries. A memo written in November 1951 commented on the fact that such broad and comprehensive undertakings as delineated by the NSC could only be accomplished by the establishment of a worldwide structure for covert operations on a much grander scale than OPC had previously contemplated. The memo stated:

> It would be a task similar in concept, magnitude and complexity to the creation of widely deployed military forces together with the logistical support required to conduct manifold, complex and delicate operations in a wide variety of overseas locations.

On October 21, 1951 NSC 10/5 replaced NSC 10/2 as the governing directive for covert action. It once again called for an intensification of covert action and reaffirmed the responsibility of the DCI in the conduct of covert operations. Each of these policy directives provided the broadest justification for large-scale covert activity.

Second, OPC operations had to meet the very different policy needs of the State and Defense Departments. The State Department encouraged political action and propaganda activities to support its diplomatic objectives, while the Defense Department requested paramilitary activities to support the Korean War effort and to counter communist-associated guerrillas. These distinct missions required OPC to develop and maintain different capabilities, including manpower and support material.

The third factor contributing to OPC's expansion was the organizational arrangements that created an internal demand for projects. The decision to undertake covert political action and to lodge that responsibility in a group distinct from the Departments required the creation of a permanent structure. OPC required regular funding to train and pay personnel, to maintain overseas stations (and provide for the supporting apparatus), and to carry out specific projects. That funding could not be provided on an *ad hoc* basis. It had to be budgeted for in advance. With budgeting came the need for ongoing activities to justify future allocations—rather than leaving the flexibility of responding to specific requirements.

To fulfill the different State and Defense requirements OPC adopted a "project" system rather than a programmed financial system. This meant that operations were organized around projects—individual activities, e.g. funding to a political candidate—rather than general programs or policy objectives, and that OPC budgeted in terms of anticipated numbers of projects. The project system had important internal effects. An individual within OPC judged his own performance, and was judged by others, on the importance and number of projects he initiated and managed. The result was competition among individuals and among the OPC divisions to generate the maximum number of projects. Projects remained the fundamental units around which clandestine activities were organized, and two generations of Agency personnel have been conditioned by this system.

The interaction among the OPC components reflected the internal competition that the project system generated. OPC was divided between field personnel stationed overseas and Headquarters personnel stationed in Washington. Split into four functional staffs (dealing with political warfare, psychological warfare, paramilitary operations and economic warfare) and six geographical divisions, Headquarters was to retain close control over the initiation and implementation of projects to insure close policy coordination with State and Defense. Field stations were to serve only as standing mechanisms for the performance of tasks assigned from Washington.

The specific relationship between the functional staffs, the geographical divisions and the overseas stations was intended to be as follows: With guidance from the NSC, the staffs would generate project outlines for the divisions. In turn, the divisions would provide their respective overseas stations with detailed instructions on project action. Very soon, however, each of the three components was attempting to control project activities. Within the functional staffs proprietary attitudes developed toward particular projects at the point when the regional divisions were to take them over. The staffs were reluctant to adopt an administrative support role with respect to the divisions in the way that was intended. Thus, the staffs and the divisions began to look upon each other as competitors rather than joint participants. In November 1949 an internal study of OPC concluded that:

> ...the present organization makes for duplication of effort and an extensive amount of unnecessary coordination and competition rather than cooperation and teamwork....

A reorganization in 1950 attempted to rectify the problem by assigning responsibility for planning single-country operations to the appropriate geographical division. This meant that the divisions assumed real operational control. The staffs were responsible for coordinating multiple country operations as well as providing the guidance function. In principle the staffs were to be relegated to the support role they were intended to serve. However, the break was never complete. The distinctions themselves were artificial, and staffs seized on their authority over multiple country activities to maintain an operational role in such areas as labor operations. This tension between the staffs and the divisions continued through the late 1960's as some staffs achieved maximum operational independence. The situation is a commentary on the project orientation which originated with OPC and the recognition that promotion and rewards were derived from project management—not from disembodied guidance activities.

The relationship between Washington and the field was subject to pressures similar to those that influenced the interaction between the divisions and the staffs. Predictably, field personnel began to develop their own perspective on suitable operations and their mode of conduct. Being "there," field personnel could and did argue that theirs was the most realistic and accurate view. Gradually, as the number of overseas personnel grew and as the number of stations increased, the stations assumed the initiative in project development.

The regional divisions at Headquarters tended to assume an administrative support role but still retained approval authority for projects of particular sensitivity and cost. The shift in initiative first from the staffs to the divisions, then to the stations, affected the relative desirability of assignments. Since fulfillment of the OPC mission was measured in terms of project development and management, the sought-after places were those where the projects originated. Individuals who were assigned those places rose quickly within the Directorate.

## C. POLICY GUIDANCE

Responsibility for coordination with the State and Defense Departments rested with Frank G. Wisner, appointed Assistant Director for Policy Coordination (ADPC) on September 1, 1948. Described almost unanimously by those who worked with him as "brilliant," Wisner possessed the operational instincts, the activist temperament, and the sheer physical energy required to develop and establish OPC as an organization. Wisner also had the advantages of independent wealth and professional and social contacts which he employed skillfully in advancing OPC's position within the Washington bureaucracy.

Wisner was born into a prominent Southern family and distinguished himself as an undergraduate and a law student at the University of Virginia. Following law school, Wisner joined a New York law firm where he stayed for seven years. After a brief stint in the Navy, Wisner was assigned to OSS and spent part of his time serving under Allen Dulles in Wiesbaden, Germany. At the end of the war he returned to law practice, but left again in 1947 to accept the post of Deputy to the Assistant Secretary of State for Occupied Areas. It was from this position that Wisner was tapped to be ADPC.

Although the stipulation of NSC 10/2 that the Secretary of State designate the ADPC was intended to insure the ADPC's primary identification with State, that did not occur. Wisner quickly developed an institutional loyalty to OPC and its mission and drew on the web of New York law firm connections that existed in postwar Washington as well as on his State Department ties to gain support for OPC's activities.

The guidance that State and Defense provided OPC became very general and allowed the maximum opportunity for project development. Approximately once a week Wisner met with the designated representatives of State and Defense. Given that Kennan had been a prime mover in the establishment of OPC, it was unlikely that as the State Department's designated representative from 1948 to 1950 he would discourage the overall direction of the organization he had helped create. From 1948 to 1949 Defense was represented by General Joseph T. McNarney, the former Commander of U.S. Forces in Europe. Having stood "eyeball to eyeball" with the Russians in Germany, McNarney was highly sympathetic to the OPC mission.

With the broad objectives laid out in NSC 10/2, the means of implementation were left to OPC. The representatives were not an approval body, and there was no formal mechanism whereby individual projects had to be brought before them for discussion. Because it was assumed that covert action would be exceptional, strict provisions for specific project authorization were not considered necessary. With minimal supervision from State and Defense and with a shared agreement on the nature of the OPC mission, individuals in OPC could take the initiative in conceiving and implementing projects. In this context, operational tasks, personnel, money and material tended to grow in relation to one another with little outside oversight.

In 1951, DCI Walter Bedell Smith took the initiative in requesting more specific high-level policy direction. In May of that year, after a review of NSC 68, Smith sought a clarification of the OPC mission from the NSC.[26] In a paper dated May 8, 1951, entitled the "Scope and Pace of Covert Operations" Smith called for NSC restatement or

---

[26] Soon after his appointment as DCI in October 1950, Smith succeeded in having OPC placed directly under the jurisdiction of the DCI, making Wisner responsible to him rather than to the Department of State and Defense. See pp. 37–38.

redetermination of the several responsibilities and authorities involved in U.S. covert operations. More importantly, Smith proposed that the newly created Psychological Strategy Board provide CIA guidance on the conduct of covert operations.[27]

The NSC adopted Smith's proposal making the Psychological Strategy Board the approval body for covert action. The body that had been responsible for exercising guidance over the CIA had received it from the DCI. Whatever the dimensions of the growth in OPC operations, the NSC had not attempted to limit the expansion.

## D. OPC ACTIVITIES

At the outset OPC activities were directed toward four principal operational areas: refugee programs, labor activities, media development, and political action. Geographically, the area of concentration was Western Europe. There were two reasons for this. First, Western Europe was the area deemed most vulnerable to Communist encroachment; and second, until 1950 both CIA (OSO) and OPC were excluded from the Far East by General Douglas MacArthur, who refused to concede any jurisdiction to the civilian intelligence agency in the Pacific theater—just as he had done with OSS during the war.

OPC inherited programs from both the Special Procedures Group (SPG) and the Economic Cooperation Administration (ECA). After the issuance of NSC 10/2 SPG turned over to OPC all of its resources, including an unexpended budget of over $2 million, a small staff, and its communications equipment. In addition to SPG's propaganda activities OPC acquired the ECA's fledgling labor projects as well as the accompanying funds. Foreign labor operations continued and became a major focus of CIA activity on a worldwide basis throughout the 1950's and into the mid-1960's.

The national elections in Europe in 1948 had been a primary motivation in the establishment of OPC. By channeling funds to center parties and developing media assets, OPC attempted to influence election results—with considerable success. These activities formed the basis for covert political action for the next twenty years. By 1952 approximately forty different covert action projects were underway in one central European country alone. Other projects were targeted against what was then referred to as the "Soviet bloc."

During his term in the State Department Wisner had spent much of his time on problems involving refugees in Germany, Austriaa and Trieste. In addition, his service with OSS had been oriented toward Central Europe. The combination of State's continuing interest and Wisner's personal experience led to OPC's immediate emphasis on Central European refugee operations. OPC representatives made contact with thousands of Soviet refugees and emigrés for the purpose of influencing their political leadership. The National Committee for Free Europe, a group of prominent American businessmen, lawyers, and philanthropists, and Radio Free Europe were products of the OPC program.

Until 1950 OPC's paramilitary activities (also referred to as preventive direct action) were limited to plans and preparations for stay-behind nets in the event of future war. Requested by the Joint Chiefs of Staff, these projected OPC operations focused, once again, on Western Europe and were designed to support NATO forces against Soviet attack.

---

[27] The Psychological Strategy Board (PSB) was an NSC subcommittee established on April 4, 1951 to exercise direction over psychological warfare programs. Its membership included departmental representatives and PSB staff members.

The outbreak of the Korean War significantly altered the nature of OPC's paramilitary activities as well as the organization's overall size and capability. Between fiscal year 1950 and fiscal year 1951, OPC's personnel strength jumped from 584 to 1531. Most of that growth took place in paramilitary activities in the Far East. In the summer of 1950, following the North Korean invasion of South Korea, the State Department requested the initiation of paramilitary and psychological operations on the Chinese mainland. Whatever MacArthur's preferences, the JCS were also eager for support activities in the Far East. This marked the beginning of OPC's active paramilitary engagement. The Korean War established OPC's and CIA's jurisdiction in the Far East and created the basic paramilitary capability that the Agency employed for twenty years. By 1953, the elements of that capability were "in place"—aircraft, amphibious craft, and an experienced group of personnel. For the next quarter century paramilitary activities remained the major CIA covert activity in the Far East.

## E. OPC INTEGRATION AND THE OPC-OSO MERGER

The creation of OPC and its ambiguous relationship to the Agency precipitated two major administrative problems, the D'CI's relationship to OPC and antagonism between OPC and the Agency's clandestine collection component, the Office of Special Operations. DCI Walter Bedell Smith acted to rectify both problems.

As OPC continued to grow, Smith's predecessor, Admiral Hillenkoetter, resented the fact that he had no management authority over OPC, although its budget and personnel were being allocated through the CIA. Hillenkoetter's clashes with the State and Defense Departments as well as with Wisner, the Director of OPC, were frequent. Less than a week after taking office Smith announced that as DCI he would assume administrative control of OPC and that State and Defense would channel their policy guidance through him rather than through Wisner. On October 12, 1950, the representatives of State, Defense and the Joint Chiefs of Staff formally accepted the change. The ease with which the shift occurred was primarily a result of Smith's own position of influence with the Departments.

OPC's anomalous position in the Agency revealed the difficulty of maintaining two separate organizations for the execution of varying but overlapping clandestine activities. The close "tradecraft" relationship between clandestine collection and covert action, and the frequent necessity for one to support the other was totally distorted with the separation of functions in OSO and OPC. Organizational rivalry rather than interchange dominated the relationship between the two components.

On the operating level the conflicts were intense. Each component had representatives conducting separate operations at each station. Given the related missions of the two, OPC and OSO personnel were often competing for the same agents and, not infrequently, attempting to wrest agents from each other. In 1952 the outright hostility between the two organizations in Bangkok required the direct intervention of the Assistant Director for Special Operations, Lyman Kirkpatrick. There an important official was closely tied to OPC, and OSO was trying to lure him into its employ.

The OPC-OSO conflict was only partially the result of overseas competition for assets. Salary differentials and the differences in mission were other sources of antagonism. At the time of its creation in 1948 OPC was granted liberal funding to attract personnel quickly in order to get its operation underway. In addition, the burgeoning activities enabled people, once hired, to rise rapidly. The result was that OPC personnel held higher-ranking, better-paid positions, than their OSO counterparts.

Many OSO personnel had served with OSS, and their resentment of OPC was intensified by the fact that they regarded themselves as the intelligence "purists," the professionals who engaged in collection rather than action and whose prewar experience made them more knowledgeable and expert than the OPC recruits. In particular, OSO personnel regarded OPC's high-risk operations as a threat to the maintenance of OSO security and cover. OPC's favored position with State and Defense, its generous budget, and its visible accomplishments all contrasted sharply with OSO's silent, long-term objectives in espionage and counterespionage. By June 1952 OPC had overtaken OSO in personnel and budget allocation. Soon after his appointment as DCI, Smith addressed the problem of the OPC-OSO conflict. Lawrence Houston, the CIA's General Counsel, had raised the issue with him and recommended a merger of the two organizations.[28] Sentiment in OSO and OPC favored the principle of a merger. Lyman Kirkpatrick, the Executive Assistant to the DCI, Major General W. G. Wyman, Assistant Director for Special Operations, Wisner, and William Jackson all appeared to have favored a merger—although there was disagreement on the form it should take.

Between 1951 and 1952 Smith made several cosmetic changes to foster better coordination between OPC and OSO. Among them was the appointment of Allen W. Dulles as Deputy Director for Plans in January 1951.[29] Dulles was responsible for supervising both OPC and OSO, although the two components were independently administered by their own Directors. During this period of "benign coordination" Smith consulted extensively with senior officials in OPC and OSO. OPC's rapid growth and its institutional dynamism colored the attitude of OSO toward a potential merger. In the discussions which Bedell Smith held, senior OSO personnel, specifically Lyman Kirkpatrick and Richard Helms, argued for an integration of OPC functions under OSO control rather than an integrated chain of command down to station level. Fundamentally, the OSO leadership feared being engulfed by OPC in both operations and in personnel. However, by this time Bedell Smith was committed to the idea of an integrated structure.

Although some effort was made to combine the OSO and OPC Western Hemisphere Divisions in June 1951, real integration at the operations level did not occur until August 1952, when OSO and OPC became the Directorate of Plans (DDP). Under this arrangement, Wisner was named Deputy Director for Plans and assumed the command functions of the ADSO and ADPC. Wisner's second in command, Chief of Operations, was Richard Helms, drawn from the OSO side to strike a balance at the senior level. At this time Dulles replaced Jackson as DDCI.

The merger resulted in the maximum development of covert action over clandestine collection. There were several reasons for this. First was the orientation of Wisner himself. Wisner's OSS background and his OPC experience had established his interests in the operational side of clandestine activities. Second, for people in the field, rewards came more quickly through visible operational accomplishments than through the silent, long-term development of agents required for clandestine collection. In the words of one former high-ranking DDP official, "Collection is the hardest thing of all; it's much easier to plant an article in a local newspaper."

---

[28] The Dulles-Jackson-Correa survey had also advised a merger of OPC, OSO and the Office of Operations, the Agency's overt collection component.

[29] Dulles had been serving as an advisor to successive DCIs since 1947. Smith and Jackson prevailed upon him to join the Agency on a full-time basis.

## F. CONGRESSIONAL REVIEW

The CIA was conceived and organized as an agent of the Executive branch. Traditionally, Congress' only formal relationship to the Agency was through the appropriations process. The concept of Congressional oversight in the sense of scrutinizing and being fully informed of Agency activities did not exist. The international atmosphere, Congress relationship to the Executive branch and the Congressional committee structure determined the pattern of interaction between the Agency and members of the legislature. Acceptance of the need for clandestine activities and of the need for secrecy to protect those activities contributed to Congress' relatively unquestioning and uncritical attitude regarding the CIA, as did the Executive branch's ascendancy in foreign policy for nearly two decades following World War II. The strong committee system which accorded enormous power to committee chairmen and limited the participation of less senior members in committee business resulted in informal arrangements whereby selected members were kept informed of Agency activities primarily through one-to-one exchanges with the DCI.

In 1946, following a Joint Committee review Congress enacted the Legislative Reorganization Act which reduced the number of committees and realigned their jurisdictions.[30] The prospect of a unified military establishment figured into the 1946 debates and decisions on Congressional reorganization. However, Congress did not anticipate having to deal with the CIA. This meant that after the passage of the National Security Act in 1947 CIA affairs had to be handled within a committee structure which had not accommodated itself to the existence of a central intelligence agency.

In the House and Senate the Armed Services and Appropriations Committees were granted jurisdiction over the Agency. No formal CIA subcommittees were organized until 1956. Until then small *ad hoc* groups composed of a few senior committee members reviewed the budget, appropriated funds, and received annual briefings on CIA activities. The DCIs kept senior committee members informed of large-scale covert action projects at the approximate time of implementation. There was no formal review or approval process involved; it was simply a matter of courtesy to the senior members. The initiative in gaining information on specific activities rested with the members.

For nearly twenty years a small group of ranking members dominated these relationships with the Agency. As Chairman of the House Armed Services Committee, Representative Carl Vinson, a Democrat from Georgia, presided over CIA matters from 1949 to 1953 and from 1955 to 1965. Clarence Cannon served as chairman of the House Appropriations Committee from 1949 to 1953 and from 1955 to 1964 and chaired the Defense Subcommittee which had supervising authority over CIA appropriations. Cannon organized a special group of five members to meet informally on CIA appropriations. In the Senate between 1947 and 1954 chairmanship of the Armed Services Committee was held by Chan Gurney, Millard Tydings, Richard Russell and Leverett Saltonstall. In 1955 Russell assumed the chairmanship and held the position until 1968.

Because the committee chairmen maintained their positions for extended periods of time, they established continuing relationships with DCIs and preserved an exclusivity in their knowledge of Agency activities. They were also able to develop relationships of

---

[30] The Act limited members' committee assignments, provided for professional staffing, tried to regularize meetings, and made some changes in the appropriations process as well as legislating other administrative modifications.

mutual trust and understanding with the DCIs which allowed informal exchanges to prevail over formal votes and close supervision.

Within the Congress procedures governing the Agency's budget assured maximum secrecy. The DCI presented his estimate of the budget for the coming fiscal year broken down into general functional categories. Certification by the subcommittee chairmen constituted approval. Exempt from floor debate and from public disclosure, CIA appropriations were and are concealed in the Department of Defense budget. In accordance with the 1949 Act the DCI has only to certify that the money as appropriated has been spent. He does not have to account publicly for specific expenditures, which would force him to reveal specific activities.

To allow greater flexibility for operational expenditures the Contingency Reserve Fund was created in 1952. The Fund provided a sum independent of the regular budget to be used for unanticipated large projects. For example, the initial funding for the development of the U-2 reconnaissance aircraft was drawn from the Contingency Reserve Fund. The most common use of the Fund was for covert operations.

Budgetary matters rather than the specific nature of CIA activities were the concern of Congressional members, and given the perception of the need for action against the Soviet Union, approval was routine. A former CIA Legislative Counsel characterized Congressional attitudes in the early 1950s in this way:

> In the view of the general public, and of the Congress which in the main reflected the public attitude, a national intelligence service in those days was more or less a part and parcel of our overall defense establishment. Therefore, as our defense budget went sailing through Congress under the impact of the Soviet extension of power into Eastern Europe, Soviet probes into Iran and Greece, the Berlin blockade, and eventually the Korean War, the relatively modest CIA budget in effect got a free ride, buried as it was in the Defense and other budgets. When Directors appeared before Congress, which they did only rarely, the main concern of the members was often to make sure that we [the CIA] had what we needed to do our job.

Limited information-sharing rather than rigorous oversight characterized Congress relationship to the Agency. Acceptance of the need for secrecy and Congressional procedures would perpetuate what amounted to mutual accommodation.

---

By 1953 the Agency had achieved the basic structure and scale it retained for the next twenty years.[30a] The Korean War, United States foreign policy objectives, and the Agency's internal organizational arrangements had combined to produce an enormous impetus for growth. The CIA was six times the size it had been in 1947.

Three Directorates had been established. In addition to the DDP and the DDI, Smith created the Deputy Directorate for Administration (DDA). Its purpose was to consolidate the management functions required for the burgeoning organization. The Directorate was responsible for budget, personnel, security, and medical services Agency-wide. However, one quarter of DDA's total personnel strength was assigned to logistical support for overseas operations. The DDP commanded the major share of the Agency's budget, personnel, and resources; in 1952 clandestine collection and covert action accounted for 74 percent of

---

[30a] For chart showing CIA organization as of 1953, see p. 98.

the Agency's total budget;[31] its personnel constituted 60 percent of the CIA's personnel strength. While production rather than coordination dominated the DDI, operational activities rather than collection dominated the DDP. The DDI and the DDP emerged at different times out of disparate policy needs. There were, in effect, separate organizations. These fundamental distinctions and emphases were reinforced in the next decade.

---

[31] This did not include DDA budgetary allocations in support of DDP operations.

# APPENDIX B

# THE HUGHES-RYAN ACT, 1974

*Editor's note:* The Hughes-Ryan Act, the first statutory tightening of controls over the CIA since the National Security Act of 1947, aimed at improving accountability for covert action through two steps: first, requiring that the president approve all important covert actions with a "finding" ("the president finds that each such operation is important") and, second, requiring that each finding be reported to lawmakers on the congressional Intelligence Committees. The law was passed on the last day of 1974, in the throes of the Watergate scandal and allegations that the CIA was involved in domestic spying and inappropriate covert actions against the democratically elected regime of President Salvador Allende of Chile.

### THE 1974 HUGHES-RYAN ACT

Also known as Section 662 (a) of the Foreign Assistance Act of 1974, the amendment states:

No funds appropriated under the authority of this or any other Act may be expended by or on behalf of the Central Intelligence Agency for operations in foreign countries other than activities intended solely for obtaining necessary intelligence unless and until the President finds that each such operation is important to the national security of the United States and reports, in a timely fashion, a description and scope of each operation to the appropriate committees of Congress.

# COVERT ACTION DECISION AND REPORTING PATHWAY

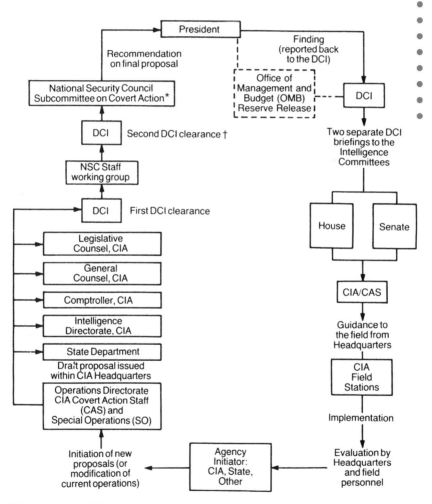

*Known as the Special Coordination Committee (SCC) during the Carter administration and the National Security Planning Group (NSPG) during the Reagan administration.

†Since 2005, the Director of National Intelligence (DNI) reveiws covert action proposals at this stage.

*Editor's note:* Since passage of the Hughes-Ryan Act in 1974, the pathway that a decision in favor of a covert action must follow is much more complicated than used to be the case. Before Hughes-Ryan, the Director of Central Intelligence (DCI) and the national security adviser would sometimes decide on covert actions without the involvement of anyone else, other than the intelligence officers and foreign assets engaged in the planning and implementation of the operation: no congressional involvement and often no presidential involvement. Now, as the diagram illustrates, covert actions must run a gauntlet of critics—valuable from the point of view of accountability, but, arguably, reducing efficiency and timeliness. Yet, as a staff intelligence overseer in the House of Representatives, the editor has seen this process take less than an hour in times of emergency, as a result of rapid and secure telephone conversations among the key participants in the review. The diagram presented here is from 1989 but remains valid today, except for the addition of another layer: the new Director of National Intelligence (replacing the DCI in 2005), placed between the NSC Staff working group and the NSC Subcommittee on Covert Action. One other related change: the Director of the Central Intelligence Agency (D/CIA) now provides the CIA's clearance before the proposal travels to the NSC Staff working group. The entry of the Department of Defense into the covert action domain is worrisome to many observers, who fear that the Hughes-Ryan checks on the wisdom of any particular covert action may be bypassed by the Pentagon, on grounds that the law applies to the CIA and not to the military—a dubious argument.

*Source*: Adapted from Loch K. Johnson, *America's Secret Power: The CIA in a Democratic Society* (New York: Oxford University Press, 1989), p. 113.

# EXAMPLES OF PRESIDENTIAL FINDINGS
# FOR COVERT ACTION

*Editor's note:* The findings presented below were approved by President Ronald Reagan, the first regarding Central America on March 9, 1981, which received written approval; and the second regarding Iran on January 17, 1986, which received only an oral approval. Both were originally top secret, then declassified in the context of the congressional inquiry into the Iran-*contra* affair in 1987. Notice how in each instance, the "purpose" or "description" is succinct, leaving considerable leeway for the CIA to fill in the details during implementation of the covert action.

*Example No. 1: Central America*

Finding Pursuant to Section 662 of the Foreign Assistance Act of 1961, As Amended, Concerning Operations Undertaken by the Central Intelligence Agency in Foreign Countries, Other Than Those Intended Solely for the Purpose of Intelligence Collection

I hereby find that the following operations in foreign countries (including all support necessary to such operations) are important to the national security of the United States, and direct the Director of Central Intelligence, or his designee, to report this Finding to the

*Sources*: *Public Papers of the President: Ronald Reagan* (Washington, DC: U.S. Government Printing Office, 1986); Presidential Finding on Central America, N16574; Iran Finding, 1/17/86, Hearings, Ex. JMP-29-D, *Report of the Congressional Committees Investigating the Iran-Contra Affair,* S. Rept. No. 100–216 and H. Rept. No. 100–433, 100th Cong., 1st Sess, U.S. Senate Select Committee on Secret Military Assistance to Iran and the Nicaraguan Opposition and U.S. House of Representatives Select Committee to Investigate Covert Arms Transactions with Iran (the Inouye-Hamilton Committee), November 1987.

concerned committees of the Congress pursuant to law, and to provide such briefings as necessary.

| SCOPE | PURPOSE |
|-------|---------|
| Central America | Provide all forms of training, equipment and related assistance to cooperating governments throughout Central America in order to counter foreign-sponsored subversion and terrorism. [still-classified section missing here] Encourage and influence foreign governments around the world to support all of the above objectives. |

*Example No. 2: Iran*

Finding Pursuant to Section 662 of The Foreign Assistance Act of 1961 As Amended. Concerning Operations Undertaken by the Central Intelligence Agency in Foreign Countries. Other Than Those Intended Solely for the Purpose of Intelligence Collection

I hereby find that the following operation in a foreign country (including all support necessary to such operation) is important to the national security of the United States, and due to its extreme sensitivity and security risks. I determine it is essential to limit prior notice, and direct the Director of Central Intelligence to refrain from reporting this Finding to the Congress as provided in Section 501 of the National Security Act of 1947, as amended, until I otherwise direct.

| SCOPE | DESCRIPTION |
|-------|-------------|
| Iran | Assist selected friendly foreign liaison services, third countries and third parties which have established relationships with Iranian elements, groups, and individuals sympathetic to U.S. Government interests and which do not conduct or support terrorist actions directed against U.S. persons, property or interests, for the purpose of: (1) establishing a more moderate government in Iran, (2) obtaining from them significant intelligence not otherwise obtainable, determine the current Iranian Government's methods with respect to its neighbors and with respect to terrorist acts, and (3) furthering the release of the American hostages held in Beirut and preventing additional terrorist acts by these groups. Provide funds, intelligence, counter-intelligence, training, guidance and communications and other necessary assistance to these elements, groups, individuals, liaison services and third countries in support of these activities. |
| | The USG will act to facilitate efforts by third parties and third countries to establish contact with moderate elements within and outside the Government of Iran by providing these elements with arms, equipment and related material in order to enhance the credibility of these elements in their effort to achieve a more pro-U.S. |

government in Iran by demonstrating their ability to obtain requisite resources to defend their country against Iraq and intervention by the Soviet Union. This support will be discontinued if the U.S. Government learns that these elements have abandoned their goals of moderating their government and appropriated the material for purposes other than that provided by this finding.

# THE ORGANIZATION DURING THE COLD WAR OF THE CIA'S DIRECTORATE OF OPERATIONS— HOME BASE FOR COVERT OPERATIONS

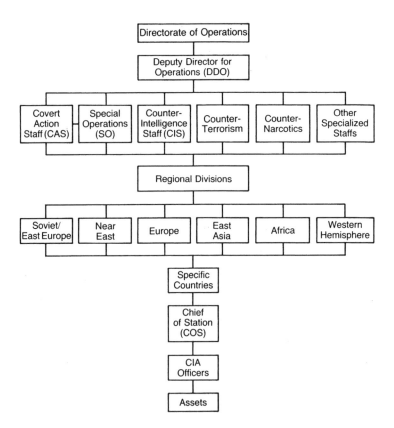

*Editor's note:* The phrase "Special Operations" (SO) in the chart refers to paramilitary activities, a subset of covert action; the word "assets" refers to foreign nationals employed secretly by the CIA.

---

*Source*: Loch K. Johnson, *America's Secret Power: The CIA in a Democratic Society* (New York: Oxford University Press, 1989), p. 46.

# APPENDIX F

# THE CIA ASSASSINATION PLOT IN THE CONGO, 1960–61

## III. ASSASSINATION PLANNING AND THE PLOTS

### A. CONGO

#### 1. Introduction

The Committee has received solid evidence of a plot to assassinate Patrice Lumumba. Strong hostility to Lumumba, voiced at the very highest levels of government may have been intended to initiate an assassination operation; at the least it engendered such an operation. The evidence indicates that it is likely that President Eisenhower's expression of strong concern about Lumumba at a meeting of the National Security Council on August 18, 1960, was taken by Allen Dulles as authority to assassinate Lumumba.[1] There is, however, testimony by Eisenhower Administration officials, and ambiguity and lack of clarity in the records of high-level policy meetings, which tends to contradict the evidence that the President intended an assassination effort against Lumumba.

The week after the August 18 NSC meeting, a presidential advisor reminded the Special Group of the "necessity for very straightforward action" against Lumumba and prompted a decision not to rule out consideration of "any particular kind of activity which might contribute to getting rid of Lumumba." The following day, Dulles cabled

---

*Source*: "Alleged Assassination Plots Involving Foreign Leaders," *An Interim Report,* Select Committee to Study Governmental Operations with Respect to Intelligence Activities (the Church Committee), U.S. Senate, 94th Cong., 2d Sess (1975), pp. 13–70.

[1] Indeed, one NSC staff member present at the August 18 meeting, believed that he witnessed a presidential order to assassinate Lumumba.

a CIA Station Officer in Leopoldville, Republic of the Congo,[2] that "in high quarters" the "removal" of Lumumba was "an urgent and prime objective." Shorty thereafter the CIA's clandestine service formulated a plot to assassinate Lumumba. The plot proceeded to the point that lethal substances and instruments specifically intended for use in an assassination were delivered by the CIA to the Congo Station. There is no evidence that these instruments of assassination were actually used against Lumumba.

A thread of historical background is necessary to weave these broad questions together with the documents and testimony received by the Committee.

In the summer of 1960, there was great concern at the highest levels in the United States government about the role of Patrice Lumumba in the Congo. Lumumba, who served briefly as Premier of the newly independent nation, was viewed with alarm by United States policymakers because of what they perceived as his magnetic public appeal and his leanings toward the Soviet Union.

Under the leadership of Lumumba and the new President, Joseph Kasavubu, the Congo declared its independence from Belgium on June 30, 1960.[3] In the turbulent month that followed, Lumumba threatened to invite Soviet troops to hasten the withdrawal of Belgian armed forces. The United Nations Security Council requested Belgium's withdrawal and dispatched a neutral force to the Congo to preserve order. In late July, Lumumba visited Washington and received pledges of economic aid from Secretary of State Christian Herter. By the beginning of September, Soviet airplanes, trucks, and technicians were arriving in the province where Lumumba's support was strongest.

In mid-September, after losing a struggle for the leadership of the government to Kasavubu and Joseph Mobutu, Chief of Staff of the Congolese armed forces, Lumumba sought protection from the United Nations forces in Leopoldville. Early in December, Mobutu's troops captured Lumumba while he was traveling toward his stronghold at Stanleyville and imprisoned him. On January 17, 1961, the central government of the Congo transferred Lumumba to the custody of authorities in Katanga province, which was then asserting its own independence from the Congo. Several weeks later, Katanga authorities announced Lumumba's death.

Accounts of the circumstances and timing of Lumumba's death vary. The United Nations investigation concluded that Lumumba was killed on January 17, 1961.[4]

---

[2] Since the period in which the events under examination occurred, the names of many geographical units and governmental institutions have changed. For instance, the nation formerly known as the Republic of the Congo is now the Republic of Zaire and the present capital city, Kinshasa, was known then as Leopoldville. For the sake of clarity in dealing with many of the documents involved in this section, the names used in this report are those which applied in the early 1960's.

[3] For detailed reporting of the events in the Congo during this period, see the *New York Times,* especially July 7, 1960, 7:3; July 14, 1960, 1:1; July 16, 1960, 1:1 and 3:2; July 28, 1960, 3:7; September 3, 1960, 3:2; September 6, 1960, 1:8; December 3, 1960, 1:8; January 18, 1961, 3:1; February 14, 1961, 1:1.

[4] Report of the Commission of Investigation. U.N. Security Council, Official Records, Supplement for October, November, and December, 11/11/61, p. 117. (Cited hereinafter as "U.N. Report, 11/11/61.")

## 2. DULLES CABLE TO LEOPOLDVILLE: AUGUST 26, 1960

The Congo declared its independence from Belgium on June 30, 1960. Shortly thereafter, the CIA assigned a new officer to its Leopoldville Station. The "Station Officer"[5] said that assassinating Lumumba was not discussed during his CIA briefings prior to departing for the Congo, nor during his brief return to Headquarters in connection with Lumumba's visit to Washington in late July. (Hedgman, 8/21/75, pp. 8–9)

During August, there was increasing concern about Lumumba's political strength in the Congo among the national security policymakers of the Eisenhower Administration.[6] This concern was nurtured by intelligence reports such as that cabled to CIA Headquarters by the Station Officer:

> EMBASSY AND STATION BELIEVE CONGO EXPERIENCING CLASSIC COMMUNIST EFFORT TAKEOVER GOVERNMENT. MANY FORCES AT WORK HERE: SOVIETS ∗∗∗ COMMUNIST PARTY, ETC. ALTHOUGH DIFFICULT DETERMINE MAJOR INFLUENCING FACTORS TO PREDICT OUTCOME STRUGGLE FOR POWER, DECISIVE PERIOD NOT FAR OFF. WHETHER OR NOT LUMUMBA ACTUALLY COMMIE OR JUST PLAYING COMMIE GAME TO ASSIST HIS SOLIDIFYING POWER, ANTI-WEST FORCES RAPIDLY INCREASING POWER CONGO AND THERE MAY BE LITTLE TIME LEFT IN WHICH TAKE ACTION TO AVOID ANOTHER CUBA. (CIA Cable, Leopoldville to Director, 8/18/60)

This cable stated the Station's operational "objective [of] replacing Lumumba with pro Western Group." Bronson Tweedy, who was Chief of the Africa Division of CIA's clandestine services, replied that he was seeking State Department approval for the proposed operation based upon "your and our belief Lumumba must be removed if possible." (CIA Cable, Tweedy to Leopoldville, 8/18/60) On August 19, DDP Richard Bissell, Director of CIA's covert operations branch, signed a follow-up cable to Leopoldville, saying: "You are authorized proceed with operation." (CIA Cable, Director to Leopoldville, 8/19/60)

Several days later, the Station Officer reported:

> ANTI-LUMUMBA LEADERS APPROACHED KASAVUBU WITH PLAN ASSASSINATE LUMUMBA ∗∗∗ KASAVUBU REFUSED AGREE SAYING HE RELUCTANT RESORT VIOLENCE AND NO OTHER LEADER SUFFICIENT STATURE REPLACE LUMUMBA. (CIA Cable, Leopoldville to Director, 8/24/60)

On August 25, Director of Central Intelligence, Allen Dulles attended a meeting of the Special Group—the National Security Council subcommittee responsible for the planning of covert operations.[7] In response to the outline of some CIA plans for political actions

---

[5] Victor Hedgman was one of the CIA officers in Leopoldville attached to the Congo Station and will be referred to hereinafter as "Station Officer."

[6] See Section 7, *infra,* for a full discussion of the prevailing anti-Lumumba attitude in the United States government as shown by minutes of the National Security Council and Special Group and the testimony of high Administration officials.

[7] The August 25th Special Group meeting and the testimony about its significance for the issue of authorization is discussed in detail in Section 7(a) (iii), *infra.*

That meeting was preceded by an NSC meeting on August 18, at which an NSC staff executive heard the President make a statement that impressed him as an order for the assassination of Lumumba. (Johnson, 6/18/75, pp. 6–7) The testimony about this NSC meeting is set forth in detail at Section 7 (a) (ii), *infra.*

against Lumumba, such as arranging a vote of no confidence by the Congolese Parliament, Gordon Gray, the Special Assistant to the President for National Security Affairs reported that the President "had expressed extremely strong feelings on the necessity for very straightforward action in this situation, and he wondered whether the plans as outlined were sufficient to accomplish this." (Special Group Minutes, 8/25/60) The Special Group "finally agreed that planning for the Congo would not necessarily rule out 'consideration' of any particular kind of activity which might contribute to getting rid of Lumumba." (Special Group Minutes, 8/25/60)

The next day, Allen Dulles signed a cable[8] to the Leopoldville Station Officer stating:

> IN HIGH QUARTERS HERE IT IS THE CLEAR-CUT CONCLUSION THAT IF [LUMUMBA] CONTINUES TO HOLD HIGH OFFICE, THE INEVITABLE RESULT WILL AT BEST BE CHAOS AND AT WORST PAVE THE WAY TO COMMUNIST TAKEOVER OF THE CONGO WITH DISASTROUS CONSEQUENCES FOR THE PRESTIGE OF THE UN AND FOR THE INTERESTS OF THE FREE WORLD GENERALLY. CONSEQUENTLY WE CONCLUDE THAT HIS REMOVAL MUST BE AN URGENT AND PRIME OBJECTIVE AND THAT UNDER EXISTING CONDITIONS THIS SHOULD BE A HIGH PRIORITY OF OUR COVERT ACTION. (CIA Cable, Dulles to Station Officer, 8/26/60)[9]

The cable said that the Station Officer was to be given "wider authority"—along the lines of the previously authorized operation to replace Lumumba with a pro-Western group—"including even more aggressive action if it can remain covert . . . we realize that targets of opportunity may present themselves to you." Dulles' cable also authorized the expenditure of up to $100,000 "to carry out any crash programs on which you do not have the opportunity to consult HQS," and assured the Station Officer that the message had been "seen and approved at competent level" in the State Department. (CIA Cable, 8/26/60) The cable continued:

> TO THE EXTENT THAT AMBASSADOR MAY DESIRE TO BE CONSULTED, YOU SHOULD SEEK HIS CONCURRENCE. IF IN ANY PARTICULAR CASE, HE DOES NOT WISH TO BE CONSULTED YOU CAN ACT ON YOUR OWN AUTHORITY WHERE TIME DOES NOT PERMIT REFERRAL HERE.

This cable raises the question of whether the DCI was contemplating action against Lumumba for which the United States would want to be in a position to "plausibly deny" responsibility. On its face, the cable could have been read as authorizing only the "removal" of Lumumba from office. DDP Richard Bissell was "almost certain" that he was informed about the Dulles cable shortly after its transmission. He testified that it was his

---

[8] Cables issued under the personal signature of the DCI are a relative rarity in CIA communications and call attention to the importance and sensitivity of the matter discusseed. By contrast, cable traffic to and from CIA field stations routinely refers to the sender or recipient as "Director" which simply denotes "CIA Headquarters."

[9] The bracketed words in cables throughout this section signify that a cryptonym, pseudonym, or other coded reference has been translated in order to maintain the security of CIA communications and to render the cable traffic comprehensible. The translations were provided to the Committee by the CIA Review Staff and by various witnesses.

"belief" that the cable was a circumlocutious means of indicating that the President wanted Lumumba killed.[10] (Bissell, 9/10/75, pp. 12, 33, 64–65)

Bronson Tweedy testified that he may have seen Dulles' cable of August 26, before it was transmitted and that he "might even have drafted it." Tweedy called this cable the "most authoritative statement" on the "policy consensus in Washington about the need for the removal of Lumumba" by any means, including assassination. He said that he "never knew" specifically who was involved in formulating this policy. But he believed that the cable indicated that Dulles had received authorization at the "policy level" which "certainly * * * would have involved the National Security Council." Tweedy testified that the $100,000 was probably intended for "political operations against Lumumba * * * not assassination-type programs." (Tweedy, 10/9/75 1, p. 5, II, pp. 5–7, 24, 26)

### 3. CIA Encouragement of Congolese Efforts to "Eliminate" Lumumba

On September 5, 1960, President Kasavubu dismissed Premier Lumumba from the government despite the strong support for Lumumba in the Congolese Parliament. After losing the ensuing power struggle with Kasavubu and Mobutu, who seized power by a military coup on September 14, Lumumba asked the United Nations peace-keeping force for protection.

The evidence indicates that the ouster of Lumumba did not alleviate the concern about him in the United States government. Rather, CIA and high Administration officials[11] continued to view him as a threat.

During this period, CIA officers in the Congo advised and aided Congolese contacts known to have an intent to assassinate Lumumba. The officers also urged the "permanent disposal" of Lumumba by some of these Congolese contacts. Moreover, the CIA opposed reopening Parliament after the coup because of the likelihood that Parliament would return Lumumba to power.

The day after Kasavubu deposed Lumumba, two CIA officers met with a high-level Congolese politician who was in close contact with the Leopoldville Station. The Station reported to CIA Headquarters:

> TO [STATION OFFICER] COMMENT THAT LUMUMBA IN OPPOSITION IS ALMOST AS DANGEROUS AS IN OFFICE, [THE CONGOLESE, POLITICIAN] INDICATED UNDERSTOOD AND IMPLIED MIGHT PHYSICALLY ELIMINATE LUMUMBA. (CIA Cable, Leopoldville to Director, 9/7/60)

The cable also stated that the Station Officer had offered to assist this politician "in preparation new government program" and assured him that the United States would supply technicians. (CIA Cable, 9/7/60)

As the struggle for power raged, Bronson Tweedy summarized the prevalent apprehension of the United States about Lumumba's ability to influence events in the Congo by virtue of his personality, irrespective of his official position:

---

[10] See Section 7(c), *infra* for additional testimony by Bissell on the question of authorization for the assassination effort against Lumumba. Bissell testified, *inter alia*, that Dulles would have used the phrase "highest quarters" to refer to the President.

[11] A detailed treatment of the expressions of continued concern over Lumumba at the National Security Council level is set forth in Section 7, *infra*.

LUMUMBA TALENTS AND DYNAMISM APPEAR OVERRIDING FACTOR IN RE-
ESTABLISHING HIS POSITION EACH TIME IT SEEMS HALF LOST. IN OTHER
WORDS EACH TIME LUMUMBA HAS OPPORTUNITY HAVE LAST WORD HE
CAN SWAY EVENTS TO HIS ADVANTAGE. (CIA Cable, Director to Leopoldville,
9/13/60)

The day after Mobutu's coup, the Station Officer reported that he was serving as an
advisor to a Congolese effort to "eliminate" Lumumba due to his "fear" that Lumumba
might, in fact, have been strengthened by placing himself in U.N. custody, which afforded a
safe base of operations. Hedginan concluded: "Only solution is remove him from scene
soonest." (CIA Cable, Leopoldville to Director, 9/15/60)

On September 17, another CIA operative in the Congo met with a leading Congolese
senator. The cable to CIA Headquarters concerning the meeting reported:

[CONGOLESE SENATOR] REQUESTED CLANDESTINE SUPPLY SMALL ARMS TO
EQUIP * * * TROOPS RECENTLY ARRIVED [LEOPOLDVILLE] AREA * * * [THE SEN-
ATOR] SAYS THIS WOULD PROVIDE CORE ARMED MEN WILLING AND ABLE TAKE
DIRECT ACTION * * * [SENATOR] RELUCTANTLY AGREES LUMUMBA MUST GO
PERMANENTLY. DISTRUSTS [ANOTHER CONGOLESE LEADER] BUT WILLING
MAKE PEACE WITH HIM FOR PURPOSES ELIMINATION LUMUMBA. (CIA Cable,
Leopoldville to Director, 9/17/60)

The CIA operative told the Congolese senator that, "he would explore possibility obtaining
arms" and he recommended to CIA headquarters that they should:

HAVE [ARMS] SUPPLIES READY TO GO AT NEAREST BASE PENDING [UNITED
STATES] DECISION THAT SUPPLY WARRANTED AND NECESSARY. (CIA Cable, 9/17/
60)[12]

Several days later, the Station Officer warned a key Congolese leader about coup plots
led by Lumumba and two of his supporters, and: "Urged arrest or other more permanent
disposal of Lumumba, Gizenga, and Mulele." (CIA Cable, Leopoldville to Director, 9/20/
61) Gizenga and Mulele Were Lumumba's lieutenants who led his supporters while Lumumba was in U.N. custody.

---

[12] This recommendation proved to be in line with large scale planning at CIA Headquarters for
clandestine paramilitary support to anti-Lumumba elements. On October 6, 1960, Richard Bissell
and Bronson Tweedy signed a cable concerning plans which the Station Officer was instructed not to
discuss with State Department representatives or operational contacts:
     [IN] VIEW UNCERTAIN OUTCOME CURRENT DEVELOPMENTS [CIA] CONDUCTING
     CONTINGENCY PLANNING FOR CONGO AT REQUEST POLICY ECHELONS. THIS
     PLANNING DESIGNED TO PREPARE FOR SITUATION IN WAY [UNITED STATES]
     WOULD PROVIDE CLANDESTINE SUPPORT TO ELEMENTS IN ARMED OPPOSITION
     TO LUMUMBA. CONTEMPLATED ACTION INCLUDES PROVISION ARMS, SUPPLIES
     AND PERHAPS SOME TRAINING TO ANTI-LUMUMBA RESISTANCE GROUPS. (CIA
     Cable, Director in Leopoldville, 10/6/60)

Throughout the fall of 1960, while Lumumba remained in U.N. protective custody,[13] the CIA continued to view him as a serious political threat. One concern was that if Parliament were re-opened and the moderates failed to obtain a majority vote, the "pressures for [Lumumba's] return will be almost irresistible." (CIA Cable, Leopoldville to Director, 10/26/60).[14] Another concern at CIA Headquarters was that foreign powers would intervene in the Congo and bring Lumumba to power. (CIA Cable, Director to Leopoldville, 10/17/60) Lumumba was also viewed by the CIA and the Administration as a stalking horse for "what appeared to be a Soviet effort to take over the Congo." (Hedgman, 8/21/75, pp. 10, 45)[15]

After Lumumba was in U.N. custody, the Leopoldville Station continued to maintain close contact with Congolese who expressed a desire to assassinate Lumumba.[16] CIA officers encouraged and offered to aid these Congolese in their efforts against Lumumba, although there is no evidence that aid was ever provided for the specific purpose of assassination.

## 4. THE PLOT TO ASSASSINATE LUMUMBA

### SUMMARY

In the Summer of 1960, DDP Richard Bissell asked the Chief of the Africa Division, Bronson Tweedy, to explore the feasibility of assassinating Patrice Lumumba. Bissell also asked a CIA scientist, Joseph Scheider, to make preparations to assassinate or incapacitate an unspecified "African leader." According to Scheider, Bissell said that the assignment

---

[13] Both Richard Bissell and Bronson Tweedy confirmed that the CIA continued to view Lumumba as a threat even after he placed himself in U.N. custody. (Bissell, 9/10/75, pp. 68–69, 79: Tweedy, 9/9/75, pp. 48–50) Two factors were mentioned consistently in testimony by government officials to substantiate this view: first, Lumumba was a spellbinding orator with the ability to stir masses of people to action; and second, the U.N. forces did not restrain Lumumba's freedom of movement and the Congolese army surrounding them were often lax in maintaining their vigil. (Mulroney, 9/11/75, pp. 22–24; Dillon, 9/2/75. p. 49) As CIA officer Michael J. Mulroney put it, the fact that Lumumba was in United Nations custody "did not result in a cessation of his political activity." (Mulroney, 9/11/75, p. 23)

[14] A CIA Cable from Leopoldville to the Director on November 3, 1960 returned to this theme: the opening of the Congolese Parliament by the United Nations is opposed because it "WOULD PROBABLY RETURN LUMUMBA TO POWER."

[15] See Section 7, infra, for a treatment of the expression of this viewpoint at high-level policy meetings.

Tweedy expressed an even broader "domino theory" about the impact of Lumumba's leadership in the Congo upon events in the rest of Africa:

"The concern with Lumumba was not really the concern with Lumumba as a person. It was concern at this very pregnant point in the new African development [with] the effect on the balance of the Continent of a disintegration of the Congo. [I]t was the general feeling that Lumumba had it within his power to bring about this dissolution, and this was the fear that it would merely be the start—the Congo, after all, was the largest geographical expression. Contained in it were enormously important mineral resources * * *. The Congo itself, is adjacent to Nigeria, which at that point was considered to be one of the main hopes of the future stability of Africa. [I]f the Congo had fallen, then the chances were Nigeria would be seized with the same infection.

"This was why Washington * * * was so concerned about Lumumba, not because there was something unique about Lumumba, but it was the Congo." (Tweedy. 10/9/75 II. p. 42)

[16] A Congolese in contact with the CIA "IMPLIED HE TRYING HAVE [LUMUMBA] KILLED BUT ADDED THIS MOST DIFFICULT AS JOB WOULD HAVE BE DONE BY AFRICAN WITH NO APPARENT INVOLVEMENT WHITE MAN." (CIA Cable, Leopoldville to Director, 10/28S/60)

had the "highest authority." Scheider procured toxic biological materials in response to Bissell's request, and was then ordered by Tweedy to take these materials to the Station Officer in Leopoldville. According to Scheider, there was no explicit requirement that the Station check back with Headquarters for final approval before proceeding to assassinate Lumumba. Tweedy maintained, however, that whether or not he had explicitly levied such a requirement, the Station Officer was not authorized to move from exploring means of assassination to actually attempting to kill Lumumba without referring the matter to Headquarters for a policy decision.

In late September, Scheider delivered the lethal substances to the Station Officer in Leopoldville and instructed him to assassinate Patrice Lumumba. The Station Officer testified that after requesting and receiving confirmation from CIA Headquarters that he was to carry out Scheider's instructions, he proceeded to take "exploratory steps" in furtherance of the assassination plot. The Station Officer also testified that he was told by Scheider that President Eisenhower had ordered the assassination of Lumumba. Scheider's testimony generally substantiated this account, although he acknowledged that his meetings with Bissell and Tweedy were the only bases for his impression about Presidential authorization. Scheider's mission to the Congo was preceded and followed by cables from Headquarters urging the "elimination" of Lumumba transmitted through an extraordinarily restricted "Eyes Only" channel—including two messages bearing the personal signature of Allen Dulles.

The toxic substances were never used. But there is no evidence that the assassination operation was terminated before Lumumba's death. There is, however, no suggestion of a connection between the assassination plot and the events which actually led to Lumumba's death.[17]

### (a) Bissell/Tweedy Meetings on Feasibility of Assassinating Lumumba

Bronson Tweedy testified that Richard Bissell initiated a discussion with him in the summer of 1960 about the feasibility of assassinating Patrice Lumumba, and that they discussed the subject "more than once" during the following fall. Tweedy said the first such conversation probably took place shortly before Dulles' cable of August 26, instructing the Station Officer that Lumumba's "removal" was a "high priority of our covert action."[18] Whether his talk with Bissell was "shortly before or shortly after" the Dulles cable, it was clear to Tweedy that the two events "were totally in tandem." (Tweedy, 9/9/75, pp. 14–15; 10/9/75 II, p. 6)

Tweedy testified that he did not recall the exact exchange but the point of the conversation was clear:

What Mr. Bissell was saying to me was that there was agreement, policy agreement, in Washington that Lumumba must be removed from the position of control and influence in the Congo * * * and that among the possibilities of that elimination was indeed assassination.

* * * The purpose of his conversation with me was to initiate correspondence with the Station for them to explore with Headquarters the possibility of * * * assassination, or indeed any other means of removing Lumumba from power * * * to have the Station start reviewing possibilities, assets, and discussing them with Headquarters in detail in the same way we would with any operation. (Tweedy, 10/9/75 II, pp. 6, 8)

---

[17] See Section 6, infra, for a discussion of the evidence about the circumstances surrounding Lumumba's death in Katanga.

[18] See Section 2, supra.

Tweedy was "sure" that in his discussions with Bissell poisoning "must have" been mentioned as one means of assassination that was being considered and which the Station Officer should explore. (Tweedy, 9/9/75, pp. 26–27)

Tweedy testified that Bissell assigned him the task of working out the "operational details," such as assessing possible agents and the security of the operation, and of finding "some solution that looked as if it made sense, and had a promise of success." Tweedy stated that Bissell "never said ∗ ∗ ∗ go ahead and do it in your own good time without any further reference to me." Rather, Tweedy operated under the impression that if a feasible means of assassinating Lumumba were developed, the decision on proceeding with an assassination attempt was to be referred to Bissell. (Tweedy, 10/9/75 I, pp. 7, 17–18)

Tweedy stated that he did not know whether Bissell had consulted with any "higher authority" about exploring the possibilities for assassinating Lumumba. Tweedy said, that generally, when he received an instruction from Bissell:

I would proceed with it on the basis that he was authorized to give me instructions and it was up to him to bloody well know what he was empowered to tell me to do. (Tweedy, 9/9/75, p. 13)[19]

*(b) Bissell/Scheider Meetings on Preparations for Assassinating "An African Leader"*

Joseph Scheider[20] testified that he had "two or three conversations" with Richard Bissell in 1960 about the Agency's technical capability to assassinate foreign leaders. In the late spring or early summer, Bissell asked Scheider generally about technical means of assassination or incapacitation that could be developed or procured by the CIA. Scheider informed Bissell that the CIA had access to lethal or potentially lethal biological materials that could be used in this manner. Following their initial "general discussion," Scheider said he discussed assassination capabilities with Bissell in the context of "one or two meetings about Africa." (Scheider, 10/7/75, pp. 6–7, 41)

Scheider testified that in the late summer or early fall, Bissell asked him to make all preparations necessary for having biological materials ready on short notice for use in the assassination of an unspecified African leader, "in case the decision was to go ahead."[21]

---

[19] When asked whether he considered declining Bissell's assignment to move toward the assassination of Lumumba, Tweedy responded:

TWEEDY: I certainly did not attempt to decline it, and I felt, in view of the position of the government on the thing, that at least the exploration of this, or possibility of removing Lumumba from power in the Congo was an objective worth pursuing.

Q:       Including killing him?

TWEEDY: Yes. I suspect I was ready to consider this ∗ ∗ ∗ Getting rid of him was an objective worth pursuing, and if the government and my betters wished to pursue it, professionally, I was perfectly willing to play my role in it, yes ∗ ∗ ∗. Having to do it all over again, it would be my strong recommendation that we not get into it. (Tweedy, 10/9/75, II, pp. 39–41)

[20] During the events discussed in the Lumumba case, Joseph Scheider served as Special Assistant to the DDP (Bissell) for Scientific Matters. Scheider holds a degree in bio-organic chemistry. (Scheider, 10/7/75, pp. 13, 25–29)

[21] Scheider said it was possible that Bissell subsequently gave him the "go signal" for his trip to the Congo and specified Lumumba as the target of the assassination operation. (Scheider, 10/7/75, pp. 65, 113–114; 10/7/75, p. 8) Scheider had a clearer memory, however, of another meeting, where the top officers of CIA's Africa Division, acting under Bissell's authority, actually dispatched to the Congo. (See Section 4(c), *infra*)

Scheider testified that Bissell told him that "he had direction from the highest authority * * * for getting into that kind of operation." Scheider stated that the reference to "highest authority" by Bissell "signified to me that he meant the President."[22] (Scheider, 10/7/75, pp. 51–55, 58; 10/9/75, p. 8)

Scheider said that he "must have" outlined to Bissell the steps he planned to take to execute Bissell's orders. (Scheider, 10/7/75, p. 58) After the meeting, Scheider reviewed a list of biological materials available at the Army Chemical Corps installation at Fort Detrick, Maryland which would produce diseases that would "either kill the individual or incapacitate him so severely that he would be out of action." (Scheider, 10/7/75, pp. 63–64; 10/9/75, pp. 8–9, 12)[23] Scheider selected one material from the list which "was supposed to produce a disease that was * * * indigenous to that area [of Africa] and that could be fatal." (Scheider, 10/7/75, p. 63) Scheider testified that he obtained this material and made preparation for its use:

> We had to get it bottled and packaged in a way that it could pass for something else and I needed to have a second material that could absolutely inactivate it in case that is what I desired to do for some contingency. (Scheider, 10/7/75, p. 64)

Scheider also "prepared a packet of * * * accessory materials," such as hypodermic needles, rubber gloves, and gauze masks, "that would be used in the handling of this pretty dangerous material." (Scheider, 10/7/75, p. 59)

*(c) Scheider Mission to the Congo on an Assassination Operation*

Scheider testified that he remembered "very clearly" a conversation with Tweedy and the Deputy Chief of the Africa Division in September 1960 which "triggered" his trip to the Congo after he had prepared toxic biological materials and accessories for use in an assassination operation. (Scheider, 10/7/75, pp. 41, 65) According to Scheider, Tweedy and his Deputy asked him to take the toxic materials to the Congo and deliver instructions from Headquarters to the Station Officer: "to mount an operation, if he could do it securely * * * to either seriously incapacitate or eliminate Lumumba." (Scheider, 10/7/75, p. 66)

Scheider said that he was directed to provide technical support to the Station Officer's attempt to find a feasible means of carrying out the assassination operation:

> They urged me to be sure that * * * if these technical materials were used * * * I was to make the technical judgments if there were any reasons the things shouldn't go, that was my responsibility. (Scheider, 10/7/75, p. 68)[24]

---

[22] See Section 7(d), *infra* for additional testimony by Scheider about the question of Presidential authorization for the assassination of Lumumba.

[23] Schieder said that there were "seven or eight materials" on the list, including tularemia ("rabbit fever"), brucellosis (undulant fever), tuberculosis, anthrax, smallpox, and Venezuelan equine encephalitis ("sleeping sickness"). (Scheider, 10/7/75, p. 64; 10/9/75, p. 9)

[24] When asked if he had considered declining to undertake the assignment to provide technical support to an assassination operation, Scheider stated:

"I think that my view of the job at the time and the responsibilities I had was in the context of a silent war that was being waged, although I realize that one of my stances could have been * * * as a conscientious objector to this war. That was not my view. I felt that a decision had been made * * * at the highest level that this be done and that as unpleasant a responsibility as it was, it was my responsibility to carry out my part of that." (Scheider, 10/9/75, p. 63)

According to Scheider, the Station Officer was to be responsible for "the operations aspects, what assets to use and other non-technical considerations." Scheider said that in the course of directing him to carry instructions to the Station Officer in the Congo, Tweedy and his Deputy "referred to the previous conversation I had with Bissell," and left Scheider with, "the impression that Bissell's statements to me in our previous meeting held and that they were carrying this message from Bissell to me." (Scheider, 10/9/75, pp. 13, 15, 69)

Although he did not have a specific recollection, Scheider stated that it was "probable" that he would have "checked with Bissell" to validate the extraordinary assignment he received from Tweedy and his Deputy, if indeed he had not actually received the initial assignment itself from Bissell. (Scheider, 10/7/75, pp. 113–114)

After being informed of Scheider's testimony about their meeting, and reviewing the contemporaneous cable traffic, Tweedy stated that it was "perfectly clear" that he had met with Scheider. He assumed that he had ordered Scheider to deliver lethal materials to the Leopoldville Station Officer and to serve as a technical adviser to the Station Officer's attempts to find a feasible means of assassinating Lumumba. (Tweedy, 10/9/75 I, pp. 18–21; 10/9/75 II, p. 9)

Tweedy said that his Deputy Chief was the only other person in the Africa Division who would have known that the assassination of Lumumba was being considered. (Tweedy, 9/9/75. p. 64) Tweedy assumed Scheider had "already been given his marching orders to go to the Congo by Mr. Bissell, not by me." (Tweedy, 10/9/75 II, p. 11)

Scheider testified that he departed for the Congo within a week of his meeting with Tweedy and his Deputy (Scheider, 10/9/75, p. 15)

*(d) Congo Station Officer Told To Expect Scheider: Dulles Cables About "Elimination" of Lumumba*

On September 19, 1960, several days after Lumumba placed himself in the protective custody of the United Nations peacekeeping force in Leopoldville, Richard Bissell and Bronson Tweedy sent a cryptic cable to Leopoldville to arrange a clandestine meeting between the Station Officer and "Joseph Braun," who was traveling to the Congo on an unspecified assignment. Joseph Scheider testified that "Joseph Braun" was his alias and was used because this was "an extremely sensitive operation." (Scheider, 10/7/75, pp. 78, 80) The cable informed the Station Officer:

["JOE"] SHOULD ARRIVE APPROX 27 SEPT * * * WILL ANNOUNCE HIMSELF AS "JOE FROM PARIS" * * * IT URGENT YOU SHOULD SEE ["JOE"] SOONEST POSSIBLE AFTER HE PHONES YOU. HE WILL FULLY IDENTIFY HIMSELF AND EXPLAIN HIS ASSIGNMENT TO YOU. (CIA Cable, Bissell, Tweedy to the Station Officer, 9/19/60)

The cable bore the codeword "PROP," which indicated extraordinary sensitivity and restricted circulation at CIA headquarters to Dulles, Bissell, Tweedy, and Tweedy's Deputy. The PROP designator restricted circulation in the Congo to the Station Officer. (Tweedy, 10/9/75 I, pp. 14–15; II, pp. 9, 37)

Tweedy testified that the PROP channel was established and used exclusively for the assassination operation. (Tweedy, 10/9/75 II, p. 37; 10/9/75 I, pp. 48–49) The Bissell/Tweedy cable informed the Station Officer that the PROP channel was to be used for:

ALL [CABLE] TRAFFIC THIS OP, WHICH YOU INSTRUCTED HOLD ENTIRELY TO YOURSELF. (CIA Cable, 9/19/60)

Tweedy testified that the fact that he and Bissell both signed the cable indicated that authorization for Scheider's trip to the Congo had come from Bissell. Tweedy stated that Bissell "signed off" on cables originated by a Division Chief "on matters of particular sensitivity or so important that the DDP wished to be constantly informed about correspondence." Tweedy said that Bissell read much of the cable traffic on this operation and was "generally briefed on the progress of the planning." (Tweedy, 10/9/75 I, pp. 14, 54)

The Station Officer, Victor Hedgman testified to a clear, independent recollection of receiving the Tweedy/Bissell cable. He stated that in September of 1960 he received a "most unusual" cable from CIA Headquarters which advised that:

> someone who I would have recognized would arrive with instructions for me ∗ ∗ ∗ I believe the message was also marked for my eyes only ∗ ∗ ∗ and contained instructions that I was not to discuss the message with anyone.

He said that the cable did not specify the kind of instructions he was to receive, and it "did not refer to Lumumba in any way." (Hedgman, 8/21/75, pp. 11–13, 43)

Three days after the Bissell/Tweedy cable, Tweedy sent another cable through the PROP channel which stated that if it was decided that "support for prop objectives [was] essential" a third country national should be used as an agent in the assassination operation to completely conceal the American role.[25] (CIA Cable, 9/22/60) Tweedy testified that "PROP objectives" referred to an assassination attempt. (Tweedy, 10/9/75 I, p. 30) Tweedy also indicated to the Station Officer and his "colleague" Scheider:

> YOU AND COLLEAGUE[26] UNDERSTAND WE CANNOT READ OVER YOUR SHOULDER AS YOU PLAN AND ASSESS OPPORTUNITIES. OUR PRIMARY CONCERN MUST BE CONCEALMENT [AMERICAN] ROLE, UNLESS OUTSTANDING OPPORTUNITY EMERGES WHICH MAKES CALCULATED RISK FIRST CLASS BET. READY ENTERTAIN ANY SERIOUS PROPOSALS YOU MAKE BASED OUR HIGH REGARD BOTH YOUR PROFESSIONAL JUDGMENTS. (CIA Cable, 9/22/60)

On September 24, the DCI personally sent a cable to Leopoldville stating:

> WE WISH GIVE EVERY POSSIBLE SUPPORT IN ELIMINATING LUMUMBA FROM ANY POSSIBILITY RESUMING GOVERNMENTAL POSITION OR IF HE FAILS IN LEOPOLDVILLE, SETTING HIMSELF IN STANLEYVILLE OR ELSEWHERE. (CIA Cable, Dulles to Leopoldville, 9/24/60)

Dulles had expressed a similar view three days before in President Eisenhower's presence at an NSC meeting.[27]

---

[25] Tweedy also expressed reservations about two agents that the Station Officer was considering for this operation and said "WE ARE CONSIDERING A THIRD NATIONAL CUTOUT CONTACT CANDIDATE AVAILABLE HERE WHO MIGHT FILL BILL." (CIA Cable, 9/22/60) This is probably a reference to agent OJ/WIN, who was later dispatched to the Congo. His mission is discussed in Sections 5(b)–5(c), *infra*.

[26] Tweedy identified Scheider as the "colleague" referred to in this cable. (Tweedy, 10/9/75 I, p. 32) Scheider was en route to the Congo at this point.

[27] Dulles' statement at the NSC meeting of September 21, 1960 is discussed in detail at Section 7(a) (v), *infra*.

Scheider recalled that Tweedy and his Deputy had told him that the Station Officer would receive a communication assuring him that there was support at CIA Headquarters for the assignment Scheider was to give him. (Scheider, 10/7/75, pp. 88–90)

*(e) Assassination Instructions Issued to Station Officer and Lethal Substances Delivered: September 26, 1960*

Station Officer Hedgman reported through the PROP channel that he had contacted Scheider on September 26. (CIA Cable, Leopoldville to Tweedy, 9/27/60)

According to Hedgman:

HEDGMAN: It is my recollection that he advised me, or my instructions were, to eliminate Lumumba.

Q:    By eliminate, do you mean assassinate?

HEDGMAN: Yes, I would say that was * * * my understanding of the primary means. I don't think it was probably limited to that, if there was some other way of * * * removing him from a position of political threat. (Hedgman, 8/21/75, pp. 17–18)

Hedgman said that he and Scheider also may have discussed non-lethal means of removing Lumumba as a "political threat," but he could not "recall with certainty on that." (Hedgman, 8/21/75, p. 28)

Scheider testified:

I explained to him [Station Officer] what Tweedy and his Deputy had told me, that Headquarters wanted him to see if he could use this [biological] capability I brought against Lumumba [and] to caution him that it had to be done * * * without attribution to the USA. (Scheider, 10/9/75, p. 16)

The Station Officer testified that he received "rubber gloves, a mask, and a syringe" along with lethal biological material from Scheider, who also instructed him in their use.[28] Hedgman indicated that this paraphernalia was for administering the poison to Lumumba for the purpose of assassination. (Hedgman, 8/21/75, pp. 18–21, 24) Scheider explained that the toxic material was to be injected into some substance that Lumumba would ingest: "it had to do with anything he could get to his mouth, whether it was food or a toothbrush, * * * [so] that some of the material could get to his mouth." (Scheider, 10/7/75, p. 100)

Hedgman said that the means of assassination was not restricted to use of the toxic material provided by Scheider. (Hedgman, 8/21/75, p. 19)

He testified that he may have "suggested" shooting Lumumba to Scheider as an alternative to poisoning. (Hedgman, 8/21/75, pp. 19, 27–29) Scheider said it was his "impression" that Tweedy and his Deputy empowered him to tell the Station Officer that he could pursue other means of assassination. (Scheider, 10/7/75, pp. 100–101) Station Officer Hedgman testified that, although the selection of a mode of assassination was left to his judgment, there was a firm requirement that:

---

[28] Scheider testified that he sent the medical paraphernalia via diplomatic pouch. (Schelder, 10/7/75, pp. 59, 99)

[I]f I implemented these instructions ∗∗∗ it had to be a way which could not be traced back ∗∗∗ either to an American or the United States government. (Hedgman, 8/21/75, p. 19)

Hedgman said Scheider assured him that the poisons were produced to: [leave] normal traces found in people that die of certain diseases." (Hedgman, 8/21/75, p. 23.)

Hedgman said that he had an "emotional reaction of great surprise" when it first became clear that Scheider had come to discuss an assassination plan. (Hedgman, 8/21/75, p. 30) He told Scheider he "would explore this." (Hedgman, 8/21/75, p. 46) and left Scheider with the impression "that I was going to look into it and try and figure if there was a way ∗∗∗ I believe I stressed the difficulty of trying to carry out such an operation." (Hedgman, 8/21/75, p. 47) Scheider said that the Station Officer was "sober [and] grim" but willing to proceed with the operation. (Scheider, 10/7/75, pp. 98, 121)

The Station Officer's report of his initial contact with Scheider was clearly an affirmative response to the assignment, and said that he and Scheider were "on same wavelength." (CIA Cable, Leopoldville to Tweedy, 9/27/60) Hedgman was "afraid" that the central government was "weakening under" foreign pressure to effect a reconciliation with Lumumba, and said:

HENCE BELIEVE MOST RAPID ACTION CONSISTENT WITH SECURITY INDICATED. (CIA Cable, 9/27/60)[29]

### (f) Hedgman's Impression That President Eisenhower Ordered Lumumba's Assassination

Station Officer Hedgman testified that Scheider indicated to him that President Eisenhower had authorized the assassination of Lumumba.[30] Hedgman had a "quite strong recollection" of asking about the source of authority for the assignment:

HEDGMAN: I must have ∗∗∗ pointed out that this was not a common or usual Agency tactic ∗∗∗ never in my training or previous work in the Agency had I ever heard any references to such methods. And it is my recollection I asked on whose authority these instructions were issued.

Q:       And what did Mr. Scheider reply?

HEDGMAN: It is my recollection that he identified the President ∗∗∗ and I cannot recall whether he said "the President," or whether he identified him by name. (Hedgman, 8/21/75, pp. 30–31)

Hedgman explained that Scheider told him "something to the effect that the President had instructed the Director" to assassinate Lumumba. (Hedgman, 8/21/75, pp. 32, 34)

Scheider stated that he had an "independent recollection" of telling the Station Officer about his meetings with Bissell, Tweedy, and Tweedy's Deputy, including Bissell's reference to "the highest authority." (Scheider, 10/7/75, p. 102) Scheider believed that he left

---

[29] Scheider interpreted this cable to mean that Hedgman was informing Headquarters: "that he has talked to me and that he is going to go ahead and see if he could mount the operation ∗∗∗ [H]e believes we ought to do it, if it is going to be done, as quickly as we can." (Scheider, 10/7/75, p. 121)

[30] See Section 7(d), infra, for a more detailed treatment of the testimony of the Station Officer and Scheider on the question of Presidential authorization for the assassination of Lumumba.

the Station Officer with the impression that there was presidential authorization for an assassination attempt against Lumumba. (Scheider, 10/7/75, pp. 90, 102–103)

*(g) Steps in Furtherance of the Assassination Operation*

(i) Hedgman's Testimony About Confirmation From Headquarters of the Assassination Plan.

Hedgman's testimony, taken fifteen years after the events in question and without the benefit of reviewing the cables discussed above, was compatible with the picture presented by the cables of a fully authorized and tightly restricted assassination operation. The only variance is that the cables portray Hedgman as taking an affirmative, aggressive attitude toward the assignment, while he testified that his pursuit of the operation was less vigorous.

The Station Officer testified that soon after cabling his request for confirmation that he was to carry out the assassination assignment, he received a reply from Headquarters, which he characterized as follows:

I believe I received a reply which I interpreted to mean yes, that he was the messenger and his instructions were * * * duly authorized. (Hedgman, 8/21/75, pp. 37–38)

Despite the cryptic nature of the cables, Hedgman said "I was convinced that yes, it was right," but he had no "desire to carry out these instructions." (Hedgman, 8/21/75, pp. 44, 50, 106) Hedgman stated:

"I think probably that I would have gone back and advised that I intended to carry out and sought final approval before carrying it out had I been going to do it, had there been a way to do it. I did not see it as * * * a matter which could be accomplished practically, certainly. (Hedgman, 8/21/75, pp. 51–52)

Hedgman said that his reason for seeking a final approval would have been to receive assurances about the practicality of the specific mode of assassination that he planned to use. (Hedgman, 8/21/75, p. 53)

All CIA officers involved in the plot to kill Lumumba testified that, by virtue of the standard operating procedure of the clandestine services, there was an implicit requirement that a field officer check back with Headquarters for approval of any major operational plan.[31] Moreover, Hedgman's cable communications with Headquarters indicate that he consistently informed Tweedy of each significant step in the formulation of assassination plans, thus allowing Headquarters the opportunity to amend or disapprove the plans. The personal cable from Dulles to the Station Officer on August 26, made it clear, however, that if Lumumba appeared as a "target of opportunity" in a situation where time did not permit referral to headquarters, Hedgeman was authorized to proceed with the assassination.

The Station Officer testified that for several months after receiving Scheider's instructions he took "exploratory steps in furtherance of the assassination plot." He sent several cables to CIA Headquarters which "probably reflected further steps I had taken," and stated that his cables to Headquarters were essentially "progress reports" on his attempts to find access to Lumumba. (Hedgman, 8/21/75, pp. 50, 59–60)

---

[31] See Tweedy, 10/9/75, I, pp. 10, 24–27; Hedgman, 8/21/75, pp. 39, 51–53; Scheider, 10/7/75, p. 92; Deputy Chief, Africa Division, affidavit, 10/17/75, p. 5.

The cable traffic conforms to the Station Officer's recollection. For two months after Scheider's arrival in the Congo, a regular stream of messages assessing prospects for the assassination operation flowed through the PROP channel between Headquarters and Leopoldville.

(ii) "Exploratory Steps"

On the basis of his talks with Scheider, Station Officer Hedgman listed a number of "possibilities" for covert action against Lumumba. At the top of the list was the suggestion that a particular agent be used in the following manner:

> HAVE HIM TAKE REFUGE WITH BIG BROTHER. WOULD THUS ACT AS INSIDE MAN TO BRUSH UP DETAILS TO RAZOR EDGE. (CIA Cable, 9/27/60)

Tweedy testified that "Big Brother" referred to Lumumba. (Tweedy, 10/9/75 II, p. 13) Tweedy and Scheider both said that this cable indicated that Hedgman's top priority plan was to instruct his agent to infiltrate Lumumba's entourage to explore means of poisoning Lumumba. (Tweedy, 10/9/75 I, p. 38, II, pp. 13–14; Scheider, 10/7/75, pp. 124–125) The Station Officer reported that he would begin to follow this course by recalling the agent to Leopoldville, and informed Headquarters:

> BELIEVE MOST RAPID ACTION CONSISTENT WITH SECURITY INDICATED * * * PLAN PROCEED ON BASIS PRIORITIES AS LISTED ABOVE, UNLESS INSTRUCTED TO CONTRARY. (CIA Cable, 9/27/60)

Scheider testified that at this point the Station Officer was reporting to Headquarters that he was proceeding to "go ahead" to carry out Scheider's instructions as quickly as possible. (Scheider, 10/7/75, pp. 121–123) Tweedy's Deputy stated that the form of the Station Officer's request would have satisfied the standard requirement for confirmation of an operational plan

> * * * it is my professional opinion that, under normal operational procedure at that time, the Station Officer would have been expected to advise Headquarters that he was preparing to implement the plan unless advised to the contrary. (Deputy Chief, Africa Division, affidavit, 10/17/75, p. 5)

On September 30, the Station Officer specifically urged Headquarters to authorize "exploratory conversations" to launch his top priority plan:

> NO REALLY AIRTIGHT OP POSSIBLE WITH ASSETS NOW AVAILABLE. MUST CHOOSE BETWEEN CANCELLING OP OR ACCEPTING CALCULATED RISKS OF VARYING DEGREES.
> * * * [IN] VIEW NECESSITY ACT IMMEDIATELY, IF AT ALL, URGE HQS AUTHORIZE EXPLORATORY CONVERSATIONS TO DETERMINE IF [AGENT] WILLING TAKE ROLE AS ACTIVE AGENT OR CUT-OUT THIS OP. (WOULD APPROACH ON HYPOTHETICAL BASIS AND NOT REVEAL PLANS.) IF HE APPEARS WILLING ACCEPT ROLE, WE BELIEVE IT NECESSARY REVEAL OBJECTIVE OP TO HIM.
> * * * REQUEST HQS REPLY [IMMEDIATELY]. (CIA Cable, Leopoldville to Tweedy, 9/30/60)

Headquarters replied:

YOU ARE AUTHORIZED HAVE EXPLORATORY TALKS WITH [AGENT] TO ASSESS
HIS ATTITUDE TOWARD POSSIBLE ACTIVE AGENT OR CUTOUT ROLE ∗ ∗ ∗ IT DOES
APPEAR FROM HERE THAT OF POSSIBILITIES AVAILABLE [THIS AGENT] IS BEST
∗∗∗ WE WILL WEIGH VERY CAREFULLY YOUR INITIAL ASSESSMENT HIS
ATTITUDE AS WELL AS ANY SPECIFIC APPROACHES THAT MAY EMERGE ∗∗∗
APPRECIATE MANNER YOUR APPROACH TO PROBLEM "HOPE ∗∗∗ FOR MODER-
ATE HASTE" (CIA Cable, Deputy Chief, Africa Division to Leopoldville, 9/30/60)

Tweedy and his Deputy made it clear that the agent was being viewed as a potential
assassin. (Tweedy, 10/9/75 I, p. 41; Deputy Chief, Africa Division, affidavit, 10/17/75,
p. 4) Tweedy stated that it would have been proper for his Deputy to issue this cable
authorizing the Station Officer to take the assassination operation "one step further" and
it was "quite possible" that Richard Bissell was informed of this directive. (Tweedy, 10/9/
75, pp. 42–43)

On October 7, the Station Officer reported to Headquarters on his meeting with the
agent who was his best candidate for gaining access to Lumumba:

CONDUCTED EXPLORATORY CONVERSATION WITH [AGENT] ∗∗∗ AFTER EX-
PLORING ALL POSSIBILITIES [AGENT] SUGGESTED SOLUTION RECOMMENDED BY
HQS. ALTHOUGH DID NOT PICK UP BALL, BELIEVE HE PREPARED TAKE ANY ROLE
NECESSARY WITHIN LIMITS SECURITY ACCOMPLISH OBJECTIVE. (CIA Cable,
Station Officer to Tweedy, 10/7/60)

The Station Officer testified that the subject "explored was the agent's ability to find a
means to inject the toxic material into Lumumba's food or toothpaste:

I believe that I queried the agent who had access to Lumumba, and his entourage, in detail about
just what access he actually had, as opposed to speaking to people. In other words, did he have
access to the bathroom did he have access to the kitchen, things of that sort.
I have a recollection of a having queried him on that without specifying why I wanted to know
this. (Hedgman, 8/21/75, pp. 48, 60)

The Station Officer said that he was left with doubts about the wisdom or practicality
of the assassination plot:

[C]ertainly I looked on it as a pretty wild scheme professionally. I did not think that it ∗∗∗ was
practical professionally, certainly, in a short time, if you were going to keep the U.S. out of
it ∗∗∗ I explored it, but I doubt that I ever really expected to carry it out. (Hedgman, 8/21/75,
p. 11)

(iii) The Assassination Operation Moves Forward After Scheider's Return to
Headquarters: October 5–7, 1960

Despite the Station Officer's testimony about the dubious practicality of the assassination operation, the cables indicate that he planned to continue his efforts to implement the
operation and sought the resources to do so successfully. For example, he urged Headquarters to send an alternate agent:

IF HQS BELIEVE [AGENT'S CIRCUMSTANCES] BAR HIS PARTICIPATION, WISH STRESS NECESSITY PROVIDE STATION WITH QUALIFIED THIRD COUNTRY NATIONAL. (CIA Cable, Leopoldville to Tweedy, 10/7/60)

Tweedy cabled the Station Officer that he "had good discussion your colleague 7 Oct"—referring to a debriefing of Scheider upon his return to the United States. Tweedy indicated that he continued to support the assassination operation and advised (Tweedy, 10/9/75 II, pp. 48–49):

BE ASSURED DID NOT EXPECT PROP OBJECTIVES BE REACHED IN SHORT PERIOD * * * CONSIDERING DISPATCHING THIRD COUNTRY NATIONAL OPERATIVE WHO, WHEN HE ARRIVES, SHOULD BE ASSESSED BY YOU OVER PERIOD TO SEE WHETHER HE MIGHT PLAY ACTIVE OR CUTOUT ROLE ON FULL TIME BASIS. IF YOU CONCLUDE HE SUITABLE AND BEARING IN MIND HEAVY EXTRA LOAD THIS PLACES ON YOU, WOULD EXPECT DISPATCH [TEMPORARY DUTY] SENIOR CASE OFFICER RUN THIS OP * * * UNDER YOUR DIRECTION. (CIA Cable, Tweedy to Station Officer, 10/7/60)[32]

According to the report of the Station Officer, Joseph Scheider left the Congo to return to Headquarters on October 5 in view of the "expiration date his material" (CIA Cable, Leopoldville to Tweedy, 10/7/60)—a reference to the date beyond which the substances would no longer have lethal strength. (Scheider, 10/7/75, pp. 132–133) The cable from the Station Officer further stated that:

[JOE] LEFT CERTAIN ITEMS OF CONTINUING USEFULNESS. [STATION OFFICER] PLANS CONTINUE TRY IMPLEMENT OP. (CIA Cable, Leopoldville to Tweedy, 10/7/60)

Notwithstanding the influence of the Station Officer's October 7 cable that some toxic substances were left with Hedgman, Scheider specifically recalled that he had "destroyed the viability" of the biological material and disposed of it in the Congo River before he departed for the United States on October 5, 1960. (Scheider, 10/7/75, pp. 133, 117, 135–136; 10/9/75, p. 20) In the only real conflict between his testimony and Schieder's, Hedgman testified that the toxic material was not disposed of until after Lumumba was imprisoned by the Congolese in early December. (Hedgman, 8/21/75, pp. 85–86)[33]

---

[32] See Sections 5(b)–5(c), *infra,* for a detailed account of the activities in the Congo of two "third country national" agents: QJ/WIN and WI/ROGUE. See Section 5(a), *infra,* for discussion of the temporary duty assignment in the Congo of senior case officer" Michael Mulroney.

[33] Scheider said he destroyed and disposed of the toxic materials: "for the reason that it didn't look like on this trip he could mount the operational * * * assets to do the job and * * * the material was not refrigerated and unstable." He said that he and the Station Offices "both felt that we shouldn't go ahead with this until there were no doubts." (Scheider, 10/7/75, p. 116) The Station Officer had been unable "to find a secure enough agent with the right access" to Lumumba before the potency of the biological material was "no longer reliable." (Scheider, 10/9/75, p. 28: 10/7/75, pp. 132–133) Scheider speculated that the Station Officer's reference to retaining "items of continuing usefulness" may have meant the gloves, mask, and hypodermic syringe left with Hedgman. Scheider said: "perhaps he is talking about leaving these accessory materials in case there will be a round two of this, and someone brings more material." (Scheider, 10/7/75, p. 135)

The central point remains that the Station Officer planned to continue the assassination effort, by whatever means, even after Scheider's departure. (Scheider, 10/7/75, p. 143) Scheider was under the impression that the Station Officer was still authorized to move ahead with an assassination attempt against Lumumba at that point, although he would have continued to submit his plans to Headquarters. (Scheider, 10/7/75, p.135; 10/9/75, pp. 20–21)[34]

(iv) Headquarters Continues to Place "Highest Priority" on the Assassination Operation

SUMMARY

The cable traffic during this period demonstrates that there was a clear intent at Headquarters to authorize and support rapid progress of the assassination operation. Even after Lumumba placed himself in the protective custody of the United Nations, CIA Headquarters continued to regard his assassination as the "highest priority" of covert action in the Congo. The cables also show an intent at Headquarters to severely restrict knowledge of the assassination operation among officers in CIA's Africa Division and among United States diplomatic personnel in the Congo, excluding, even those who were aware of, and involved in, other covert activities.

The Station Officer, despite the burden of his other operational responsibilities, was actively exploring, evaluating, and reporting on the means and agents that might be used in an attempt to assassinate Lumumba. When his implementation of the assassination operation was thwarted by the failure of his prime candidate to gain access to Lumumba, Hedgman requested additional operational and supervisory personnel to help him carry out the assignment, which he apparently pursued until Lumumba was imprisoned by Congolese authorities.

On October 15, 1960, shortly after Tweedy offered additional manpower for the assassination operation, a significant pair of cables were sent from CIA Headquarters to Leopoldville.

One cable was issued by a desk officer in CIA's Africa Division, released under Bronson Tweedy's signature, and transmitted through standard CIA channels, thus permitting distribution of the message to appropriate personnel in the CIA Station and the

---

In support of his position the Station Officer speculated that it was "possible" that be had preserved the poisons in his safe until after Lumumba's death. (Hedgman, 8/21/75, p. 85) He said that after Scheider's visit, he locked the toxic material in the bottom drawer of his safe, "probably" sealed in an envelope marked "Eyes Only" with his name on it. (Hedgman, 8/21/75, pp. 48–49) He did not recall taking the materials out of his safe except when he disposed of them months later. (Hedgman, 8/21/75, p. 84)

Both Scheider and the Station Officer specifically recalled disposing of the toxic material in the Congo River and each recalled performing the act alone. (Scheider, 10/7/75, pp. 117–118; Hedgman, 8/21/75, p. 84)

The Station Officer's testimony is bolstered by Michael Malroney's account that when he arrived in the Congo nearly a month after Scheider had returned to Headquarters. Hedgman informed him that there was a lethal virus in the station safe. (See Section 5(a) (iii), *infra.*) Moreover, the Station Officer distinctly remembered disposing of the medical paraphernalia. (Hedgman, 8/21/75, p. 84) This would indicate that, at the least, the operation had not been "stood down" to the point of disposing of all traces of the plot until long after Scheider's departure from the Congo.

[34] For Tweedy's testimony about the operational authority possessed by the Station Officer on October 7, see Section 4(h), *infra.*

United States Embassy. (Tweedy, 10/9/75 I, pp. 60–62) The cable discussed the possibility of covertly supplying certain Congolese leaders with funds and military aid and advised:

> ONLY DIRECT ACTION WE CAN NOW STAND BEHIND IS TO SUPPORT IMMOBILIZING OR ARRESTING [LUMUMBA], DESIRABLE AS MORE DEFINITIVE ACTION MIGHT BE. ANY ACTION TAKEN WOULD HAVE TO BE ENTIRELY CONGOLESE. (CIA Cable, Director to Leopoldville, 10/15/60)

On the same day Tweedy dispatched, a second cable, via the PROP channel for Hedgman's "Eyes Only," which prevented the message from being distributed to anyone else, including the Ambassador.[35] Tweedy's Deputy stated that "the cable which carried the PROP indicator would have controlling authority as between the two cables." (Deputy Chief, Africa Division affidavit, 10/17/75, p. 4) The second cable stated:

> YOU WILL NOTE FROM CABLE THROUGH NORMAL CHANNEL CURRENTLY BEING TRANSMITTED A PARA[GRAPH] ON PROP TYPE SUGGESTIONS. YOU WILL PROBABLY RECEIVE MORE ALONG THESE LINES AS STUMBLING BLOC [LUMUMBA] REPRESENTS INCREASINGLY APPARENT ALL STUDYING CONGO SITUATION CLOSELY AND HIS DISPOSITION SPONTANEOUSLY BECOMES NUMBER ONE CONSIDERATION.
>
> RAISE ABOVE SO YOU NOT CONFUSED BY ANY APPARENT DUPLICATION. THIS CHANNEL REMAINS FOR SPECIFIC PURPOSE YOU DISCUSSED WITH COLLEAGUE AND ALSO REMAINS HIGHEST PRIORITY. (CIA Cable, Tweedy to Station Officer, 10/15/60)

Tweedy testified that the "specific purpose discussed with colleague" referred to the Station Officer's discussion of "assassination with Scheider." He stated that the premise of his message was that "there is no solution to the Congo as long as Lumumba stays in a position of power or influence there." (Tweedy, 10/9/75 I, pp. 59, 60)[36]

Tweedy went on to request the Station Officer's reaction to the prospect of sending a senior CIA case officer to the Congo on a "direct assignment * * * to concentrate entirely this aspect" (CIA Cable, Tweedy to Station Officer, 10/15/60).[37]

The cable also provided an insight into why the assassination operation had not progressed more rapidly under the Station Officer:

> SEEMS TO US YOUR OTHER COMMITMENTS TOO HEAVY GIVE NECESSARY CONCENTRATION PROP.

---

[35] Hedgman testified that he did not discuss the assassination operation with anyone at the United States embassy in Leopoldville. Moreover, he testified that he never discussed the prospect of assassinating Lumumba with Clare H. T. Timberlake, who was the Ambassador to the Congo at that time. (Hedgman, 8/21/75, p. 91)

[36] See Section 4(h), *infra*, for Tweedy's testimony on the conditions under which he believed the operation was authorized to proceed.

This referred to CIA officer Michael Mulroney (Tweedy, 10/9/75 I, p. 56), who testified that in late October he was asked by Richard Bissell to undertake the mission of assassinating Lumumba.

[37] For a full account of the meeting between Bissell and Mulroney and Mulroney's subsequent activities in the Congo, see Section 5 (a), *infra*.

In contradiction of the limitations on anti-Lumumba activity outlined in the cable sent through normal channels, Tweedy's cable suggested:

> POSSIBILITY USE COMMANDO TYPE GROUP FOR ABDUCTION [LUMUMBA], EITHER VIA ASSAULT ON HOUSE UP CLIFF FROM RIVER OR, MORE PROBABLY, IF [LUMUMBA] ATTEMPTS ANOTHER BREAKOUT INTO TOWN * * * REQUEST YOUR VIEWS. (CIA Cable, Tweedy to Station Officer, 10/15/60)

Two days later the Station Officer made a number of points in a reply to Tweedy. First, the agent he had picked for the assassination operation had difficulty infiltrating Lumumba's inner circle:[38]

> HAS NOT BEEN ABLE PENETRATE-ENTOURAGE. THUS HE HAS NOT BEEN ABLE PROVIDE OPS INTEL NEEDED THIS JOB. * * * ALTHOUGH MAINTAINING PRIORITY INTEREST THIS OP, ABLE DEVOTE ONLY LIMITED AMOUNT TIME, VIEW MULTIPLE OPS COMMITMENTS. * * * BELIEVE EARLY ASSIGNMENT SENIOR CASE OFFICER HANDLE PROP OPS EXCELLENT IDEA * * * IF CASE OFFICER AVAILABLE [STATION OFFICER] WOULD DEVOTE AS MUCH TIME AS POSSIBLE TO ASSISTING AND DIRECTING HIS EFFORTS, (CIA Cable, 10/17/60)

The Station Officer concluded this cable with the following cryptic recommendation, reminiscent of his testimony that he may have "suggested" shooting Lumumba to Scheider as an alternative to poisoning (Hedgman, 8/21/75, pp. 27–29):

> IF CASE OFFICER SENT, RECOMMEND HQS POUCH SOONEST HIGH POWERED FOREIGN MAKE RIFLE WITH TELESCOPIC SCOPE AND SILENCER. HUNTING GOOD HERE WHEN LIGHTS RIGHT. HOWEVER AS HUNTING RIFLES NOW FORBIDDEN, WOULD KEEP RIFLE IN OFFICE PENDING OPENING OF HUNTING SEASON. (CIA Cable, 10/17/60)

Tweedy testified that the Station Officer's recommendation clearly referred to sending to the Congo via diplomatic pouch a weapon suited for assassinating Lumumba. (Tweedy, 10/9/75 I, p. 64) Senior case officer Mulroney stated that lie never heard discussion at Headquarters of sending a sniper-type weapon to the Congo, nor did he have any knowledge that such a weapon had been "pouched" to the Congo. (Mulroney affidavit, 11/7/75)

The oblique suggestion of shooting Lumumba at the "opening of hunting season" could be interpreted as a plan to assassinate Lumumba as soon as lie was seen outside the residence where he remained in U.N. protective custody. Tweedy interpreted the cable to mean that "an operational plan involving a rifle" had not yet been formulated by the Station Officer and that the "opening of hunting season" would depend upon approval of such a plan by CIA headquarters. (Tweedy, 10/9/75 1, pp. 64–65)

A report sent the next month by the Station Officer through the PROP channel for Tweedy's "Eyes Alone" indicated that, whatever the intention about moving forward with a plan for assassination by rifle fire, Lumumba was being viewed as a "target" and his movements were under close surveillance. Hedgman's cable described the stalemate which prevailed from mid-September until Lumumba's departure for Stanleyville on November 27; Lumumba was virtually a prisoner in U.N. custody, and inaccessible to CIA agents and the Congolese:

---

[38] This agent left Leopoldville "sometime in October" and their discussions terminated. (Hedgman, 8/21/75, p. 61)

TARGET HAS NOT LEFT BUILDING IN SEVERAL WEEKS. HOUSE GUARDED DAY AND NIGHT BY CONGOLESE AND UN TROOPS * * *. CONGOLESE TROOPS ARE THERE TO PREVENT TARGET'S ESCAPE AND TO ARREST HIM IF HE ATTEMPTS. UN TROOPS THERE TO PREVENT STORMING OF PALACE BY CONGOLESE. CONCEN-TRIC RINGS OF DEFENSE MAKE ESTABLISHMENT OF OBSERVATION POST IMPOSSIBLE. ATTEMPTING GET COVERAGE OF ANY MOVEMENT INTO OR OUT OF HOUSE BY CONGOLESE * * *. TARGET HAS DISMISSED MOST OF SERVANTS SO ENTRY THIS MEANS SEEMS REMOTE. (CIA Cable, Station Officer to Tweedy, 11/14/60)

*(h) Tweedy/Bissell Testimony: Extent of Implementation; Extent o f Authorization*

### SUMMARY

The testimony of Richard Bissell and Bronson Tweedy is at some variance from the picture of the assassination plot presented by the Station Officer and by the cable traffic from the period.

The cables demonstrate that CIA Headquarters placed the "highest priority" on the effort to assassinate Lumumba. They also show that the assassination operation involving Scheider and the Station Officer was initiated by a cable signed personally by Bissell and Tweedy and transmitted in a specially restricted cable channel established solely for communications about this operation. Bissell and Tweedy both testified to an absence of independent recollection of Scheider's assignment in the Congo and of any specific op-eration to poison Lumumba.

The cables appear to indicate that the Station Officer was authorized to proceed with an assassination attempt if he determined it to be a feasible, secure operation and if time did not permit referral to Headquarters for approval. Tweedy alone testified that the Station Officer was empowered only to explore and assess the means of assassinating Lumumba and not to proceed with an assassination attempt even when "time did not permit" referral to Head-quarters.

*(i) Tweedy's Testimony About the Scope of the Assassination Operation*

As Chief of the Africa Division, Bronson Tweedy had the principal supervisory re-sponsibility at CIA Headquarters for the operations of the Station Officer Hedgman in Leopoldville. Most of the reports and recommendations cabled by Hedgman on the as-sassination operation were marked for Tweedy's "Eyes Only." Through Tweedy, in-structions were issued, plans were approved, and progress reports were assessed concerning the effort to assassinate Lumumba.[39]

---

[39] Tweedy personally signed both the cable which initially informed the Station Officer that "JOE" would arrive in Leopoldville with an assignment (CIA Cable, Bissell, Tweedy to Station Officer, 9/19/60) and the cable of October 7 indicating that he had debriefed Scheider upon his return from the Congo. (CIA Cable, Tweedy to Station Officer, 10/7/60) Tweedy was also the "Eyes Only" recipient of Hedgman's reports on Scheider's arrival in the Congo (CIA Cable, Station Officer to Tweedy, 9/27/60) and of subsequent communications about the top priority plan that emerged from the discussions between Scheider and Hedgman: i.e., infiltrating an agent into Lumumba's entourage to administer a lethal poison to the Congolese leader, (CIA Cable, Station Officer to Tweedy, 9/30/60; CIA Cable, Station Officer to Tweedy, 10/7/60; CIA Cable, Station Officer to Tweedy, 10/17/60) See Sections 4(a)–4(e) *supra* for a full treatment of the cables sent in the PROP channel between Tweedy and the Station Officer in Leopoldville.

Before reviewing all of the cables, Tweedy testified that he had no knowledge of the plot to poison Lumumba. (Tweedy, 9/9/75, pp. 30–31) He stated that if Scheider went to the Congo as a courier carrying lethal biological material, "I will bet I knew it, but I don't recall it." (Tweedy, 9/9/75, p. 35)

Tweedy commented that rather than questioning the truth of the Station Officer's testimony,[40] the discrepancies between their testimony could be attributed to his own lack of recall.[41]

Even after he reviewed the cables on the PROP operation, Tweedy said that he did not recall talking to Scheider about an assignment to the Congo, although he assumed he had done so. Tweedy's review enabled him to "recall the circumstances in which these things occurred; and there's no question that Mr. Scheider went to the Congo." (Tweedy, 10/9/75 I, p. 13; II, pp. 5–6)[42]

Despite Tweedy's lack of recollection about the actual plot to poison Lumumba, he recalled discussing the feasibility of an assassination attempt against Lumumba with Bissell and communicating with the Station Officer about gaining access to Lumumba for this purpose. (Tweedy, 9/9/75, pp. 14–15, 19–21)

Tweedy characterized his discussions with Bissell about assassinating Lumumba as "contingency planning" (Tweedy, 9/9/75, p. 28):

TWEEDY.  * * * I think it came up in the sense that Dick would have said we probably better be thinking about whether it might ever be necessary or desirable to get rid of Lumumba, in which case we presumably should be in position to assess whether we could do it or not successfully.

Q.  Do it, meaning carry off an assassination?

TWEEDY.  Yes, but it was never discussed with him in any other sense but a planning exercise. * * * never were we instructed to do anything of this kind. We were instructed to ask whether such a thing would be feasible and to have the Station Officer thinking along those lines as well. (Tweedy, 9/9/75, pp. 15, 28)

Tweedy testified that Bissell never authorized him to proceed beyond the planning stage to move forward with an assassination attempt. (Tweedy, 10/9/75 I, p. 17)

Tweedy characterized the entire assassination operation as "exploratory":

This involved the launching of the idea with the field so they could make the proper operational explorations into the feasibility of this, reporting back to Headquarters for guidance. At no point

---

[40] Tweedy expressed a high regard for the credibility of the Station Officer. Tweedy said that he never had occasion to doubt Hedgman's veracity or integrity, adding, "I would trust his memory and I certainly trust his integrity." (Tweedy, 9/9/75, p. 36)

[41] Tweedy explained his difficulty in recalling the assassination operation:
"[T]he things that I recall the most vividly about all my African experiences were * * * the things I was basically concerned with all the time, which was putting this Division together and the rest of it. When it comes to operational detail I start getting fuzzy and you would have thought with something like thinking about Mr. Lumumba in these terms that I would have gone to bed and got up thinking about Lumumba, I can assure you this wasn't the case." (Tweedy, 9/9/75, p 34)

[42] For a detailed treatment of Tweedy's testimony on Scheider's assignment to the Congo and the assassination operation against Lumumba, see Sections 4(a)–(g), *supra.*

was the field given carte blanche if they thought they had found a way to do the job, just to carry it out with no further reference. (Tweedy, 10/9/75 II, p. 22)

He testified that the period of exploration of access to Lumumba remained "a planning interval and at no point can I recall that I ever felt it was imminent that somebody would say 'go.' " (Tweedy, 9/9/75, pp. 18–19)

Tweedy stated that, despite his inability to specifically recall his directive to Scheider, he would not have given the Station Officer an instruction "to use this [toxic] material and go ahead and assassinate Lumumba, as if * * * that is all the authority that was necessary." He said that:

> Under no circumstances would that instruction have been given by me without reference to higher authority up through the chain of command * * * my higher authority, in the first instance, would be Mr. Bissell * * * and I know Mr. Bissell would have talked to Mr Dulles. (Tweedy, 10/9/75 I, pp. 17–18; 10/9/75 II, pp. 25, 33)

It is difficult to reconcile some of the cables and the testimony of Scheider and Hedgman with Tweedy's testimony that there was "no misunderstanding" that the PROP operation was purely exploratory "contingency planning" and that no authorization was granted for attempting an assassination without checking back with headquarters.

For example, Dulles' August 26 directive appeared to indicate wide latitude for making operational decisions in the field "where time does not permit referral" to Headquarters.

Tweedy testified that sending a potentially lethal biological material with a short period of toxicity to the Congo did not mean that the Station Officer was empowered to take action without seeking final approval from Headquarters.

TWEEDY: If, as a result of the Station focusing on the problem for the first time, as a result of Headquarters' request, they had come up with a plan that they thought was exceedingly solid and which Headquarters approved, it is not surprising, perhaps, that we wanted the materials there to take advantage of such * * * an unlikely event.

Q: Because Scheider took lethal materials to the Congo with him that had such a short period of lethality, were you not contemplating at that tine that the operation might well move from the exploration phase to the implementation phase just as soon as Scheider and Hedgman determined that it was feasible?

TWEEDY: I think I would put it quite differently. I think that I would say that we would have been remiss in not being in a position to exploit, if we reached the point where we all agreed that the thing was possible. (Tweedy, 10/9/75 I, pp. 49–50)

The dispatch of toxic material and medical paraphernalia to the Congo certainly demonstrates that the "exploration" of the feasibility of assassinating Lumumba had progressed beyond mere assessment and "contingency planning."

Tweedy further disagreed that the Station Officer's October 7 message that he would "continue try implement op[eration]" signified that the Officer was prepared to proceed to "implement" an assassination attempt:

> He would continue to explore the possibilities of this operation and continue to report to Headquarters. That is all this means. It does not mean that * * * he would try to pull off the

operation without further reference to Headquarters * * * [H]e was to continue to explore it to determine whether or not there was a feasible means. (Tweedy, 10/9/75 II, pp. 14–15)

Finally, Tweedy's recollection that a "go ahead" on the assassination operation was never imminent is brought into question by the cable he sent for Hedgman's "Eyes Only" on October 15 to assure him that there was a policy-level consensus that Lumumba's "disposition spontaneously becomes number one consideration" and that the PROP operation "remains highest priority." (CIA Cable, Tweedy to Station, 10/15/60)

(ii) Bissell's Testimony About Moving the Assassination Operation From Planning to Implementation

Richard Bissell testified that he did not remember discussing the feasibility of assassinating Lumumba with Bronson Tweedy, but it seemed "entirely probable" to him that such discussions took place. Bissell, who did not review the cable traffic, said he "may have" given Tweedy specific instructions about steps to further an assassination plan, but he did not remember doing so. He said that seeking information from the Station Officer about access for poisoning or assassinating Lumumba by other means would "almost certainly" have been a "major part" of his "planning and preparatory activity" but he had no specific recollection of cable communications on this subject. He did recall that the Station Officer had an agent who supposedly had direct access to Lumumba. (Bissell, 9/10/75, pp. 3, 4, 6–8, 80)

Bissell testified that he "most certainly" approved any cables that Tweedy sent to the Station Officer seeking information about gaining access to Lumumba because in "a matter of this sensitivity," Tweedy probably would have referred cables to him for final dispatch. But Bissell added:

I think Mr. Tweedy, on the basis of an oral authorization from me, would have had the authority to send such a cable without my signing off on it. (Bissell, 9/10/75, p. 8)

Bissell's failure to recall discussing his assignment to Michael Mulroney[43] with Tweedy provided a basis for his speculation that Tweedy might also have been unaware of the true purpose of Scheider's visit. (Bissell, 9/10/75, pp. 20–22)

Bissell did not recall cables concerning Scheider's mission, and confirming that Scheider's instructions were to be followed; but he said "this sounds highly likely * * * I would expect, given the background, that the confirmation would have been forthcoming." (Bissell, 9/10/75, p. 43)

Bissell said that it was "very probable" that he discussed the assassination of Lumumba with Scheider, who was then his science advisor. On a number of occasions he and Scheider had discussed "the availability of means of incapacitation, including assassination." Although he had no "specific recollection," Bissell assumed that, if Scheider went to the Congo, Bissell would have approved the mission, which "might very well" have dealt with the assassination of Lumumba. (Bissell, 9/10/75, pp. 14, 60, 18, 20, 44)

Bissell testified that it would not have been against CIA policy in the fall of 1960 to send poisons to the Congo. He characterized "the act of taking the kit to the Congo * * * as still in the planning stage." (Bissell, 9/10/75, pp. 35, 49). He acknowledged, however, that:

---

[43] Bissell's assignment to Mulroney is discussed in Sections 5(a) (i) and 5(a) (ii), *infra*.

It would indeed have been rather unusual to send such materials—a specific kit ∗ ∗ ∗ of this sort—
out to a relatively small Station, unless planning for their use was quite far along. (Bissell, 9/10/7,
p. 37)

Nonetheless, Bissell said that he "probably believed" that he had sufficient authority
at that point to direct CIA officers to move from the stage of planning to implementation.
(Bissell, 9/10/75, pp. 60–61) Although he did not have a specific recollection, Bissell
assumed that if Scheider had instructed Hedgman to assassinate Lumumba, Scheider would
not have been acting beyond the mandate given to him by Bissell and the assassination plot
would then have "passed into an implementation phase." (Bissell, 9/10/75, pp. 39, 41, 49)

## 5. The Question of a Connection Between the Assassination Plot and Other Actions of CIA Officers and Their Agents in the Congo

### SUMMARY

Michael Mulroney, a senior CIA officer in the Directorate for Plans, testified that in
October 1960 he had been asked by Richard Bissell to go to the Congo to carry out the
assassination of Lumumba. Mulroney said he refused to participate in an assassination
operation, but proceeded to the Congo to attempt to draw Lumumba away from the protective custody of the U.N. guard and place him in the hands of Congolese authorities.
(Mulroney, 6/9/75, pp. 11–14)

Shortly after Mulroney's arrival in the Congo, he was joined by QJ/WIN, a CIA agent
with a criminal background.[44] Late in 1960, WI/ROGUE, one of Hedgman's operatives
approached QJ/WIN with a proposition to join an "execution squad." (CIA Cable, Leopoldville to Director, 12/7/60)

It is unlikely that Mulroney was actually involved in implementing the assassination
assignment. Whether there was any connection between the assassination plot and either of
the two operatives—QJ/WIN and WI/ROGUE—is less clear.

*(a) Mulroney's Assignment in the Congo*

(i) Mulroney's Testimony That He Went to the Congo After Refusing an Assassination
    Assignment From Bissell

In early October, 1960, several PROP cables discussed a plan to send a "senior case
officer" to the Congo to aid the overburdened Station Officer with the assassination operation.[45] Shortly after the Station Officer's request on October 17, for a senior case officer
to concentrate on the assassination operation. Bissell broached the subject with Mulroney.
At the time, Mulroney was the Deputy Chief of an extraordinarily secret unit within the
Directorate of Plans. (Mulroney, 6/9/75, p. 8)

Mulroney testified that in October of 1960, Bissell asked him to undertake the mission
of assassinating Patrice Lumumba:

MULRONEY: He called me in and told me he wanted to go down to the Belgian Congo, the
            former Belgian Congo, and to eliminate Lumumba ∗ ∗ ∗.

---

[44] See Part III, Section c, of this Report for a discussion of the CIA's use of QJ/WIN in developing a
stand-by assassination capability in the Executive Action project.

[45] See Section 4(g), *supra*, for full treatment of these cables.

Q:          What did you understand him to mean by eliminate?

MULRONEY: To kill him and thereby eliminate his influence.

Q:          What was the basis for your interpreting his remarks, whatever his precise
            language, as meaning that he was talking about assassination rather than
            merely neutralizing him through some other means?

MULRONEY: It was not neutralization * * * clearly the context of our talk was to kill him.
            (Mulroney, 6/9/75, pp. 11–12, 19, 43)

Mulroney testified:

> I told him that I would absolutely not have any part of killing Lumumba. He said, I want you to go
> over and talk to Joseph Scheider. (Mulroney, 6/9/75, p. 12)

Mulroney said that it was "inconceivable that Bissell would direct such a mission
without the personal permission of Allen Dulles":

> I assumed that he had authority from Mr. Dulles in such as important issue, but it was not
> discussed [with me], nor did he purport to have higher authority to do it. (Mulroney, 9/9/75,
> pp. 15, 44)

Mulroney then met promptly with Scheider and testified that he was "sure that Mr.
Bissell had called Scheider and told him I was coming over" to his office. Scheider told
Mulroney "that there were four or five * * * lethal means of disposing of Lumumba
* * *. One of the methods was a virus and the others included poison." Mulroney said
that Scheider "didn't even hint * * * that he had been in the Congo and that he had
transported any lethal agent to the Congo." (Mulroney, 6/9/75, pp. 12–13; 9/11/75, pp.
7–7A)

Mulroney testified that after speaking with Scheider:

> I then left his office, and I went back to Mr. Bissell's office, and I told him in no way would I have
> any part in the assassination of Lumumba * * * and reasserted in absolute terms that I would not be
> involved in a murder attempt. (Mulroney, 9/11/75, p. 43)[46]

---

[46] When asked at the conclusion of his testimony to add anything to the record that he felt was
necessary to present a full picture of the operation against Lumumba, Mulroney volunteered a statement about the moral climate in which it took place:

"All the people that I knew acted in good faith. I think they acted in the light of * * * maybe not their
consciences, but in the light of their concept of patriotism. [T]hey felt that this was in the best interests
of the U.S. I think that we have to much of the 'good German' in us, in that we do something because the
boss says it is okay. And they are not essentially evil people. But you can do an awful lot of wrong in
this.

"* * * This is such a dishonest business that only honest people can be in it. That is the only thing that
will save the Agency and make you trust the integrity of what they report * * *. An intelligence officer
* * * must be scrupulous and he must be moral * * * he must have personal integrity * * *. They must be
particularly conscious of the moral element in intelligence operations." (Mulroney, 9/11/75, pp. 57, 61)

Earlier in his testimony, Mulroney succinctly summarized his philosophical opposition to assassinating Lumumba: "murder corrupts." (Mulroney, 9/11/75, p. 9)

Mulroney said that in one of his two conversations with Bissell about Lumumba, he raised the prospect "that conspiracy to commit murder being done in the District of Columbia might be in violation of federal law." He said that Bissell "airily dismissed" this prospect. (Mulroney, 6/9/75, p. 14)

Although he refused to participate in assassination, Mulroney agreed to go to the Congo on a general mission to "neutralize" Lumumba "as a political factor" (Mulroney, 9/11/75, pp. 43–44):

> I said I would go down and I would have no compunction about operating to draw Lumumba out [of UN custody], to run an operation to neutralize his operations which were against Western interests, against, I thought, American interests. (Mulroney, 6/9/75, p. 13)[47]

Although Mulroney did not formulate a precise plan until he reached the Congo, he discussed a general strategy with Bissell:

MULRONEY: I told Mr. Bissell that I would be willing to go down to neutralize his activities and operations and try to bring him out [of UN custody] and turn him over to the Congolese authorities.

Senator MONDALE: Was it discussed then that his life might be taken by the Congolese authorities?

MULRONEY: It was, I think, considered * * * not to have him killed, but then it would have been a Congolese being judged by Congolese for Congolese crimes. Yes, I think it was discussed. (Mulroney, 6/9/75, p. 38)

According to Mulroney there was a "very, very high probability" that Lumumba would receive capital punishment at the hands of the Congolese authorities. But he "had no compunction about bringing him out and then having him tried by a jury of his peers." (Mulroney, 6/9/75, pp. 24, 14)

Despite Mulroney's expressed aversion to assassination and his agreement to undertake a more general mission to "neutralize" Lumumba's influence, Bissell continued pressing him to consider an assassination operation:

> In leaving at the conclusion of our second discussion * * * he said, well, I wouldn't rule out that possibility—meaning the possibility of the elimination or the killing of Lumumba * * *. In other words, even though you have said this, don't rule it out * * *. There is no question about it, he said, I wouldn't rule this other out, meaning the elimination or the assassination. (Mulroney, 9/11/75, p. 45)

Mulroney distinctly recalled that after his second discussion with Bissell, he meet with Richard Helms, who was then Deputy to the DDP and Chief of Operations in the clandestine services division, in order to make his opposition to assassinating Lumumba a matter of record (Mulroney, 9/11/75, pp. 44–45):

---

[47] Bissell also recalled that, after discussing assassination with Mulroney, Mulroney went to the Congo "with the assignment * * * of looking at other ways of neutralizing Lumumba." (Bissell, 9/10/75, p. 53)

[I]n the Agency, since you don't have documents, you have to be awfully canny and you have to get things on record, and I went into Mr. Helms' office, and I said, Dick, here is what Mr. Bissell proposed to me, and I told him that I would under no conditions do it, and Helms said, 'you're absolutely right.' (Mulroney 6/9/75, pp. 15–16)

Helms testified that it was "likely" that he had such a conversation with Mulroney and he assumed that Mulroney's version of their conversation was correct. (Helms, 9/16/75, pp. 22–23)[48]

William Harvey was Mulroney's immediate superior at that time[49] He testified:

Mr. Mulroney came to me and said that he had been approached by Richard Bissell * * * to undertake an operation in the Congo, one of the objectives of which was the elimination of Patrice Lumumba. He also told me that he had declined to undertake this assignment. (Harvey, 6/25/75, p. 9)

Harvey said that in a later conversation with Bissell, Bissell told him that he had asked Mulroney to undertake such an operation. (Harvey, 6/25/75, p. 9)

Tweedy's Deputy, who aided in making preparations for Mulroney's trip to the Congo, recalled that Mulroney had "reacted negatively" to Bissell's request to undertake an assassination operation. (Deputy Chief, Africa Division affidavit, 10/17/75, p. 2) He stated:

Despite the fact that Mulroney had expressed a negative reaction to this assignment, it was clear to me that when Mulroney went to the Congo, exploration of the feasibility of assassinating Lumumba was part of his assignment from Bissell. As far as I know, Mulroney was not under assignment to attempt to assassinate Lumumba, but rather merely to make plans for such an operation. (Deputy Chief, Africa Division affidavit, 10/17/75, p. 2)

In Tweedy's mind, Mulroney's eventual mission to the Congo was also linked to assessing the possibility for assassinating Lumumba rather than to a general plan to draw Lumumba out of U.N. custody. (Tweedy, 9/9/75, pp. 24, 26)

Mulroney testified, however, that because he was "morally opposed to assassination" he would "absolutely not" have explored the means by which such access could be gained, nor would he have undertaken a mission to the Congo to assess an assassination operation even if it were directed by someone else. (Mulroney, 9/11/75, p. 26)

Mulroney said that he departed for the Congo within forty-eight hours of his second discussion with Bissell. (Mulroney, 9/11/75, pp. 45–46)

(ii) Bissell's Testimony About the Assignment to Mulroney

Bissell remembered "very clearly" that he and Mulroney discussed the assassination of Lumumba in the fall of 1960 (Bissell, 6/9/75, pp. 74–750 and the Mulroney reacted negatively. (Bissell 9/11/75, p. 18) Accrodingly to Bissell, Mulroney said that assassination

---

[48] Helms testified that he did not inquire further into the subject of this conversation in any way. He did not recall why Mulroney had gone to the Congo or what his mission was. (Helms, 9/16/75, pp. 32–33)

[49] Harvey was later centrally involved in the Castro case and the Executive Action project. See Parts III (B) and Part III (C), *infra*.

"was an inappropriate action and that the desired object could be accomplished better in other ways." (Bissell, 6/11/75, p. 54)

Bissell's testimony differs from Mulroney's account on only one important point—the degree to which Bissell's initial assignment to Mulroney contemplated the mounting of an operation as opposed to contingency planning. Mulroney flatly testified that Bissell requested him to attempt to kill Lumumba. In his first testimony on the subject, Bissell said that he asked Mulroney "to investigate the possibility of killing Lumumba." (Bissell, 6/11/75, p. 54; *see also* pp. 55, 75) In a later appearance, however, Bissell stated that Mulroney "had been asked to plan and prepare for" the assassination of Lumumba. (Bissell, 9/10/75, p. 24)

Bissell said that after his conversations with Mulroney, he considered "postponing" the assassination operation:

> I seem to recollect that after this conversation with him, I wanted this put very much on the back burner and inactivated for quite some time. Now that doesn't rule out the possibility that some action through completely different channels might have gone forward. But the best of my recollection is, I viewed this not only as terminating the assignment for him, but also as reason for at least postponing anything further along that line. (Bissell, 9/10/75, pp. 25–26)

(iii) Mulroney Informed of Virus in Station Safe Upon Arriving in Congo: November 3, 1960

On October 29, the Station Officer was informed that Michael Mulroney would soon arrive in Leopoldville "in furtherance this project." (CIA Cable Deputy Chief, Africa Division, to Station Officer 10/29/60) On November 3, Mulroney arrived in Leopoldville. (CIA Cable, Leopoldville to Director, 11/4/60) Hedgman said it was "very possible" that he regarded the dispatch to the Congo of a senior officer as a signal that CIA Headquarters was "dissatisfied with my handling" of Scheider's instructions. (Hedgman, 8/21/75, p. 42)

Hedgman had only a general picture of Mulroney's assignment:

> I understood it to be that—similar to mine, that is, the removal or neutralization of Lumumba * * * I have no clear recollection of his discussing the assassination. (Hedgman, 8/21/75, p. 54)

Station Officer Hedgman said that he did not recall if Mulroney indicated whether he was considering assassination as a means of "neutralizing" Lumumba. Hedgman said, "in view of my instructions, I may have assumed that he was" considering assassination. Generally, however, the Station Officer perceived Mulroney as unenthusiastic about his assignment. (Hedgman, 8/21/75, pp. 55, 56, 88–89)

When Mulroney arrived in the Congo, he met with the Station Officer, who informed him that there was "a virus in the safe." (Mulroney, 9/11/75, p. 7–A; 6/9/75, p. 16) Mulroney said he assumed it was a "lethal agent," although the Station Officer was not explicit:

> I knew it wasn't for somebody to get his polio shot up to date. (Mulroney, 6/9/75, pp. 16, 37)[50]

---

[50] Mulroney added that if the virus was to be used for medical purposes, "It would have been in the custody of the State Department" personnel, not the CIA Station. (Mulroney, 6/9/75, p. 36)

Mulroney said that he did not recall the Station Officer's mentioning the source of the virus, but:

> It would have had to come from Washington, in my estimation, and I would think, since it had been discussed with Scheider that it probably would have emanated from his office. (Mulroney, 6/9/75, p. 28)[51]

Hedgman did not recall discussing Scheider's trip to the Congo with Mulroney, but "assumed" that he did so. (Hedgman, 8/21/75, pp. 60–61)

Mulroney was "certain" that the virus had arrived before he did. (Mulroney, 6/9/75, p. 24) He was surprised to learn that such a virus was at the Leopoldville Station because he had refused an assassination mission before departing for the Congo. (Mulroney, 6/9/75, p. 17)

Mulroney stated that he knew of no other instance where a CIA Station had possessed lethal biological substances. He assumed that its purpose was assassination, probably targeted against Lumumba. (Mulroney, 9/11/75, p. 50):

> My feeling definitely is that it was for a specific purpose, and was just not an all-purpose capability there, being held for targets of opportunity, unspecified targets. (Mulroney, 9/11/75, p. 49)

Mulroney said that the Station Officer never indicated that Mulroney was to employ the virus, that he "never discussed his assassination effort, he never even indicated that this was one." (Mulroney, 9/11/75, pp. 52, 54)

While Station Officer Hedgman had no direct recollection of discussing the assassination operation with Mulroney, he "assumed" that he had at least mentioned the problem of gaining access to Lumumba for the purpose of assassinating him. (Hedgman, 8/21/75, pp. 55, 60)

Mulroney was "sure" that he "related everything" to Hedgman about his conversations with Bissell concerning the assassination of Lumumba. (Mulroney, 9/11/75, p. 46) Hedgman, however, did not recall learning this from Mulroney. (Hedgman, 8/21/75, p. 56)

Mulroney said that his discussions of assassination with Hedgman were general and philosophical, dealing with "the morality of assassinations. (Mulroney, 9/11/75, pp. 46, 54):

> From my point of view I told him I had moral objections to it, not just qualms, but objections. I didn't think it was the right thing to do. (Mulroney, 9/11/75, p. 9)

When asked to characterize Hedgman's attitude toward assassination based on those discussions, Mulroney said:

> He would not have been opposed in principle to assassination in the interests of national security * * *. I know that he is a man of great moral perception and decency and honor * * *. And

---

[51] When Mulroney was informed about Hedgman's testimony concerning Scheider's trip to the Congo and the plot to poison Lumumba, he said, "I believe absolutely in its credibility. Mulroney found nothing in the facts as he knew them, nor in Hedgman's character, to raise a question about that testimony. He regarded Hedgman as "an honest and a decent man—a totally truthful man." (Mulroney, 9/11/75, pp. 19, 53, 56)

that it would disturb him to be engaged in something like that. But I think I would have to say that in our conversations, my memory of those, at no time would he rule it out as being a possibility. (Mulroney, 9/11/75, p. 18)

### (iv) Mulroney's Plan to "Neutralize" Lumumba

After Mulroney arrived in the Congo, he formulated a plan for "neutralizing" Lumumba by drawing him away from the custody of the U.N. force which was guarding his residence:

MULRONEY: [W]hat I wanted to do was to get him out, to trick him out, if I could, and then turn him over ∗∗∗ to the legal authorities and let him stand trial. Because he had atrocity attributed to him for which he could very well stand trial.

Q:      And for which he could very well have received capital punishment?

MULRONEY: Yes. And I am not opposed to capital punishment. (Mulroney, 9/11/75, pp. 20–21)[52]

To implement his plan, Mulroney made arrangements to rent "an observation post over the palace in which Lumumba was safely ensconced." He also made the acquaintance of a U.N. guard to recruit him for an attempt to lure Lumumba outside U.N. protective custody. (Mulroney, 6/9/75, p. 20; 9/11/75, p. 21) Mulroney said that he cabled progress reports to CIA Headquarters, and kept the Station Officer informed about his activities. (Mulroney, 9/11/75, pp. 26–27, 56)

Mulroney arranged for CIA agent QJ/WIN, to come to the Congo to work with him:

What I wanted to use him for was ∗∗∗ counter-espionage. ∗∗∗ I had to screen the U.S. participation in this ∗∗∗ by using a foreign national whom we knew, trusted, and had worked with ∗∗∗ the idea was for me to use him as an alter ego. (Mulroney, 6/9/75, pp. 19–20)

In mid-November, two cables from Leopoldville urged CIA Headquarters to send QJ/WIN:

LOCAL OPERATIONAL CIRCUMSTANCES REQUIRE IMMEDIATE EXPEDITION OF QJ/WIN TRAVEL TO LEOPOLDVILLE. (CIA Cable, Leopoldville to Director, 11/13/60; see also 11/11/60)

The cables did not explain the "operational circumstances."

---

[52] When Mulroney's mission to draw Lumumba out of the hands of the U.N. was described to C. Douglas Dillon, who was Undersecretary of State at that time, Dillon testified that it conformed to United States policy toward Lumumba. (Dillon, 9/21/75, p. 50)

According to an earlier report from the Station Officer, it was the view of the Special Representative of the Secretary General of the United Nations that arrest by Congolese authorities was "JUST A TRICK TO ASSASSINATE LUMUMBA." (CIA Cable, Station Officer to Director, 10/11/60) The Station Officer proceeded to recommend Lumumba's arrest in the same cable:

STATION HAS CONSISTENTLY URGED [CONGOLESE] LEADERS ARREST LUMUMBA IN BELIEF LUMUMBA WILL CONTINUE BE THREAT TO STABILITY CONGO UNTIL REMOVED FROM SCENE.

(b) QJ/WIN's Mission in the Congo: November–December 1960

QJ/WIN was a foreign citizen with a criminal background, recruited in Europe. (Memo to CIA Finance Division, Re: Payments to QJ/WIN, 1/31/61) In November 1960, agent QJ/WIN was dispatched to the Congo to undertake a mission that "might involve a large element of personal risk." (CIA Cable, 11/2/60)[53]

A cable from Headquarters to Leopoldville stated:

> In view of the extreme sensitivity of the objective for which we want [QJ/WIN] to perform his task, he was not told precisely what we want him to do ∗∗∗. Instead, he was told ∗∗∗ that we would like to have him spot, assess, and recommend some dependable, quick-witted persons for our use ∗∗∗. It was thought best to withhold our true, specific requirements pending the final decision to use [him]. (CIA Cable, 11/2/60)

This message itself was deemed too sensitive to be retained at the station: "this dispatch should be reduced to cryptic necessary notes and destroyed after the first reading." (CIA Cable, 11/2/60)

QJ/WIN arrived in Leopoldville on November 21, 1960, and returned to Europe in late December 1960. (CIA Cable, 11/29/60; CIA Cable, Director to Leopoldville, 12/9/60)

Mulroney described QJ/WIN as follows:

MULRONEY: ∗∗∗ I would say that he would not be a man of many scruples.

Q:     So he was a man capable of doing anything?

MULRONEY: I would think so, yes.

Q:     And that would include assassination?

MULRONEY: I would think so. (Mulroney, 9/11/75, pp. 35–36)

But Mulroney had no knowledge that QJ/WIN was ever used for an assassination operation. (Mulroney, 9/11/75, pp. 36, 42)

Mulroney said that, as far as he knew, he was the only CIA officer with supervisory responsibility for QJ/WIN, and QJ/WIN did not report independently to anyone else. When asked if it was possible that QJ/WIN had an assignment independent of his operations for Mulroney, he said:

> Yes, that is possible—or it could have been that somebody contacted him after he got down there, that they wanted him to do something along the lines of assassination. I don't know. (Mulroney, 9/11/75, pp. 28, 29)

---

[53] An additional purpose in dispatching QJ/WIN was to send him from the Congo to another African country for an unspecified mission. QJ/WIN's mission to this country is not explained in the cable traffic between CIA Headquarters and the various stations that dealt with him.

There is no indication in CIA files as to whether QJ/WIN completed this operation. Mulroney said he had no knowledge of any assignment that would have taken QJ/WIN to this other country. (Mulroney, 9/11/75, pp. 32–33) William Harvey stated that he recalled that QJ/WIN might have been sent to an African country other than the Congo, but Harvey was "almost certain that this was not connected in any way to an assassination mission." (Harvey affidavit, 9/14/75, p. 5)

Mulroney discounted this possibility as "highly unlikely" because it would be a departure from standard CIA practice by placing an agent in a position of knowledge superior to that of his supervising officer. (Mulroney, 9/11/75, p. 29)

Despite Mulroney's doubt that QJ/WIN had an independent line of responsibility to Station Officer Hedgman, Hedgman's November 29 cable to Tweedy reported that QJ/WIN had begun implementing a plan to "pierce both Congolese and U.N. guards" to enter Lumumba's residence and "provide escort out of residence." (CIA Cable, Station Officer to Tweedy, 11/29/60) Mulroney said that he had directed QJ/WIN to make the acquaintance of the member of U.N. force. (Mulroney, 9/11/75, p. 21) By this point, Lumumba had already left U.N. custody to travel toward his stronghold at Stanleyville. This did not deter QJ/WIN:

VIEW CHANGE IN LOCATION TARGET, QJ/WIN ANXIOUS GO STANLEYVILLE AND EXPRESSED DESIRE EXECUTE PLAN BY HIMSELF WITHOUT USING ANY APPARAT (CIA Cable, 11/29/60)

It is unclear whether this latter "plan" contemplated assassination as well as abduction. Headquarters replied affirmatively the next day in language which could have been interpreted as an assassination order:

CONCUR QJ/WIN GO STANLEYVILLE * * * WE ARE PREPARED CONSIDER DIRECT ACTION BY QJ/WIN BUT WOULD LIKE YOUR READING ON SECURITY FACTORS. HOW CLOSE WOULD THIS PLACE [UNITED STATES] TO THE ACTION? (CIA Cable, Chief of Africa Division to Station Officer, 11/30/60)

Mulroney said that QJ/WIN's stay in the Congo was "coextensive with my own, allowing for the fact that he came after I did." (Mulroney, 6/9/75, p. 19)

In a memorandum to arrange the accounting for QJ/WIN's activities in the Congo, William Harvey, Mulroney's immediate superior in the Directorate of Plans, noted: "QJ/WIN was sent on this trip for a specific, highly sensitive operational purpose which has been completed." (Memo for Finance Division from Harvey, 1/11/61) Mulroney explained Harvey's reference by saying that once Lumumba was in the hands of the Congolese authorities "the reason for the mounting of the project * * * had become moot." When asked if he and QJ/WIN were responsible for Lumumba's departure from U.N. custody and subsequent capture, Mulroney replied: "Absolutely not." (Mulroney, 9/11/75, p. 35)[54]

Despite the suggestive language of the cables at the end of November about the prospect of "direct action" by QJ/WIN and an indication in the Inspector General's Report that QJ/WIN may have been recruited initially for an assassination mission[55] there is no clear evidence that QJ/WIN was actually involved in any assassination plan or attempt. The Inspector General's Report may have accurately reported a plan for the use of QJ/WIN

---

[54] Harvey did not recall the meaning of the memorandum, but he assumed that the mere fact that Mulroney had returned from the Congo would have constituted the "completion" of QJ/WIN's mission. (Harvey affidavit, 9/14/75, p. 2)

[55] The CIA Inspector General's Report said that QJ/WIN "had been recruited earlier * * * for use in a special operation in the Congo (the assassination of Patrice Lumumba) to be run by Michael Mulroney." (I.G. Report, p. 38)

As explained above, Bissell and Mulroney testified that Mulroney had refused to be associated with an assassination operation. See sections 5(a) (ii) and (iii).

which predated Mulroney's refusal to accept the assassination assignment from Bissell. But there is no evidence from which to conclude that QJ/WIN was actually used for such an operation.

Station Officer Hedgman had a "vague recollection" that QJ/WIN was in the Congo working for Mulroney. But Hedgman did not recall why QJ/WIN was in the Congo and said that QJ/WIN was not one of his major operatives. (Hedgman, 8/21/75, p. 95) Bissell and Tweedy did not recall anything about QJ/WIN's activities in the Congo. (Bissell, 9/10/75, pp. 54–57; Tweedy, 9/9/75, pp. 54, 61)

Harvey, whose division "loaned" QJ/ WIN to the Congo Station, testified:

> I was kept informed of the arrangements for QJ/WIN's trip to the Congo and, subsequently, of his presence in the Congo. I do not know specifically what QJ/WIN did in the Congo. I do not think that I ever had such knowledge * * *. If QJ/WIN were to be used on an assassination mission, it would have been cleared with me. I was never informed that he was to be used for such a mission. (Harvey affidavit, 9/14/75, pp. 3–4)[56]

A 1962 CIA cable indicates the value the CIA accorded QJ/WIN and the inherent difficulty for an intelligence agency in employing criminals. The CIA had learned that QJ/WIN was about to go on trial in Europe on smuggling charges and Headquarters suggested:

> If * * * INFOR[MATION] TRUE WE MAY WISH ATTEMPT QUASH CHARGES OR ARRANGE SOMEHOW SALVAGE QJ/WIN FOR OUR PURPOSES. (CIA Cable, 1962)

(c) WI/ROGUE Asks QJ/WIN to Join "Execution Squad": December 1960

The only suggestion that QJ/WIN had any connection with assassination was a report that WI/ROGUE, another asset of the Congo Station, once asked QJ/WIN to join an "execution squad."

WI/ROGUE was an "essentially stateless" soldier of fortune, "a forger and former bank robber." (Inspector General Memo, 3/14/75)[57] The CIA sent him to the Congo after providing him with plastic surgery and a toupee so that Europeans traveling in the Congo would not recognize him. (I.G. Memo, 3/14/75) The CIA characterized WI/ROGUE as a man who "learns quickly and carries out any assignment without regard for danger." (CIA Cable, Africa Division to Leopoldville, 10/27/60) CIA's Africa Division recommended WI/ROGUE as an agent in the following terms:

> He is indeed aware of the precepts of right and wrong, but if he is given an assignment which may be morally wrong in the eyes of the world, but necessary because his case officer ordered him to

---

[56] Harvey stated that the memoranda concerning QJ/WIN were probably written for his signature by the officer who supervised QJ/WIN's activities in Europe. (Harvey affidavit, 9/14/75, pp. 1, 4)

Harvey said that in later discussions he held with Scheider concerning the development of a general assassination capability, Scheider never mentioned QJ/WIN's activities in the Congo, nor did Scheider refer to his own trip to Leopoldville. Harvey also stated that before the formation of that project, QJ/WIN's case officer had not previously used him "as an assassination capability or even viewed him as such." (Harvey affidavit, 9/14/75, pp. 7, 8) *See* discussion in Part III, Section C.

[57] This information was derived from a report on WI/ROGUE'S assignment to the Congo prepared by a former Africa Division officer on March 14, 1975 at the request of the CIA Office of the Inspector General.

carry it out, then it is right, and he will dutifully undertake appropriate action for its execution without pangs of conscience. In a word, he can rationalize all actions.

Station Officer Hedgman described WI/ROGUE as "a man with a rather unsavory reputation, who would try anything once, at least." Hedgman used him as "a general utility agent" because "I felt we needed surveillance capability, developing new contacts, various things." Hedgman supervised WI/ROGUE directly and did not put him in touch with Mulroney. (Hedgman, 8/21/75, pp. 96–97)

A report on agent WI/ROGUE, prepared for the CIA Inspector General's Office in 1975, described the training he received:

> On 19 September 1960 two members of Africa Division met with him to discuss "an operational assignment in Africa Division." In connection with this assignment, WI/ROGUE was to be trained in demolitions, small arms, and medical immunization. (I.G. Memo, 3/14/75)[58]

The report also outlined WI/ROGUE'S assignment to the Congo and recorded no mention of the use to which WI/ROGUE'S "medical immunization" training would be put:

> In October 1960 a cable to Leopoldville stated that ∗ ∗ ∗ Headquarters [had] ∗ ∗ ∗ intent to use him as utility agent in order to (a) organize and conduct a surveillance team; (b) intercept packages; (c) blow up bridges; and (d) execute other assignments requiring positive action. His utilization is not to be restricted to Leopoldville." (I.G. Memo, 3/14/75)

WI/ROGUE made his initial contact with Hedgman in Leopoldville on December 2, 1960. Hedgman instructed him to 'build cover during initial period;" and to "spot persons for [a] surveillance team" of intelligence agents in the province where Lumumba's support was strongest. (CIA Cable, 12/17/60)

Soon thereafter Hedgman cabled Headquarters:

> QJ/WIN WHO RESIDES SAME HOTEL AS WI/ROGUE REPORTED ∗ ∗ ∗ WI/ROGUE SMELLED AS THOUGH HE IN INTEL BUSINESS. STATION DENIED ANY INFO ON WI/ ROGUE. 14 DEC QJ/WIN REPORTED WI/ROGUE HAD OFFERED HIM THREE HUNDRED DOLLARS PER MONTH TO PARTICIPATE IN INTEL NET AND BE MEMBER "EXECUTION SQUAD." WHEN WI/ROGUE ADDED THERE WOULD BE BONUSES FOR SPECIAL JOBS. UNDER QJ/WIN QUESTIONING, WI/ROGUE LATER SAID HE WORK-ING FOR [AMERICAN] SERVICE.
>    ∗ ∗ ∗ IN DISCUSSING LOCAL CONTACTS, WI/ROGUE MENTIONED QJ/WIN BUT DID NOT ADMIT TO HAVING TRIED RECRUIT HIM. WHEN [STATION OFFICER] TRIED LEARN WHETHER WI/ROGUE HAD MADE APPROACH LATTER CLAIMED HAD TAKEN NO STEPS. [STATION OFFICER] WAS UNABLE CONTRADICT, AS DID NOT WISH REVEAL QJ/WIN CONNECTION [WITH CIA]. (CIA Cable, Leopoldville to Director, 12/17/60)

---

[58] A case officer who prepared WI/ROGUE for his mission in the Congo stated that he had no knowledge that WI/ROGUE received any training in "medical immunization." The case officer assumed that an unclear cable reference to the fact that WI/ROGUE received innoculations before his journey was misinterpreted in the memorandum prepared for the Inspector General's Office on March 14, 1975. (WI/ROGUE Case Officer affidavit, 11/14/75)

The cable also expressed Hedgman's concern about WI/ROGUE's actions:

> *** LEOP CONCERNED BY WI/ROGUE FREE WHEELING AND LACK SECURITY. STATION HAS ENOUGH HEADACHES WITHOUT WORRYING ABOUT AGENT WHO NOT ABLE HANDLE FINANCES AND WHO NOT WILLING FOLLOW INSTRUCTIONS. IF HQS DESIRES, WILLING KEEP HIM ON PROBATION, BUT IF CONTINUE HAVE DIFFICULTIES, BELIEVE WI/ROGUE RECALL BEST SOLUTION. (CIA Cable, Leopoldville to Director, 12/17/60)

Hedgman explained WI/ROGUE's attempt to recruit QJ/WIN for an execution squad as an unauthorized unexpected contact. He testified that he had not instructed WI/ROGUE to make this kind of proposition to QJ/WIN or anyone else:

> I would like to stress that I don't know what WI/ROGUE was talking about as an "execution squad," and I am sure he was never asked to go out and execute anyone. (Hedgman, 8/21/75, p. 100)

Hedgman suggested that WI/ROGUE had concocted the idea of an execution squad:

> His idea of what an intelligence operative should do, I think, had been gathered by reading a few novels or something of the sort. (Hedgman, 8/21/75, p. 100)

Mulroney said he knew of no attempt by anyone connected with the CIA to recruit an execution squad and he did not remember WI/ROGUE. (Mulroney, 9/11/75, pp. 39–42) He stated that QJ/WIN was considered for use on "strong arm squad[s]," unrelated to assassinations:

> Surveillance teams where you have to go into crime areas *** where you need a fellow that if he gets in a box can fight his way out of it. (Mulroney, 9/11/75, p. 36)

Richard Bissell recalled nothing about WI/ROGUE's approach to QJ/WIN. (Bissell, 9/11/75, p. 71) Bronson Tweedy remembered that WI/ROGUE was "dispatched on a general purpose mission" to the Congo. But Tweedy testified that WI/ROGUE would "absolutely not" have been used on an assassination mission against Lumumba because " he was basically dispatched, assessed and dealt with by the balance of the Division" rather than by the two people in the Africa Division, Tweedy and his Deputy, who would have known that the assassination of Lumumba was being considered. (Tweedy, 9/9/75, pp. 63–65)

The Station Officer said that if WI/ROGUE had been involved in an actual assassination plan, he would have transmitted messages concerning WI/ROGUE in the PROP channel. Instead, he limited distribution of the cable about WI/ROGUE in a routine manner—as a CIA officer would "normally do *** when you speak in a derogatory manner of an asset." (Hedgman, 8/21/75, pp. 101–102)

Hedgman maintained that WI/ROGUE's proposition to QJ/WIN to join an "execution squad" could be attributed to WI/ROGUE's "freewheeling" nature:

> I had difficulty controlling him in that he was not a professional intelligence officer as such. He seemed to act on his own without seeking guidance or authority *** I found he was rather an unguided missile *** the kind of man that could get you in trouble before you knew you were in trouble. (Hedgman, 8/21/75, pp. 96–97)

But Hedgman did not disavow all responsibility for WI/ROGUE's actions:

> [I]f you give a man an order and he carries it out and causes a problem for the Station, then you accept responsibility. (Hedgman, 8/21/75, p. 97)

In sum, the testimony of the CIA officers involved in the PROP operation and the concern about WI/ROGUE'S "freewheeling" in Hedgman's cable suggests that agent WI/ROGUE's attempt to form an "execution squad" was an unauthorized, maverick action, unconnected to any CIA operation. However, the fact that WI/ROGUE was to be trained in "medical immunization" (I.G. Report Memo, 3/14/75) precludes a definitive conclusion to that effect.

### 6. The Question of Whether the CIA Was Involved in Bringing About Lumumba's Death in Katanga Province

The CIA officers most closely connected with the plot to poison Lumumba testified uniformly that they knew of no CIA involvement in Lumumba's death. The Congo Station had advance knowledge of the central government's plan to transport Lumumba into the hands of his bitterest enemies, where he was likely to be killed. But there is no evidentiary basis for concluding that the CIA conspired in this plan or was connected to the events in Katanga that resulted in Lumumba's death.

*(a) Lumumba's Imprisonment After Leaving U.N. Custody: November 27–December 3, 196*

The only suggestion that the CIA may have been involved in the capture of Lumumba by Mobutu's troops after Lumumba left U.N. custody on November 27, is a PROP cable from the Station Officer to Tweedy on November 14. The cable stated that a CIA agent had learned that Lumumba's

> POLITICAL FOLLOWERS IN STANLEYVILLE DESIRE THAT HE BREAK OUT OF HIS CONFINEMENT AND PROCEED TO THAT CITY BY CAR TO ENGAGE IN POLITICAL ACTIVITY. * * * DECISION ON BREAKOUT WILL PROBABLY BE MADE SHORTLY. STATION EXPECTS TO BE ADVISED BY [AGENT] OF DECISION WAS MADE. * * * STATION HAS SEVERAL POSSIBLE ASSETS TO USE IN EVENT OF BREAKOUT AND STUDYING SEVERAL PLANS OF ACTION. (CIA Cable, Station Officer to Tweedy, 11/14/60)

There is no other evidence that the CIA actually learned in advance of Lumumba's plan to depart for Stanleyville. In fact, a cable from Leopoldville on the day after Lumumba's escape evidenced the Station's complete ignorance about the circumstances of Lumumba's departure. (CIA Cable, Leopoldville to Director, 11/28/60) However, the same cable raises a question concerning whether the CIA was involved in Lumumba's subsequent capture en route by Congolese troops:

> [STATION] WORKING WITH [CONGOLESE GOVERNMENT] TO GET ROADS BLOCKED AND TROOPS ALERTED [BLOCK] POSSIBLE ESCAPE ROUTE. (CIA Cable, 11/28/60)

Station Officer Hedgman testified that he was "quite certain that there was no Agency involvement in any way" in Lumumba's departure from U.N. custody and that he had no advance knowledge of Lumumba's plan. He stated that he consulted with Congolese officers about the possible routes Lumumba might take to Stanleyville, but he was "not a major assistance" in tracking down Lumumba prior to his capture. (Hedgman, 8/21/75, pp. 63–65)

Mulroney, who had planned to draw Lumumba out of U.N. custody and turn him over to Congolese authorities, testified that Lumumba escaped by his own devices and was not tricked by the CIA. (Mulroney, 9/11/75, p. 22)

*(b) Lumumba's Death*

The contemporaneous cable traffic shows that the CIA was kept informed of Lumumba's condition and movements in January of 1961 by the Congolese and that the CIA continued to consider Lumumba a serious political threat. Despite the fact that the Station Officer knew of a plan to deliver Lumumba into the hands of his enemies at a time when the CIA was convinced that "drastic steps" were necessary to prevent Lumumba's return to power, there is no evidence of CIA involvement in this plan or in bringing about the death of Luntumba in Katanga.

There is no doubt that the CIA and the Congolese government shared a concern in January 1961 that Lumumba might return to power, particularly since the Congolese army and police were threatening to mutiny if they were not given substantial pay raises. Station Officer Hedgman reported that a mutiny "almost certainly would ∗ ∗ ∗ bring about [Lumumba] return power" and said he had advised the Congolese government of his opinion that the army garrison at Leopoldville

WILL MUTINY WITHIN TWO OR THREE DAYS UNLESS DRASTIC ACTION TAKEN SATISFY COMPLAINTS. (CIA Cable, Leopoldville to Director, 1/12/61)

Hedgman urged Headquarters to consider an immediate reaction to the crisis. (CIA Cable, 1/12/61) This cable, which was sent through the ordinary channel, made no reference, even indirectly, to assassination, and instead recommended a different course of action.

The next day, Hedgman cabled Headquarters:

STATION AND EMBASSY BELIEVE PRESENT GOVERNMENT MAY FALL WITHIN FEW DAYS. RESULT WOULD ALMOST CERTAINLY BE CHAOS AND RETURN [LUMUMBA] TO POWER. (CIA Cable, Leopoldville to Director, 1/13/61)

Hedgman advised that reopening the Congolese Parliament under United Nations supervision was unacceptable because:

THE COMBINATION OF [LUMUMBA'S] POWERS AS DEMAGOGUE, HIS ABLE USE OF GOON SQUADS AND PROPAGANDA AND SPIRIT OF DEFEAT WITHIN [GOVERNMENT] COALITION WHICH WOULD INCREASE RAPIDLY UNDER SUCH CONDITIONS WOULD ALMOST CERTAINLY INSURE [LUMUMBA] VICTORY IN PARLIAMENT. ∗ ∗ ∗ REFUSAL TAKE DRASTIC STEPS AT THIS TIME WILL LEAD TO DEFEAT OF [UNITED STATES] POLICY IN CONGO. (CIA Cable, Leopoldville to Director, 1/13/61)

On January 14, Hedgman was advised by a Congolese government leader that Lumumba was to be transferred from the Thysville military camp, where he had been held since shortly after Mobutu's troops captured him, to a prison in Bakwanga, the capital of another Congolese province reported to be the "home territory of ∗ ∗ ∗ Lumumba's sworn enemy." (CIA Cable, Leopoldville to Director, 1/17/61; CIA Information Report, 1/17/61)

On January 17, authorities in Leopoldville placed Lumumba and two of his leading supporters, Maurice Mpolo and Joseph Okito aboard an airplane bound for Bakwanga. Appparently the aircraft was redirected in midflight to Elisabethville in Katanga Province "when it was learned that United Nations troops were at Bakwanga airport." On February 13, the government of Katanga reported that Lumumba and his two companions escaped the previous day and died at the hands of hostile villagers. (U.N. Report, 11/12/61, pp. 98–100; 109)

The United Nations Commission on Investigation was "not convinced by the version of the facts given by the provincial government of Katanga." The Commission concluded instead, that Lumumba was killed on January 17, almost immediately after his arrival in Katanga, probably with the knowledge of the central government and at the behest of the Katanga authorities. (U.N. Report, 11/11/61, pp. 100, 117):

> The Commission wishes to put on record its view that President Kasavubu and his aides, on the one hand, and the provincial government of Katanga headed by Mr. Tshombe on the other, should not escape responsibility for the death of Mr. Lumumba, Mr. Okito, and Mr. Mpolo. For Mr. Kasavubu and his aides had handed over Mr. Lumumba and his colleagues to the Katanga authorities knowing full well, in doing so, that they were throwing them into the hands of their bitterest political enemies. The government of the province of Katanga in turn not only failed to safeguard the lives of the three prisoners but also had, by its action, contributed, directly or indirectly, to the murder of the prisoners. (U.N. Report, 11/11/61, p. 118)

Cables from the Station Officer demonstrated no CIA involvement in the plan to transport Lumumba to Bakwanga. But the Station Officer clearly had prior knowledge of the plan to transfer Lumumba to a state where it was probable that he would be killed. Other supporters of Lumumba who had been sent to Bakwanga earlier by Lepoldville authorities

> Were killed there in horrible circumstances, and the place was known as the 'slaughterhouse.' It was therefore improbable that Mr. Lumumba and his companions would have met a different fate at Bakwanga if they had been taken there. (U.N. Report, 11/11/61, p. 109)

After learning that Lumumba was to be flown to Bakwanga, the Station Officer cabled:

> IT NOW MORE IMPORTANT THAN EVER SUPPORT THOSE SINGLE ELEMENTS WHICH CAN STRENGTHEN FABRIC OVERALL * * * OPPOSITION [LUMUMBA]. WISH ASSURE HQS WE TRYING SHORE UP * * * DEFENSES ONLY IN TERMS OUR OWN OBJECTIVES DENY CONGO GOVT CONTROL [LUMUMBA]. (CIA Cable, 1/16/61)

Despite his perception of an urgent need to prevent Lumumba's return to power at this time, the Station Officer testified that the CIA was not involved in bringing about Lumumba's death in Katanga and that he did not have any first-hand knowledge of the circumstances of Lumumba's death. (Hedgman, 8/25/75, pp. 31, 33)[59]

---

[59] Hedgman also testified that he had no discussions with the Congolese central government, after Lumumba was in its custody, about executing Lumumba or sending him to Katanga. Hedgman said:

To the best of my knowledge, neither the Station nor the Embassy had any input in the decision to send him to Katanga * * * I think there was a general assumption, once we learned he had been sent to Katanga, that his goose was cooked, because Tshombe hated him and looked on him as a danger and rival. (Hedgman, 8/21/75, p. 78)

In late November, Hedgman attended a meeting of CIA officers from African Stations with Bissell and Tweedy. Hedgman testified that he briefed Bissell and Tweedy on developments in the Congo, including Lumumba's flight from Leopoldville, but he could not recall any discussion at the meeting of the possibility of assassinating Lumumba. (Hedgman, 8/21/75, pp. 66, 68)

Two days after Lumumba was flown to Katanga, the CIA Base Chief in Elisabethville sent an unusual message to headquarters:

> THANKS FOR PATRICE. IF WE HAD KNOWN HE WAS COMING WE WOULD HAVE BAKED A SNAKE.

The cable also reported that the Base's sources had provided "no advance word whatsoever" of Lumumba's flight to Katanga and that the Congolese central government "does not plan to liquidate Lumumba." (CIA Cable, Elisabethville to Director, 1/19/61)

This cable indicates that the CIA did not have knowledge of the central government's decision to transfer Lumumba from Thysville military camp to a place where he would be in the hands of his avowed enemies. This cable indicates that the CIA was not kept informed of Lumumba's treatment after he arrived in Katanga because, according to the report of the United Nations Commission, Lumumba had already been killed when the cable was sent.[60]

On February 10, several weeks after Lumumba died, but before his death was announced by the Katanga government, the Elisabethville Base cabled Headquarters that "Lumumba fate is best kept secret in Katanga." (CIA Cable, Elisabethville to Director, 2/10/61) The cable gave different versions from several sources about Lumumba's death. Hedgman testified that the cable conformed to his recollection that the CIA "did not have any hard information" as of that date about Lumumba's fate after arrival in Katanga. (Hedgman, 8/25/75, p. 34)

Hedgman acknowledged that the CIA was in close contact with some Congolese officials who "quite clearly knew" that Lumumba was to be shipped to Katanga "because they were involved." But Hedgman said that these Congolese contacts "were not acting under CIA instructions if and when they did this." (Hedgman, 8/21/75, p. 35)

Tweedy and Mulroney agreed with Hedgman's account that the CIA was not involved in the events that led to Lhmumba's death.[61]

### 7. The Question of The Level at Which The Assassination Plot Was Authorized

#### SUMMARY

The chain of events revealed by the documents and testimony is strong enough to permit a reasonable inference that the plot to assassinate Lumumba was authorized by

---

[60] Hedgman testified that neither he nor the Elisabethville Base knew of a Congolese plan to send Lumumba to Katanga. (Hedgman, 8/25/75, pp. 25–26)

[61] When asked if there was any CIA involvement, Tweedy replied that there was "none whatsoever." Tweedy stated that "the fate of Lumumba in the end was purely an African event." (Tweedy, 9/9/75, p. 53) Mulroney testified "CIA had absolutely no connection, to my certain knowledge, with the death of Patrice Lumumba." (Mulroney, 6/9/75, p. 20)

During his tenure as DCI, several years after Lumumba's death, Richard Helms was told by CIA investigators that "it was clear that the Agency had not murdered Lumumba," and that "the Agency had no involvement" in the events that led to Lumumba's death. (Helms, 9/16/75, p. 26)

President Eisenhower. Nevertheless, there is enough countervailing testimony by Eisenhower Administration officials and enough ambiguity and lack of clarity in the records of high-level policy meetings to preclude the Committee from making a finding that the President intended an assassination effort against Lumumba.

It is clear that the Director of Central Intelligence, Allen Dulles, authorized an assassination plot. There is, however, no evidence of United States involvement in bringing about the death of Lumumba at the hands of Congolese authorities in Katanga.

Strong expressions of hostility toward Lumumba from the President and his national security assistant, followed immediately by CIA steps in furtherance of an assassination operation against Lumumba, are part of a sequence of events that, at the least, make it appear that Dulles believed assassination was a permissible means of complying with pressure from the President to remove Lumumba from the political scene.

---

The chain of significant events in the Lumumba case begins with the testimony that President Eisenhower made a statement at a meeting of the National Security Council in the summer or early fall of 1960 that came across to one staff member in attendance as an order for the assassination of Patrice Lumumba. The next link is a memorandum of the Special Group meeting of August 25, 1960, which indicated that when the President's "extremely strong feelings on the necessity for very straightforward action" were conveyed, the Special Group

> * * * agreed that planning for the Congo would not necessarily rule out "consideration" of any particular kind of activity which might contribute to getting rid of Lumumba. (Special Group Minutes, 8/25/60)

The following day, CIA Director Allen Dulles, who had attended the Special Group meeting, personally cabled to the Station Officer in Leopoldville that Lumumba's

> REMOVAL MUST BE AN URGENT AND PRIME OBJECTIVE * * * A HIGH PRIORITY OF OUR COVERT ACTION. YOU CAN ACT ON YOUR OWN AUTHORITY WHERE TIME DOES NOT PERMIT REFERRAL HERE. (CIA Cable, Dulles to Station Officer, 8/26/60)

Although the Dulles cable does not explicitly mention assassination, Richard Bissell—the CIA official under whose aegis the assassination effort against Lumumba took place—testified that, in his opinion, this cable was a direct outgrowth of the Special Group meeting and signaled to him that the President had authorized assassination as one means of effecting Lumumba's "removal." (Bissell, 9/10/75, pp. 33–34 61–62; see Section 7(c), *infra*) Bronson Tweedy, who had direct operational responsibility at Headquarters for activities against Lumumba, testified that the Dulles cable confirmed the policy that no measure, including assassination, was to be overlooked in the attempt to remove Lumumba from a position of influence. (Tweedy, 10/9/75, pp. 4–5)

On September 19, 1960, Bissell and Tweedy cabled Station Officer Hedgman to expect a messenger from CIA Headquarters. Two days later, in the presence of the President at a meeting of the National Security Council, Allen Dulles stated that Lumumba "would remain a grave danger as long as he was not yet disposed of." (Memorandum, 460th NSC Meeting, 9/21/60) Five days after this meeting, CIA scientist, Joseph Scheider, arrived in Leopoldville and provided the Station Officer with toxic biological substances, instructed him to assassinate Lumumba, and informed him that the President had authorized this operation.

Two mitigating factors weaken this chain just enough so that it will not support an absolute finding of Presidential authorization for the assassination effort against Lumumba.

First, the two officials of the Eisenhower Administration responsible to the President for national security affairs and present at the NSC meetings in question testified that they knew of no Presidential approval for, or knowledge of, an assassination operation.

Second, the minutes of discussions at meetings of the National Security Council and its Special Group do not record an explicit Presidential order for the assassination of Lumumba. The Secretary of the Special Group maintained that his memoranda reflected the actual language used at the meetings without omission or euphemism for extremely sensitive statements. (Parrott, 7/10/75, p. 19) All other NSC staff executives stated however, that there was a strong possibility that a statement as sensitive as an assassination order would have been omitted from the record or handled by means of euphemism. Several high Government officials involved in policymaking and planning for covert operations testified that the language in these minutes clearly indicated that assassination was contemplated at the NSC as one means of eliminating Lumumba as a political threat; other officials testified to the contrary.

*(a) High-Level Meetings at which "Getting Rid of Lumumba" Was Discussed*

(i) Dillon's Testimony About Pentagon Meeting: Summer 1960

In late July 1960, Patrice Lumumba visited the United States and met with Secretary of State Christian Herter and Undersecretary of State C. Douglas Dillon. While Lumumba was in Washington, D.C., Secretary Herter pledged aid to the newly formed Government of the Republic of the Congo.

According to Dillon, Lumumba impressed American officials as an irrational, almost "psychotic" personality:

> When he was in the State Department meeting, either with me or with the Secretary in my presence ✽ ✽ ✽ he would never look you in the eye. He looked up at the sky. And a tremendous flow of words came out. He spoke in French, and he spoke it very fluently. And his words didn't ever have any relation to the particular things that we wanted to discuss ✽ ✽ ✽. You had a feeling that he was a person that was gripped by this fervor that I can only characterize as messianic ✽ ✽ ✽. [H]e was just not a rational being. (Dillon, 9/2/75, p. 24)

Dillon said that the willingness of the United States government to work with Lumumba vanished after these meetings:

> [T]he impression that was left was ✽ ✽ ✽ very bad, that this was an individual whom it was impossible to deal with. And the feelings of the Government as a result of this sharpened very considerably at that time ✽ ✽ ✽. We [had] hoped to see him and see what we could do to come to a better understanding with him. (Dillon, 9/2/75, pp. 23–24)

Dillon testified that shortly after Lumumba's visit in late July or August, he was present at a meeting at the Pentagon attended by representatives of the State Department, Defense Department, Joint Chiefs of Staff and the CIA. (Dillon, 9/2/75, pp. 17–20, 25–26)[62]

---

[62] Dillon was unable to recall the precise date of this meeting. (Dillon, 9/2/75, pp. 25–26)

According to Dillon, "a question regarding the possibility of an assassination attempt against Lumumba was briefly raised. Dillon did not recall anything about the language used in raising the question. Dillon assumed that when the subject of Lumumba's assassination was raised, "it was turned off by the CIA" because "the CIA people, whoever they were, were negative to any such action." This opposition "wasn't moral," according to Dillon, but rather an objection on the grounds that it was "not a possible thing." Dillon said the CIA reaction "might have been" made out of the feeling that the group was too large for such a sensitive discussion. (Dillon, 9/2/75, pp. 15–17, 25, 30, 60)

Dillon did not remember who lodged the negative reaction to the assassination question although he thought it "would have to have been either Allen Dulles, or possibly [General] Cabell ∗ ∗ ∗ most likely Cabell."[63] (Dillon, 9/2/75, pp. 22, 25) Dillon thought it was "very likely that Richard Bissell attended the meeting. (Dillon, 9/2/75, p. 21)

Dillon stated that this discussion could not have served as authorization for an actual assassination effort against Lumumba, but he believed that the CIA:

> Could have decided they wanted to develop the capability ∗ ∗ ∗ just by knowing the concern that everyone had about Lumumba. ∗ ∗ ∗ They wouldn't have had to tell anyone about that. That is just developing their own internal capability, and then they would have to come and get permission. (Dillon, 9/2/75, pp. 30, 31)

Dillon testified that he had never heard any mention of the plot to poison Lumumba nor, even a hint that the CIA asked permission to mount such an operation. (Dillon, 9/2/75, p. 50) But after he was informed of the poison plot, Dillon made the following comment about the Pentagon meeting:

> I think it is ∗ ∗ ∗ likely that it might have been the beginning of this whole idea on the CIA's part that they should develop such a capacity. And maybe they didn't have it then and went to work to develop it beginning in August. (Dillon, 9/2/75, p. 61)

Dillon said that it was unlikely that formal notes were taken at the meeting or preserved because it was a small "ad hoc" group rather than an official body. Such interdepartmental meetings were "not unusual," according to Dillon. (Dillon, 9/2/75, p. 18)

The only officials Dillon named as probable participants other than the CIA representatives were Deputy Secretary of Defense James Douglas and Assistant Secretary of Defense John N. Irwin II. (Dillon, 9/2/75, pp. 19, 21) Douglas stated that it was possible that he attended such a meeting at the Pentagon, but he did not recall it. Nor did he recall the question of Lumumba's assassination ever being raised in his presence. (Douglas affidavit, 9/5/75) Irwin stated that it was "likely" that he attended the meeting to which Dillon referred, but he did not remember whether he was present "at any meeting at the Pentagon where the question of assassinating Patrice Lumumba was raised." (Irwin affidavit, 9/22/75, p. 3)

(ii) Robert Johnson's Testimony That He Understood the President to Order Lumumba's Assassination at an NSC Meeting

Robert H. Johnson, a member of the National Security Council staff from 1951 to January 1962, offered what he termed a "clue" to the extent of Presidential involvement in

---

[63] General Cabell was Allen Dulles' Deputy DCI at this time.

the decision to assassinate Lumumba. (Johnson, 6/18/75, pp. 4–5)[64] Johnson recounted the following occurrence at an NSC meeting, in the summer of 1960, which began with a briefing on world developments by the DCI:

> At some time during that discussion, President Eisenhower said something—I can no longer remember his words—that came across to me as an order for the assassination of Lumumba who was then at the center of political conflict and controversy in the Congo. There was no discussion; the meeting simply moved on. I remember my sense of that moment quite clearly because the President's statement came as a great shock to me. I cannot, however, reconstruct the moment more specifically.
>
> Although I was convinced at the time—and remained convinced when I thought about it later—that the President's statement was intended as an order for the assassination of Lumumba, I must confess that in thinking about the incident more recently I have had some doubts. As is well known, it was quite uncharacteristic of President Eisenhower to make or announce policy decisions in NSC meetings. Certainly, it was strange if he departed from that normal pattern on a subject so sensitive as this. Moreover, it was not long after this, I believe, that Lumumba was dismissed as premier by Kasavubu in an action that was a quasi-coup. I have come to wonder whether what I really heard was only an order for some such political action. All I can tell you with any certainty at the present moment is my sense of that moment in the Cabinet Room of the White House. (Johnson, 6/18/75, pp. 6–7)

Johnson "presumed" that the President made his statement while "looking toward the Director of Central Intelligence." (Johnson, 6/18/75, p. 11) He was unable to recall with any greater specificity the words used by the President. (Johnson, 9/13/75, p. 10) Johnson was asked:

Q:       * * * Would it be fair to say that although you allow for the possibility that a coup or some more general political action was being discussed, it is your clear impression that you had heard an order for the assassination of Lumumba?

JOHNSON: It was my clear impression at the time.

Q:       And it remains your impression now?

---

[64] Robert Johnson introduced his testimony before the Committee with the following statement:

"* * * I would like to preface my remarks by pointing out that my decision to offer testimony to this committee has involved for me a profound personal, moral dilemma. In my role as a member of the NSC Staff for ten and one-half years, I was privy to a great deal of information that involved relationships of confidentiality with high officials of the United States government. I have always taken very seriously the responsibilities implied in such relationships.

"These responsibilities extend, in my view, far beyond questions of security classification or other legal or foreign policy concerns. They relate to the very basis of human society and government—to the relationships of trust without which no free society can long survive and no government can operate.

"I have been forced by recent developments, however to weigh against these considerable responsibilities, my broader responsibilities as a citizen on an issue that involves major questions of public morality, as well as questions of sound policy. Having done so, I have concluded, not without a great deal of reluctance, to come to your committee with information bearing upon your inquiry into government decisions relating to the assassination of foreign leaders." (Johnson, 6/18/75, pp. 4–5)

After his tenure on the staff of the National Security Council, Robert Johnson served from 1962 to 1967 on the Policy Planning Council at the Department of State.

JOHNSON: It remains my impression now. I have reflected on this other kind of possibility; but that is the sense ∗∗∗ that persists. (Johnson, 9/13/75, pp. 24–25)[65]

Johnson stated that the incident provoked a strong reaction from him:

I was surprised ∗∗∗ that I would ever hear a President say anything like this in my presence or the presence of a group of people. I was startled. (Johnson, 6/18/75, p. 13)

A succinct summary of Johnson's testimony was elicited by Senator Mathias in the following exchange:

Senator MATHIAS: ∗∗∗ What comes across is that you do have a memory, if not of exact words, but of your own reaction really to a Presidential order which you considered to be an order for an assassination.

JOHNSON: That is correct.

Senator MATHIAS: And that although precise words have escaped you in the passage of fifteen years, that sense of shock remains?

JOHNSON: Right. Yes, Sir. (Johnson, 6/18/75, p. 8)

After the meeting, Johnson, who was responsible for writing the memorandum of the discussion, consulted with a senior official on the NSC staff to determine how to handle the President's statement in the memorandum and in the debriefing of the NSC Planning Board that followed each meeting:

I suspect—but no longer have an exact recollection—that I omitted it from the debriefing. I also do not recall how I handled the subject in the memo of the meeting, though I suspect that some kind of reference to the President's statement was made. (Johnson, 6/18/75, p. 7)

In his second appearance before the Committee, Johnson stated that it was "quite likely that it [the President's statement] was handled through some kind of euphemism or may have been omitted altogether." (Johnson, 9/13/75, p. 21)[66]

---

[65] Johnson further explained that his allowance for the possibility that he had heard an order for a coup did not disturb his recollection of hearing an assassination order:

"It was a retrospective reflection on what I had heard, and since this coup did occur, it occurred to me that it was possible that that is what I heard, but that would not change my sense of the moment when I heard the President speak, which I felt then, and I continue to feel, was a statement designed to direct the disposal, assassnation, of Lumumba." (Johnson, 9/13/75, p. 12)

[66] In 1960 Johnson was Director of the Planning Board Secretariat—third in command on the NSC staff. He attended NSC meetings to take notes on the discussions whenever one of the two senior NSC officials was absent.

Johnson testified that the person with whom he consulted about the manner of recording the President's statement in the minutes was one of the two top NSC staff officials at that time: NCS Executive Secretary James Lay or Deputy Executive Secretary Marion Boggs. (Johnson, 9/13/75, pp. 12–13) Johnson could not recall which of the two officials he had consulted, but he "inferred" that it must have been the "top career NSC staff person present" at the meeting where he heard the President's statement. (Johnson, 9/13/75, p. 12) At both of the NSC meetings where the President and Johnson were present for a discussion of Lumumba—August 18 and September 7—James Lay was absent and Marion Boggs served as Acting Executive Secretary.

As Johnson stated, his testimony standing alone is "a clue, rather than precise evidence of Presidential involvement in decision making with respect to assassinations." (Johnson, 6/18/75, p. 5) To determine the significance of this "clue," it must be placed in the context of the records of the NSC meetings attended by Johnson, testimony about those meetings, and the series of events that preceded the dispatch of poisons to the Congo for Lumumba's assassination.

In the summer of 1960, Robert Johnson attended four NSC meetings at which developments in the Congo were discussed. The President was not in attendance on two of those occasions—July 15 and July 21. (NSC Minutes, 7/15/60; NSC Minutes, 7/21/60) The attitude toward Lumumba at these first two meetings was vehement:

> Mr. Dulles said that in Lumumba we were faced with a person who was a Castro or worse * * *
> Mr. Dulles went on to describe Mr. Lumumba's background which he described as "harrowing"
> * * * It is safe to go on the assumption that Lumumba has been bought by the Communists; this also, however, fits with his own orientation. (NSC Minutes, 7/21/60)

The President presided over the other two NSC meetings—on August 18 and September 7. After looking at the records of those meetings, Johnson was unable to determine with certainty at which meeting he heard the President's statement.[67] (Johnson, 9/13/75, p. 16)

The chronology of meetings, cables, and events in the Congo during this period makes it most likely that Johnson's testimony refers to the NSC meeting of August 18, 1960.

The meeting of August 18 took place at the beginning of the series of events that preceded the dispatch of Scheider to Leopoldville with poisons for assassinating Lumumba.[68] The September 7 meeting took place in the midst of these events.

---

Marion Bogg's statement about his method of handling the situation described by Johnson is in accord with Johnson's testimony:

"I have no independent recollection of being consulted by Mr. Johnson about how to handle in the memorandum of discussion any sensitive statement regarding Lumumba. I am not saying I was not consulted; merely that I do not remember such an incident. If I had been consulted, I would almost certainly have directed Mr. Johnson to omit the matter from the memorandum of discussion." (Boggs affidavit, 10/10/75, p. 2)

James Lay, who attended other NSC meetings where Lumumba was discussed (*e.g.*, September 21, 1960), also confirmed the fact that NSC minutes would not be likely to record a statement as sensitive as a Presidential order for an assassination, if such an order were given:

"If extremely sensitive matters were discussed at an NSC meeting, it was sometimes the practice that the official NSC minutes would record only the general subject discussed without identifying the specially sensitive subject of the discussion. In highly sensitive cases, no reference to the subject would be made in the NSC minutes." (Lay affidavit, 9/8/75, p. 2)

[67] Johnson testified without benefit of review of the complete Memorandum of Discussion of the meeting of September 7 because the Committee had not received it at that point. Instead, he reviewed the Record of Action which summarized the decisions made at that meeting. As discussed at Section (7)(a) (iv), *infra,* when the complete minutes of the meetings of August 18 and September 7 are compared, it is clear that the subject of Lumumba's role in the Congo received far more attention at the meeting of August 18.

[68] Each of the major events in this series is discussed in detail in other sections of the report and summarized at the beginning of section 7, *supra.*

The NSC meeting of August 18, 1960 was held three weeks before Lumumba's dismissal by Kasavubu, which Johnson remembers as taking place "not long after" he heard the President's statement. The only other meeting at which Johnson could have heard the statement by the President was held two days after this event, on September 7.[69]

Robert Johnson's memorandum of the meeting of August 18, 1960 indicates that Acting Secretary of State C. Douglas Dillon[70] introduced the discussion of United States policy toward the Congo. In the course of his remarks, Dillon maintained that the presence of United Nations troops in the Congo was necessary to prevent Soviet intervention at Lumumba's request:

> If * * * Lumumba carried out his threat to force the U.N. out, he might then offer to accept help from anyone. * * * The elimination of the U.N. would be a disaster which, Secretary Dillon stated, we should do everything we could to prevent. If the U.N. were forced out, we might be faced by a situation where the Soviets intervened by invitation of the Congo.
>
> * * * Secretary Dillon said that he [Lumumba] was working to serve the purposes of the Soviets and Mr. Dulles pointed out that Lumumba was in Soviet pay. (NSC Minutes, 8/18/60)

Dillon's remarks prompted the only statements about Lumumba attributed to the President in the Memorandum of the August 18 meeting:

> The President said that the possibility that the U.N. would be forced out was simply inconceivable. We should keep the U.N. in the Congo even if we had to ask for European troops to do it. We should do so even if such action was used by the Soviets as the basis for starting a fight. Mr. Dillon indicated that this was State's feeling but that the Secretary General and Mr. Lodge doubted whether, if the Congo put up really determined opposition to the U.N., the U.N. could stay in. In response, the President stated that Mr. Lodge was wrong to this extent—we were talking of one man forcing us out of the Congo; of Lumumba supported by the Soviets. There was no indication, the President stated, that the Congolese did not want U.N. support and the maintenance of order. Secretary Dillon reiterated that this was State's feeling about the matter. The situation that would be created by a U. N. withdrawal was altogether too ghastly to contemplate. (NSC Minutes, 8/18/60)

As reported, this statement clearly does not contain an order for the assassination of Lumumba. But the statement does indicate extreme Presidential concern focused on Lumumba: the President was so disturbed by the situation in the Congo that he was willing to risk a fight with the Soviet Union and he felt that Lumumba was the "one man" who was responsible for this situation, a man who did not represent the sentiment of the Congolese people in the President's estimation.

After reviewing NSC documents and being informed of Robert Johnson's testimony, Douglas Dillon stated his "opinion that it is most likely that the NSC meeting of August 18,

---

[69] See Section 7(a) (iv), *infra*, for an analysis of the substance of the NSC discussion on September 7, 1960.

[70] In 1960, Dillon served as Undersecretary of State, the "number two position in the State Department." The title was subsequently changed to Deputy Secretary of State. In this post, Dillon frequently served as Acting Secretary of State and either attended or was kept informed about NSC and Special Group meetings. Dillon later served as Secretary of the Treasury under President Kennedy. (Dillon, 9/2/75, pp. 2–4)

1960 is the meeting referred to by Mr. Johnson." (Dillon affidavit, 9/15/75, p. 2) However, Dillon testified that he did not "remember such a thing" as a "clearcut order" from the President for the assassination of Lumumba. (Dillon, 9/2/75, pp. 32–33) Dillon explained how he thought the President may have expressed himself about Lumumba:

DILLON: It could have been in view of this feeling of everybody that Lumumba was [a] very difficult if not impossible person to deal with, and was dangerous to the peace and safety of the world, that the President expressed himself, we will have to do whatever is necessary to get rid of him. I don't know that I would have taken that as a clearcut order as Mr. Johnson apparently did. And I think perhaps others present may have interpreted it other ways. (Dillon, 9/2/75, pp. 32–33)

Q: Did you ever hear the President make such a remark about Lumumba, let's get rid of him, or let's take action right away on this?

DILLON: I don't remember that. But certainly this was the general feeling of Government at that time, and it wouldn't have been if the President hadn't agreed with it. (Dillon, 9/2/75, p. 33)

Dillon said that he would have thought that such a statement "was not a direct order to have an assassination." But he testified that it was "perfectly possible" that Allen Dulles would have translated such strong Presidential language about "getting rid of" Lumumba into authorization for an assassination effort. (Dillon, 9/2/75, pp. 33, 34–35):

I think that Allen Dulles would have been quite responsive to what he considered implicit authorization, because he felt very strongly that we should not involve the President directly in things of this nature. And he was perfectly willing to take the responsibility personally that maybe some of his successors wouldn't have been. And so I think that this is a perfectly plausible thing, knowing Allen Dulles. (Dillon, 9/2/75, p. 34)

According to President Eisenhower's national security advisor, Gordon Gray, Dulles would have placed the CIA in a questionable position if he mounted an assassination operation on the basis of such "implicit authorization." Gray testified that the CIA would have been acting beyond its authority if it undertook an assassination operation without a specific order to do so. (Gray, 9/9/75, p. 18)

Marion Boggs, who attended the meeting of August 18, as Acting Executive Secretary of the NSC, stated after reviewing the Memorandum of Discussion at that Meeting:

I recall the discussion at that meeting, but have no independent recollection of any statements or discussion not summarized in the memorandum. Specifically, I have no recollection of any statement, order or reference by the President (or anyone else present at the meeting) which could be interpreted as favoring action by the United States to bring about the assassination of Lumumba.[71] (Boggs affidavit, 10/10/75, pp. 1–2)

---

[71] Boggs added:

"Based on my whole experience with the NSC, I would have considered it highly unusual if a matter of this nature had been referred to in a Council meeting where a number of persons with no 'need to know' were present." (Boggs affidavit, 10/10/75, p. 2)

There are at least four possible explanations of the failure of NSC records to reveal whether the President ordered the assassination of Lumumba at one of the meetings where Robert Johnson was present.

First, an assassination order could have been issued but omitted from the records. Johnson testified that it was "very likely" that the Presidential statement he heard would have been handled by means of a euphemistic reference or by complete omission "rather than given as [a] * * * direct quotation" in the Memorandum of Discussion. (Johnson, 9/13/75, p. 14) NSC staff executives Marion Boggs and James Lay substantiated Johnson's testimony about the manner of handling such a statement in the records.

Second, as illustrated by Douglas Dillon's testimony, the President could have made a general statement about "getting rid of" Lumumba with the intent to convey to Allen Dulles implicit authorization for an assassination effort.

Third, despite general discussions about removing Lumumba, the President may not have intended to order the assassination of Lumumba even though Allen Dulles may have thought it had been authorized. The three White House staff members responsible to the President for national security affairs testified that there was no such order.[72]

Fourth, whatever language he used, the President may have intended to authorize "contingency planning" for an assassination effort against Lumumba, while reserving decision on whether to authorize an actual assassination attempt. This interpretation can be supported by a strict construction of the decision of the Special Group on August 25, in response to the "strong feelings" of the President, not to rule out " 'consideration' of any particular kind of activity which might contribute to getting rid of Lumumba" and by the testimony of Bronson Tweedy that the assassination operation was limited to "exploratory activity."[73]

(iii) Special Group Agrees to Consider Anything That Might Get Rid of Lumumba: August 25, 1960

On August 25, 1960, five men[74] attended a meeting of the Special Group, the subcommittee of the National Security Council responsible for planning covert operations. Thomas Parrott, a CIA officer who served as Secretary to the Group, began the meeting by outlining the CIA operations that had been undertaken in "mounting an anti-Lumumba campaign in the Congo." (Special Group Minutes, 8/25/60) This campaign involved covert operations through certain labor groups and "the planned attempt * * * to arrange a vote of no confidence in Lumumba" in the Congolese Senate. (Special Group Minutes, 8/25/60) The outline of this campaign evoked the followed dialogue:

---

[72] See Section 7 (b), *infra*, for a general treatment of the testimony of Gray, Goodpaster, and Eisenhower.

[73] This interpretation of the Special Group minutes must be posed against the testimony of other witnesses who construed the minutes as authorizing action, as well as planning an assassination operation. (Special Group Minutes, 8/25/60, p. 1; see Section 7 (a) (ii) *infra*) See Section 4 (h) (ii), *supra*, for a detailed discussion of Tweedy's testimony.

[74] The four standing members of the Special Group were in attendance: Allen Dulles, Director of Central Intelligence; Gordon Gray, Special Assistant to the President for National Security Affairs; Livingston Merchant, Undersecretary of State for Political Affairs; and John N. Irwin II, Assistant Secretary of Defense. Also in attendance was Thomas A. Parrott, Secretary to the Special Group.

The Group agreed that the action contemplated is very much in order. Mr. Gray commented, however, that his associates had expressed extremely strong feelings on the necessity for very straightforward action in this situation, and he wondered whether the plans as outlined were sufficient to accomplish this. Mr. Dulles replied that he had taken the comments referred to seriously and had every intention of proceeding as vigorously as the situation permits or requires, but added that he must necessarily put himself in a position of interpreting instructions of this kind within the bounds of necessity and capability. It was finally agreed that planning for the Congo would not necessarily rule out "consideration" of any particular kind of activity which might contribute to getting rid of Lumumba. (Special Group Minutes, 8/25/60, p. 1)

Both Gordon Gray and Thomas Parrott testified that the reference to Gray's "associates" was a euphemism for President Eisenhower which was employed to preserve "plausible deniability" by the President of discussion of covert operations memorialized in Special Group Minutes. (Gray, 7/9/75, p. 27; Parrott, 7/10/75, pp. 8–9)

The four living participants at the meeting have all stated that they do not recall any discussion of or planning for the assassination of Lumumba. Gray said that he did not consider the President's desire for "very straightforward action" to include "any thought in his mind of assassination." Parrott testified to the same effect, maintaining that he would have recorded a discussion of assassination in explicit terms in the Special Group Minutes if such a discussion had taken place. (Gray, 7/9/75, pp. 27, 32; Parrott, 7/10/75, pp. 25–26; Merchant affidavit, 9/8/75, p. 1; Irwin affidavit, 9/22/75, pp. 1–2) John N. Irwin II acknowledged, however, that while he did not have "any direct recollection of the substance of that meeting," the reference in the minutes to the planning for "getting rid of Lumumba" was "broad enough to cover a discussion of assassination." (Irwin affidavit, 9/22/75, p. 2)

Irwin's interpretation was shared by Douglas Dillon and Richard Bissell who were not participants at this Special Group meeting but were involved in the planning and policy-making for covert operations in the Congo during this period.

As a participant in NSC meetings of this period, Dillon said that he would read the Special Group minutes of August 25 to indicate that assassination was within the bounds of the kind of activity that might be used to "get rid of" Lumumba. Dillon noted that the reference in the minutes to Dulles' statement that he "had taken the comments referred to seriously" probably pointed to the President's statement at the NSC meeting on August 18. (Dillon, 9/2/75, pp. 39–42) When asked whether the CIA would have the authority to mount an assassination effort against Lumumba on the basis of the discussion at the Special Group, Dillon said:

They would certainly have the authority to plan. It is a close question whether this would be enough to actually go ahead with it. But certainly the way this thing worked, as far as I know, they didn't do anything just on their own. I think they would have checked back at least with the senior people in the State Department or the Defense Department. (Dillon, 9/2/75, p. 43)

Dillon said that if the CIA checked with the State Department, it might have done so in a way that would not appear on any record. (Dillon, 9/2/75, p. 43) Dillon added that "to protect the President as the public representative of the U.S. from any bad publicity in connection with this," Allen Dulles "wouldn't return to the President" to seek further approval if an assassination operation were mounted. (Dillon, 9/2/75, pp. 42–43)

Bissell stated that in his opinion the language of the August 25 Special Group Minutes indicated that the assassination of Lumumba was part of a general NSC strategy and was within the CIA's mandate for removing Lumumba from the political scene. (Bissell, 9/10/75, pp. 29, 32) He added:

> The Agency had put a top priority, probably, on a range of different methods of getting rid of Lumumba in the sense of either destroying him physically, incapacitating him, or eliminating his political influence. (Bissell, 9/10/75, p. 29)

Bissell pointed to the Special Group Minutes of August 25 as a "prime example" of the circumlocutious manner in which a topic like assassination would be discussed by high government officials:

> When you use the language that no particular means were ruled out, that is obviously what it meant, and it meant that to everybody in the room. * * * Meant that if it had to be assassination, that that was a permissible means.
>      You don't use language of that kind except to mean in effect, the Director is being told, get rid of the guy, and if you have to use extreme means up to and including assassination, go ahead. (Bissell, 9/10/75, pp. 32–33)

Bissell added that this message was, "in effect," being given to Dulles by the President through his representative, Gordon Gray. (Bissell, 9/10/75, p. 33)

(iv) Dulles Reminded by Gray of "Top-Level Feeling" That "Vigorous Action" Was Necessary in the Congo: September 7–8, 1960

The Memorandum of Discussion from the NSC meeting of September 7, 1960—the only other meeting at which Johnson could have heard the President's statement—records only a brief, general discussion of developments in the Congo. As part of Allen Dulles' introductory intelligence briefing on world events, the Memorandum contained his remarks on the situation in the Congo following Kasavubu's dismissal of Lumumba from the government. Neither the length nor the substance of the record of this discussion indicates that Lumumba's role in the Congo received the same intense consideration as the NSC had given it on August 18.[75] There is no record of any statement by the President during the September 7 discussion. (NSC Minutes, 9/7/60, p. 4–5)

In the course of Dulles' briefing, he expressed his continuing concern over the amount of personnel and equipment that was being sent to the Congo by the Soviet Union, primarily to aid Lumumba. Dulles concluded this part of his briefing with an observation that demonstrated that Lumumba's dismissal from the government had not lessened the extent to which he was regarded at the NSC as a potent political threat in any power struggle in the Congo:

> Mr. Dulles stated that Lumumba always seemed to come out on top in each of these struggles. (NSC Minutes, 9/7/60, p. 5)

At a Special Group Meeting the next day, Gordon Gray made a pointed reminder to Allen Dulles of the President's concern about the Congo:

---

[75] The NSC minutes of the meeting of September 7 deal with the discussion of the Congo in two pages. (NSC Minutes, 9/7/60, pp. 4–5). By comparison, the August 18 meeting required an extraordinarily lengthy (fifteen pages) summary of discussion on the Congo and related policy problems in Africa, indicating that this topic was the focal point of the meeting. (NSC Minutes, 8/18/60, pp. 1–15)

Mr. Gray said that he hoped that Agency people in the field are fully aware of the top-level feeling in Washington that vigorous action would not be amiss. (Special Group Minutes, 9/8/60)

(v) Dulles Tells NSC That Lumumba Remains a Grave Danger Until "Disposed of": September 21, 1960

In the course of his intelligence briefing to the NSC on September 21, 1960, Allen Dulles stressed the danger of Soviet influence in the Congo. Despite, the fact that Lumumba had been deposed as Premier and was in U.N. custody, Dulles continued to regard him as a threat, especially in light of reports of an impending reconciliation between Lumumba and the post-coup Congolese government. In the presence of the President, Dulles concluded:

Mobutu appeared to be the effective power in the Congo for the moment but Lumumba was not yet disposed of and remained a grave danger as long as he was not disposed of. (NSC Minutes, 9/21/60)

Three days after this NSC meeting, Dulles sent a personal cable to the Station Officer in Leopoldville which included the following message:

WE WISH GIVE EVERY POSSIBLE SUPPORT' IN ELIMINATING LUMUMBA FROM ANY POSSIBILITY RESUMING GOVERNMENTAL POSITION OR IF HE FAILS IN LEOP[OLDVILLE], SETTING HIMSELF IN STANLEYVILLE OR ELSEWHERE (CIA Cable, Dulles, Tweedy to Leopoldville, 9/24/60)

On September 26, Joseph Scheider, under assignment from CIA Headquarters, arrived in Leopoldville, provided the Station Officer with poisons, conveyed Headquarters' instruction to assassinate Lumumba, and assured him that there was Presidential authorization for this mission.[76]

Marion Boggs, the NSC Deputy Executive Secretary, who wrote the Memorandum of Discussion of September 21, did not interpret Dulles' remark as referring to assassination:

I have examined the memorandum (which I prepared) summarizing the discussion of the Congo at the September 21, 1960 meeting of the NSC. I recall the discussion and believe it is accurately and adequately summarized in the memorandum. I have no recollection of any discussion of a possible assassination of Lumumba at this meeting. With specific reference to the statement of the Director of Central Intelligence * * * I believe this is almost a literal rendering of what Mr. Dulles said. My own interpretation of this statement * * * was that Mr. Dulles was speaking in the context of efforts being made within the Congolese government to force Lumumba from power. I did not interpret it as referring to assassination.[77] (Boggs affidavit, 10/10/75, pp. 2–3)

Boggs, however, was not in a position to analyze Dulles' remark in the context of the actual planning for covert operations that took place during this period because Boggs was not privy to most such discussions. (Boggs affidavit, 10/10/75, p. 2)

---

[76] See Sections 4(e)–4(f), *supra.*

[77] NSC Executive Secretary James Lay, who was also present at the meeting of September 21, 1960, stated: "I cannot recall whether there was any discussion of assassinating Lumumba at any NSC meetings." (Lay affidavit, 9/8/75, p. 1)

Dillon, who attended this NSC meeting as Acting Secretary of State, did not recall the discussion. Dillon said that the minutes "could mean that" assassination would have been one acceptable means of "disposing of" Lumumba, although he felt that "getting him out [of the Congo] or locking him up" would have been a preferable disposition of Lumumba at that point since he was already out of office. (Dillon, 9/2/75, pp. 47–48)[78] When reminded of the fact that Lumumba's movement and communications were not restricted by the U.N. force and that the Congolese army continued to seek his arrest after the September 21 meeting, Dillon acknowledged that during this period Lumumba continued to be viewed by the United States as a potential threat and a volatile force in the Congo:

> * * * He had this tremendous ability to stir up a crowd or a group. And if he could have gotten out and started to talk to a battalion of the Congolese Army, he probably would have had them in the palm of his hand in five minutes. (Dillon, 9/20/75, p. 49)

Irwin, who attended the NSC meeting as Assistant Secretary of Defense, stated that although he had no recollection of the discussion, the language of these minutes, like that of the August 25 minutes, was "broad enough to cover a discussion of assassination." (Irwin affidavit, 9/22/75, p. 2)

Bissell testified that, based upon his understanding of the policy of the NSC toward Lumumba even after Lumumba was in U.N. custody, he would read the minutes of September 21 to indicate that assassination was contemplated "as one possible means" of "disposing of" Lumumba[79] (Bissell, 9/10/75, p. 70)

Bissell's opinion stands in opposition to Gordon Gray's testimony. Gray stated that he could not remember the NSC discussion, but he interpreted the reference to "disposing of" Lumumba as "in the same category as 'get rid of,' 'eliminate'." (Gray, 7/9/75, p. 59) He said: "It was not my impression that we had in mind the assassination of Lumumba.") (Gray, 7/9/75, p. 60)[80]

*(b) Testimony of Eisenhower White House Officials*

Gordon Gray and Andrew Goodpaster—the two members of President Eisenhower's staff who were responsible for national security affairs—both testified that they had no knowledge of any Presidential consideration of assassination during their tenure.[81]

---

[78] See Section 3, *supra,* for discussion of CIA cable traffic indicating that Lumumba continued to be regarded as capable of taking over the government after he was deposed and that pressure to "eliminate" him did not cease until his death.

[79] Bissell was not present at the NSC meeting. (NSC Minutes, 9/21/60)

[80] John Eisenhower, the President's son, who attended the NSC meeting as Assistant White House Staff Secretary, said that he had no "direct recollection" of the discussion but he found the minutes of the meeting consonant with his "recollection of the atmosphere" at the time: "The U.S. position was very much anti-Lumumba." He said:

"I would not conjecture that the words 'disposed of' meant an assassination, if for no other reason than if I had something as nasty as this to plot, I wouldn't do it in front of 21 people * * * the number present [at] the meeting." (Eisenhower, 7/18/75, pp. 9–10)

[81] For a more detailed treatment of the testimony of Gray, Goodpaster, and other Eisenhower Administration officials on the general question of discussion of assassination by the President, see Part 3, Section B(3) (a), *infra.*

Gray served as Special Assistant to the President for National Security Affairs, in which capacity he coordinated the National Security Council and represented the President at Special Group meetings. Gray testified that despite the prevalent attitude of hostility toward Lumumba in the Administration, he did not recall President Eisenhower "ever saying anything that contemplated killing Lumumba." (Gray, 7/9/75, p. 28)[82] When asked to interpret phrases such as "getting rid of" or "disposing of" Lumumba from the minutes of particular NSC and Special Group Meetings, Gray stated:

> It is the intent of the user of the expression or the phrase that is controlling and there may well have been in the Central Intelligence Agency plans and/or discussions of assassinations, but * * * at the level of the Forty Committee [Special Group] or a higher level than that, the National Security Council, there was no active discussion in any way planning assassination.
>
> * * * I agree that assassination could have been on the minds of some people when they used these words 'eliminate' or 'get rid of' * * * I am just trying to say it was not seriously considered as a program of action by the President or even the Forty [Special] Group. (Gray, 7/9/75, pp. 16–17)

Goodpaster, the White House Staff Secretary to President Eisenhower, said that he and Gray were the "principal channels" between the President and the CIA, outside of NSC meetings. Goodpaster was responsible for "handling with the President all matters of day-to-day operations in the general fields of international affairs and security affairs." He regularly attended NSC meetings and was listed among the participants at the NSC meetings of August 18, 1960 and September 21, 1960. (Goodpaster, 7/17/75, pp. 3, 4)

When asked if he ever heard about any assassination effort during the Eisenhower Administration, Goodpaster replied unequivocally:

> * * * at no time and in no way did I ever know of or hear about any mention of such an activity. * * * [I]t is my belief that had such a thing been raised with the President other than in my presence, I would have known about it, and * * * it would have been a matter of such significance and sensitivity that I am confident that * * * I would have recalled it had such a thing happened. (Goodpaster, 7/17/75, p. 5)

John Eisenhower, the President's son who served under Goodpaster as Assistant White House Staff Secretary, stated that the use of assassination was contrary to the President's philosophy that "no man is indispensable." As a participant at NSC meetings who frequently attended Oval Office discussions relating to national security affairs, John Eisenhower testified that nothing that came to his attention in his experience at the White House "can be construed in my mind in the remotest way to mean any Presidential knowledge of our concurrence in any assassination plots or plans." (Eisenhower, 7/18/75, pp. 4, 14)

Each of the other Eisenhower Administration officials who was active in the Special Group in late 1960—Assistant Secretary of Defense John N. Irwin II, Undersecretary of State for Political Affairs Livingston Merchant, and Deputy Secretary of Defense James

---

[82] At the outset of his testimony on the subject, Gordon Gray acknowledged that he did not have a clear, independent recollection of Lumumba's role in the Congo. (Gray, 7/9/75, pp. 25–26)

Douglas—stated that he did not recall any discussion about assassinating Lumumba. (Irwin affidavit, 9/22/75; Merchant affidavit, 9/8/75; Douglas affidavit, 9/5/75)[83]

Even if the documentary record is read to indicate that there was consideration of assassination at high-level policy meetings, there is no evidence that any officials of the Eisenhower Administration outside the CIA were aware of the specific operational details of the plot to poison Lumumba.[84]

*(c) Bissell's Assumptions About Authorization by President Eisenhower and Allen Dulles*

Richard Bissell's testimony on the question of high-level authorization for the effort to assassinate Lumumba is problematic. Bissell stated that he had no direct recollection of receiving such authorization and that all of his testimony on this subject "has to be described as inference." (Bissell, 9/10/75, p. 48)

Bissell began his testimony on the subject by asserting that on his own initiative he instructed Michael Mulroney to plan the assassination of Lumumba. (Bissell, 6/11/75, pp. 54–55)[85] Nevertheless, Bissell's conclusion—based on his inferences from the totality of circumstances relating to the entire assassination effort against Lumumba—was that an assassination attempt had been authorized at the highest levels of the government. (Bissell, 9/10/75, pp. 32–33, 47–49, 60–62, 65)

As discussed above, Bissell testified that the minutes of meetings of the Special Group on August 25, 1960 and the NSC on September 21, 1960 indicate that assassination was contemplated at the Presidential level as one acceptable means of "getting rid of Lumumba."[86]

There was "no question," according to Bissell, that the cable from Allen Dulles to the Station Officer in Leopoldville on August 26—which called for Lumumba's "removal" and authorized Hedgman to take action without consulting Headquarters if time did not

---

[83] Douglas Dillon testified that the subject of assassination never arose in his "direct dealings with either President Eisenhower or President Kennedy." (Dillon, 9/2/75, p. 22) He was asked by a member of the Committee, however, to speculate upon the general philosophical approach that Presidents Eisenhower and Kennedy would have taken to decision-making on the question of using assassination as a tool of foreign policy:

"SENATOR HART (Colorado): I would invite your speculation at this point as a sub-Cabinet officer under President Eisenhower, and as a Cabinet Officer under President Kennedy, I think the Committee would be interested in your view as to the attitude of each of them toward this subject, that is to say, the elimination, violent elimination of foreign leaders.

"DILLON: Well, that is a difficult thing to speculate on in a totally different atmosphere. But I think probably both of them would have approached it in a very pragmatic way, most likely, simply weighed the process and consequence rather than in a way that was primarily of a moral principle. That is what would probably have been their attitude in a few cases. Certainly the idea that this was going to be a policy of the U.S., generally both of them were very much opposed to it." (Dillon, 9/2/75, pp. 22–23)

Dillon served as Undersecretary of State in the Eisenhower Administration and as Secretary of the Treasury under Kennedy.

[84] Although several CIA officers involved in the PROP operation to poison Lumumba testified that the operation was within the scope of actions authorized by the NSC and Special Group, there is no testimony that any official of the Eisenhower Administration outside the CIA had specific knowledge of the operational planning and progress.

[85] See Sections 5 (a) (i) and 5 (a) (ii), *supra.*

[86] See Sections 7 (a) (iii) and 7 (a) (v).

permit—was a direct outgrowth of the Special Group meeting Dulles had attended the previous day. (Bissell, 9/10/75, pp. 31–32) Bissell was "almost certain" that he had been informed about the Dulles cable shortly after its transmission. (Bissell, 9/10/75, p. 12) Bissell said that he assumed that assassination was one of the means of removing Lumumba from the scene that was contemplated by Dulles' cable, despite the fact that it was not explicitly mentioned. (Bissell, 9/10/75, p. 32)

> It is my belief on the basis of the cable drafted by Allen Dulles that he regarded the action of the Special Group as authorizing implementation [of an assassination] if favorable circumstances presented themselves, if it could be done covertly. (Bissell, 9/10/75, pp. 64–65)[87]

Dulles' cable signaled to Bissell that there was Presidential authorization for him to order action to assassinate Lumumba. (Bissell, 9/10/75, pp. 61–62):

Q:            Did Mr. Dulles tell you that President Eisenhower wanted Lumumba killed?
Mr. BISSELL: I am sure he didn't.
Q:            Did he ever tell you even circumlocutiously through this kind of cable?
Mr. BISSELL: Yes, I think his cable says it in effect. (Bissell, 9/10/75, p. 33)

As for discussions with Dulles about the source of authorization for an assassination effort against Lumumba, Bissell stated:

> I think it is probably unlikely that Allen Dulles would have said either the President or President Eisenhower even to me. I think he would have said, this is authorized in the highest quarters, and I would have known what he meant. (Bissell, 9/10/75, p. 48)

When asked if he had sufficient authority to move beyond the consideration or planning of assassination to order implementation of a plan, Bissell said, "I probably did think I had [such] authority." (Bissell, 9/10/75, pp. 61–62)

When informed of the Station Officer's testimony about the instructions he received from Scheider, Bissell said that despite his absence of a specific recollection:

> I would strongly infer in this case that such an authorization did pass through me, as it were, if Joe Scheider gave that firm instruction to the Station Officer. (Bissell, 9/10/75, p. 40)[88]

Bissell said that the DCI would have been the source of this authorization. (Bissell, 9/10/75, p. 40)

Bissell did not recall being informed by Scheider that Scheider had represented to the Station Officer that Lumumba's assassination had been authorized by the President. But he said that assuming he had instructed Scheider to carry poison to the Congo, "there was no possibility" that he would have issued such an instruction without authorization from

---

[87] Joseph Scheider also testified that, in the context of the Dulles cable, "removal" would signify to someone familiar with "intelligence terminology" a "range of things, from just getting him out of office to killing him." (Scheider, 10/9/75, pp. 45–48)

[88] See Section 7 (d), infra, for Scheider's testimony on his impression that Bissell had authorized his assignment to the Congo.

Dulles. Likewise Bissell said he "probably did" tell Scheider that the mission had the approval of President Eisenhower. (Bissell, 9/10/75, pp. 46, 47) This led to Bissell's conclusion that if, in fact, the testimony of the Station Officer about Scheider's actions was accurate, then Scheider's actions were fully authorized.[89] Bissell further stated:

> Knowing Mr. Scheider, it is literally inconceivable to me that we would have acted beyond his instructions. (Bissell, 9/10/75, p. 41)

Bronson Tweedy functioned as a conduit between Bissell and Scheider for instructions relating to the PROP operation. Scheider's impression about the extent of authorization for the assassination operation stemmed ultimately from his conversation with Bissell which was referred to by Tweedy during the meeting in which Scheider was ordered to the Congo.[90]

Tweedy testified that Bissell never referred to the President as the source of authorization for the assassination operation. Tweedy said, however, that the "impression" he derived from his meetings with Bissell and from the Dulles cable of August 26 was that the Agency had authorization at the highest level of the government. But Tweedy found it "very difficult ∗∗∗ to judge whether the President*per se*had been in contact with the Agency" because he was not involved in decisionmaking at "the policy level." (Tweedy, 10/9/75 I, pp. 9, 10)

Concerning the assignment of Mulroney to "plan and prepare for" the assassination of Lumumba, Bissell testified that "it was my own idea to give Mulroney this assignment." But he said that this assignment was made only after an assassination mission against Lumumba already had authorization above the level of DDP. (Bissell, 9/10/75, pp. 24, 50; see also pp. 32–33, 47–48, 60–62)

*(d) The Impression of Scheider and Hedgman That the Assassination Operation had Presidential Authorization*

The Station Officer and Scheider shared the impression that the President authorized an assassination effort against Lumumba.[91] This impression was derived solely from conversations Scheider had with Bissell and Tweedy. Thus, the testimony of Scheider and the Station Officer does not, in itself, establish Presidential authorization. Neither Scheider nor the Station Officer had first-hand knowledge of any statements by Allen Dulles about Presidential authorization—statements which Bissell assumed he had heard, although he had no specific recollection. Moreover, Scheider may have misconstrued Bissell's reference to "highest authority."

Station Officer Hedgman testified that Scheider indicated to him that President Eisenhower had authorized the assassination of Lumumba by an order to Dulles. Hedgman stated that Scheider initially conveyed this account of Presidential authorization when

---

[89] Q:   in light of the entire atmosphere at the Agency and the policy at the Agency at the time Mr. Scheider's representation to the Station Officer that the President bad instructed the DCI to carry out this mission would not have been beyond the pale of Mr. Scheider's authority, at that point?

BISSELL. No, it would not. (Bissell, 9/10/75, p. 65)

[90] See Section 7 (d), *infra*.

[91] See Section 4 (f), *infra*, for additional testimony of the Station Officer and Scheider on this issue.

Hedgman asked him about the source of authority for the Lumumba assassination assignment. (Hedgman, 8/21/75, pp. 30–34)

Hedgman was under the clear impression that the President was the ultimate source of the assassination operation:

Q:          Your understanding then was that these instructions were instructions coming to you from the office of the President?

HEDGMAN: That's correct.

Q:          Or that he had instructed the Agency, and they were passed on to you?

HEDGMAN: That's right.

Q:          You are not the least unclear whether ✳ ✳ ✳ the President's name had been invoked in some fashion?

HEDGMAN: At the time, I certainly felt that I was under instructions from the President, yes. (Hedgman, 8/21/75, pp. 32–33)

Hedgman cautioned:

[A]fter fifteen years, I cannot be 100 percent certain, but I have always, since that date, had the impression in my mind that these orders had come from the President. (Hedgman, 8/21/75, p. 34; *accord,*p. 102)

Hedgman testified that he was under the impression that a "policy decision" had been made—that assassination had been "approved" as "one means" of eliminating Lumumba as a political threat (Hedgman 8/21/75, p. 52):

I thought the policy decision had been made in the White House, not in the Agency, and that the Agency had been selected as the Executive agent if you will, to carry out a political decision. (Hedgman, 8/21/75, p. 52.)

Although Hedgman assumed that the President had not personally selected the means of assassination, he testified that he was under the impression that the President had authorized the CIA to proceed to take action:

HEDGMAN: ✳ ✳ ✳ I doubt that I thought the President had said, you use this system. But my understanding is the President had made a decision that an act should take place, but then put that into the hands of the Agency to carry out his decision.

Q:          Whatever that act was to be, it was clearly to be assassination or the death of the foreign political leader?

HEDGMAN: Yes. (Hedgman, 8/21/75, p. 104)

The Station Officer's impression about Presidential authorization stemmed from his conversations with Scheider in the Congo and from his reading of the cable traffic from CIA Headquarters which, in fact, never explicitly mentioned the President although it referred to "high quarters."[92]

---

[92] See Section 7 (c) for Bissell's interpretation of the reference to "high quarters" in the Dulles cable of August 26, 1960.

Joseph Scheider's testimony about these discussions is compatible with Hedgman's account. (Scheider, 10/7/75, pp. 107–108) Despite the fact that he did not recall mentioning the President by name to Hedgman, Scheider believed that he left Hedgman with the impression that there was Presidential authorization for an assassination attempt against Lumumba. (Scheider, 10/7/75, pp. 103–104, 110; 10/9/75, p. 17) However, Scheider made it clear that the basis for his own knowledge about Presidential authorization for the assassination of Lumumba were the statements to him by Bissell, Tweedy, and Tweedy's Deputy. (Scheider, 10/9/75, pp. 10;/7/75, p. 90)

Scheider testified that in the late summer or early fall of 1960, Richard Bissell asked him to make all the preparations necessary for toxic materials to be ready on short notice for use in the assassination of an unspecified African leader, "in case the decision was to go ahead."[93] (Scheider, 10/7/75, pp. 51–55; 10/9/75, p. 8) Scheider had a specific recollection that Bissell told him that "he had direction from the highest authority" for undertaking an assassination operation. (Scheider, 10/7/75, pp. 51–52, 58):

SCHEIDER: The memory I carry was that he indicated that he had the highest authority for getting into that kind of an operation.

Q: Getting into an operation which would result in the death or incapacitation of a foreign leader?

SCHEIDER: Yes, yes, yes. (Scheider, 10/7/75, p. 52)

Scheider acknowledged the possibility that he "may have been wrong" in his assumptions of Presidential authorization which he based on Bissell's words:

The specific words, as best I can recollect them, [were] "on the highest authority." (Scheider, 10/9/75, p. 11).

Scheider testified that there was a basis of experience for his assumption that "highest authority" signified the President. He said he "had heard it before" at the CIA and had always interpreted it to denote the President. (Scheider, 10/9/75, p. 51) Likewise, Bronson Tweedy testified that " 'highest authority' was a term that we used in the Agency and it was generally recognized as meaning 'the President'." (Tweedy, 10/9/75 II, p. 20)

According to Scheider, Allen Dulles would have approved the assassination operation before Bissell broached the subject with other CIA officers:

I would have assumed that Bissell would never have told me that it was to be undertaken under the highest authority until his line ran through Dulles and until Dulles was in on it. (Scheider, 10/7/75, p. 76)

Scheider said that he left the meeting with Bissell under the impression that the Presidential authorization extended only to making preparations to carry out an assassination mission and that the implementation of such a plan might require a separate "go ahead." (Scheider, 10/7/75, pp. 53, 56–8) As far as Scheider was concerned, the "go ahead" on the assassination operation was given to him shortly thereafter by Tweedy and

---

[93] See section 4 (b), *infra,* for a full treatment of Scheider's meetings with Bissell and his preparation of toxic biological materials and medical paraphernalia pursuant to Bissell's directive.

his Deputy.[94] When they instructed him on his Congo trip, Scheider said Tweedy and his Deputy "referred to the previous conversation I had with Bissell" and they conveyed to Scheider the impression that Bissell "felt the operation had Presidential authority." (Scheider, 10/7/75, pp. 65, 69, 71; 10/9/75, p. 13)[95] Scheider interpreted the statements by Tweedy and his Deputy to mean that Bissell's reference to "highest authority" for the operation had carried over from planning to the implementation stage. (Scheider, 10/7/75, p. 90)

Scheider's impression that there was Presidential authorization for the assassination operation clearly had a powerful influence on the Station Officer's attitude toward undertaking such an assignment.

Hedgman had severe doubts about the wisdom of a policy of assassination in the Congo. At the conclusion of his testimony about the assassination plot, he was asked to give a general characterization of the advisability of the plot and the tenor of the times in which it took place. His response indicated that although he was willing to carry out what he considered a duly authorized order, he was not convinced of the necessity of assassinating Lumumba:

> I looked upon the Agency as an executive arm of the Presidency * * *. Therefore, I suppose I thought that it was an order issued in due form from an authorized authority.
>
> On the other hand, I looked at it as a kind of operation that I could do without, that I thought that probably the Agency and the U.S. government could get along without. I didn't regard Lumumba as the kind of person who was going to bring on World War III.
>
> I might have had a somewhat different attitude if I thought that one man could bring on World War III and result in the deaths of millions of people or something, but I didn't see him in that light. I saw his as a danger to the political position of the United States in Africa, but nothing more than that. (Hedgman, 8/21/75, pp. 110–111)

---

[94] See Section 4 (c), *infra*, for a detailed account of the testimony about the meeting of Tweedy, his Deputy, and Scheider.

[95] Tweedy was unable to shed much light on the discussion of authorization at his meeting with Scheider:

I do not recall that Scheider and I ever discussed higher authority and approval. I do not say that it did not occur." (Tweedy, 10/9/75, p. 65)

# THE EXECUTIVE ORDER PROHIBITING ASSASSINATION PLOTS, 1976

## PRESIDENT GERALD R. FORD'S EXECUTIVE ORDER 11905: UNITED STATES FOREIGN INTELLIGENCE ACTIVITIES

February 18, 1976

....*(g) Prohibition of Assassination.* No employee of the United States Government shall engage in, or conspire to engage in, political assassination....

*Source*: *Weekly Compilation of Presidential Documents*, vol. 12 (February 23, 1976), p. 15.

# WHEN COVERT ACTION SUBVERTS U.S. LAW: THE IRAN-*CONTRA* CASE

*Tower Commission*

In the aftermath of the Iran-*contra* scandal involving questionable arms sales to Iran and the funneling of the profits to the *contras* for a covert war in Nicaragua, President Ronald Reagan established a blue-ribbon panel to investigate the affair. The president selected a former U.S. senator, Republican John Tower of Texas, to head up the inquiry. This selection summarizes the commission's findings, which were highly critical of both the president and the NSC staff.

## WHAT WAS WRONG

The arms transfers to Iran and the activities of the NSC staff in support of the Contras are case studies in the perils of policy pursued outside the constraints of orderly process.

The Iran initiative ran directly counter to the Administration's own policies on terrorism, the Iran/Iraq war, and military support to Iran. This inconsistency was never re-

*Sources*: Report of the President's *Special Review Board* (Tower Commission), Washington, DC, February 26, 1987), pp. IV, 1–13; and witness testimony, *Hearings,* Select Committee on Secret Military Assistance to Iran and the Nicaraguan Opposition (the Inouye-Hamilton Joint Committee, co-chaired by Senator Daniel K. Inouye, D-Hawaii, and Representative Lee Hamilton, D-Indiana), July and August 1987. The Tower Commission members included the chair, John Tower (R-Texas); Edmund Muskie, former Democratic Senator from Maine and secretary of state in the Carter administration; and Brent Scowcroft, national security adviser in the Ford and first Bush administrations. In the second part of this appendix, the congressional testimony is from national security adviser Vice Admiral John M. Poindexter and NSC staff aide Lieut. Col. Oliver L. North, as well as Secretary of State George P. Shultz.

solved, nor were the consequences of this inconsistency fully considered and provided for. The result taken as a whole was a U.S. policy that worked against itself.

The Board believes that failure to deal adequately with these contradictions resulted in large part from the flaws in the manner in which decisions were made. Established procedures for making national security decisions were ignored. Reviews of the initiative by all the NSC principals were too infrequent. The initiatives were not adequately vetted below the cabinet level. Intelligence resources were underutilized. Applicable legal constraints were not adequately addressed. The whole matter was handled too informally, without adequate written records of what had been considered, discussed, and decided.

This pattern persisted in the implementation of the Iran initiative. The NSC staff assumed direct operational control. The initiative fell within the traditional jurisdictions of the Departments of State, Defense, and CIA. Yet these agencies were largely ignored. Great reliance was placed on a network of private operators and intermediaries. How the initiative was to be carried out never received adequate attention from the NSC principals or a tough working-level review. No periodic evaluation of the progress of the initiative was ever conducted. The result was an unprofessional and, in substantial part, unsatisfactory operation.

In all of this process, Congress was never notified. . . .

## A. A FLAWED PROCESS

### 1. CONTRADICTORY POLICIES WERE PURSUED

The arms sales to Iran and the NSC support for the Contras demonstrate the risks involved when highly controversial initiatives are pursued covertly.

#### ARMS TRANSFERS TO IRAN

The initiative to Iran was a covert operation directly at odds with important and well-publicized policies of the Executive Branch. But the initiative itself embodied a fundamental contradiction. Two objectives were apparent from the outset: a strategic opening to Iran, and release of the U.S. citizens held hostage in Lebanon. The sale of arms to Iran appeared to provide a means to achieve both these objectives. It also played into the hands of those who had other interests—some of them personal financial gain—in engaging the United States in an arms deal with Iran.

In fact, the sale of arms was not equally appropriate for achieving both these objectives. Arms were what Iran wanted. If all the United States sought was to free the hostages, then an arms-for-hostages deal could achieve the immediate objectives of both sides. But if the U.S. objective was a broader strategic relationship, then the sale of arms should have been contingent upon first putting into place the elements of that relationship. An arms-for-hostages deal in this context could become counter-productive to achieving this broader strategic objective. In addition, release of the hostages would require exerting influence with Hizballah, which could involve the most radical elements of the Iranian regime. The kind of strategic opening sought by the United States, however, involved what were regarded as more moderate elements.

The U.S. officials involved in the initiative appeared to have held three distinct views. For some, the principal motivation seemed consistently a strategic opening to Iran. For others, the strategic opening became a rationale for using arms sales to obtain the release of the hostages. For still others, the initiative appeared clearly as an arms-for-hostages deal from first to last.

Whatever the intent, almost from the beginning the initiative became in fact a series of arms-for-hostages deals. . . .

While the United States was seeking the release of the hostages in this way, it was vigorously pursuing policies that were dramatically opposed to such efforts. The Reagan Administration in particular had come into office declaring a firm stand against terrorism, which it continued to maintain. In December of 1985, the Administration completed a major study under the chairmanship of the Vice President. It resulted in a vigorous re-affirmation of U.S. opposition to terrorism in all its forms and a vow of total war on terrorism whatever its source. The Administration continued to pressure U.S. allies not to sell arms to Iran and not to make concessions to terrorists.

No serious effort was made to reconcile the inconsistency between these policies and the Iran initiative. No effort was made systematically to address the consequences of this inconsistency—the effect on U.S. policy when, as it inevitably would, the Iran initiative became known. . . .

## NSC STAFF SUPPORT FOR THE CONTRAS

The activities of the NSC staff in support of the Contras sought to achieve an important objective of the Administration's foreign policy. The President had publicly and empha-tically declared his support for the Nicaragua resistance. That brought his policy in direct conflict with that of the Congress, at least during the period that direct or indirect support of military operations in Nicaragua was barred.

Although the evidence before the Board is limited, no serious effort appears to have been made to come to grips with the risks to the President of direct NSC support for the Contras in the face of these Congressional restrictions. Even if it could be argued that these restrictions did not technically apply to the NSC staff, these activities presented great political risk to the President. The appearance of the President's personal staff doing what Congress had forbade other agencies to do could, once disclosed, only touch off a firestorm in the Congress and threaten the Administration's whole policy on the Contras.

## 2. THE DECISION-MAKING PROCESS WAS FLAWED

Because the arms sales to Iran and the NSC support for the Contras occurred in settings of such controversy, one would expect that the decisions to undertake these activities would have been made only after intense and thorough consideration. In fact, a far different picture emerges.

## ARMS TRANSFERS TO IRAN

The Iran initiative was handled almost casually and through informal channels, always apparently with an expectation that the process would end with the next arms-for-hostages exchange. It was subjected neither to the general procedures for interagency consideration and review of policy issues nor the more restrictive procedures set out in NSDD 159 for handling covert operations. This had a number of consequences.

*(i) The opportunity for a full hearing before the President was inadequate.* In the last half of 1985, the Israelis made three separate proposals to the United States with respect to

the Iran initiative (two in July and one in August). In addition, Israel made three separate deliveries of arms to Iran, one each in August, September, and November. Yet prior to December 7, 1985, there was at most one meeting of the NSC principals, a meeting which several participants recall taking place on August 6. There is no dispute that full meetings of the principals did occur on December 7, 1985, and on January 7, 1986. But the proposal to shift to direct U.S. arms sales to Iran appears not to have been discussed until later. It was considered by the President at a meeting on January 17 which only the Vice President, Mr. Regan, Mr. Fortier, and VADM Poindexter attended. Thereafter, the only senior-level review the Iran initiative received was during one or another of the President's daily national security briefings. These were routinely attended only by the President, the Vice President, Mr. Regan, and VADM Poindexter. There was no subsequent collective consideration of the Iran initiative by the NSC principals before it became public 11 months later.

This was not sufficient for a matter as important and consequential as the Iran initiative. Two or three cabinet-level reviews in a period of 17 months was not enough. The meeting on December 7 came late in the day, after the pattern of arms-for-hostages exchanges had become well established. The January 7 meeting had earmarks of a meeting held after a decision had already been made. Indeed, a draft Covert Action Finding authorizing the initiative had been signed by the President, though perhaps inadvertently, the previous day.

At each significant step in the Iran initiative, deliberations among the NSC principals in the presence of the President should have been virtually automatic. This was not and should not have been a formal requirement, something prescribed by statute. Rather, it should have been something the NSC principals desired as a means of ensuring an optimal environment for Presidential judgment. The meetings should have been preceded by consideration by the NSC principals of staff papers prepared according to the procedures applicable to covert actions. These should have reviewed the history of the initiative, analyzed the issues then presented, developed a range of realistic options, presented the odds of success and the costs of failure, and addressed questions of implementation and execution. Had this been done, the objectives of the Iran initiative might have been clarified and alternatives to the sale of arms might have been identified.

*(ii) The initiative was never subjected to a rigorous review below the cabinet level.* Because of the obsession with secrecy, interagency consideration of the initiative was limited to the cabinet level. With the exception of the NSC staff and, after January 17, 1986, a handful of CIA officials, the rest of the executive departments and agencies were largely excluded.

As a consequence, the initiative was never vetted at the staff level. This deprived those responsible for the initiative of considerable expertise—on the situation in Iran; on the difficulties of dealing with terrorists; on the mechanics of conducting a diplomatic opening. It also kept the plan from receiving a tough, critical review.

Moreover, the initiative did not receive a policy review below cabinet level. Careful consideration at the Deputy/Under Secretary level might have exposed the confusion in U.S. objectives and clarified the risks of using arms as an instrument of policy in this instance.

The vetting process would also have ensured better use of U.S. intelligence. As it was, the intelligence input into the decision process was clearly inadequate. First, no independent evaluation of other Israeli proposals offered in July and August appears to have been sought or offered by U.S. intelligence agencies. The Israelis represented that they for some time had had contacts with elements in Iran. The prospects for an opening to Iran depended heavily on these contacts, yet no systematic assessment appears to have been made by U.S. intelligence agencies of the reliability and motivations of these contacts, and the identity and objectives of the elements in Iran that the opening was supposed to reach. Neither was any systematic assessment made of the motivation of the Israelis.

Second, neither Mr. Ghorbanifar nor the second channel seem to have been subjected to a systematic intelligence vetting before they were engaged as intermediaries. Mr. Ghorbanifar had been known to the CIA for some time and the agency had substantial doubts as to his reliability and truthfulness. Yet the agency did not volunteer that information or inquire about the identity of the intermediary if his name was unknown. Conversely, no early request for a name check was made of the CIA, and it was not until January 11, 1986, that the agency gave Mr. Ghorbanifar a new polygraph, which he failed. Notwithstanding this situation, with the signing of the January 17 Finding, the United States took control of the initiative and became even more directly involved with Mr. Ghorbanifar. The issues raised by the polygraph results do not appear to have been systematically addressed. In similar fashion, no prior intelligence check appears to have been made on the second channel.

Third, although the President recalled being assured that the arms sales to Iran would not alter the military balance with Iran, the Board could find no evidence that the President was ever briefed on this subject. The question of the impact of any intelligence shared with the Iranians does not appear to have been brought to the President's attention.

A thorough vetting would have included consideration of the legal implications of the initiative. There appeared to be little effort to face squarely the legal restrictions and notification requirements applicable to the operation. At several points, other agencies raised questions about violations of law or regulations. These concerns were dismissed without, it appears, investigating them with the benefit of legal counsel.

Finally, insufficient attention was given to the implications of implementation. The implementation of the initiative raised a number of issues: should the NSC staff rather than the CIA have had operational control; what were the implications of Israeli involvement; how reliable were the Iranian and various other private intermediaries; what were the implications of the use of Mr. Secord's private network of operatives; what were the implications for the military balance in the region; was operational security adequate. Nowhere do these issues appear to have been sufficiently addressed.

The concern for preserving the secrecy of the initiative provided an excuse for abandoning sound process. Yet the initiative was known to a variety of persons with diverse interests and ambitions—Israelis, Iranians, various arms dealers and business intermediaries, and Lt. Col. North's network of private operatives. While concern for secrecy would have justified limiting the circle of persons knowledgeable about the initiative, in this case it was drawn too tightly. As a consequence, important advice and counsel were lost.

In January of 1985, the President had adopted procedures for striking the proper balance between secrecy and the need for consultation on sensitive programs. These covered the institution, implementation, and review of covert operations. In the case of the Iran initiative, these procedures were almost totally ignored.

The only staff work the President apparently reviewed in connection with the Iran initiative was prepared by NSC staff members, under the direction of the National Security Advisor. These were, of course, the principal proponents of the initiative. A portion of this staff work was reviewed by the Board. It was frequently striking in its failure to present the record of past efforts—particularly past failures. Alternative ways of achieving U.S. objectives—other than yet another arms-for-hostages deal—were not discussed. Frequently it neither adequately presented the risks involved in pursuing the initiative nor the full force of the dissenting views of other NSC principals. On balance, it did not serve the President well.

*(iii) The process was too informal.* The whole decision process was too informal. Even when meetings among NSC principals did occur, often there was no prior notice of the agenda. No formal written minutes seem to have been kept. Decisions subsequently taken by the President were not formally recorded. An exception was the January 17 Finding, but even this was apparently not circulated or shown to key U.S. officials.

The effect of this informality was that the initiative lacked a formal institutional record. This precluded the participants from undertaking the more informed analysis and reflection that is afforded by a written record, as opposed to mere recollection. It made it difficult to determine where the initiative stood, and to learn lessons from the record that could guide future action. This lack of an institutional record permitted specific proposals for arms-for-hostages exchanges to be presented in a vacuum, without reference to the results of past proposals. Had a searching and thorough review of the Iran initiative been undertaken at any stage in the process, it would have been extremely difficult to conduct. The Board can attest first hand to the problem of conducting a review in the absence of such records. Indeed, the exposition in the wake of public revelation suffered the most.

## NSC STAFF SUPPORT FOR THE CONTRAS

It is not clear how Lt. Col. North first became involved in activities in direct support of the Contras during the period of the Congressional ban. The Board did not have before it much evidence on this point. In the evidence that the Board did have, there is no suggestion at any point of any discussion of Lt. Col. North's activities with the President in any forum. There also does not appear to have been any interagency review of Lt. Col. North's activities at any level.

This latter point is not surprising given the Congressional restrictions under which the other relevant agencies were operating. But the NSC staff apparently did not compensate for the lack of any interagency review with its own internal vetting of these activities. Lt. Col. North apparently worked largely in isolation, keeping first Mr. McFarlane and then VADM Poindexter informed.

The lack of adequate vetting is particularly evident on the question of the legality of Lt. Col. North's activities. The Board did not make a judgment on the legal issues raised by his activities in support of the Contras. Nevertheless, some things can be said.

If these activities were illegal, obviously they should not have been conducted. If there was any doubt on the matter, systematic legal advice should have been obtained. The political cost to the President of illegal action by the NSC staff was particularly high, both because the NSC staff is the personal staff of the President and because of the history of serious conflict with the Congress over the issue of Contra support. For these reasons, the President should have been kept apprised of any review of the legality of Lt. Col. North's activities.

Legal advice was apparently obtained from the President's Intelligence Oversight Board. Without passing on the quality of that advice, it is an odd source. It would be one thing for the Intelligence Oversight Board to review the legal advice provided by some other agency. It is another for the Intelligence Oversight Board to be originating legal advice of its own. That is a function more appropriate for the NSC staff's own legal counsel.

### 3. IMPLEMENTATION WAS UNPROFESSIONAL

The manner in which the Iran initiative was implemented and Lt. Col. North undertook to support the Contras are very similar. This is in large part because the same cast of characters was involved. In both cases the operations were unprofessional, although the Board has much less evidence with respect to Lt. Col. North's Contra activities.

#### ARMS TRANSFERS TO IRAN

With the signing of the January 17 Finding, the Iran initiative became a U.S. operation run by the NSC staff. Lt. Col. North made most of the significant operational decisions. He conducted the operation through Mr. Secord and his associates, a network of private individuals already involved in the Contra resupply operation. To this was added a handful of selected individuals from the CIA.

But the CIA support was limited. Two CIA officials, though often at meetings, had a relatively limited role. One served as the point man for Lt. Col. North in providing logistics and financial arrangements. The other (Mr. Allen) served as a contact between Lt. Col. North and the intelligence community. By contrast, George Cave actually played a significant and expanding role. However, Clair George, Deputy Director for Operations at CIA, told the Board: "George was paid by me and on the paper was working for me. But I think in the heat of the battle, . . . George was working for Oliver North."

Because so few people from the departments and agencies were told of the initiative, Lt. Col. North cut himself off from resources and expertise from within the government. He relied instead on a number of private intermediaries, businessmen and other financial brokers, private operators, and Iranians hostile to the United States. Some of these were individuals with questionable credentials and potentially large personal financial interests in the transactions. This made the transactions unnecessarily complicated and invited kickbacks and payoffs. This arrangement also dramatically increased the risks that the initiative would leak. Yet no provision was made for such an eventuality. Further, the use of Mr. Secord's private network in the Iran initiative linked those operators with the resupply of the Contras, threatening exposure of both operations if either became public.

The result was a very unprofessional operation. . . .

The implementation of the initiative was never subjected to a rigorous review. Lt. Col. North appears to have kept VADM Poindexter fully informed of his activities. In addition, VADM Poindexter, Lt. Col. North, and the CIA officials involved apparently apprised Director Casey of many of the operational details. But Lt. Col. North and his operation functioned largely outside the orbit of the U.S. Government. Their activities were not subject to critical reviews of any kind.

After the initial hostage release in September, 1985, it was over 10 months before another hostage was released. This despite recurring promises of the release of all the hostages and four intervening arms shipments. Beginning with the November shipment, the United States increasingly took over the operation of the initiative. In January, 1986, it decided to transfer arms directly to Iran.

Any of these developments could have served as a useful occasion for a systematic reconsideration of the initiative. Indeed, at least one of the schemes contained a provision for reconsideration if the initial assumptions proved to be invalid. They did, but the reconsideration never took place. It was the responsibility of the National Security Advisor and the responsible officers on the NSC staff to call for such a review. But they were too involved in the initiative both as advocates and as implementors. This made it less likely that they would initiate the kind of review and reconsideration that should have been undertaken.

### NSC STAFF SUPPORT FOR THE CONTRAS

As already noted, the NSC activities in support of the Contras and its role in the Iran initiative were of a piece. In the former, there was an added element of Lt. Col. North's intervention in the customs investigation of the crash of the SAT aircraft. Here, too, selected CIA officials reported directly to Lt. Col. North. The limited evidence before the Board suggested that the activities in support of the Contras involved unprofessionalism much like that in the Iran operation.

*iv. Congress was never notified.* Congress was not apprised either of the Iran initiative or of the NSC staff's activities in support of the Contras.

In the case of Iran, because release of the hostages was expected within a short time after the delivery of equipment, and because public disclosure could have destroyed the operation and perhaps endangered the hostages, it could be argued that it was justifiable to defer notification of Congress prior to the first shipment of arms to Iran. The plan apparently was to inform Congress immediately after the hostages were safely in U.S. hands. But after the first delivery failed to release all the hostages, and as one hostage release plan was replaced by another, Congress certainly should have been informed. This could have been done during a period when no specific hostage release plan was in execution, Consultation with Congress could have been useful to the President, for it might have given him some sense of how the public would react to the initiative. It also might have influenced his decision to continue to pursue it. . . .

## B. FAILURE OF RESPONSIBILITY

The NSC system will not work unless the President makes it work. After all, this system was created to serve the President of the United States in ways of his choosing. By his actions, by his leadership, the President therefore determines the quality of its performance.

By his own account, as evidenced in his diary notes, and as conveyed to the Board by his principal advisors, President Reagan was deeply committed to securing the release of the hostages. It was this intense compassion for the hostages that appeared to motivate his steadfast support of the Iran initiative, even in the face of opposition from his Secretaries of State and Defense.

In his obvious commitment, the President appears to have proceeded with a concept of the initiative that was not accurately reflected in the reality of the operation. The President did not seem to be aware of the way in which the operation was implemented and the full consequences of U.S. participation.

The President's expressed concern for the safety of both the hostages and the Iranians who could have been at risk may have been conveyed in a manner so as to inhibit the full functioning of the system.

The President's management style is to put the principal responsibility for policy review and implementation on the shoulders of his advisors. Nevertheless, with such a complex, high-risk operation and so much at stake, the President should have ensured that the NSC system did not fail him. He did not force his policy to undergo the most critical review of which the NSC participants and the process were capable. At no time did he insist upon accountability and performance review. Had the President chosen to drive the NSC system, the outcome could well have been different. As it was, the most powerful features of the NSC system—providing comprehensive analysis, alternatives and follow-up—were not utilized.

The Board found a strong consensus among NSC participants that the President's priority in the Iran initiative was the release of U.S. hostages. But setting priorities is not enough when it comes to sensitive and risky initiatives that directly affect U.S. national security. He must ensure that the content and tactics of an initiative match his priorities and objectives. He must insist upon accountability. For it is the President who must take responsibility for the NSC system and deal with the consequences.

Beyond the President, the other NSC principals and the National Security Advisor must share in the responsibility for the NSC system.

President Reagan's personal management style places an especially heavy responsibility on his key advisors. Knowing his style, they should have been particularly mindful of the need for special attention to the manner in which this arms sale initiative developed and proceeded. On this score, neither the National Security Advisor nor the other NSC principals deserve high marks.

It is their obligation as members and advisors to the Council to ensure that the President is adequately served. The principal subordinates to the President must not be deterred from urging the President not to proceed on a highly questionable course of action even in the face of his strong conviction to the contrary.

In the case of the Iran initiative, the NSC process did not fail, it simply was largely ignored. The National Security Advisor and the NSC principals all had a duty to raise this issue and insist that orderly process be imposed. None of them did so.

All had the opportunity. While the National Security Advisor had the responsibility to see that an orderly process was observed, his failure to do so does not excuse the other NSC principals. It does not appear that any of the NSC principals called for more frequent consideration of the Iran initiative by the NSC principals in the presence of the President. None of the principals called for a serious vetting of the initiative by even a restricted group of disinterested individuals. The intelligence questions do not appear to have been raised, and legal considerations, while raised, were not pressed. No one seemed to have complained about the informality of the process. No one called for a thorough reexamination once the initiative did not meet expectations or the manner of execution changed. While one or another of the NSC principals suspected that something was amiss, none vigorously pursued the issue.

Mr. Regan also shares in this responsibility. More than almost any Chief of Staff of recent memory, he asserted personal control over the White House staff and sought to extend this control to the National Security Advisor. He was personally active in national security affairs and attended almost all of the relevant meetings regarding the Iran initiative.

He, as much as anyone, should have insisted that an orderly process be observed. In addition, he especially should have ensured that plans were made for handling any public disclosure of the initiative. He must bear primary responsibility for the chaos that descended upon the White House when such disclosure did occur.

Mr. McFarlane appeared caught between a President who supported the initiative and the cabinet officers who strongly opposed it. While he made efforts to keep these cabinet officers informed, the Board heard complaints from some that he was not always successful. VADM Poindexter on several occasions apparently sought to exclude NSC principals other than the President from knowledge of the initiative. Indeed, on one or more occasions Secretary Shultz may have been actively misled by VADM Poindexter.

VADM Poindexter also failed grievously on the matter of Contra diversion. Evidence indicates that VADM Poindexter knew that a diversion occurred, yet he did not take the steps that were required given the gravity of that prospect. He apparently failed to appreciate or ignored the serious legal and political risks presented. His clear obligation was either to investigate the matter or take it to the President—or both. He did neither. Director Casey shared a similar responsibility. Evidence suggests that he received information about the possible diversion of funds to the Contras almost a month before the story broke. He, too, did not move promptly to raise the matter with the President. Yet his responsibility to do so was clear.

The NSC principals other than the President may be somewhat excused by the insufficient attention on the part of the National Security Advisor to the need to keep all the principals fully informed. Given the importance of the issue and the sharp policy divergences involved, however, Secretary Shultz and Secretary Weinberger in particular distanced themselves from the march of events. Secretary Shultz specifically requested to be informed only as necessary to perform his job. Secretary Weinberger had access through intelligence to details about the operation. Their obligation was to give the President their full support and continued advice with respect to the program or, if they could not in conscience do that, to so inform the President. Instead, they simply distanced themselves from the program. They protected the record as to their own positions on this issue. They were not energetic in attempting to protect the President from the consequences of his personal commitment to freeing the hostages.

Director Casey appears to have been informed in considerable detail about the specifics of the Iranian operation. He appears to have acquiesced in and to have encouraged North's exercise of direct operational control over the operation. Because of the NSC staff's proximity to and close identification with the President, this increased the risks to the President if the initiative became public or the operation failed.

There is no evidence, however, that Director Casey explained this risk to the President or made clear to the President that Lt. Col. North, rather than the CIA, was running the operation. The President does not recall ever being informed of this fact. Indeed, Director Casey should have gone further and pressed for operational responsibility to be transferred to the CIA.

Director Casey should have taken the lead in vetting the assumptions presented by the Israelis on which the program was based and in pressing for an early examination of the reliance upon Mr. Ghorbanifar and the second channel as intermediaries. He should also have assumed responsibility for checking out the other intermediaries involved in the operation. Finally, because Congressional restrictions on covert actions are both largely directed at and familiar to the CIA, Director Casey should have taken the lead in keeping the question of Congressional notification active.

Finally, Director Casey, and, to a lesser extent, Secretary Weinberger, should have taken it upon themselves to assess the effect of the transfer of arms and intelligence to Iran on the Iran/Iraq military balance, and to transmit that information to the President. . . .

*Inouye—Hamilton Committee*

> In response to the Iran-*contra* scandal, the Congress created an investigative
> panel to examine what had happened. The House-Senate Joint Committee
> heard from twenty-eight witnesses in public hearings, including Lieut. Col.
> Oliver L. North, Vice Admiral John N. Poindexter (President Reagan's
> national security adviser at the time), and Secretary of State George P. Shultz.
> Their testimony, excerpted in this selection, takes us behind the scenes of the
> Iran-*contra* affair, disclosing many of the intrigues that occurred inside the
> NSC during this period, as well as the systematic attempts by several key NSC
> officials to conceal them from lawmakers.

## THE COMMITTEE HEARD FROM LIEUT. COL. OLIVER L. NORTH IN JULY OF 1987

### JULY 7, 1987

John W. Nields Jr., chief counsel for the House.

Q   The American people were told by this Government that our Government had nothing
to do with the Hasenfus airplane [a secret CIA military-supply flight which crashed in
Nicaragua in 1986], and that was false. And it is a principal purpose of these hearings
to replace secrecy and deception with disclosure and truth. And that's one of the
reasons we have called you here, sir. And one question the American people would
like to know the answer to is what did the President know about the diversion of the
proceeds of Iranian arms sales to the contras. Can you tell us what you know about
that, sir?

A   You just took a long leap from Mr. Hasenfus's airplane.

As I told this committee several days ago—and if you will indulge me, counsel,
in a brief summary of what I said: I never personally discussed the use of the residuals
or profits from the sale of U.S. weapons to Iran for the purpose of supporting
the Nicaraguan resistance with the President. I never raised it with him and he
never raised it with me during my entire tenure with the National Security Council
staff.

Throughout the conduct of my entire tenure at the National Security Council,
I assumed that the President was aware of what I was doing and had, through my
superiors, approved it. I sought approval of my superiors for every one of my actions,
and it is well documented.

I assumed, when I had approval to proceed from either Judge Clark, Bud
McFarlane or Admiral Poindexter, that they had indeed solicited and obtained the
approval of the President. To my recollection, Admiral Poindexter never told me that
he met with the President on the issue of using residuals from the Iranian sales to
support the Nicaraguan resistance. Or that he discussed the residuals or profits for use
by the contras with the President. Or that he got the President's specific approval.

Nor did he tell me that the President had approved such a transaction.

But again, I wish to reiterate throughout I believed that the President had indeed
authorized such activity.

No other person with whom I was in contact with during my tenure at the White House told me that he or she ever discussed the issue of the residuals or profits with the President.

In late November, two other things occurred which relate to this issue. On or about Friday, Nov. 21, [1986] I asked Admiral Poindexter directly: Does the President know? He told me he did not. And on Nov. 25, the day I was reassigned back to the United States Marine Corps for service, the President of the United States called me. In the course of that call, the President said to me words to the effect that: I just didn't know.

Those are the facts as I know them, Mr. Nields. I was glad that . . . you said that you wanted to hear the truth. I came here to tell you the truth, the good, the bad and the ugly. I am here to tell it all, pleasant and unpleasant. And I am here to accept responsibility for that which I did. I will not accept responsibility for that which I did not do. . . .

Q   I'm not asking you about words now, Colonel. I am asking you whether you didn't continue to send memoranda seeking approval of diversions or residuals—whatever the word—for the benefit of the contras up to the President for approval?

A   I did not send them to the President, Mr. Nields. This memorandum went to the National Security Adviser, seeking that he obtain the President's approval. There is a big difference. This is not a memorandum to the President.

Q   And my question to you is: Didn't—isn't it true that you continued to send them up to the National Security Adviser, seeking the President's approval?

A   Is it my recollection that I did, yes sir.

Q   And Admiral Poindexter never told you: Stop sending those memoranda?

A   I do not recall the admiral saying that. It is entirely possible, Mr. Nields, that that did happen.

Q   Well if it had happened, then you would have stopped sending them, isn't that true?

A   Yes.

Q   But you didn't stop sending them. You've just testified you sent them on five different occasions.

A   I testified that to my recollection there were about five times when we thought we had an arrangement that would result in the release of American hostages and the opening of a dialogue with Iran. And that we thought the deal was sufficiently framed that we could proceed with it. And that I thought—because I don't have those records before me—that I had sent memoranda forward, as I always did, seeking approval.

That's what I think and that's what I recall.

Q   And was there ever a time when Admiral Poindexter said: Don't send them up for the President's approval; just send them up for my approval?

A   Again, I don't recall such a conversation.

Q   Well in fact, isn't it true that it was Admiral Poindexter that wanted you to send these memoranda up for the President to approve?

A   I don't recall Admiral Poindexter instructing me to do that, either. . . .

Q   So far from telling you to stop sending memoranda up for the President's approval, Admiral Poindexter was specifically asking you to send memoranda up for the President's approval?

A    Well, again, in this particular case that's true, Mr. Nields. And I don't believe that I have said that Admiral Poindexter told me to stop. Did I?

Q    Where are these memoranda?

A    Which memoranda?

Q    The memoranda that you sent up to Admiral Poindexter, seeking the President's approval?

A    Well, they're probably in these books to my left that I haven't even looked through yet. And if I try to guess, I'm going to be wrong. But I think I shredded most of that. Did I get them all. I'm not trying to be flippant, I'm just—

Q    Well, that was going to be my very next question, Colonel North. Isn't it true that you shredded them?

A    I believe I did. . . .

Q    Well, that's the whole reason for shredding documents, isn't it, Colonel North—so that you can later say you don't remember whether you had them and you don't remember what's in them?

A    No, Mr. Nields. The reason for shredding documents and the reason the Government of the United States gave me a shredder—I mean, I didn't buy it myself—was to destroy documents that were no longer relevant; that did not apply or that should not be divulged.

     And again, I want to go back to the whole intent of a covert operation. Part of a covert operation is to offer plausible deniability of the association of the Government of the United States with the activity. Part of it is to deceive our adversaries. Part of it is to insure that those people who are at great peril carrying out those activities are not further endangered.

     All of those are good and sufficient reasons to destroy documents. And that's why the Government buys [and] gives them to people running [a] covert operation. Not so that they can have convenient memories. I came here to tell you the truth; to tell you and this committee and the American people the truth. And I'm trying to do that, Mr. Nields. And I don't like the insinuation that I'm up here having a convenient memory lapse like perhaps some others have had. . . .

Q    Is it correct to say that following the enactment of the Boland Amendment, our support for the war in Nicaragua did not end and that you were the person in the United States Government who managed it?

A    Starting in the spring of 1984, well before the Boland proscription of no appropriated funds made available to the D.O.D. and the C.I.A., etc., I was already engaged in supporting the Nicaraguan resistance and the democratic outcome in Nicaragua.

     I did so as part of a covert operation. It was carried out starting as early as the spring of '84, when we ran out of money and people started to look in Nicaragua, in Honduras and Guatemala, El Salvador and Costa Rica for some sign of what the Americans were really going to do, and that that help began much earlier than the most rigorous of the Boland proscriptions. And yes, it was carried out covertly, and it was carried out in such a way as to insure that the heads of state and the political leadership in Nicaragua—in Central America—recognized the United States was going to meet the commitments of the President's foreign policy.

     And the President's foreign policy was that we are going to achieve a democratic outcome in Nicaragua and that our support for the Nicaraguan freedom fighters was going to continue, and that I was given the job of holding them together in body and soul. And it slowly transitioned into a more difficult task as time went on and as the C.I.A. had to withdraw further and further from that support, until finally we got to the point in October when I was the only person left talking to them. . . .

Q   Well maybe it would be most useful to get into specifics of the areas of your support. I take it one area of your support was to endeavor to raise money from sources other than the U.S. Treasury?

A   That's correct. Boland proscriptions do not allow us to do so, and so we sought a means of complying with those Boland proscriptions by going elsewhere for those monies.

Q   And you went to foreign countries?

A   I did not physically go to those foreign countries.

Q   Representatives of—

A   Representatives of foreign countries and I had discussions about those matters, yes.

Q   And you asked them for money for the contras?

A   I want to be a little bit more specific about that. I don't recall going hat in hand to anybody asking for money. I do recall sitting and talking about how grateful this country would be if the issue that they had discussed with others were indeed brought to fruition. For example, a representative of Country 3 and I met and we talked about an issue that had been raised with him beforehand by others outside the Government, and I told him that I thought that was a dandy idea. And I told him where he could send the money. And he did so. . . .

Q   Now, my next question is you've indicated that the national security advisers, for whom you worked, authorized you to seek support from foreign countries, both financial and operational?

A   Yes.

Q   Was your—were your activities, in that respect, known to others in the White House, other than the national security advisers?

A   Well, I want to go back to something I said at the very beginning of all of this, Mr. Nields. I assumed that those matters which required the attention and decision of the President of the United States did indeed get them.

    I assumed that. I never asked that. I never walked up to the President and said, oh by the way Mr. President, yesterday I met with so-and-so from Country 4. Nor did he ever say, I'm glad you had a meeting with Country 4 and it went well.

Q   Do you know whether or not the President was aware of your activities seeking funds and operational support for the contras, from third countries?

A   I do not know.

Q   Were you ever—

A   I assumed that he did.

Q   Were you ev—what was the basis of your assumption?

A   Just that there was a lot going on and it was very obvious that the Nicaraguan resistance survived—I sent forward innumerable documents, some of which you've just shown us as exhibits, that demonstrated that I was keeping my superiors fully informed, as to what was going on. . . .

Q   Mr. McFarlane has testified that he gave you instructions not to solicit money from foreign countries or private sources. Did he give you those instructions?

A   I never carried out a single act—not one, Mr. Nields—in which I did not have authority from my superiors. I haven't, in the 23 years that I have been in the uniformed services of the United States of America ever violated an order—not one.

Q   But that wasn't the question. The question was—

A   That *is* the answer to your question.

Q   No, the question was did Mr. McFarlane give you such instructions?

A   No. I never heard those instructions.

Q   And I take it that it was your understanding, from what you've just said, that quite to the contrary, you were authorized to seek money from foreign countries?

A   I was authorized to do everything that I did.

Q   Well, again, that isn't the question.

A   I was authorized to have a meeting, in this particular case by Mr. McFarlane, for the purpose of talking to the man about a suggestion that had been made to him by others, and to encourage that process along. And I did so. I had already provided to Mr. McFarlane a card with the address of an account, an offshore account which would support the Nicaraguan resistance. And thank God, somebody put money into that account and the Nicaraguan resistance didn't die—as perhaps others intended. Certainly the Sandinistas and Moscow and Cuba intended that. And they didn't die, they grew in strength and numbers and effectiveness as a consequence. And I think that is a good thing. . . .

I get the sense that somehow or another we've tried to create the impression that Oliver North picked up his hat and wandered around Washington and foreign capitals begging for money, and I didn't do that. I didn't have to do it because others were more willing to put up the money than the Congress because they saw well what was happening to us in Central America, and the devastating consequences of a contra wipeout and an American walkaway and write-off; to what was going to happen to this country and to democracy elsewhere in the world.

I didn't have to wander around and beg. There were other countries in the world, and other people in this country, who were more willing to help the Nicaraguan resistance survive, and cause democracy to prosper in Central America, than this body here. And that is an important factor in all of what you do, counsel, and in what this committee is going to do. It's got to be part of your assessment, as to why is it that other countries in the world were willing to step up and help in a desperate cause when we were not willing to do so ourselves.

That has got to be something that is debated not just by pulling people before this group and hammering at them and haranguing them and reducing it to pettiness. It has got to be something that the American people come to understand, how desperately important it was not just to us, not just to Ollie North and not just to President Ronald Reagan. It was important to these other people who put forth that money. And I didn't beg them, they offered. And that's important, sir. . . .

## JULY 8, 1987

Q   You testified about Admiral Poindexter and the President. Who else, if anyone—and I don't mean to imply anything in the question. But leaving those two people aside, who else in the Government was aware of either the plan or the fact of using proceeds of arms sales to Iran for the contras?

A   Well I, if I may clarify what I testified to yesterday, it is my assumption the President knew and then I subsequently testified that I was told he did not know. I know that Admiral Poindexter knew. I know that Mr. McFarlane knew at a point in time when he was no longer in the Government. And [CIA] Director [William J.] Casey knew.

Aside from that, I can't speak with certainty as to who else, inside the government, knew for sure. . . . But the only ones that I know for sure, who I confirmed it with, were those three. . . .

Q   When did Director Casey first learn of it?

A   Actually, I—my recollection is Director Casey learned about it before the fact. Since I'm confessing to things, I may have raised it with him before I raised it with Admiral Poindexter. Probably when I returned from the February—from the January discussions.

Q   You're referring now to the discussions, the trip, during which you had the discussion with Mr. [Nanucher] Ghorbanifar [a go-between in the Iranian arms deal] in the bathroom?

A   Yes, I don't recall raising the bathroom [discussion], specifically, with the Director, but I do recall talking with the Director and I don't remember whether it was before or after I talked to Admiral Poindexter about it. But I—I was not the only one who was enthusiastic about this idea. And I—Director Casey used several words to describe how he felt about it, all of which were effusive.

He referred to it as the ultimate irony, the ultimate covert operation kind of thing, and was very enthusiastic about it. He also recognized that there were potential liabilities. And that there was risk involved. . . .

Q   What kinds of risks did he identify to you?

A   This very political risk that we see being portrayed out here now; that it could indeed be dangerous, or not dangerous so much as politically damaging.

Q   Do you have any reason to believe that Director Casey, given the political risk, ever discussed the matter with the President?

A   I have no reason to believe that he did because he never addressed that to me. I never, as I indicated yesterday, no one ever told me that they had discussed it with the President. . . .

Q   And there came a time, did there not, when you had an interview with members of the House Intelligence Committee?

A   I did. . . .

Q   And they were interested in finding out the answers to the questions raised by the resolution of inquiry?

A   Exactly.

Q   Your fund-raising activities, military support for the contras?

A   That's right. . . .

Q   But I take it you did considerably more which you did not tell the committee about?

A   I have admitted that here before you today. . . . I will tell you right now, counsel, and all the members here gathered, that I misled the Congress. . . .

Q    You made false statements to them about your activities in support of the contras?

A    I did. Furthermore, I did so with a purpose. And I did so with the purpose of hopefully avoiding the very kind of thing that we have before us now, and avoiding a shut-off of help for the Nicaraguan resistance, and avoiding an elimination of the resistance facilities in three Central American countries, wherein we had promised those heads of state on my specific orders—on specific orders to me I had gone down there and assured them of our absolute and total discretion.

      And I am admitting to you that I participated in the preparation of documents to the Congress that were erroneous, misleading, evasive and wrong. And I did it again here when I appeared before that committee convened in the White House Situation Room. And I make no excuses for what I did. I will tell you now that I am under oath and I was not then.

Q    We do live in a democracy, don't we?

A    We do sir, thank God.

Q    In which it is the people not one marine lieutenant colonel that get to decide the important policy decisions for the nation?

A    Yes, and I would point out that part of that answer is that this marine lieutenant colonel was not making all of those decisions on his own. As I indicated yesterday in my testimony, Mr. Nields, I sought approval for everything that I did.

Q    But you denied Congress the facts?

A    I did.

Q    You denied the elected representatives of our people the facts, upon which, which they needed—

A    I did.

Q    —to make a very important decision for this nation?

A    I did, because of what I have just described to you as our concerns. And I did it because we have had incredible leaks from discussions with closed committees of the Congress.

## THE CONGRESSIONAL COMMITTEE HEARD FROM REAR ADM. JOHN M. POINDEXTER. HERE ARE EXCERPTS FROM HIS TESTIMONY, AS RECORDED BY THE NEW YORK TIMES

### JULY 15, 1987

Arthur L. Liman, chief counsel to the Senate committee.

      Now let's turn to the Iran initiative. Were you advised sometime in August of 1985 by Mr. McFarlane that the President had approved some Israeli transactions with Iran?

      Admiral Poindexter Mr. Liman, that is a very fuzzy time period for me. . . . The period of time you're asking about, August of 1985, I was the deputy, and I did not have primary responsibility on this issue. . . .

Q    But you did become aware that there was an Iran initiative?

A    Yes, I did.

Q    And you became aware of that from a conversation with Mr. McFarlane?

A   I did. . . .

Q   Now, admiral, did there come a time in connection with this transaction, when the C.I.A. sent over to you a proposed finding for the President to sign?

A   Yes, Mr. Liman. That is the finding that I discussed with you earlier on the second of May.

Q   Did you receive the letter of Nov. 26, 1985, from William Casey addressed to you which says, pursuant to our conversation, this should go to the President for his signature and should not be passed around in any hands below our level?

A   I did receive that.

Q   And you received the finding with it. Is that correct?

A   Well, I must say that I don't actually remember getting it, but I'm sure that I did. I'm sure they came together.

Q   Now, Admiral, when you saw the finding, am I correct that the finding itself was essentially a straight arms-for-hostage finding?

A   That is correct. It had been prepared essentially by the C.I.A. as a what we call a C.Y.A. effort.

Q   Did the President of the United States sign that finding?

A   As I've testified before, he did, on or about the 5th of December. I'm vague on the date. . . .

Q   Do you recall who was present when the President signed the finding?

A   No, I don't. One of the reasons that I think my recollection is very poor on the circumstances of the President's actually signing this is that, recall that, that was a day or so after Mr. McFarlane had resigned and the President had just—I guess we had announced it on the fourth. Mr. McFarlane actually resigned, I think, on the 30th of November, we announced it on the fourth of December, and my recollection is that he signed this the following day on the fifth. My recollection now is that the C.I.A., especially the Deputy Director, John McMahon, was very anxious to get this signed. I frankly was never happy with it, because it was not fully staffed, and I frankly can't recall when I showed it to the President who was there or exactly what the discussion was or even what I recommended to him at this point. I simply can't remember that.

Q   But you do recall that whatever you recommended, the President read it and he signed it.

A   Yes, he did. He did sign it.

Q   And there was, in fact, the recommendation from Bill Casey that he sign it, and Bill Casey was a person whose advice the President valued.

A   He did.

Q   Now what happened to that finding?

A   As I said earlier, I destroyed that by tearing it up on the 21st of November because I thought it was a significant political embarrassment to the President. And I wanted to protect him from possible disclosure of this. To get into the details of exactly how it happened, which I assume you're interested in—

Q   Yes. When you say the 21st of November, you're talking about the 21st of November 1986.

A   1986. That's correct.

Q   Now, would you tell the panel the circumstances of your destroying this finding because you thought it would be a significant political embarrassment to the President?

A   I will. The finding, the existence of the finding I had completely forgotten in early November 1986. As I said before, the finding initially was prepared by the C.I.A. for the reason that I stated. I can recall in my time at the White House one or possibly two other findings that had a retroactive nature to them. I frankly was always uncomfortable with that because I thought it didn't particularly make a lot of sense.

The finding was very narrow. It was prepared before there had been thorough discussion of the issue. As I said earlier, I came into the issue in a full, responsible way in early December of 1985. Prior to that time, Mr. McFarlane had handled it. I felt that it was important that we improve on this finding so that we clearly lay out what the objectives were in the Iranian . . . After this finding was signed, it was retained in my immediate office and at some point after it was signed I had apparently given it to Commander Thompson, my military assistant, to put in an envelope in his safe to keep.

I had, as I said, completely forgotten about it. On November the 21st, when Ed Meese [the Attorney General] called me and said—well, to go back a step, we'd run into a problem in November of what had actually happened in 1985. It was very dim in people's memories. We didn't think we had much in writing.

As I think you've heard Colonel North testify, we frankly did not realize the old PROF notes [the White House electronic message system] existed. My policy was to erase them, and I apparently did it the right way, and I don't think Colonel North did it the right way. So we didn't have the benefit that these committees have in going back over these old PROF notes, or we didn't realize that we had that opportunity.

But Ed Meese and I talked many times during the month of November, and when it became clear that there was a disagreement between Cabinet-level officials as to what had happened in November of 1985, he indicated that he wanted to come over and ask the President to have a fact-finding session primarily with the Cabinet-level officials involved to try to sort out what had happened, actually happened in November of 1985. And he called me early in the morning on the 21st of November and told me this, and he said he had an appointment to see the President at 11:30, and he wanted me and Don Regan [the White House chief of staff] to go with him, which we did at 11:30.

He told the President about the controversy, not really controversy, the different recollections as to what had happened in November. And he said he thought it would be useful if he would have a couple of his people that were close to him look into the matter to see if they could piece together what had happened. The President readily agreed. . . .

So Ed called me after lunch. . . . and he asked if I would have the appropriate documents pulled together so they could take a look at them. I said I would do that. After he called, I called Commander Thompson, my military assistant, and asked him to take charge of pulling these documents together.

And then I called Colonel North and told him of my conversation with Mr. Meese and asked him to cooperate with Commander Thompson and Mr. Meese's people. . . .

Later in the afternoon or early evening, Commander Thompson brought into my office the envelopes that I had given him earlier containing the material we had on the

Iranian project in the immediate office, which was essentially the various findings. And he pulled out this November finding—it was actually signed in December. And my recollection is that he said something to the effect that they'll have a field day with this, or something to that effect. . . . The import of his comment was that up until that time in November of 1986, the President was being beaten about the head and shoulders, that this was, the whole Iranian project, was just an arms-for-hostage deal.

Well, this finding, unfortunately, gave that same impression. And I, frankly, didn't see any need for it at the time. I thought it was politically embarrassing, and so I decided to tear it up. And I tore it up, put it in the burn basket behind my desk.

I can't recall, but I believe that Colonel North was there in the office, but I'm a little fuzzy on that point.

Q   Was Commander Thompson there when you tore it up?

A   I believe he was, but I can't swear to it. I know he brought it in, and I can recall his comment, but exactly how long it took me, because I—when he made his comment he said, I said, well let me see the finding. And he pulled it out and gave it to me, and I read it and at some point after that I tore it up, but it was within a short period of time.

Q   Admiral, you talked about the fact that the President was being beaten around the head and shoulders by the media for sanctioning an arms-for-hostage deal and that this finding seemed to corroborate it, and you therefore destroyed it in order to prevent significant political embarrassment. Did you regard one of the responsibilities of the national security adviser to protect the President from political embarrassment?

A   I think that it's always the responsibility of a staff to protect their leader and certainly in this case where the leader is the Commander in Chief. I feel very strongly that that's one of the roles. And I don't mean that in any sense of covering up, but one has to always put things in the President's perspective and to make sure that he's not put in a position that can be politically embarrassing.

Q   Now, Admiral, a finding represents a decision of the President of the United States, correct?

A   A finding, I don't believe, is discussed in any statute. It is discussed in various Presidential directives. It is an artifact of what the statute calls a Presidential determination.

Q   And the President, when he signed this finding, was making a determination?

A   That's correct, but it's important to point out that the finding, that early finding was designed for a very specific purpose, and was not fully staffed and did not in any way ever represent the total thinking on the subject.

Q   The President didn't authorize you to destroy the finding, correct?

A   He certainly did not.

## MEETING OF THE N.S.C.

Q   Let's go to the—on Dec. 7, 1985, after the finding had been signed by the President, there was a meeting, was there not, between the principals of the National Security Council?

A   Yes, there was.

Q   And you recall Mr. Weinberger was there, and Secretary Shultz was there, Don Regan was there, Mr. McMahon of the C.I.A. was there, do you recall that?

A   Yes, I do.

Q   . . . At this meeting, there was a discussion again, or there was a discussion of the Iran initiative? Is that so? . . .

A   Yes, yes, there was. . . .

Q   And the subject on the table was an Israeli initiative, under which the Israelis would ship arms to the Iranians and we would replenish the arms. Hopefully there would be better relations with Iran. And as a token of good faith, the American hostages would be released. Is that a fair summary?

A   Well, I think it's a partial summary.

Q   Well, why don't you complete it?

A   We had been concerned, in the National Security Council, for some period of time, with the situation in Iran. Unfortunately, we have very poor intelligence on what's happening in Iran. The National Security Council staff had prepared a draft finding, earlier in 1985, to try to get the Government focused on what we saw as a very significant, looming problem in Iran, as Ayatollah Khomeini eventually passed from the scene and there was some sort of succession.

   We didn't want a repeat of the 1970's, when things were happening in Iran that we weren't aware of, and eventually went out of our control, and out of control of the Government there.

   . . . We felt that we needed to take an initiative to get closer to people in the Iranian Government, so that we could find out what's happening and hopefully have some influence in the future or, at least, have information on which to base the United States policy.

Q   Admiral, see if this part is correct: that the currency for trying to get that influence that was being demanded, as reported by the Israelis, involved arms?

A   That is often the currency of any sort of business in the Middle East.

Q   And in this case that was the currency being demanded?

A   Yes, that is correct.

Q   And it is also true that we did not want to authorize arms shipments to the Iranians, unless we were assured of getting our hostages back, is that so?

A   As I was trying to lay out a moment ago, what our concerns were, what our major objective was, the President was clearly also concerned about the hostages. The President is a very sensitive person, and he is concerned about individuals when they're in difficulty. And so he, just as a human being, was concerned about the hostages.

   I don't think that the President is overly concerned about them, but he recognized that we did have an opportunity here to try to get the hostages back. And there was no way that we could carry on discussions with Iranian officials about broader objectives, until we got over the first obstacle. And the first obstacle was to get the hostages back. And the President felt that, that it was worth taking some risks here.

Q   Now, did the Secretary of State and the Secretary of Defense express objections?

A   They expressed, as opposed to some reports, very strong, vociferous objection and clearly laid out for the President the other side of the issue.

Q    And without going into undue detail, could you just tick off the points they made?

A    Well, there are the obvious points that have been made since this all has become public. Secretary Shultz was concerned about our operation to staunch the flow of arms into Iran, which is one of the methods that we are using to try to stop the war between Iran and Iraq. . . .

But in its simplest terms, what was being proposed here was not in accordance with that particular method that we were using. He was concerned that if the European countries found out about it, that it would lessen their willingness to cooperate. In reality though, in my opinion, we've never had good cooperation from anybody on Operation Staunch. The European countries continue to send military equipment and supplies into Iran. Iran's been able to carry on the war for six, going on seven, years now, I guess.

Other objections were that of it was contrary to the Arms Export Control Act. Secretary Weinberger had slightly different reasons, but they're generally along the same lines.

Q    And there's no doubt in your mind that the President listened to, and understood, those objections?

A    . . . The President listened to all of this very carefully. And at the end of the discussion, at least the first round, he sat back and he said something to the effect—and I, this is not a direct quote—but it was something to the effect that, I don't feel that we can leave any stone unturned in trying to get the hostages back. We clearly have a situation here where there are larger strategic interests. But it's also an opportunity to get the hostages back. And I think that we ought to at least take the next step. . . .

Q    Now, one other question which just has been handed to me, that Colonel North apparently testified that Secretary Shultz and Secretary Weinberger's opposition was not vigorously expressed in this January period. I take it that it was vigorously expressed at the January 7th meeting, and it was expressed by the Secretary of State at that January 16th meeting and that no one had any doubt about where both of them stood.

A    That's true of the earlier meetings. On the 16th of January, I think it was pretty clear to George [Shultz] that the President wanted to go ahead with this at that point, and so although he voiced objection, I wouldn't say that, and this is probably why Colonel North's recollection is as it was. In fact, I think probably the 16 January meeting may have been the only meeting that Colonel North was in attendance where he may have heard the other Cabinet officers give their views. But it is accurate that both George Shultz and Cap Weinberger vigorously made this case as to why we should not do this.

## LEGALITY AND APPROVAL

Q    Right. Now, admiral, is it correct that in the discussions that you had leading up to the January 17th finding, there was no discussion with the President of the United States about the possibility of using proceeds of the sale to support the contras?

A    There was none.

Q    And there was none with you.

A    There was none with me.

Q   Now, would you tell us, and I'm going to break this into different questions, when was the first time that you were told by Colonel North about this possibility?

A   My best recollection is that this took place sometime in February of 1986.

Q   And would you tell us what Colonel North said to you?

A   My recollection is that he had just come back from a meeting in London, and he was giving me a general update on the situation as he saw it. And he was reviewing the status of the work that was in progress at C.I.A. and Defense in addition to the results of his meeting in London. And near the end of the conversation, my recollection is that he said something to the effect that, Admiral, I think we can, I have found a way that we can legally provide some funds to the democratic resistance or as they have been called here—and I frankly agree with Congressman [Henry J.] Hyde [R.-Illinois] that I have no problem with calling them contras—through funds that will accrue from the arms sales to the Iranians.

Q   Did he use the word legally?

A   My best recollection is that he did, but of course I know that Colonel North is not a lawyer, and so I was taking that in a layman's sense that that was his conclusion.

Q   Do you recall in reciting this in your deposition you didn't use the word legally?

A   I don't recall that, that I didn't. I believe that he did, he may not have.

Q   Now, did he tell you what the method would be for doing this?

A   This was a very general discussion, but this was clearly a new aspect that I had not thought about before. To make a long story short, in the end I thought it was a very good idea at the end of this conversation, and I personally approved it.

Q   Did he ask you for your approval?

A   I don't recall how he phrased his request, but he was clearly looking for a signal from me whether or not to proceed ahead along this line.

Q   And you gave it.

A   And I gave it to him. . . .

In order to put this in perspective, and I think it's important to understand my state of mind at the time and what things were of concern to us. The President's policy with regard to support for the contras had not changed since 1981. The various versions of the Boland Amendment came and went. But the President was steadfast in his support for the contras. . . . So I was absolutely convinced as to what the President's policy was with regard to support for the contras.

I was aware that the President was aware of third-country support, that the President was aware of private support. And the way Colonel North described this to me at the time, it was obvious to me that this fell in exactly the same category that these funds could either be characterized as private funds because of the way that we had, that Director Casey and I had agreed to carry out the finding. They could be characterized as private funds or they could be characterized as third-country funds. In my view, it was a matter of implementation of the President's policy, with regard to support for the contras.

We were in the process of working on our legislative plan to get $100 million from Congress for essentially unrestricted support to the contras. . . .

The President was bound and determined and still is, that he will not sit still for the consolidation of a Communist government on the mainland of America. And in order to prevent that, he feels that the most effective way, with which I also agree, is to keep pressure on the Communist Sandinista Government. And the most effective way to do that, given all of the factors considered and because we don't want to send U.S. soldiers to Nicaragua, is to provide support to the contras and keep them alive until we can get the $100 million. . . .

And so after weighing all of these matters—and I also felt that I had the authority to approve it because I had a commission from the President which was in very broad terms. My role was to make sure that his policies were implemented. In this case, the policy was very clear, and that was to support the contras. After working with the President for five and a half years, the last three of which were very close and probably closer than any other officer in the White House except the chief of staff, I was convinced that I understood the President's thinking on this and that if I had taken it to him that he would have approved it.

Now I was not so naïve as to believe that it was not a politically volatile issue; it clearly was because of the divisions that existed within the Congress on the issue of support for the contras. And it was clear that there would be a lot of people that would disagree, that would make accusations that indeed have been made. So although I was convinced that we could properly do it and that the President would approve if asked, I made a very deliberate decision not to ask the President so that I could insulate him from the decision and provide some future deniability for the President if it ever leaked out. Of course, our hope was that it would not leak out.

Q   When you say deniability, are you saying that your decision was not to tell the President so that he would be able to deny that he knew of it?

A   That's correct.

Q   And did you at any time prior to the Attorney General's finding this on November 22d tell the President of the United States of the fact that proceeds from the Iranian arms sale were being used to support the contras?

A   I don't—I did not. I want to make this very clear because I understand it's an important issue. I did not talk to anybody else except Colonel North about this decision until, to my knowledge, my best recollection—and I don't want to quibble here over times in late November 1986—but my recollection is the first mention that I made to anybody besides Colonel North was on November 24, 1986, to Ed Meese.

Q   And so that the answer is you did not tell the President of the United States.

A   I did not.

Q   And that for a period of whatever it is, nine months, you kept it from the President of the United States, for the reasons you've given.

A   Mr. Liman, this clearly was an important decision but it was also an implementation of very clear policy. If the President had asked me, I very likely would have told him about it. But he didn't. And I think—you know, an important point here is that on this whole issue, you know, the buck stops here with me. I made the decision; I felt that I had the authority to do it. I thought it was a good idea. I was convinced that the President would in the end think it was a good idea. But I did not want him to be associated with the decision. . . .

Q   Were there any other examples during your term as national security adviser where you withheld a decision from the President that you had made in order to give him deniability?

A    Well, this again—this decision, in my view, was a matter of implementation, and there were many details of implementation that were not discussed with the President. This particular detail was the only one of its kind in terms of the disagreements and the controversy that existed over the issue.

Q    Were there any other decisions that you withheld from the President that you had made because they were politically explosive?

A    I don't recall anything else that fell in that same category, although there were lots—I want to make a distinction here between what I felt my authority was and why I didn't discuss it with the President. Number one, I felt that it was within my authority because it was an implementation of a policy that was well understood, that the President felt very strongly about. It was not a secret foreign policy, the President's policy with regard to the contras was clearly understood by every member of the Congress and the American people. So it wasn't matter of going out and making a secret foreign policy. . . .

    You know, frankly, as Colonel North has testified, I thought it was a neat idea, too. And I'm sure the President would have enjoyed knowing about it. But on the other hand, because it would be controversial—and I must say that I don't believe that I estimated how controversial it would be accurately—but I knew very well that it would be controversial, and I wanted the President to have some deniability so that he would be protected and at the same time we'd be able to carry out his policy and provide the opposition to the Sandinista Government. . . .

## AIDING THE CONTRAS

Q    Now as I understand your testimony, you genuinely believed that in approving the diversion, that it was consistent with the policies of the President, in terms of third-country support. You've already testified to that. And I'd like to ask you some questions about that. Is it a fact that the Administration had gone to Congress in 1985 and gotten permission from Congress to solicit third-country support?

A    Yes, we worked with members of Congress to get that provision.

Q    And is it a fact that that provision for obtaining third-country support was limited to humanitarian aid?

A    Since leaving the White House and going back over this material, that is correct. I can't say that during the discussions, that I can recall in the White House, there was great distinction made between humanitarian aid or any other kind of aid, at that particular time. There was with respect to the $27 million. But I just simply don't recall great distinctions being made.

Q    Well, are you saying that when Congress worked out the legislation with the Administration that authorized solicitation for humanitarian aid, the Administration interpreted that as meaning that it could solicit for lethal aid?

A    No, I'm not saying that at all. I'm just giving you my recollection of the time.

Q    Now, and you also understood that that bill provided that it was only the State Department that could do the solicitation, do you recall that, sir?

A    Yes, I recall that.

Q    Now, was the money that you were getting from the Ayatollah, or [Gen. Richard]

Secord [another go-between], however you viewed it, was that money to be limited to being disbursed for humanitarian aid?

A    In no way. You see the distinction here is that—and this is contrary to what you have heard before, from other witnesses. But I never believed, and I don't believe today, that the Boland Amendment ever applied to the National Security Council staff or the President's personal staff. But the problem was that the Boland Amendment did apply to the State Department. It did apply to C.I.A. And it did apply to the Defense Department.

We had been running this operation, on our own, for a long period of time because there was no other alternative, in order to keep the contras alive. And we wanted help. We wanted also a more public recognition of the fact that the U.S. was supporting the contras in some way.

I frankly, I personally still wanted that to be done in—the public support to be done in such way that we could slowly turn back to a covert program, run by the C.I.A. But it was important to me, and to others, that we get the State Department back into the game.

Q    I understand you. Did you ever discuss, with the President of the United States, that the N.S.C. was raising money for lethal aid?

A    Mr. Liman does—are you, if I may ask to clarify the question—are you saying that raising money is soliciting money?

Q    I don't want to get into a semantic debate about solicitation. I mean every day in the newspapers, in the financial sections, they have announcements of offerings, and they say this is not a solicitation. So please do not get me into that semantic debate. Let's talk about raising money, obtaining money, for lethal aid. That the N.S.C. was obtaining money for lethal aid?

A    The President was aware that we were encouraging, I guess would be a fair way to describe it, third countries to contribute to the cause of the contras in Central America, in their fight against the Communist Sandinistas. And, of course, we were doing that primarily by pointing out to them the dangers that we saw. And, as Colonel North has testified, it wasn't very difficult. They clearly understood the problem. The Central American countries understood, the neighboring countries. The other countries that are on your list, that I've heard you talk about up here. . . .

## FINANCING COVERT PROJECTS

Q    Colonel North testified that in addition to the use of the proceeds of the Iranian arms sale for the contras, it was to be used for a series of other covert projects. Do you remember that testimony of his?

A    I heard that testimony.

Q    Was that the first time you ever heard about that?

A    It's the first time that I heard it discussed in that depth. I must say there was, as far as I was concerned, no such plan. I don't at all doubt that Colonel North and Director Casey may have discussed that. Frankly, it's an idea that has some attractive features in my mind, but there was no plan that was brought to me or that I took to the President to proceed in that kind of direction. That would have required substantial discussion. . . .

Q   You testified this morning that if the President had asked you about what countries were helping, you probably would have told him about this. Do you recall that?

A   That would have been a difficult situation, and I don't—

Q   But you wouldn't lie to the President?

A   I wouldn't lie to the President, and if he had outright asked me about it, I would have told him. He didn't.

Q   Are you saying that with the interest the President had in the contra movement and his concern about the dire straits it was in financially that he never asked you which countries were helping?

A   That's correct. The President is—as I've said—is not a man for great detail. He—and I don't mean that in any sort of funny way—I don't think a President ought to get involved in details—he has to maintain a strategic perspective, and he's got enough to worry about. I think by and large the President has the same sort of management philosophy that I do, and that is that he picks good people for the job and gives them a lot of authority to carry out that job, and he wanted the contras supported. We were reporting to him on the status of the contras, in general terms, and he knew that they were surviving and that was the thing that was important to him.

## AT THE CONCLUSION OF POINDEXTER'S APPEARANCE, REPRESENTATIVE LEE H. HAMILTON, DEMOCRAT OF INDIANA, THE CHAIRMAN OF THE HOUSE COMMITTEE, ADDRESSED HIM ABOUT HIS TESTIMONY DURING THE HEARINGS:

### JULY 21, 1987

Representative Hamilton. . . . Admiral Poindexter, I want to say that we have indeed appreciated your testimony. . . . None of us, I think, can know all of the circumstances that you confronted as the national security adviser to the President.

. . . It is, however, . . . our job to examine your role in the decision-making process. . . .

Now, your comments about secrecy in government . . . concerned me . . . a great deal. You have testified that you intentionally withheld information from the President, denied him the opportunity to make, probably, the most fateful decision of his Presidency— whether to divert the funds from the Iranian arms sales to aid the contras.

You said your objective was to withhold information from the Congress. And apparently, so far as I understood the testimony, without direction or authority to do so. As many have mentioned, you destroyed the Dec. 5, '85, finding. You apparently intended to have original documents, relating to the contras, either altered or removed. You were unwilling to speak candidly with senior Justice and C.I.A. officials about the Hawk missile shipments to Iran. And you kept the . . . Secretaries of State and Defense, uninformed. . . .

All of us who work with our system of government sometimes feel impatient with its painstaking procedures. . . . Yet, your comment about Congress, and I quote it directly: I simply did not want any outside interference, reflects an attitude which makes, in my judgment at least, our constitutional system of checks and balances unworkable.

Instead of bringing each agency dealing with foreign policy into the process, you cut those agencies out of the process. You told the committees, I firmly believe in very tight compartmentation. You compartmentalized not only the President's senior advisers, but in effect, you locked the President himself out of the process.

You began your testimony by saying that the function of a national security adviser is to present options and to advise the President. Yet, you told the committees the buck stops here with me. That is not where the buck is supposed to stop.

You wanted to deflect blame from the President but that is another way of saying you wanted to deflect responsibility from the President. And that should not be done in our system of government.

You testified that diverting funds to the contras was a detail, a matter of implementation of the President's policies. And you felt that you had the authority to approve it. Yet, this was a major foreign policy initiative, as subsequent events have shown, with very far-reaching ramifications. And this member, at least, wonders what else could be done in the President's name, if this is mere implementation of policy. . . .

Probably more important, secrecy contributed to disarray in the Oval Office. The President apparently did not know that you were making some of the most important foreign policy decisions of his Presidency. You've testified, I was convinced that the President would, in the end, think the diversion was a good idea. Yet, the President has stated that he would not've approved the diversion.

Excessive secrecy placed the President in an untenable position and caused him to make false and contradictory public statements. Let me cite some of them:

On Nov. 6, 1986, the President said, the speculation, the commenting and all, on a story that came out of the Middle East has no foundation.

A week later, the President said, we did not, repeat, we did not, trade weapons, or anything else, for hostages.

But on March 4, the President said: A few months ago, I told the American people I did not trade arms for hostages. My heart and my best intentions still tell me that's true but the facts and the evidence tell me it is not.

Turning to the solicitation of private aid for the contras, the President said, on May 5, I don't know how that money was to be used. And I have no knowledge that there was ever any solicitation by our people with these people.

But on May 15, the President altered his view. He said: As a matter of fact, I was definitely involved in the decisions about support to the freedom fighters. It was my idea to begin with.

May I suggest that the President was unaware of some important actions taken by his staff and, therefore, he misspoke. Because he lacked information, the President in-flicted serious and repeated political wounds upon himself. Polls continue to indicate that a majority of the American people still feels that the President, despite his state-ments to the contrary, did know that money from the Iran arms sales was channeled to the contras. . . .

POINDEXTER   I just have one brief comment.

HAMILTON   Yes, indeed.

POINDEXTER   Mr. Chairman, with regard to your closing statement I would just simply say that we'll have to agree, you and I, to disagree on your interpretation of many of the events. And finally, I leave this hearing with my head held high that I have done my very best to promote the long-term national security interests of the United States. Thank you.

## FOLLOWING ARE EXCERPTS FROM SECRETARY OF STATE GEORGE P SHULTZ'S TESTIMONY:

### JULY 24, 1987

Representative Lee H. Hamilton, chairman of the House committee. Mr. Secretary, do you have an opening statement?

MR. SHULTZ   No, I don't. But with your permission, Mr. Chairman, I'd like to make a few remarks.

Q   Please proceed.

A   ...I have on numerous occasions—including, I think, before your committee right here, Chairman [Dante B.] Fascell [D.-Florida, chairman of the House Foreign Affairs Committee]—been asked about what advice I gave the President on this, that or the other, subject. And I have always taken a position, in 10 and a half years as a member of the Cabinet, that those conversations are privileged and I would not discuss them. This is an exception, and I have made this material available on the President's instruction. But I mention it because if I'm testifying before you on some other subject sometime and you try to use this as a precedent, I won't buy it. I'm just putting you on notice right now.

Thank you, Mr. Chairman.

Q   Thank you, Mr. Secretary. We'll begin the questions this morning with Mr. Belnick....

Mark A. Belnick, executive assistant to the chief counsel of the Senate committee. Mr. Secretary, I'd like to begin this morning by reviewing certain key events that the panel has been considering in order to establish when the Secretary of State was first informed of those events....

Let me begin by this question. Mr. Secretary, when were you first informed that the President of the United States had signed a covert action finding authorizing the sale of U.S. arms to Iran?

A   On November the 10th, 1986, at a meeting in the Oval Office, with the President's principal advisers, during a briefing by Admiral Poindexter on what had transpired over the past year or so....

Q   Mr. Secretary, when were you first informed that this nation had sold weapons directly to Iran?

A   ...This all started to break in very early November 1986....

Q   Prior to then, ... had any member of the United States Government informed you that the United States had sold weapons directly ... to Iran?

A   No.

Q   Mr. Secretary, when were you first informed of the McFarlane mission to Teheran?

A   It was after the mission, but I think shortly after it was completed.

Q   And were you given the details of the mission at that time?

A   I was told that it had fizzled, ... that the whole project had been told to stand down.

Q   Were you told at that time that Mr. McFarlane had brought U.S. weapons with him to Teheran?

A   No....

Q   Mr. Secretary, when were you first informed that United States negotiations with the second channel in the early autumn of 1986 had produced agreement on a so-called nine-point agenda which provided for additional arms sales to Iran in exchange for hostages and which contained provision also with respect to actions directed at the Government of Iraq?

A   On December 13th of 1986. But if I may interrupt your questioning, I'd like to expand on that.

Q   Please.

A   In the course of the effort to come to grips with what was taking place, the President put the management of Iran matters into my hands by that time—we're talking in December—sort of at first a little bit but then for sure. And I discovered that the C.I.A. had a meeting scheduled with an Iranian for that date. And so we considered what to do. And we decided that we should go ahead with that meeting, that the C.I.A. representative who was scheduled to be the representative there, Mr. Cave, should go. But we would have accompanying him Mr. Charles Dunbar, who is a Foreign Service officer and Farsi speaker. And we would have instructions carefully written, designed to use the meeting as a means to tell that channel that there would be no more arms sales discussed in that channel or anywhere else. . . .

At the meeting, the message was delivered, but also as our representative listened, there was back and forth discussion about this agenda, nine-point agenda. And so gradually then, and in discussion with Mr. Cave, Mr. Dunbar got a reasonable idea of what was on this agenda. And then he called that back on Dec. 13, which was a Saturday, to the department. And I saw it on Saturday afternoon. And it was astonishing.

So I called the President, or I called the White House to get an appointment with the President. And there was a lot of back and forth, what did I want to see him about and so on. And I didn't seem to be getting an appointment right away, so I picked up the phone Sunday morning and I called the President. I said, "Mr. President, I have something I should bring over here and tell you about right now." So he said, 'Fine, come over.' He happened to be in Washington.

I went up to the family quarters, and Al Keel, who was then acting national security adviser, went with me, at my request. And I told the President the items on this agenda, including such things as doing something about the Dawa prisoners, which made me sick to my stomach that anybody would talk about that as something we would consider doing.

And the President was astonished. And I have never seen him so mad. He's a very genial, pleasant man and doesn't—very easy-going. But his jaw set, and his eyes flashed, and both of us, I think, felt the same way about it. And I think in that meeting I finally felt that the President deeply understands that something is radically wrong here. . . .

Q   . . . In particular, Admiral Poindexter testified that he did not withhold anything from you that you did not want withheld from you. . . . Mr. Secretary, . . . let me ask you first whether you ever told Admiral Poindexter or any other member of the Administration that you did not want to be kept informed of the Iran initiative?

A   I never made such a statement. What I did say to Admiral Poindexter was that I wanted to be informed of the things I needed to know to do my job as Secretary of State, but he didn't need to keep me posted on the details, the operational details of what he was doing. That's what I told him.... The reason for that was that there had been a great amount of discussion of leaks in the Administration, and justifiably so. And we were all very concerned about it. And there had been in connection with what to do about it, discussion of the idea of giving very large numbers of people who were—who had access to classified information, lie detector tests on a regular or random basis, which I opposed.

While I was on a trip abroad in the latter part of 1985, a directive encompassing that idea was signed. So I didn't comment on it while I was abroad, but when I got back here I did comment on it, registered my opposition, talked to the President about it. And it got changed. Now that, I recognized, put me at odds with the intelligence and national security community, to put it mildly. So . . . in terms of particulars, like who is going to go someplace to meet somebody and so forth, . . . it seemed to me in the light of the suspicions cast on me as a result, and the hostility, that I would not know that. So I felt it would probably leak, and then it wouldn't be my leak. . . .

But that doesn't mean that I just bowed out insofar as major things having to do with our foreign policy are concerned. . . . To consider that that statement would mean that I shouldn't be informed of things like that is ridiculous. . . .

Q    Do you recall what you told Admiral Poindexter about your views concerning the Iran initiative, as he described it to you in that briefing?

A    Well, I told him that I thought it was a very bad idea, that I was opposed to it. . . . I was in favor of doing things that had any potential for rear-ranging the behavior of Iran and our relationship with Iran. But I was very much opposed to arms sales in connection with that.

Q    Did you tell him at that time that in your view, the proposed policy amounted to paying for hostages and had to be stopped?

A    Yes.

Q    In that same conversation, sir, on Dec. 5, . . . did he tell you that on the very same day, the President had signed a covert action finding authorizing an arms shipment to Iran?

A    No. . . .

Q    Now do you recall another briefing, listed on the chronology by Admiral Poindexter a month later, on Feb. 28, in which he discussed the hostage situation and advised you then of a possible high-level meeting between Bud McFarlane and certain Iranian representatives?

A    Yes, I do. He told me that as a result of the discussions they had been having, that the Iranians had said they wanted a high-level meeting and if there were a proper high-level meeting, discussing our future possible relationships, that would be the occasion in which hostages . . . would be released. I said, 'Well, that sounds almost too good to be true. But anyway, if that's the case, I'm in favor of it.' . . .

Q    Did Admiral Poindexter tell you that the agenda for any meeting between Mr. McFarlane and Iranian representatives would include current deliveries of U.S. arms?

A    No. . . . This negotiation had been taking place in a manner consistent with what I thought was proper, and I thought, well, maybe I won the argument after all, with the President.

Q    In that light, did Admiral Poindexter tell you on Feb. 28 that only one day before, that was on Feb. 27, the United States had shipped 500 TOW's, TOW missiles, to Iran, and that about 10 days earlier the United States had also shipped 500 TOW missiles to Iran?

A   No, he did not....

Q   In May 1986, ... you were advised ... of an approach to a British entrepreneur by Mr. Nir about ... an arms deal to Iran ... which supposedly had White House approval which had John Poindexter as the point man and which included participants such as Mr. Adnan Khashoggi and Mr. Ghorbanifar?

A   Yes.... I received a cable from the Under Secretary of State, Mr. Armacost, ... in Tokyo....

Q   Once you received this information, you spoke to Don Regan ... and Admiral Poindexter. Am I correct?

A   That's correct.

Q   I understand that in those conversations you objected strongly to any such deal, to the United States being involved, insisted that if there was such an operation it be called off and warned that the President was seriously exposed and at risk.... Is that a fair summary?

A   Yes.... You can imagine how I felt when I read this cable.... I said more or less what you said. Don Regan seemed to me to be very upset about it. He said he would take it up with the President when he saw him.... He later told me that the President was upset and this was not anything he knew about. And Admiral Poindexter told me ... we are not dealing with these people, this is not our deal....

Q   Well, when Admiral Poindexter told you that this was not our deal, ... did he inform you that our deal involved an upcoming mission ... to Teheran, which would be led by Bud McFarlane, which would include a shipment of Hawk spare parts to Iran?

A   No....

Q   Also, Mr. Secretary, if I could, let me ask you to turn to exhibit 24. That exhibit, sir, is a PROF note dated May 17, 1986.... from Oliver North to Admiral Poindexter about the McFarlane mission to Teheran.... Colonel North suggests to Admiral Poindexter that there be a quiet meeting with Bud McFarlane and the President prior to the departure of the mission, and he queries whether the participants ... ought to include you and the Secretary of Defense and the D.C.I. [Director, Central Intelligence: William J. Casey]. Do you see that?

A   Yes, I see that.

Q   If you turn, then, please, to the next exhibit, ... you'll see Admiral Poindexter's reply to that suggestion, ... and I quote, 'I don't want a meeting with R.R., Shultz and Weinberger.' ... I take it you were unaware of this exchange, as well?

A   Obviously....

Q   Mr. Secretary, you testified earlier, ... that you had told Admiral Poindexter that while you didn't need to be informed of what you called operational details, you did want and need to be kept informed of those facts which you needed in order to do your job—correct?

A   Correct.

Q   Sir, in order to do your job as the nation's chief diplomat, and as a statutory member of the National Security Council, and at a time when, through Operation Staunch, you were in charge of attempting to persuade our allies and other nations throughout the world not to sell arms to Iran, did you need to know that the United States itself was selling arms to Iran, that the President had signed covert action findings authorizing those sales, and that the President's former national security adviser was in Teheran on a diplomatic mission, bringing with him the first installment on the delivery of U.S. Hawk parts? Did you need to know those facts?

A   Certainly. One of the many arguments that I used, and Secretary Weinberger used, in opposing having an arms sale dimension to the Iran initiative, one of the arguments, was that we felt that one way of getting the Iran-Iraq war to come to an end was to do everything we could to deny weapons to the country that was refusing to come to an end, and so we had a rather vigorous program, called Operation Staunch.

Q   Sir, did you ever express the view that Colonel North was a loose cannon?

A   No, I didn't. What I said—I think what you're referring to is an incident . . . in which I told Elliott Abrams [Assistant Secretary of State for Latin America]—the question was where, where are the freedom fighters getting their arms. . . . And Elliott said he didn't know. And I said, well, you're our pointman here, you should find out, or something like that.

Q   As I understand, that conversation took place on Sept. 4, 1985. Secretary Abrams has described that conversation here, based on a note that he took, in which he said you told him to 'monitor Ollie.' Is that your recollection? . . .

A   . . . No reason why Elliott shouldn't have taken it that way, because Colonel North was commonly seen as a principal contact with the freedom fighters.

Q   Did you have a view at that time that Colonel North, because of any information that you had about him, was someone who had to be watched closely or that Elliott ought to monitor?

A   There was talk around about erratic behavior on his part, but I had no particular knowledge about it and didn't want to pass judgment. . . . I can't get myself in the position of supervising people down the line working for others.

Q   But you did expect, based on what you told Secretary Abrams Sept. 4, 1985, that he would keep himself informed about . . . how the contras were getting supplied with arms, and not simply shut his eyes to that?

A   Yes.

Q   All right, sir, in light of what you now know, . . . regarding, for example, the role of Colonel North and other N.S.C. staff members in assisting the contras during the period of the Boland restrictions, the involvement in the Hasenfus flight, the involvement of at least one of our own ambassadors, Mr. Tams, in negotiations for an airstrip to be used in Central America for contra resupply and in helping, as he testified to this panel, on instructions from Colonel North, to open a southern military front against Nicaragua, during the period of the Boland restrictions, . . . is it your view that Secretary Abrams carried out your instruction to keep himself, and you, informed?

A   What has been brought out, in these hearings about all of the activities you mentioned, has surprised a lot of people. It surprised me. It must have been a surprise to Chairman Hamilton, who looked into this a couple of times and had assurances. So I imagine it has surprised the President. So things have come out that we didn't know about. . . .

Senator Daniel K. Inouye, chairman of the Senate Committee. Mr. Secretary, at the outset of these hearings, which began about two months ago, I made a sad prediction that when the story began to unfold, the American people will have the right to ask, how did this ever happen here? Or, how could this ever happen in the United States? And I think, at the same time, Americans would have the right to demand that it never happen again.

The story we have heard over the past 10 weeks of testimony, to some has been sad and depressing and distressing, and to many of us on this panel, many of us old-timers and a bit sophisticated, but we found it shocking and at times frightening.

And I believe that made the question that the Americans will ask, and the expectations they have, a bit more compelling.

Mr. Secretary, you and I have lived through the agony and the nightmare of Watergate. And we saw it ruin a President, ruin his senior advisers, demoralize the country and cause the American people to lose faith in their political leaders.

And therefore, it's especially troubling to me, and I'm sure it's to you, to see this nation once again faced with this breakdown of trust, between the important branches of Government, and more importantly, between the Government and the American people....

My question is a very general one, Mr. Secretary, but with your background in public service and being at the helm of the State Department, I hope you can give us a response. How did this happen again? And how did life-long public servants, and patriotic Americans, like Admiral Poindexter, Bud McFarlane and Bill Casey and Oliver North, find themselves in a position where they misled you, kept information away from the Secretary of State, from the Secretary of Defense, lied to the Congress, withheld information from the President of the United States, destroyed... Government documents to hide or cover up their activities, and involved rather shady characters—and that's an understatement, I think—in participating in the formulation of foreign policy, and the implementation of such, while, at the same time, skirting around the people who should be doing that work, to wit, the Secretary of State and the ambassadors.

And more importantly, Mr. Secretary, if you could also touch upon and advise us as to how we can prevent this from happening again....

A    I would say with respect to the revelations that were brought out this morning,... that's not the way life is in Government as I have experienced it....

Public service is a very rewarding and honorable thing, and nobody has to think they need to lie and cheat in order to be a public servant or to work in foreign policy. Quite to the contrary. If you are really going to be effective,... you have to be straightforward, and you have to conduct yourself in a basically honest way....

I think there are a lot of things to be learned myself reflecting on these events, if not from these events, that seem to me ... worth mentioning.... One that I think was most vivid in response to Senator [Sam] Nunn's [D.-Georgia] question, and that is I think the importance of separating the function of gathering and analyzing intelligence from the function of developing and carrying out policy. If the two things are mixed in together, it is too tempting to have your analysis and the selection of information that's presented favor the policy that you're advocating.

I believe that one of the reasons the President was given what I regard as wrong information, for example, about Iran and terrorism was that the agency, or the people in the C.I.A., were too involved in this. So that's one point. And I feel very clear in my mind about this point.

And I know that long before this all emerged, I had come to have grave doubts about the objectivity and reliability of some of the intelligence I was getting. . . .

Mark A. Belnick, executive assistant to the chief counsel of the Senate committee. And did you begin developing the view, particularly as of Nov. 10, . . . that the President's advisers were misleading him and not giving him the facts concerning what had actually transpired in the Iran initiative?

A    I developed a very clear opinion that the President was not being given accurate information, and I was very alarmed about it, and it became the preoccupying thing that I was working on through this period. And I felt that it was tremendously important for the President to get accurate information. . . . His judgment is excellent when he's given the right information, and he was not being given the right information.

And I felt as this went on that the people who were giving him the information . . . had a conflict of interest with the President. And they were trying to use his undoubted skills as a communicator to have him give a speech and give a press conference and say these things, and in doing so he would bail them out. . . . I don't want to try to attribute motives to other people too much, although I realize I am, but that's the way it shaped up to me. So I was in a battle to try to get what I saw as the facts to the President and get—and see that he understood them.

Now this was a very traumatic period for me because everybody was saying I'm disloyal to the President. I'm not speaking up for the policy. And I'm battling away here, and I could see people were calling for me to resign if I can't be loyal to the President, even including some of my friends and people who had held high office and should know that maybe there's more involved than they're seeing. And I frankly felt that I was the one who was loyal to the President, because I was the one who was trying to get him the facts so he could make a decision. And I must say, as he absorbed this, he did; he made the decision that we must get all these facts out. But it was a—it was a battle royal.

Q    Mr. Secretary, in that battle royal to get out the facts, which you waged and which the record reflects that you waged, who was on the other side?

A    Well, I can't say for sure, I—I feel that Admiral Poindexter was certainly on the other side of it. I felt that Director Casey was on the other side of it. And I don't know who all else, but they were the principals. . . .

Senator Inouye. Mr. Secretary, I have another question. And I ask this with great reluctance because I realize it is rather personal in nature, but I think it is relevant. . . . I've been advised that in August of 1986 you tendered a letter of resignation to the President of the United States. Is that true? And if so, can you tell us something about it?

A    . . . That is true. And I have asked the President to let me leave this office on a couple of other occasions, earlier. . . .

Q    Was that in any way related to the Iran-contra affair?

A    Well, in August of 1986 I thought that it was over. . . . I didn't know anything about the contra side of it anyway. But on the effort with Iran, I thought it was basically on a proper track.

But it was because I felt a sense of estrangement. I knew the White House was very uncomfortable with me. I was very uncomfortable with what I was getting from the intelligence community, and I knew they were very uncomfortable with me—perhaps going back to the lie-detector test business. I could feel it.

What I have learned about the various things that were being done, I suppose explains why I was not in good odor with the N.S.C. staff and some of the others in the White House. I had a terrible time. There was a kind of guerrilla warfare going on, on all kinds of little things. For example, as you know, the Congress doesn't treat the State Department very well when it comes to appropriated funds. And not only have we historically taken a beating but we've been cut brutally . . . and I think in a manner that is not in the interests of the United States. . . .

But anyway, one of the conventions that's grown up—because we have no travel money to speak of . . .—the Air Force runs a White House Presidential Wing and when the Secretary of State has a mission, that gets approved and then I get an airplane and the airplane, it is paid for out of this budget. If I had to pay for that airplane, I couldn't travel. So you have me grounded unless I can get approved.

Now it's not a problem; the system works all right and it's just assumed that that's the way it's supposed to be. But I started having trouble because some people on the White House staff decided that they were going to make my life unhappy and they stopped approving these airplane things. And we fought about it and so on. And finally, I—I hated to do this. I went to the President and I gave him little memorandums to check off—yes, no. And that's no business for the Secretary of State to be taking up with the President of the United States.

But I found out there was a character in the White House that was in charge of doing this. His name was Jonathan Miller, and you've seen him here, and he was . . . trying to knock me out of trips. . . . But this was an atmosphere that I found—I felt that I was no longer on the wavelength that I should be on. And so I told the President, "I'd like to leave and here's my letter." And he stuck it in his drawer and he said, "You're tired. It's about time to go on vacation and let's talk about it after you get back from vacation." So I said, "O.K.," and I guess everybody knows what happened. In early—beginning early September last year, it was a tremendous stretch of activity and so nothing ever happened on that. . . .

At an earlier time, in the middle of 1983, I resigned. And that was because I discovered that Bud McFarlane, who was then the deputy national security adviser, was sent on a secret trip to the Middle East . . . without my knowledge, while we're busy negotiating out there. And also I found some things happened with respect to actions on Central America that I didn't know about beforehand.

So I went to the President and I said, "Mr. President, you don't need a guy like me for Secretary of State if this is the way things are going to be done, because when you send somebody out like that McFarlane trip, I'm done." In the labor relations business—I used to be Secretary of Labor and there used to be a lot of intervention in labor disputes and we used to say, "When the President hangs out his shingle, he'll get all the business." When—when the President hangs out his shingle and says, "You don't have to go through the State Department, just come right into the White House," he'll get all the business.

That's a big signal to countries out there about how to deal with the U.S.

Government. And it may have had had something to do with how events transpired, for all I know. But it's wrong; you can't do it that way. . . .

So the other time I resigned was after my big lie-detector test flap, and again I could see that I was on the outs with everybody and so I said, "Mr. President, why don't you let me go home. I like it in California." . . . And again, he wouldn't let that happen. And that was in late 1985. Mr. McFarlane had resigned, and Mr. McFarlane and I, I think, worked very effectively together in . . . our efforts with the U.S.S.R. and . . . in the end I didn't feel, with Mr. McFarlane having left, that it was fair to the President or the country for me to leave at the same time, so I didn't.

But I do think that in jobs like the job I have, where it is a real privilege to serve in this kind of job, or the others that you recounted, that you can't do the job well if you want it too much. You have to be willing to say goodbye, and I am.

Q    I thank you very much, Mr. Secretary.

# RECOMMENDATIONS ON ORGANIZING FOR NATIONAL SECURITY*

*Tower Commission*

In selection 28 (found in Part VIII of this text), weaknesses in the NSC as discovered by the Tower Commission were laid out. Presented here are the commission's recommendations for reform.

## RECOMMENDATIONS

"Not only ... is the Federal power over external affairs in origin and essential character different from that over internal affairs, but participation in the exercise of the power is significantly limited. In this vast external realm, with its important, complicated, delicate and manifold problems, the President alone has the power to speak or listen as a representative of the nation."
—*United States v. Curtiss-Wright Export Corp., 299 U.S. 304, 319 (1936).*

Whereas the ultimate power to formulate domestic policy resides in the Congress, the primary responsibility for the formulation and implementation of national security policy falls on the President.

It is the President who is the usual source of innovation and responsiveness in this field. The departments and agencies—the Defense Department, State Department, and CIA bureaucracies—tend to resist policy change. Each has its own perspective based on long experience. The challenge for the President is to bring his perspective to bear on these bureaucracies for they are his instruments for executing national security policy, and he must work through them. His task is to provide them leadership and direction.

The National Security Act of 1947 and the system that has grown up under it affords the President special tools for carrying out this important role. These tools are the National Security Council, the National Security Advisor, and the NSC staff. These are the means through which the creative impulses of the President are brought to bear on the permanent government. The National Security Act, and custom and practice, rightly give the President wide latitude in fashioning exactly how these means are used.

There is no magic formula which can be applied to the NSC structure and process to produce an optimal system. Because the system is the vehicle through which the President formulates and implements his national security policy, it must adapt to each individual President's style and management philosophy. This means that NSC structures and processes must be flexible, not rigid. Overprescription would ... either destroy the system or render it ineffective.

Nevertheless, this does not mean there can be no guidelines or recommendations that might improve the operation of the system, whatever the particular style of the incumbent President. We have reviewed the operation of the system over the past 40 years, through good times and bad. We have listened carefully to the views of all the living former Presidents as well as those of most of the participants in their own national security systems.

*Reprinted from Report of the President's Special Review Board (the Tower Commission), Washington, D.C., February 26, 1987, pp. V-1–V-7.

With the strong caveat that flexibility and adaptability must be at the core, it is our judgment that the national security system seems to have worked best when it has in general operated along the lines set forth below.

**Organizing for National Security**   Because of the wide latitude in the National Security Act, the President bears a special responsibility for the effective performance of the NSC system. A President must at the outset provide guidelines to the members of the National Security Council, his National Security Advisor, and the National Security Council staff. These guidelines, to be effective, must include how they will relate to one another, what procedures will be followed, what the President expects of them. If his advisors are not performing as he likes, only the President can intervene.

The National Security Council principals other than the President participate on the Council in a unique capacity.[1] Although holding a seat by virtue of their official positions in the Administration, when they sit as members of the Council they sit not as cabinet secretaries or department heads but as advisors to the President. They are there not simply to advance or defend the particular positions of the departments or agencies they head but to give their best advice to the President. Their job—and their challenge—is to see the issue from this perspective, not from the narrower interests of their respective bureaucracies.

The National Security Council is only advisory. It is the President alone who decides. When the NSC principals receive those decisions, they do so as heads of the appropriate departments or agencies. They are then responsible to see that the President's decisions are carried out by those organizations accurately and effectively.

This is an important point. The policy innovation and creativity of the President encounters a natural resistance from the executing departments. While this resistance is a source of frustration to every President, it is inherent in the design of the government. It is up to the politically appointed agency heads to ensure that the President's goals, designs, and policies are brought to bear on this permanent structure. Circumventing the departments, perhaps by using the National Security Advisor or the NSC staff to execute policy, robs the President of the experience and capacity resident in the departments. The President must act largely through them, but the agency heads must ensure that they execute the President's policies in an expeditious and effective manner. It is not just the obligation of the National Security Advisor to see that the national security process is used. All of the NSC principals—and particularly the President—have that obligation.

This tension between the President and the Executive Departments is worked out through the national security process described in the opening sections of this report. It is through this process that the nation obtains both the best of the creativity of the President and the learning and expertise of the national security departments and agencies.

This process is extremely important to the President. His decisions will benefit from the advice and perspective of all the concerned departments and agencies. History offers numerous examples of this truth. President Kennedy, for example, did not have adequate consultation before entering upon the Bay of Pigs invasion, one of his greatest failures. He remedied this in time for the Cuban missile crisis, one of his greatest successes. Process will not always produce brilliant ideas, but history suggests it can at least help prevent bad ideas from becoming Presidential policy.

**The National Security Advisor**   It is the National Security Advisor who is primarily responsible for managing this process on a daily basis. The job requires skill, sensitivity, and integrity. It is his responsibility to ensure that matters submitted for consideration by the Council cover the full range of issues on which review is required; that those issues are fully analyzed; that a full range of options is considered; that the prospects and risks of each are examined; that all relevant intelligence and other information is available to the principals; that legal considerations are addressed; that difficulties in implementation are confronted. Usually, this can best be accomplished through interagency participation in the analysis of the issue and a preparatory policy review at the Deputy or Under Secretary level.

The National Security Advisor assumes these responsibilities not only with respect to the President but with respect to all the NSC principals. He must keep them informed of the President's thinking and decisions. They should have adequate notice and an agenda for all meetings. Decision papers should, if at all possible, be provided in advance.

The National Security Advisor must also ensure that adequate records are kept of NSC consultations and Presidential decisions. This is essential to avoid confusion among Presidential advisors and departmental staffs about what was actually decided and what was wanted. Those records are also essential for conducting a periodic review of a policy or initiative, and to learn from the past.

It is the responsibility of the National Security Advisor to monitor policy implementation and to ensure that policies are executed in conformity with the intent of the President's decision. Monitoring includes initiating periodic reassessments of a policy or operation, especially when changed circumstances suggest that the policy or operation no longer serves U.S. interests.

But the National Security Advisor does not simply manage the national security process. He is himself an important source of advice on national security matters to the President. He is not the President's only source of advice, but he is perhaps the one most able to see things from the President's perspective. He is unburdened by departmental responsibilities. The President is his only master. His advice is confidential. He is not subject to Senate confirmation and traditionally does not formally appear before Congressional committees.

To serve the President well, the National Security Advisor should present his own views, but he must at the same time represent the views of others fully and faithfully to the President. The system will not work well if the National Security Advisor does not have the trust of the NSC principals. He, therefore, must not use his proximity to the President to manipulate the process so as to produce his own position. He should not interpose himself between the President and the NSC principals. He should not seek to exclude the NSC principals from the decision process. Performing both these roles well is an essential, if not easy, task.

In order for the National Security Advisor to serve the President adequately, he must have direct access to the President. Unless he knows first hand the views of the President and is known to reflect them in his management of the NSC system, he will be ineffective. He should not report to the President through some other official. While the Chief of Staff or others can usefully interject domestic political considerations into national security deliberations, they should do so as additional advisors to the President.

Ideally, the National Security Advisor should not have a high public profile. He should not try to compete with the Secretary of State or the Secretary of Defense as the articulator of public policy. They, along with the President, should be the spokesmen for the policies of the Administration. While a "passion for anonymity" is perhaps too strong a term, the National Security Advisor should generally operate offstage.

The NSC principals of course must have direct access to the President, with whatever frequency the President feels is appropriate. But these individual meetings should not be used by the principal to seek decisions or otherwise circumvent the system in the absence of the other principals. In the same way, the National Security Advisor should not use his scheduled intelligence or other daily briefings of the President as an opportunity to seek Presidential decision on significant issues.

If the system is to operate well, the National Security Advisor must promote co-operation rather than competition among himself and the other NSC principals. But the President is ultimately responsible for the operation of this system. If rancorous infighting develops among his principal national security functionaries, only he can deal with them. Public dispute over external policy by senior officials undermines the process of decision-making and narrows his options. It is the President's responsibility to ensure that it does not take place.

Finally, the National Security Advisor should focus on advice and management, not implementation and execution. Implementation is the responsibility and the strength of the departments and agencies. The National Security Advisor and the NSC staff generally do not have the depth of resources for the conduct of operations. In addition, when they take on implementation responsibilities, they risk compromising their objectivity. They can no longer act as impartial overseers of the implementation, ensuring that Presidential guidance is followed, that policies are kept under review, and that the results are serving the President's policy and the national interest.

**The NSC Staff**    The NSC staff should be small, highly competent, and experienced in the making of public policy. Staff members should be drawn both from within and from outside government. Those from within government should come from the several departments and agencies concerned with national security matters. No particular department or agency should have a predominate role. A proper balance must be maintained between people from within and outside the government. Staff members should generally rotate with a stay of more than four years viewed as the exception.

A large number of staff action officers organized along essentially horizontal lines enhances the possibilities for poorly supervised and monitored activities by individual staff members. Such a system is made to order for energetic self-starters to take unauthorized initiatives. Clear vertical lines of control and authority, responsibility and accountability, are essential to good management.

One problem affecting the NSC staff is lack of institutional memory. This results from the understandable desire of a President to replace the staff in order to be sure it is responsive to him. Departments provide continuity that can help the Council, but the Council as an institution also needs some means to assure adequate records and memory. This was identified to the Board as a problem by many witnesses.

We recognize the problem and have identified a range of possibilities that a President might consider on this subject. One would be to create a small permanent executive secretariat. Another would be to have one person, the Executive Secretary, as a permanent position. Finally, a pattern of limited tenure and overlapping rotation could be used. Any of these would help reduce the problem of loss of institutional memory; none would be practical unless each succeeding President subscribed to it.

The guidelines for the role of the National Security Advisor also apply generally to the NSC staff. They should protect the process and thereby the President. Departments and agencies should not be excluded from participation in that process. The staff should not be implementors or operators and staff should keep a low profile with the press.

## PRINCIPAL RECOMMENDATION

The model we have outlined above for the National Security Council system constitutes our first and most important recommendation. It includes guidelines that address virtually all of the deficiencies in procedure and practice that the Board encountered in the Iran/Contra affair as well as in other case studies of this and previous administrations.

We believe this model can enhance the performance of a President and his administration in the area of national security. It responds directly to President Reagan's mandate to describe the NSC system as it ought to be.

**The Board recommends that the proposed model be used by Presidents in their management of the national security system.**

## SPECIFIC RECOMMENDATIONS

In addition to its principal recommendation regarding the organization and functioning of the NSC system and roles to be played by the participants, the Board has a number of specific recommendations.

**1. The National Security Act of 1947**   The flaws of procedure and failures of responsibility revealed by our study do not suggest any inadequacies in the provisions of the National Security Act of 1947 that deal with the structure and operation of the NSC system. Forty years of experience under that Act demonstrate to the Board that it remains a fundamentally sound framework for national security decision-making. It strikes a balance between formal structure and flexibility adequate to permit each President to tailor the system to fit his needs.

As a general matter, the NSC staff should not engage in the implementation of policy or the conduct of operations. This compromises their oversight role and usurps the responsibilities of the departments and agencies. But the inflexibility of a legislative restriction should be avoided. Terms such as "operation" and "implementation" are difficult to define, and a legislative proscription might preclude some future President from making a very constructive use of the NSC staff.

Predisposition on sizing of the staff should be toward fewer rather than more. But a legislative restriction cannot foresee the requirements of future Presidents. Size is best left to the discretion of the President, with the admonition that the role of the NSC staff is to review, not to duplicate or replace, the work of the departments and agencies.

**We recommend that no substantive change be made in the provisions of the National Security Act dealing with the structure and operation of the NSC system.**

**2. Senate Confirmation of the National Security Advisor**   It has been suggested that the job of the National Security Advisor has become so important that its holder should be screened by the process of confirmation, and that once confirmed he should return frequently for questioning by the Congress. It is argued that this would improve the accountability of the National Security Advisor.

We hold a different view. The National Security Advisor does, and should continue, to serve only one master, and that is the President. Further, confirmation is inconsistent with the role the National Security Advisor should play. He should not decide, only advise. He should not engage in policy implementation or operations. He should serve the President, with no collateral and potentially diverting loyalties.

Confirmation would tend to institutionalize the natural tension that exists between the Secretary of State and the National Security Advisor. Questions would increasingly arise about who really speaks for the President in national security matters. Foreign governments could be confused or would be encouraged to engage in "forum shopping."

Only one of the former government officials interviewed favored Senate confirmation of the National Security Advisor. While consultation with Congress received wide support, confirmation and formal questioning were opposed. Several suggested that if the National Security Advisor were to become a position subject to confirmation, it could induce the President to turn to other internal staff or to people outside government to play that role.

**We urge the Congress not to require Senate confirmation of the National Security Advisor.**

**3. The Interagency Process**   It is the National Security Advisor who has the greatest interest in making the national security process work, for it is this process by which the President obtains the information, background, and analysis he requires to make decisions and build support for his program. Most Presidents have set up interagency committees at both a staff and policy level to surface issues, develop options, and clarify choices. There has typically been a struggle for the chairmanships of these groups between the National Security Advisor and the NSC staff on the one hand, and the cabinet secretaries and department officials on the other.

Our review of the operation of the present system and that of other administrations where committee chairmen came from the departments has led us to the conclusion that the system generally operates better when the committees are chaired by the individual with the greatest stake in making the NSC system work.

**We recommend that the National Security Advisor chair the senior-level committees of the NSC system.**

**4. Covert Actions**   Policy formulation and implementation are usually managed by a team of experts led by policymaking generalists. Covert action requirements are no different, but there is a need to limit, sometimes severely, the number of individuals involved. The lives of many people may be at stake, as was the case in the attempt to rescue the hostages in Tehran. Premature disclosure might kill the idea in embryo, as could have been the case in the opening of relations with China. In such cases, there is a tendency to limit those involved to a small number of top officials. This practice tends to limit severely the expertise brought to bear on the problem and should be used very sparingly indeed.

The obsession with secrecy and preoccupation with leaks threaten to paralyze the government in its handling of covert operations. Unfortunately, the concern is not misplaced. The selective leak has become a principal means of waging bureaucratic warfare. Opponents of an operation kill it with a leak; supporters seek to build support through the same means.

We have witnessed over the past years a significant deterioration in the integrity of process. Rather than a means to obtain results more satisfactory than the position of any of the individual departments, it has frequently become something to be manipulated to reach a specific outcome. The leak becomes a primary instrument in that process.

This practice is destructive of orderly governance. It can only be reversed if the most senior officials take the lead. If senior decision-makers set a clear example and demand compliance, subordinates are more likely to conform.

Most recent administrations have had carefully drawn procedures for the consideration of covert activities. The Reagan Administration established such procedures in January, 1985, then promptly ignored them in their consideration of the Iran initiative.

**We recommend that each administration formulate precise procedures for restricted consideration of covert action and that, once formulated, those procedures be strictly adhered to.**

**5. The Role of the CIA**    Some aspects of the Iran arms sales raised broader questions in the minds of members of the Board regarding the role of the CIA. The first deals with intelligence.

The NSC staff was actively involved in the preparation of the May 20, 1985, update to the Special National Intelligence Estimate on Iran. It is a matter for concern if this involvement and the strong views of NSC staff members were allowed to influence the intelligence judgments contained in the update. It is also of concern that the update contained the hint that the United States should change its existing policy and encourage its allies to provide arms to Iran. It is critical that the line between intelligence and advocacy of a particular policy be preserved if intelligence is to retain its integrity and perform its proper function. In this instance, the CIA came close enough to the line to warrant concern.

**We emphasize to both the intelligence community and policymakers the importance of maintaining the integrity and objectivity of the intelligence process.**

**6. Legal Counsel**    From time to time issues with important legal ramifications will come before the National Security Council. The Attorney General is currently a member of the Council by invitation and should be in a position to provide legal advice to the Council and the President. It is important that the Attorney General and his department be available to interagency deliberations.

The Justice Department, however, should not replace the role of counsel in the other departments. As the principal counsel on foreign affairs, the Legal Adviser to the Secretary of State should also be available to all the NSC participants.

Of all the NSC participants, it is the Assistant for National Security Affairs who seems to have had the least access to expert counsel familiar with his activities.

**The Board recommends that the position of Legal Adviser to the NSC be enhanced in stature and in its role within the NSC staff.**

**7. Secrecy and Congress**    There is a natural tension between the desire for secrecy and the need to consult Congress on covert actions. Presidents seem to become increasingly concerned about leaks of classified information as their administrations progress. They blame Congress disproportionately. Various cabinet officials from prior administrations indicated to the Board that they believe Congress bears no more blame than the Executive Branch.

However, the number of Members and staff involved in reviewing covert activities is large; it provides cause for concern and a convenient excuse for Presidents to avoid Congressional consultation.

We recommend that Congress consider replacing the existing Intelligence Committees of the respective Houses with a new joint committee with a restricted staff to oversee the intelligence community, patterned after the Joint Committee on Atomic Energy that existed until the mid-1970s.

**8. Privatizing National Security Policy**  Careful and limited use of people outside the U.S. Government may be very helpful in some unique cases. But this practice raises substantial questions. It can create conflict of interest problems. Private or foreign sources may have different policy interests or personal motives and may exploit their association with a U.S. government effort. Such involvement gives private and foreign sources potentially powerful leverage in the form of demands for return favors or even blackmail.

The U.S. has enormous resources invested in agencies and departments in order to conduct the government's business. In all but a very few cases, these can perform the functions needed. If not, then inquiry is required to find out why.

We recommend against having implementation and policy oversight dominated by intermediaries. We do not recommend barring limited use of private individuals to assist in United States diplomatic initiatives or in covert activities. We caution against use of such people except in very limited ways and under close observation and supervision.

## EPILOGUE

If but one of the major policy mistakes we examined had been avoided, the nation's history would bear one less scar, one less embarrassment, one less opportunity for opponents to reverse the principles this nation seeks to preserve and advance in the world.

As a collection, these recommendations are offered to those who will find themselves in situations similar to the ones we reviewed; under stress, with high stakes, given little time, using incomplete information, and troubled by premature disclosure. In such a state, modest improvements may yield surprising gains. This is our hope.

## NOTE

1. As discussed in more detail in Part II [not reprinted in this text] the statutory members of the National Security Council are the President, Vice President, Secretary of State, and Secretary of Defense. By the phrase "National Security Council principals" or "NSC principals," the Board generally means those four statutory members plus the Director of Central Intelligence and the Chairman of the Joint Chiefs of Staff.

# GLOSSARY

| | |
|---|---|
| ACCM | Alternative or Compensatory Control Measure |
| AFIO | Association of Former Intelligence Officers |
| AG | Attorney General |
| Aman | Agaf ha-Modi'in (Israeli military intelligence) |
| ANC | African National Congress |
| BDA | Battle Damage Assessment |
| BfV | Bundesamt für Verfassungsschutz (German equivalent of the FBI) |
| BMD | Ballistic Missile Defense |
| BND | Bundesnachrichtendienst (German foreign intelligence service) |
| BSO | Black September Organization |
| BW | Biological Weapons |
| CA | Covert Action |
| CAS | Covert Action Staff (CIA) |
| CBW | Chemical/Biological Warfare |
| CCP | Consolidated Cryptographic Program |
| CDA | Congressionally Directed Action |
| CE | Counterespionage |
| CHAOS | Code name for CIA illegal domestic spying |
| CI | Counterintelligence |
| CIA | Central Intelligence Agency |
| CIFA | Counterintelligence Field Activity |
| CIG | Central Intelligence Group |
| CMS | Community Management Staff |
| CNC | Crime and Narcotics Center (CIA) |

| | |
|---|---|
| COINTELPRO | FBI Counterintelligence Program |
| COMINT | Communications Intelligence |
| Corona | Codename for first U.S. spy satellite system |
| COS | Chief of Station (CIA) |
| COSPO | Community Open Source Program Office |
| CPA | Covert Political Action |
| CPSU | Communist Party of the Soviet Union |
| CSI | Committee on Intelligence Services (Britain) |
| CT | Counterterrorism |
| CTC | Counterterrorism Center (CIA) |
| CW | Chemical Weapons |
| D & D | Denial and Deception |
| DARP | Defense Airborne Reconnaissance Program |
| DAS | Deputy Assistant Secretary |
| DBA | Dominant Battlefield Awareness |
| DC | Deputies Committee (NSC) |
| DCD | Domestic Contact Division (CIA) |
| DCI | Director of Central Intelligence |
| D/CIA | Director of Central Intelligence Agency |
| DDA | Deputy Director of Administration (CIA) |
| DDCI | Deputy Director for Central Intelligence (DDCI) |
| DD/CIA | Deputy Director, Central Intelligence Agency |
| DDO | Deputy Director for Operations (CIA) |
| DDP | Deputy Director for Plans (CIA) |
| DDS&T | Deputy Director for Science and Technology (CIA) |
| DEA | Drug Enforcement Administration |
| DGSE | Directorie Génerale de la Sécurité Extérieure (French intelligence service) |
| DHS | Department of Homeland Security |
| DI | Directorate of Intelligence (CIA) |
| DIA | Defense Intelligence Agency |
| DIA/Humint | Defense Humint Service |
| DINSUM | *Defense Intelligence Summary* |
| DNI | Director of National Intelligence |
| DO | Directorate of Operations |
| DoD | Department of Defense |
| DOD | Domestic Operations Division (CIA) |
| DOE | Department of Energy |
| DOJ | Department of Justice |
| DOT | Department of Treasury |
| DOS | Department of State |
| DP | Directorate of Plans ( CIA) |
| DST | Directoire de Surveillance Territore (France) |
| ECHR | European Convention of Human Rights |

| | |
|---|---|
| ELINT | Electronic Intelligence |
| ENIGMA | Code machine used by the Germans during World War II |
| EO | Executive Order |
| EOP | Executive Office of the President |
| ETF | Environmental Task Force (CIA) |
| FARC | Fuerzas Armadas Revolucionarias in Colombia |
| FBI | Federal Bureau of Investigation |
| FBIS | Foreign Broadcast Information Service |
| FISA | Foreign Intelligence Surveillance Act (1978) |
| FNLA | National Front for the Liberation of Angola |
| FOIA | Freedom of Information Act |
| FRD | Foreign Resources Division (CIA) |
| FSB | Federal'naya Sluzba Besnopasnoti (Federal Security Service, Russia) |
| GAO | General Accountability Office (Congress) |
| GCHQ | Government Communications Headquarters (the British NSA) |
| GEO | Geosynchronous Orbit |
| GEOINT | Geospatial Intelligence |
| GRU | Soviet Military Intelligence |
| GSG | German Counterterrorism Service |
| HEO | High Elliptical Orbit |
| HPSCI | House Permanent Select Committee on Intelligence |
| HUAC | House Un-American Activities Committee |
| HUMINT | Human Intelligence (assets) |
| I & W | Indicators and Warning |
| IAEA | International Atomic Energy Agency |
| IAF | Israel Air Force |
| IC | Intelligence Community |
| ICS | Intelligence Community Staff |
| IDF | Israeli Defense Force |
| IG | Inspector General |
| IMINT | Imagery Intelligence (photographs) |
| INR | Bureau of Intelligence and Research (Department of State) |
| INTELINK | An intelligence community computer information system |
| INTs | Collection disciplines (IMINT, SIGINT, OSINT, HUMINT, MASINT) |
| IOB | Intelligence Oversight Board (White House) |
| ISA | Israeli Security Agency |
| ISC | Intelligence and Security Committee (U.K.) |
| ISI | Inter-Services Intelligence (Pakistani intelligence agency) |
| IT | Information Technology |
| JCAE | Joint Committee on Atomic Energy |
| JCS | Joint Chiefs of Staff |
| JIC | Joint Intelligence Committee (U.K.) |

| | |
|---|---|
| JSOC | Joint Special Operations Command |
| JSTARS | Joint Surveillance Target Attack Radar Systems |
| KGB | Soviet Secret Police |
| KH | Keyhole (satellite) |
| LTTE | Tamil Tigers of Tamil Elam |
| MAGIC | Allied code-breaking operations against the Japanese in the World War II |
| MASINT | Measurement and Signatures Intelligence |
| MI5 | Security Service (U.K.) |
| MI6 | Secret Intelligence Service (U.K.) |
| MON | Memoranda of Notification |
| MONGOOSE | Code name for CIA covert actions against Fidel Castro of Cuba (1961–62) |
| Mossad | Israeli Intelligence Service |
| MPLA | Popular Movement for the Liberation of Angola |
| NAACP | National Association for the Advancement of Colored People |
| NBC | Nuclear, Biological, and Chemical (Weapons) |
| NCS | National Clandestine Service |
| NCIC | National Counterintelligence Center |
| NCTC | National Counterterrorism Center |
| NED | National Endowment for Democracy |
| NFIB | National Foreign Intelligence Board |
| NFIC | National Foreign Intelligence Council |
| NFIP | National Foreign Intelligence Program |
| NGA | National Geospatial-Intelligence Agency |
| NGO | Nongovernmental organization |
| NIA | National Intelligence Authority |
| NIC | National Intelligence Council |
| NID | *National Intelligence Daily* |
| NIE | National Intelligence Estimate |
| NIO | National Intelligence Officer |
| NOC | Nonofficial Cover |
| NPIC | National Photographic Interpretation Center |
| NRO | National Reconnaissance Office |
| NSA | National Security Agency |
| NSC | National Security Council (White House) |
| NSCID | National Security Council Intelligence Directive |
| NTM | National Technical Means |
| OB | Order of Battle |
| OC | Official Cover |
| ODNI | Office of the Director of National Intelligence |
| OMB | Office of Management and Budget |
| ONI | Office of Naval Intelligence |

| | |
|---|---|
| OPC | Office of Policy Coordination |
| OSD | Office of the Secretary of Defense |
| OSINT | Open-Source Intelligence |
| OSS | Office of Strategic Services |
| P & E | Processing and Exploitation |
| PDB | *President's Daily Brief* |
| PFIAB | President's Foreign Intelligence Advisory Board (White House) |
| PFLP | Popular Front for the Liberation of Palestine |
| PIJ | Palestinian Islamic Jihad |
| PLO | Palestine Liberation Organization |
| PM | Paramilitary |
| PRO | Public Record Office (U.K.) |
| RADINT | Radar Intelligence |
| RFE | Radio Free Europe |
| RL | Radio Liberty |
| SA | Special Activities Division (DO/CIA) |
| SAS | Special Air Service (U.K.) |
| SBS | Special Boat Service (U.K.) |
| SDO | Support to Diplomatic Operations |
| SHAMROCK | Code name for illegal NSA interception of cables |
| SIG | Senior Interagency Group |
| SIGINT | Signals Intelligence |
| SIS | Secret Intelligence Service (U.K., also known as MI6) |
| SISDE | Italian Intelligence Service |
| SMO | Support to Military Operations |
| SMS | Secretary's *Morning Summary* (Department of State) |
| SNIE | Special National Intelligence Estimate |
| SO | Special Operations (CIA) |
| SOCOM | Special Operations Command (Department of Defense) |
| SOE | Special Operations Executive (U.K.) |
| SOG | Special Operations Group (DO/CIA) |
| SOVA | Office of Soviet Analysis (CIA) |
| SSCI | Senate Select Committee on Intelligence |
| SVR | Russian Foreign Intelligence Service |
| TECHINT | Technical Intelligence |
| TELINT | Telemetery Intelligence |
| TIARA | Tactical Intelligence and Related Activities |
| TPED | Tasking, Processing, Exploitation, and Dissemination |
| UAV | Unmanned Aerial Vehicle (drone) |
| ULTRA | Code name for the Allied operation that deciphered the German ENIGMA code in World War II |
| UN | United Nations |
| UNITA | National Union for the Total Independence of Angola |

| | |
|---|---|
| UNSCOM | United Nations Special Commission |
| USIB | United States Intelligence Board |
| USTR | United States Trade Representative |
| VCI | Viet Cong Infrastructure |
| VENONA | Code name for SIGINT intercepts against Soviet spying in America |
| VOA | Voice of America |
| VX | A deadly nerve agent used in chemical weapons |
| WMD | Weapons of mass destruction |

# INDEX

Iran: Israeli arms sales to, 79; Mossadeq's downfall, 4, 126, 149; policy dilemmas, 99–100; presidential findings, 197; presidential notification for Iran-*contra*, 161; Reagan administration selling arms, 2; United States and Western power linkage, 31

Iran-*contra* affair: Committee heard from Lieut. Col. Oliver L. North, 272–78; Committee heard from Rear Adm. John M. Poindexter, 278–88; covert action subverting U.S. law, 261–306; excerpts from Secretary of State George P. Shultz's testimony, 290–98; failure of responsibility, 268–71; flawed process, 262–68; Israel covert action, 78–81; open democracy, 19; recommendations for organizing national security, 299–306; Representative Lee H. Hamilton after Poindexter appearance, 288–89

Irangate affair, Israel covert action, 78–81

Iran-Iraq war, CIA undermining Saddam Hussein, 94

Iran operation: code-named TPAJAX, 4, 6; trading arms for hostages, 13

Iraq: gray propaganda, 112; secret propaganda war, 113–14, 115

Iraqi Kurds: CIA supporting, 48; false hope, 115

Iraqi Shias, false hope, 115

Iraq War 2003, secret propaganda, 109

Ireland, covert actions, 26

Islamic Jihadists, 158

Islamic terrorism, destruction of World Trade Center towers, 149–50

Israeli covert action, 1967 Six-Day War, 64, 66; Bad Business, 61–65; categorization of operations, 80; covert rescue missions, 72–75; Entebbe Operation, 70, 70–72, 80; *Esek Ha'Bish*, 61–65; Irangate affair, 78–81; Israel Air Force (IAF) and MiG-21, 75–76; Khaled Mashal fiasco, 65; Lavon Affair, 61–65; Military Intelligence (MI), 61, 63; Operation Blanket, 72; Operation Damocles, 68–69; Operation Isorad, 78;

Operation Magic Carpet, 72; Operation Moses, 73–74; Operation Noah's Ark, 76–78; Operation Plumbat, 78; Operation Sheba, 74; Operation Solomon, 74–75; Operation Susannah, 61–65; Operation Tuchia, 73; Operation Yehonathan, 70–72; Sinai Campaign, 64; Spring of Youth Operation, 69–70; Sword of Gideon, 66; theft operations, 75–78; Uranium Ship Operation, 78; Wrath of God Operation, 65–67

Italian Christian Democrats: black propaganda, 112; CIA's first success, 3, 37–38

Italian elections, Central Intelligence Agency (CIA) funding, 37–38

Italy, political covert action, 125

Jefferson, Thomas, political covert action, 121–22

Jihad, Abu, assassination operation, 68–69

Johnson, Lock H., ladder of escalations for covert actions, 97–98

Joint Special Operations Command (JSOC): black operations, 133; creation, 132; operators opposing Pentagon emphasis, 141

Jonas, George, *Vengeance*, 67

Kennan, George F.: covert action policy document, 84; Directorate of Operations, 30; "The Sources of Soviet Conduct," 29

Kennedy, President John F.: Bay of Pigs fiasco, 90, 91; CIA overthrowing regimes, 126, 129; CIA-trained Cuban exiles, 4–5, 9; political covert action, 122

*Ker-Frisbie-Toscanino* doctrine, concept in U.S. courts, 164

KGB: assessing success, 52; covert action development, 32–33; covert political action, 36; friendly intelligence services, 46–47; front organizations, 40–42; Popular Movement for the Liberation of Angola (MPLA), 39–40; press agencies, 35; propaganda and disinformation, 34–35; reorganization, 27

# ABOUT THE EDITOR AND CONTRIBUTORS

## EDITOR

**Loch K. Johnson** is Regents Professor of Public and International Affairs at the University of Georgia and author of several books and over 100 articles on U.S. intelligence and national security. His books include *The Making of International Agreements* (1984); *A Season of Inquiry* (1985); *Through the Straits of Armageddon* (1987, coedited with Paul Diehl); *Decisions of the Highest Order* (1988, coedited with Karl F. Inderfurth); *America's Secret Power* (1989); *Runoff Elections in the United States* (1993, coauthored with Charles S. Bullock III); *America as a World Power* (1995); *Secret Agencies* (1996); *Bombs, Bugs, Drugs, and Thugs* (2000); *Fateful Decisions* (2004, coedited with Karl F. Inderfurth); *Strategic Intelligence* (2004, coedited with James J. Wirtz); *Who's Watching the Spies?* (2005, coauthored with Hans Born and Ian Leigh); *American Foreign Policy* (2005, coauthored with Daniel Papp and John Endicott); and *Seven Sins of American Foreign* Policy (2007). He has served as special assistant to the chair of the Senate Select Committee on Intelligence (1975–76), staff director of the House Subcommittee on Intelligence Oversight (1977–79), and special assistant to the chair of the Aspin-Brown Commission on Intelligence (1995–96). In 1969–70, he was an American Political Science Association Congressional Fellow. He has served as secretary of the American Political Science Association and President of the International Studies Association, South. Born in New Zealand and educated at the University of California, Johnson has taught at the University of Georgia since 1979, winning its Meigs Professorship for meritorious teaching and its Owens Award for outstanding accomplishments in the field of social science research. In 2000, he led the founding of the School of Public and

International Affairs at the University of Georgia. He is the senior editor of the international journal *Intelligence and National Security*.


## CONTRIBUTORS

**Matthew M. Aid** is Managing Director in the Washington, DC, office of Citigate Global Intelligence and Security and coeditor of *Secrets of Signals Intelligence During the Cold War and Beyond* (2001).

**James E. Baker** sits on the U.S. Court of Appeals for the Armed Forces. He previously served as Special Assistant to the President and Legal Adviser to the National Security Council and as Deputy Legal Adviser to the NSC. He has also served as Counsel to the President's Foreign Intelligence Advisory Board, an attorney at the Department of State, a legislative aide to Senator Daniel Patrick Moynihan, and as a Marine Corps infantry officer. He is the coauthor with Michael Reisman of *Regulating Covert Action* (Yale University Press, 1992).

**David M. Barrett** is Associate Professor of Political Science at Villanova University and author of *Congress and the CIA* (Kansas, 2005).

**Hans Born** is a senior fellow in democratic governance of the security sector at the Geneva Centre for Democratic Control of the Armed Forces (DCAF). He is an external member of the crisis management and security policy faculty of the Federal Institute of Technology and a guest lecturer on governing nuclear weapons at the UN Disarmament Fellowship Programme. He has written, co-authored, and co-edited various books on international relations and security policy, including the Inter-Parliamentary Union Handbook on *Parliamentary Oversight of the Security Sector: Principles, Mechanisms and Practices* (Geneva: IPU/DCAF, 2003, translated in 30 languages); *Making Intelligence Accountable: Legal Standards and Best Practice for Oversight of Intelligence Agencies* (Oslo: Publishing House of the Parliament of Norway, 2005, translated in 10 languages); *Who is Watching the Spies? Establishing Intelligence Agency Accountability* (Dulles, VA: Potomac Publishers, 2005); *Civil-Military Relations in Europe: Learning from Crisis and Institutional Change* (London: Routledge, 2006); and *The Double Democratic Deficit: Parliamentary Accountability and the Use of Force under International Auspices* (London: Ashgate Publishers: Aldershot).

**A. Denis Clift** is President of the Department of Defense Joint Military Intelligence College. He was born in New York City and educated at Friends Seminary, Phillips Exeter Academy (1954), Stanford University (B.A., 1958), and the London School of Economics and Political Science (M.Sc., 1967). He began a career of public service as a naval officer in the Eisenhower and Kennedy administrations and has served in military and civilian capacities in ten administrations, including thirteen successive years in the Executive Office of the President and the White House. From 1971–76, he served on the National Security

Council staff. From 1974–76, he was head of President Ford's National Security Council staff for the Soviet Union and Eastern and Western Europe. From 1977–81, he was Assistant for National Security Affairs to the Vice President. From 1991–94, he was Chief of Staff, Defense Intelligence Agency. From 1963–66, he was the editor of the U.S. Naval Institute *Proceedings*. His published fiction and nonfiction include the novel *A Death in Geneva* (Ballantine Books, Random House), *Our World in Antarctica* (Rand McNally), *With Presidents to the Summit* (George Mason University Press), and *Clift Notes: Intelligence and the Nation's Security* (JMIC Writing Center Press).

**William J. Daugherty** holds a doctorate in government from the Claremont Graduate School and is Associate Professor of government at Armstrong Atlantic State University in Savannah, Georgia. A retired senior officer in the CIA, he is also the author of *In the Shadow of the Ayatollah: A CIA Hostage in Iran* (Annapolis, 2001) and *Executive Secrets: Covert Action and the Presidency* (Kentucky, 2004).

**Jack Davis** served in the CIA from 1956 to 1990 as analyst, manager, and teacher of analysts. He now is an independent contractor with the Agency, specializing in analytic methodology. He is a frequent contributor to the journal *Studies in Intelligence*.

**Stuart Farson** is Lecturer, Political Science Department, Simon Fraser University, Vancouver/Surrey, Canada. He is a former Secretary-Treasurer of the Canadian Association for Security and Intelligence Studies, and served as Director of Research for the Special Committee of the House Commons (Canada) on the Review of the Canadian Security Intelligence Service Act and the Security Offences Act. He has numerous articles on security, intelligence, and policing issues and is the coeditor of *Security and Intelligence in a Changing World* (with David Stafford and Wesley K. Wark, Cass, 1991).

**Timothy Gibbs** is a final-year doctoral student in history at Robinson College, Cambridge University, and a member of the Cambridge University Intelligence Seminar. He is also a former Visiting Scholar at the University of Georgia. His doctoral dissertation, titled *British and American Intelligence and the Atom Spies*, was submitted in the summer of 2006 and was supervised by Professor Christopher Andrew.

**Peter Gill** is Reader in Politics and Security, Liverpool John Moores University, Liverpool, United Kingdom. He is coauthor of *Introduction to Politics* (1988, 2nd ed.) and *Intelligence in an Insecure World* (2006). He is currently researching the control and oversight of domestic security in intelligence agencies.

**Harold M. Greenberg** graduated with a B.A. in history from Yale University in 2005. At Yale, he participated in the Studies in Grand Strategy program, and he has recently published research on CIA covert action in the 1950s. He now works as a legislative aide in the U.S. House of Representatives.

**Daniel S. Gressang IV** is Professor at the Joint Military Intelligence College (JMIC) in Washington, DC, and serves concurrently as the National Security Agency/National Cryptologic School of Liaison to JMIC. He has researched, written, and lectured extensively on terrorism and counterinsurgency. His research focuses primarily on the application of complex adaptive systems perspectives to understanding the dynamics of terror and other forms of unconventional warfare. In 2004, he was designated Intelligence Community Officer by the Director of Central Intelligence.

**Glenn Hastedt** received his doctorate in political science from Indiana University. Until recently he was Professor and Chair of the Political Science Department at James Madison University. He is now chair of the Justice Studies Department there. Among his publications is *American Foreign Policy: Past, Present, Future*, 6th ed. (Prentice Hall).

**John Hollister Hedley,** during more than thirty years at CIA, edited the *President's Daily Brief*, briefed the *PDB* at the White House, served as Managing Editor of the *National Intelligence Daily*, and was Chairman of the CIA's Publications Review Board. Now retired, Hedley has taught intelligence at Georgetown University and serves as a consultant to the National Intelligence Council and the Center for the Study of Intelligence.

**Michael Herman** served from 1952 to 1987 in Britain's Government Communications Headquarters, with secondments to the Cabinet Office and the Ministry of Defence. Since retirement he has written extensively on intelligence matters, with official clearance. He has had academic affiliations with Nuffield and St. Antony's Colleges in Oxford and is Founder Director of the Oxford Intelligence Group and Honorary Departmental Fellow at Aberystwyth University. In 2005 he received the degree of Honorary D.Litt from Nottingham University. He is a leading British intelligence scholar and author of *Intelligence Power in Peace and War* (Cambridge, 2001).

**Frederick P. Hitz** is Lecturer (Diplomat in Residence) in Public and International Affairs, Woodrow Wilson School, Princeton University.

**Max M. Holland** is the author of *The Kennedy Assassination Tapes* (Knopf, 2004).

**Arthur S. Hulnick** is Associate Professor of International Relations at Boston University. He is a veteran of thirty-five years of intelligence service, including seven years in Air Force Intelligence and twenty-eight years in the CIA. He is author of *Fixing the Spy Machine* (Praeger, 1999) and *Keeping Us Safe* (Praeger, 2004).

**Rhodri Jeffreys-Jones** is Professor of American History at the University of Edinburgh. The author of several books on intelligence history, he is currently completing a study of the FBI.

**Ephraim Kahana** is Professor of Political Science and faculty member in the Western Galilee College, Acre, Israel. He teaches courses on international relations, national security and intelligence, and foreign policy in the National Security Program in the University of Haifa. Kahana has written numerous papers on intelligence and foreign policy. His most recent book is the *Historical Dictionary of Israeli Intelligence* (2006).

**Patrick Radden Keefe** is a graduate of the School of Law at Yale University and is presently a Fellow with the Century Foundation in New York City. He is the author of *Chatter: Uncovering the Echelon Surveillance Network and the Secret World of Global Eavesdropping* (Random House, 2006), and has published essays in *The New York Review of Books*, *The New York Times Magazine*, the *New York Times*, the *Boston Globe*, the *Yale Journal of International Law*, *Legal Affairs*, *Slate*, and *Wired*. He has been a Marshall Scholar and a 2003 fellow at the Dorothy and Lewis B. Cullman Center for Scholars and Writers at the New York Public Library.

**Jennifer D. Kibbe** is Assistant Professor of Government at Franklin and Marshall College. Between 2002 and 2004, she was a postdoctoral fellow at the Brookings Institution. Her research interests include U.S. foreign policy, intelligence and covert action, presidential decision making, and political psychology. She has published work on U.S. policy in Iraq and the Middle East, and the military's involvement in covert actions.

**Katharina von Knop** is a doctoral candidate in Political Science at Leopold-Franzens University in Innsbruck, Austria, specializing in counter- and antiterrorism, and coeditor with Heinrich Neisser and Martin van Creveld of *Countering Modern Terrorism: History, Current Issues, and Future Threats* (2005).

**Lawrence J. Lamanna** is a doctoral candidate in the School of Public and International Affairs at the University of Georgia. He holds an M.A. from Yale University and a B.A. from the University of Notre Dame.

**Ian Leigh** is Professor of Law and Codirector of the Human Rights Centre at the University of Durham. He lives in Durham, England.

**Kristin M. Lord** is Associate Dean at George Washington University's Elliott School of International Affairs. In 2005–2006, she was a Council on Foreign Relations International Affairs Fellow and Special Adviser to the Under Secretary of State for Democracy and Global Affairs. Lord is the author of *The Perils and Promise of Global Transparency: Why the Information Revolution May Not Lead to Security Democracy or Peace* (SUNY Press, 2006); coeditor, with Bernard I. Finel, of *Power and Conflict in the Age of Transparency* (Palgrave Macmillan, 2000); and the author of numerous book chapters, articles, and papers on international politics and security. Lord received her doctorate in government from Georgetown University.

328 ABOUT THE EDITOR AND CONTRIBUTORS

**Minh A. Luong** is Assistant Director of International Security Studies at Yale University, where he teaches in the Department of History. He also serves as adjunct Assistant Professor of Public Policy at the Taubman Center at Brown University.

**Cynthia M. Nolan** earned a doctorate at American University in the School of International Service, researching intelligence oversight. She is a former officer in the Directorate of Operations in the CIA and has published in the *International Journal of Intelligence and Counterintelligence*.

**Kevin A. O'Brien** is a former research associate with the Canadian Institute of Strategic Studies and is currently a senior analyst for RAND Europe.

**Mark Phythian** is Professor of International Security and Director of the History and Governance Research Institute at the University of Wolverhampton, United Kingdom. He is the author of *Intelligence in an Insecure World* (2006, with Peter Gill), *The Politics of British Arms Sales Since 1964* (2000), and *Arming Iraq* (1997), as well as numerous journal articles on intelligence and security issues.

**Harry Howe Ransom** is Professor Emeritus of Political Science at Vanderbilt University. He has a B.A. from Vanderbilt and an M.A. and Ph.D. from Princeton University. He was a Congressional Fellow of the American Political Science Association and a Fellow of the Woodrow Wilson International Center for Scholars. He taught at Princeton, Vassar College, Michigan State University, Harvard University, and the University of Leeds. His books include *Central Intelligence and National Security* (1958), *Can American Democracy Survive Cold War?* (1963), and *The Intelligence Establishment* (1970).

**Jeffrey T. Richelson** is Senior Fellow with the National Security Archive in Washington, DC, and author of *The Wizards of Langley*, *The U.S. Intelligence Community*, *A Century of Spies*, and *America's Eyes in Space*, as well as numerous articles on intelligence activities. He received his doctorate in political science from the University of Rochester and has taught at the University of Texas, Austin, and the American University, Washington, DC. He lives in Los Angeles.

**Jerel A. Rosati** is Professor of Political Science and International Studies at the University of South Carolina since 1982. His area of specialization is the theory and practice of foreign policy, focusing on the U.S. policy-making process, decision-making theory, and the political psychological study of human cognition. He is the author and editor of five books and over forty articles and chapters. He has received numerous outstanding teaching awards. He has been Visiting Professor at Somalia National University in Mogadishu and Visiting Scholar at China's Foreign Affairs College in Beijing. He also has been a Research Associate in the Foreign Affairs and National Defense Division of the Library of Congress's Congressional Research Service, President of the International

Studies Association's Foreign Policy Analysis Section, and President of the Southern region of the International Studies Association.

**Richard L. Russell** is Professor of national security studies at the National Defense University. He is also an adjunct associate professor in the Security Studies Program and research associate in the Institute for the Study of Diplomacy at Georgetown University. He previously served as a CIA political-military analyst. Russell is the author of *Weapons Proliferation and War in the Greater Middle East: Strategic Contest* (2005).

**Frederick A. O. Schwarz Jr.** received an A.B. from Harvard University and J.D. from Harvard Law School, where he was an editor of the *Law Review*. After a year's clerkship with Hon. J. Edward Lumbard, U.S. Court of Appeals for the Second Circuit, he worked one year for the Nigerian government as Assistant Commissioner for Law Revision under a Ford Foundation grant. He joined the New York City law firm of Cravath, Swaine and Moore in 1963 and was elected a partner in 1969. From 1975 through mid-1976, he served as Chief Counsel to the Senate Select Committee to Study Government Operations with Respect to Intelligence Activities (the Church Committee); from 1982–89, he served as Corporation Counsel and head of the Law Department of the City of New York. In 1989, he chaired the New York City Charter Revision Commission.

**James M. Scott** is Professor and Chair of the Department of Political Science at Oklahoma State University. His areas of specialization include foreign policy analysis and international relations, with particular emphasis on U.S. foreign policy making and the domestic sources of foreign policy. He is author or editor of four books, over forty articles, book chapters, review essays, and other publications. He has been President of the Foreign Policy Analysis section and President of the Midwest region of the International Studies Association, where he has also served as conference organizer for both sections and has been a two-time winner of the Klingberg Award for Outstanding Faculty Paper at the ISA Midwest Annual Meeting. Since 1996, he has received over two dozen awards from students and peers for his outstanding teaching and research, including his institution's highest awards for scholarship in 2000 and 2001. Since 2005, he has been Director of the Democracy and World Politics Summer Research Program, a National Science Foundation Research Experience for Undergraduates.

**Len Scott** is Professor of International Politics at the University of Wales, Aberystwyth, where he is Director of the Centre for Intelligence and International Security Studies. Among his recent publications are *Understanding Intelligence in the Twenty-First Century: Journeys in Shadows* (2004, coedited with Peter Jackson) and *Planning Armageddon: Britain, the United States and the Command of Nuclear Forces, 1943–1964* (2000, coedited with Stephen Twigge).

**Katherine A. S. Sibley** is Professor and Chair of the History Department at St. Joseph's University. She is currently working on a biography of Florence Kling

Harding, titled *America's First Feminist First Lady*. Sibley's work will revise the typical portrait of Mrs. Harding as manipulative, unhappy wife, casting new light on her public and private life. In 2004, Sibley published *Red Spies in America: Stolen Secrets and the Dawn of the Cold War* with the University Press of Kansas. She is also the author of *The Cold War* (1998) and *Loans and Legitimacy: The Evolution of Soviet-American Relations, 1919–1933* (1996). Her work has appeared in journals including *American Communist History*, *Peace and Change*, and *Diplomatic History*, and she also serves as book review editor for *Intelligence and National Security*. She is a three-term Commonwealth Speaker for the Pennsylvania Humanities Council.

**Jennifer Sims** is Director of Intelligence Studies and Visiting Professor in the Security Studies Program at Georgetown University's Edmund A. Walsh School of Foreign Service. She also consults for the U.S. government and private sector on homeland security and intelligence related matters. Prior to this, Sims was Research Professor at Johns Hopkins University's Nitze School of Advanced International Studies in Washington, DC (Fall 2001–Summer 2003). She has served as defense and foreign policy adviser to Senator John Danforth (1990–94), a professional staff member of the Senate Select Committee on Intelligence (1991–94), Deputy Assistant Secretary of State for Intelligence Coordination (1994–98), and as the Department of State's first Coordinator for Intelligence Resources and Planning in the office of the Under Secretary for Management. In 1998 Sims was awarded the U.S. Intelligence Community's Distinguished Service Medal. She received her B.A. degree from Oberlin College and her M.A. and Ph.D. in national security studies from Johns Hopkins University in 1978 and 1985, respectively. She is the author of a number of books and articles on intelligence and arms control. The most recent of these include "Foreign Intelligence Liaison: Devils, Deals and Details," *International Journal of Intelligence and Counterintelligence Affairs* (Summer 2006); *Transforming US Intelligence,* coedited with Burton Gerber (Georgetown University Press, 2005); "Transforming U.S. Espionage: A Contrarian's Approach," *Georgetown Journal of International Affairs* (Winter/Spring 2005); "Domestic Factors in Arms Control: The U.S. Case," in Jeffrey A Larson (ed.), *Arms Control: Cooperative Security in a Changing Environment* (Lynne Rienner, 2002); "What Is Intelligence? Information for Decision-Makers," in Roy Godson, Ernest R. May, and Gary Schmitt, *U.S. Intelligence at the Crossroads* (Brassey's, 1995); "The Cambridge Approach Reconsidered," *Daedalus* 120 (Winter 1991); and *Icarus Restrained: An Intellectual History of American Arms Control* (Westview Press, 1990).

**Robert David Steele** is CEO of OSS.Net, an international open source intelligence provider. As the son of an oilman, a Marine Corps infantry officer, and a clandestine intelligence case officer for the CIA, he has spent over twenty years abroad in Asia and Central and South America. As a civilian intelligence officer he spent three back-to-back tours overseas, including one tour as one of the first officers assigned full-time to terrorism, and three headquarters tours in offensive counterintelligence, advanced information technology, and satellite program management. He resigned from the CIA in 1988 to be the senior civilian founder of the Marine Corps Intelligence Command. He resigned from the Marines in 1993. He is the author of three works on intelligence, as well as the editor of a book on peacekeeping intelligence. He has earned graduate degrees in international relations and public administration, is a graduate of the Naval War College, and has a certificate in Intelligence Policy. He is also a graduate of the Marine Corps Command and Staff Course and of the CIA's Mid-Career Course 101.

**John D. Stempel** is Senior Professor of International Relations at the University of Kentucky's Patterson School of Diplomacy and International Commerce, where he was Associate Director (1988–93) and Director (1993–2003). He came to the University of Kentucky following a 24-year career in the U.S. Foreign Service. There he focused on political and economic affairs, with overseas assignments in Africa (Guinea, Burundi, Zambia), Iran, and India, concluding with three years as U.S. Consul General in Madras. His Middle East service (1975–79) in Tehran provided the material for his book *Inside the Iranian Revolution*. His subsequent academic writings have focused on religion and diplomacy, intelligence and diplomacy, and American views of negotiation. His Washington assignments featured duty for both the State and Defense Departments, including a two-year tour as Director of the State Department's Crisis Center. He has taught at George Washington and American Universities, plus two years as Diplomat in Residence at the U.S. Naval Academy, Annapolis. Stemple is a member of the New York Council on Foreign Relations and is listed in *Who's Who in the World* and *Who's Who in America*. He holds an A.B. degree from Princeton University and M.A. and Ph.D. degrees from the University of California at Berkeley.

**Stan A. Taylor** is an Emeritus Professor of Political Science at Brigham Young University in Provo, Utah. He has taught in England, Wales, and New Zealand and in 2006 was a visiting professor at the University of Otago in Dunedin, New Zealand. He is founder of the David M. Kennedy Center for International Studies at Brigham Young University. He writes frequently on intelligence, national security, and U.S. foreign policy.

**Athan Theoharis** is Professor of History at Marquette University whose research has focused on government secrecy, Cold War politics, and the history of the FBI. He is the author, coauthor, and editor of eighteen books, including *The FBI and American Democracy* (2004), *Chasing Spies* (2002), *A Culture of Secrecy* (1998), and *The FBI: A Comprehensive Reference Guide* (1998). He has received numerous awards, including the American Bar Association's Gavel Award and selection as a fellow by the Wisconsin Academy of Arts, Sciences, and Letters.

**Gregory F. Treverton** is senior analyst at the RAND Corporation. Earlier, he directed RAND's Intelligence Policy Center and its International Security and Defense Policy Center, and he is Associate Dean of the Pardee RAND Graduate School. His recent work has examined at terrorism, intelligence, and law enforcement, with a special interest in new forms of public-private partnership. He has served in government for the first Senate Select Committee on Intelligence, handling Europe for the National Security Council, and most recently as vice chair of the National Intelligence Council, overseeing the writing of America's National Intelligence Estimates. He holds an A.B. *summa cum laude* from Princeton University, a master's in public policy, and Ph.D. in economics and politics from Harvard University. His latest books are *Reshaping National Intelligence for an Age of Information* (Cambridge University Press, 2001), and *New Challenges, New Tools for Defense Decisionmaking* (edited, RAND, 2003).

**Michael A. Turner** is a political scientist who has taught international relations and national security matters in San Diego, California, for the past twelve years. Before that, he spent over fifteen years in various positions within the CIA. Turner is the author of *Why Secret Intelligence Fails* (2005; 2006) and the *Historical Dictionary of United States Intelligence* (2006).

**Michael Warner** serves as Historian for the Office of the Director of National Intelligence.

**Nigel West** is a military historian specializing in security and intelligence topics. He is the European editor of the *World Intelligence Review* and is on the faculty at the Center for Counterintelligence and Security Studies in Washington, DC. He is the author of more than two dozen works of nonfiction and recently edited *Guy Liddell Diaries*.

**Reg Whitaker** is Distinguished Research Professor Emeritus, York University, and Adjunct Professor of Political Science, University of Victoria, Canada. He has written extensively on Canadian and international security and intelligence issues.

**James J. Wirtz** is Professor in the Department of National Security Affairs at the Naval Postgraduate School, Monterey, California. He is Section Chair of the Intelligence Studies Section of the International Studies Association and President of the International Security and Arms Control Section of the American Political Science Association. Wirtz is the series editor for *Initiatives in Strategic Studies: Issues and Policies*, published by Palgrave Macmillan.

**Amy B. Zegart** is Associate Professor of Public Policy at the University of California, Los Angeles. A specialist on national and homeland security, she has served on the National Security Council staff, as a foreign policy advisor to the Bush-Cheney 2000 presidential campaign, and as a consultant to California state and local homeland security agencies. She has published articles in leading academic journals, including *International Security* and *Political Science Quarterly*, and is the author of *Flawed by Design: The Origins of the CIA, JCS, and NSC* (Stanford, 1999). She received her Ph.D. in political science from Stanford, where she studied under Condoleezza Rice, and an A.B. in East Asian Studies from Harvard University.